Regenerative Design Techniques:

Practical Applications in Landscape Design

PETE MELBY
TOM CATHCART

JOHN WILEY & SONS, INC.

This book is dedicated to our families . . .
Cindy, Hannah, and Caroline
Karen, Julia, Wendell, and Abigail
whose love and support helped us through the
composition of this book.

Library of Congress Cataloging-in-Publication Data

ISBN 0-471-41472-7

Printed in the United States of America.
10 9 8 7 6 5 4 3 2 1

CONTENTS

An extensive bibliography including books, journals and web sites can be found at www.wiley.com/go/melby.

PREFACE

Many authors have pointed out the need for humans to learn to live "more sustainably." By this, they mean living in ways that do not exhaust essential resources and do not pollute the land, water, and air. A common theme has been that we need to change the way we do things, to get away from an energy- and waste-intensive lifestyle and live more in concert with the production and assimilative capacities of our planet.

The need for basic changes has not been widely accepted (at least in the United States), and changes have been correspondingly slow and limited. This has been disturbing to many environmentalists, who argue that our cultures are more like ocean liners than bicycles and take a long time to change direction.

Human behavior appears to be both adaptable and monolithic. Under some circumstances, people learn very quickly to change their behavior. Witness the proliferation of electronic communication and commerce. Under other circumstances, old habits persist with remarkable tenacity. Our inability, in the United States, to "kick the petroleum habit" (even when it has torpedoed our balance of payments abroad and may be laying seige to our environment) has been well documented.

The speed and willingness of humans to change their behavior, and all the factors that stimulate or impede such change, appear to be related to a number of factors, including perceived advantages, perceived disadvantages, and faith in available information. Clearly, though, once people are convinced that changes are necessary, they will make the changes, or at least try to do so.

We are convinced that changes in the way people interact with their environment are essential. Our human population is growing very rapidly. The ways in which we now, as a group, meet our space and energy needs and handle our wastes are destructive. As our population grows, it is inevitable that these practices will either change or will lead to significant damage to the natural systems that support us. It is not a matter of *whether*, it is a matter of *when*.

The techniques and technologies for making substantive changes in the way we humans interact with our environment are largely available. Many are inexpensive. Many are relatively low-technology solutions and do not require impossible adjustments in the way we live. Once people accept that such changes are necessary, they will need to have access to information to make the changes, or at least start them on the path.

It is with this purpose that we offer this book. Please visit our web site at www.wiley.com/go/melby for supplementary information and links to related websites.

Pete Melby
Tom Cathcart
Starkville, Mississippi

v

ACKNOWLEDGMENTS

This resource on the many regenerative technologies contributing to sustainable human life support systems came about through our reliance on a great many experts. The major contributors are listed here. Editor Margaret Cummins talked to us by telephone several times convincing us of the need for a comprehensive resource focused on the technologies that contribute to creating sustainable environments. Even though Tom and I had been teaching classes for about five years that were creating sustainable master plans composed of regenerative technologies, this book was her idea.

Landscape architect and department head Cameron Man instilled an interest in the early 1980s on the importance in creating sustainable landscapes. This direction was very insightful. A hero, Dr. Bill Wolverton, was very generous with his knowledge of creating biologically based water and air purification systems. Dr. Charlie Wax, geographer and climatologist, has been a regular contributor to our knowledge of how climate and sun path affect energy flows in the landscape. Accounting professor Dr. Mark Lehman shared his interest in the different ways of accounting for different costs. Dr. John Hargreaves provided a direct link back to the original thinking done by the biologists with the New Alchemists in their quest for creating sustainable environments. Dr. Armondo de la Cruz assisted us with basic biology and ecology issues. Nutritionist Dr. Wanda Dodson served as a mentor on the relationship of food production to human health. Carolyn Adams, USDA Watershed Science Institute Director, provided an opportunity for us to learn about Best Management Practices pertaining to the treatment of runoff from the built landscape. Landscape architect Ernie Dorrill with NRCS provided examples of planning to accommodate water runoff in developing landscapes.

Dr. Cathcart also wishes to acknowledge fellow faculty in the Agricultural and Biological Engineering Department and Mississippi State University for allowing time to pursue the writing of this book, and would particularly like to thank Bruce Johnson for carrying part of his teaching load. We would both like to thank Jonathan Pote for encouraging us to work in this area, and to artist Kelly McCaffery who created most of the sketches for the book and did so in an untiring and pleasant manner.

It is to all of these fine people and many others, as well, who have devoted their lives to the pursuit of better ways to live with the land, that we say, thank you.

Pete Melby

PART I

Sustainability and Regeneration

Chapter 1

Introduction to Sustainability

Sustainable development: *Development that meets the needs of the present without compromising the ability of future generations to meet their own needs.*
—Brundtland Commission (U.N. Commission on Environment and Development), 1987

We have lived by the assumption that what was good for us would be good for the world. We have been wrong. We must change our lives, so that it will be possible to live by the contrary assumption that what is good for the world will be good for us. And that requires that we make the effort to know the world and to learn what is good for it. We must learn to cooperate in its processes, and to yield to its limits.
—Wendell Berry, *Recollected Essays,* 1981

Basic human needs have changed very little over time. We have always needed food, energy, air, and water. The processes that meet these needs have also remained essentially unchanged. We are dependent on photosynthesis and a variety of cyclical phenomena for the continued functioning of these processes, but this has always been the case. Why, then, are we now talking so much about "sustainability"?

The answer to this question lies in the increased population of humans on earth (Figure 1-1). This book is not about overpopulation or population control. The earth's actual carrying capacity for humans is debatable. What is no longer debatable is whether humans have the capacity to significantly degrade processes on which we depend for our well-being and, indeed, our survival. There is ample evidence that we are able to temporarily or permanently disrupt these processes. In the following sections, we will consider some of the systems and processes that we need for survival, ways in which we can disrupt them, and how we may avoid such disruptions.

CYCLES AND REGENERATIVE SYSTEMS

Chemical cycles form the basis for our continued survival on earth. Photosynthesis is a process in which plants and certain bacteria trap solar energy. The energy is stored in

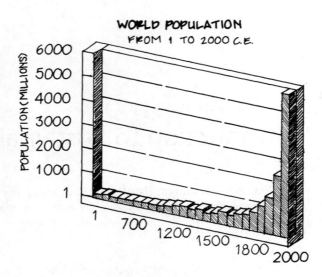

Figure 1-1 World population increase from 1 to 2000 C.E.

chemical bonds that join carbon dioxide (CO_2) to water in order to produce carbohydrate (CH_2O, a basic organic molecule) and oxygen (O_2):

$$\text{sunlight}$$
$$CO_2 + H_2O \rightarrow CH_2O + O_2$$
(carbon dioxide + water yields carbohydrate + oxygen)

Once bound in the carbohydrate, the trapped solar energy becomes available to other organisms that depend on it for their own metabolic functioning.

For this process to continue, there must be solar energy, adequate CO_2 (a gas, derived from the atmosphere), and water (in liquid form). Because plants and photosynthetic bacteria are living organisms, their immediate environment must be free of toxic materials and at a temperature that falls within the upper and lower limits that the plants and bacteria can tolerate.

There is not an infinite store of CO_2 in the atmosphere (air is 79% nitrogen, 20% oxygen, and less than 1% carbon dioxide). Carbon dioxide is continually replenished from a number of sources. For example, in the aerobic digestion of carbohydrates (which liberates energy stored in carbohydrate bonds):

$$CH_2O + O_2 \rightarrow CO_2 + H_2O$$
(carbohydrate + oxygen yields carbon dioxide + water)

Similarly, in terrestrial environments, there is not an infinite store of water. Water must be continually replenished, usually through precipitation. Such precipitation becomes available as a result of evaporation from surface waters and condensation in the atmosphere.

None of these facts are startling. They do, however, illustrate two essential concepts. First, the processes that make solar energy, water, oxygen, and carbon dioxide available are linked. Disrupting one process can have an impact on the others. Second, the processes are "regenerative." The carbon, oxygen, and water (hydrologic) cycles can continue indefinitely because each end product (such as carbohydrate in photosynthesis) is a source for another process that occurs elsewhere in the cycle (such as carbohydrate in digestion).

DISRUPTION OF REGENERATIVE CYCLES

The linkages between natural cycles, and their regenerative nature, are both strengths and weaknesses. This finely tuned arrangement can, and has, continued essentially unchanged for vast periods of time. That is good for organisms, like us, that need stability to persist. The arrangement is apparently quite robust, having been disrupted and reestablished multiple times in the past (assuming the correctness of postulated collisions with meteors or comets that disrupted the cycles for a time). This is good for the biological history of our planet, though less good for the multitude of species made extinct by such events.

These are strengths of the linked and regenerative cycles. A weakness, however, is that the system was formed, shaped, and modified by events that occurred in earth's history. The regenerative cycles are robust with respect to most perturbations that would be expected to occur naturally (without the intervention of something unexpected), even to the point of minor cosmic collisions.

Yet this robustness probably does not extend to all possible perturbations. Very large cosmic events (such as our sun "going nova"—exploding at the end of its existence) would permanently disrupt all regenerative cycles on earth. Conceivably, the introduction of a powerful toxin or some other major change in our environment could produce the same result.

From our perspective (that of a single species), we need to be concerned about less dramatic disruptions as well. Events that do not permanently disrupt the linked cycles may, in fact, disrupt us. As a species, we depend on the stability of our environment for our continued well-being. Ironically, as our dependence on technology grows, so does our dependence on stability. Witness the recent speculation about the potential effects of a programming error that we collectively called "Y2K" and the outwardly rippling effects of the tragic events of September 11, 2001.

These issues may be valid, but they still do not explain the recent emergence of "sustainability" and "sustainable design" as areas of concern. The reason is the perception among many people that humans may be in the process of creating their own perturbations to the systems on which they depend.

HUMAN PERTURBATIONS TO THE LANDSCAPE

For much of our history, our ability to disrupt regenerative cycles was limited. Occasionally, as we congregated in towns and cities, our wastes would overwhelm the capacity of nearby waters to process the waste load (convert the organic molecules to water, carbon dioxide, and inorganic nutrients). When that happened, the waters became smelly, unsafe to use, and sometimes a source of contagious diseases. Our agricultural practices have often degraded the soil, but when that happened our ancestors would clear another site or move as a group to an unspoiled location.

As our technical proficiency increased (in agriculture, manufacturing, energy production, health care, etc.), both our population and our per capita ability to alter our environment increased. When our numbers were small and our technical proficiency limited, the worst we could do was fairly insignificant to the earth as a whole. There is a growing consensus that we are now in a position to disrupt, permanently or temporarily, some regenerative systems on a global scale. As our population and technical ability continue to expand, the likelihood of such problems occurring will increase. Like the giraffe growing up in a garage, we will eventually have to consider our limits.

Large-Scale Human Perturbations

There are a variety of ways that human activities can interrupt essential regenerative cycles. An extreme example is the potential of our weapons of destruction. Although as yet untested, the "nuclear winter" postulated to occur following a limited exchange of nuclear weapons is an example of how our activities could induce a global-scale breakdown of photosynthesis that would be similar to the posited effect of a collision with an asteroid. There are, however, other examples that are less unthinkable and more pertinent to the subject of this book.

Eutrophication (Nutrient Enrichment) of Water Bodies

As late as the 1960s, we (in the United States) regarded bodies of water as convenient receptacles of raw wastes. Much of our sewage and all of the waste that ran off our land with storm water ended up in receiving waters (streams, rivers, lakes, coastal waters). The effects of raw and nearly raw sewage on receiving waters (that is, the overwhelming of the water's ability to process such waste) was sufficiently obvious that we applied our technical ability to the treatment of sewage and avoided the problem of organic overloading at the point of discharge.

Unfortunately, implementing sewage treatment did not completely solve the problem. Nutrients (mainly nitrogen and phosphorus) from treated sewage and from other sources (farms, cities, suburbs) continue to cause organic overloading. Now, however, the problem usually occurs downstream or offshore from its point of origin.

The causes and effects are fairly straightforward. Nutrients enter waterways through the discharge of treated sewage, via runoff from farms and other managed landscapes (agricultural fields, yards, parks, golf courses). The nutrients increase the rate of photosynthesis by single-celled algae called phytoplankton, causing their populations to increase beyond normal levels. At this point, several things can happen (depending on the severity of the nutrient increase).

The increased plankton concentrations can shade plants that grow below the surface. Submerged aquatic vegetation (SAV) provides food and a place for many organisms (including commercially valuable animals) to live. Loss of SAV due to shading can profoundly affect aquatic ecosystems.

The increased nutrient concentrations can cause a shift in the types of phytoplankton that occur in an area. Shifting the types of phytoplankton, which are basic to the food chain, can affect the species that depend on them for food. Sometimes harmful species become more prevalent. "Red tide" and other undesirable organisms appear to occur more frequently in coastal areas experiencing nutrient enrichment.

When conditions are right, nutrient enrichment can cause an explosive growth in phytoplankton, called a "bloom." The bloom will eventually subside when one or more nutrients are used up (often a minor nutrient not being supplied). When this limiting nutrient is exhausted, the phytoplankton die, sink to the bottom, and are digested by aerobic bacteria. The bacteria, now experiencing their own population increase, can quickly use up the available oxygen in the water. This can lead to fish kills and greatly altered ecological systems.

The process of nutrient overenrichment, called eutrophication, has become a widespread problem in the world's water bodies. On the east coast of the United States, the Chesapeake Bay has experienced eutrophication with associated habitat loss and species alterations. In the northern Gulf of Mexico, eutrophication has resulted in a persistent area of low oxygen, called the "dead zone," of approximately 7000 mi^2. There are numerous other examples. Nutrient enrichment caused by humans is already causing widespread degradation of essential regenerative cycles.

Consequences of Eutrophication for Ecological Systems

- Eutrophication can destabilize existing aquatic systems. Complex and enduring regenerative cycles can be altered or disrupted.
- The abundance and diversity of organisms may decrease.
- In extreme cases, die-offs and habitat loss may occur.

Consequences of Eutrophication for Humans

- Loss of commercially important species
- Loss of jobs
- Introduction of nuisance species
- Aesthetic damage

Global Warming—The Greenhouse Effect

There has been an ongoing debate about the extent of human involvement in the general warming trend of the last 50 years. The complexity of atmospheric processes and uncertainty in the data have fueled skepticism about the involvement of human activities, but the consensus in the scientific community is swinging strongly toward at least some human complicity in the earth's warming. Our opinion is that the circumstantial evidence that warming is at least partly due to human activity is strong enough to accept.

The term "greenhouse effect" is based on the perceived similarity of earth's atmospheric processes to the workings of a greenhouse. In a greenhouse, the glass allows most of the visible light from the sun to pass through. Because most of the sun's radiation to earth is in the visible range, most of the incident solar radiation gets into the greenhouse, where much of it is absorbed by the plants and other solid objects. The absorbed solar radiation causes the solid objects to heat up. Some of the absorbed heat is then reradiated to the surroundings (all objects on earth radiate to their surroundings; the warmer they are, the greater the energy they radiate), but this time the radiation is called "long-wave" or infrared radiation. We can't see it, but we can measure it. Glass is not transparent to long-wave radiation. It absorbs it and reradiates much of it back in to the greenhouse. This is why greenhouse temperatures become elevated during the day.

"Greenhouse" gases in our atmosphere are analogous to the glass of a real greenhouse. They allow short-wave (visible) solar radiation from the sun to pass to the earth's surface but absorb a portion of the long-wave radiation that the earth radiates back toward space. Constituents of the atmosphere that behave this way include water vapor, carbon dioxide, methane, nitrous oxide, and hydrofluorocarbons, among others.

The earth's atmosphere has behaved like a greenhouse from its early history (water vapor and carbon dioxide have long been present). In general, this has been a good thing. Trapping and holding solar radiation has helped to moderate and stabilize the earth's climate, which has been beneficial to life. In the vast coldness of space, being able to hold onto heat can be very helpful.

Being a greenhouse can become a problem, however, if the earth retains too much heat. The regenerative cycling of nutrients, gases, and water often includes essential biological components (plants, bacteria, and other organisms). Many organisms thrive only within fairly narrow temperature ranges. Shifting temperatures out of these ranges can seriously impair cycle functioning. The impairments may be temporary (until the population adapts or is replaced by another population that fulfills the same ecological role). There may be permanent impairment (if replacement species function at a significantly different level or if the original population persists impaired). There may be complete loss of function (if no other species fulfills a similar role in the cycle or if other factors change the nature of the habitat).

In addition to directly affecting living organisms, warming may indirectly alter habitat and cycle functions. Temporary changes in ocean currents, blamed on ocean warming, have reduced nutrient contents in areas that have historically supported large populations of fish. Loss of the nutrients reduces the amount of food that supports such populations, thus decreasing population numbers. This phenomenon, characterized by a flow of unusually warm waters, called "El Nino," has caused temporary declines in fisheries located in the eastern Pacific (mainly Peru, Ecuador, and Chile).

As discussed earlier, the large human population and high degree of specialization in our cultures make us particularly susceptible to the effects of disruptive events. Impairment of agricultural production, for the same reasons mentioned, is also a cause for concern in the event of warming. Rosy scenarios ("production will increase due to carbon dioxide enrichment"; "the corn belt will become the rice belt") ignore the interdependence of many factors inherent in agriculture. Complex interdependent systems, such as agriculture, may take more time to recover from perturbations than humans can afford. It should also be noted that this argument ignores the catastrophic scenarios that are often included in discussions of global warming (melting ice caps that may cause loss of coastal habitat; increasingly violent weather patterns due to the increased energy content of the lower atmosphere; increased prevalence of droughts and floods).

Consequences of Global Warming for Ecological Systems

- Loss of populations and diversity as temperatures exceed species' tolerance
- Population shifts with uncertain effects on the previous habitat functions
- Altered weather patterns and ocean currents

Consequences of Global Warming for Humans

- Potential disruptions to agriculture
- Potential disruptions to fishing
- Some loss of habitat
- Increasingly violent weather patterns

This chapter has discussed two ways in which human activities can affect regenerative cycles. There are many other examples (heavy metal pollution, the effect of DDT on various systems, and degradation of the protective ozone layer, among others). But this book is not about "gloom and doom." It is about finding ways to live within the rules that govern regenerative cycles or, failing that, to minimize the extent that we stray from those rules.

LEARNING TO LIVE WITHIN EARTH'S LIMITS: SUSTAINABILITY AND SUSTAINABLE PRACTICES

Sustainability literally means the ability to persist; the capacity to continue. When applied to the relationship of humans with their environment, sustainability means the ability to persist for an extended time period; for as far as we can see into the future.

There are (at least) two aspects of sustainability to consider. First, to persist as a species, we must meet our basic needs (food, water, shelter, and so on). Second, to be indefinitely sustainable, we must avoid "killing the goose that laid the golden eggs." We must, as Wendell Berry pointed out, *make the effort to know the world and to learn what is good for it . . . to cooperate in its processes, and to yield to its limits.* Only by learning to live within these limits can we achieve sustainability.

The remaining chapters of this book address sustainable practices. A sustainable practice is a method to meet a basic human need that is consistent with sustainability. The practices presented in this book are quite diverse, but they share common elements, including:

- Use of resources that are renewable
- Creation of wastes that become resources for other processes
- Use of resources and creation of wastes at rates that are consistent with the rates at which resources become available and wastes can be processed

Environmentally sustainable practices are like the pieces of a puzzle that, taken as a whole, can help to make us sustainable.

Can we learn to *cooperate in* [the earth's] *processes, and to yield to its limits?* Of course we can. Humans are remarkably adaptable creatures. The knowledge base of "how to" information is broad and growing. The good news is that many sustainable practices are relatively easy and inexpensive to implement. The real question is: are we willing to change our habits? We believe that, with knowledge, all things are possible. The purpose of this book is to put useful knowledge before the reader in a form that is convenient to use. The chapters provide references to a broad range of materials on sustainable development and regenerative practices. We believe that people want and need this information. The measure of this book's success will be whether it proves to be a good conduit for its delivery.

Chapter 2

Blending the Human Landscape with the Natural Ecological System

Designing and managing human developments based on the regenerative capacities of the natural ecological system will contribute to the health of global natural systems, instead of degrading their well-being and integrity.

This chapter discusses how we have to live if we are going to survive. To blend human development with nature, we must understand how ecosystems exist in their normally healthy state, never seeming to be out of balance, ill in any way, or without food for growth. The indefinitely sustainable ecosystem is earth-friendly and continually improves environmental conditions, rather than degrading environments as do most human landscapes. It is our hope to impart a method to design and manage human developments based on the processes used in the indefinitely sustainable natural ecosystem. These processes allow nature to flourish in a sustainable way, without creating wastes and without using massive amounts of fossil fuels for survival, as do most human landscapes.

ECOSYSTEM AS A MODEL FOR DESIGN AND MANAGEMENT OF THE LANDSCAPE

In his book *Fundamentals of Ecology,* noted ecologist Eugene Odum says, "Any area of nature that includes living organisms and nonliving substances interacting to produce an exchange of materials between the living and nonliving parts is an ecological system or ecosystem." The four interacting components constituting an ecosystem are:

- *Compounds* in the environment, both organic and inorganic
- *Producing organisms,* usually plants, that make food from inorganic compounds
- *Consuming organisms,* usually animals, that eat plants or other animals
- *Decomposing organisms,* usually bacteria and fungi, that break down compounds and release minerals usable by the producers

Examples of ecosystems are a pond, a lake, a forest, an aquarium, a desert, the tundra, and a prairie grassland. The three environments in which ecosystems exist are freshwater, saltwater—also known as marine—and land-based or terrestrial environments. To better understand what an ecosystem is, let us look at the ecology of a pond, a deciduous forest, and a grassland.

Pond Ecosystem

When examining a pond landscape (Figure 2-1), notice that it is a place where there are plants, animals, water, and mud. In the pond there are living organisms and non-living materials. Looking back at the four components that make up an ecosystem, we see that there are organic and inorganic compounds present in the water. Both types of compounds contain oxygen, carbon dioxide, nitrogen, calcium, and phosphorus. There are producers making food from the organic and inorganic compounds, including plants growing in the mud where the water is shallow and plants floating in the water. Plants use inorganic material that bacteria must mineralize before it becomes available. There are also small algae plants, called phytoplankton, that are suspended in the water, and they are making food as well. In fact, the algae are significant food producers in a water landscape, often outproducing the larger plants. These phytoplankton usually exist as deeply as light can penetrate into the water. Next, consumer organisms in the pond environment eat the plants and the algae, and each other. These include fish, crawfish, snails, and insects. Consumers that eat only plants are called herbivores. Consumers that eat other animals are called carnivores. Finally, the bacteria and fungi decomposers feed on the dead plant and animal matter, creating a mineral or nutrient pool for use by the producer plants to grow more biomass. This decomposition usually happens in the lower level of the pond, which ecologist Odum calls the "decomposition-nutrient regeneration" zone. By contrast, sunlight and compounds in the upper level of the pond are being used by producers for plant biomass production, thereby creating a "production zone." This composition of living organisms and nonliving compounds, and their dependence on each other for survival and health, is what is called the pond ecosystem.

Deciduous Forest Ecosystem

In a deciduous forest ecosystem with abundant rainfall of 30 to 60 in. (762 to 1524 mm) per year, there are large hardwood plants that form a canopy or an overstory (Figure 2-2). Small trees, shrubs, and forbs are located beneath, in what is called the understory. The trees and shrubs produce a large amount of fruit and nuts that attract and support deer, bears, squirrels, racoons, foxes, and bobcats. Birds also attracted to this environment include turkeys, woodpeckers, and a large number of small songbirds. The forest floor is covered with plant detritus that is full of bacteria, fungi, and insects. The forest floor humus provides food for the plants and acts as a sponge, soaking up rainfall and storing water for later use. The flow of nutrients from the plants to the consumers, then to the decomposers and back to the producers, forms a loop that demonstrates a sustainable flow of materials in the ecosystem. In this ecosystem, as in all ecosystems, the water, materials, and energy flow in a closed loop where waste products are always used to sustain life.

Figure 2-1   Pond or freshwater wetland landscape.

Grassland Ecosystem

A grassland ecosystem (Figure 2-3) has low rainfall, generally from 10 to 30 in. (254 to 762 mm) per year. This is the reason trees are not present. Grasses can exist with less water. The soil of the grassland is composed of large amounts of organic matter that provides nutrients and stores water for later use. Many of the grasses produce a thick sod covering over the soil that also protects it from wind erosion. Root systems of grasses go deep, often two to three times the height and mass of the aboveground portion of the plant. Plants other than the grasses, such as sunflowers, do grow here, but these are only a small part of the grassland ecosystem. Grasslands provide homes, or habitat, and food for ground squirrels, prairie dogs, and gophers. Birds attracted to the prairie grasslands include prairie chickens and meadowlarks. Grazing animal inhabitants include American bison and antelope. Carnivores attracted to grassland inhabitants include foxes, badgers, coyotes, and hawks.

The sun, and the nutrients provided by the decomposers, enable plants to grow. The plants provide food for the herbivores, such as the bison and prairie dogs. The herbivores become food for the carnivores, such as the coyote and the hawk. From the dead plants and animals and their waste matter, decomposers create minerals, or nutrients, that become food for the producers to continue production of plant biomass. Thus, the circle of life continues on and on. This is why the natural ecosystem is called the indefinitely sustainable ecosystem, and this is why the ecosystem is a great model for consideration in creating human landscapes. It is also the only model for sustainable living.

Figure 2-2 Deciduous forest and overstory canopy.

THE RELATIONSHIP BETWEEN NATURE AND THE DEVELOPMENTS OF HUMANKIND

Ecosystems are influenced by humans and most also have human presence within them. For this reason, it is important that we understand ecosystem processes and determine how to design and manage our own landscapes so that they become a part of the ecosystem. As the designer/manager works toward blending human developments with these natural processes, a human landscape evolves that is regenerative and in harmony with the natural ecosystem. Regeneration and regenerative technologies are important to all design and management. Let us define a few terms important to understand when creating sustainable landscapes.

Landscape—The landscape is an assemblage of all the living species and nonliving materials within and upon the land, both natural and human-made. It also includes the

Figure 2-3 Grassland or prairie type ecosystem.

natural processes that occur, such as nutrient uptake, chemical transformation, and energy transfer. The landscape is buildings, roads, agriculture, parks, and everything else on the land. The human landscape includes both human-made developments and their management practices.

Ecosystem—Simply stated, an ecological system (ecosystem) is a system in which living species and nonliving materials interact with one another in a given area. A given ecosystem can be of any size, ranging from the whole earth to a pond, a forest, the shaded area under a porch, or a square foot of turf.

Regeneration—Regeneration refers to the ability for something to happen again and again. Regeneration means to bring into existence again, to reproduce, to be able to continue to exist through continually applying certain processes. When applied to environmental systems, regeneration is the creation of a resource through the reassembly of waste products. Regenerative systems use the natural cycling of materials to continually provide essential resources.

Renewable Resources—Renewable resources are constantly being produced and made available as a result of natural processes. The sun, wind, and surface runoff water are renewable resources that are continually recurring. The trees of the forest, grasses, crops, and soil are also continually renewable, just like the humus from yard waste and manure from the animal kingdom.

Nonrenewable Resources—These are resources that are not being constantly produced and are not available for continuous use. They include groundwater reserves, minerals in the ground, and fossil fuels like oil, coal, and gas that have taken millions of years to form.

Sustainability—Sustainability means the ability to continue in existence or in a certain state; to keep up or prolong. Sustainable development allows the current needs of people to be met without compromising the ability of future generations to meet their own needs. Although we must change the natural landscape to meet the needs of humankind, we can do so while respecting the natural order, structure, and function of the ecosystem and making sure that humans' life-support systems blend with the natural, regenerative processes of the ecosystem. With this approach, we will not deplete resources, create pollution, or harm natural ecosystems.

Processes of Regeneration

Species in any environment perform consistent sets of activities or processes in order to maintain life. These processes enable the natural ecological system to sustain itself through regeneration. This ability to regenerate is based on five commonly occurring activities that take place within a natural ecosystem. These five functions, or processes of regeneration, are key to sustaining life in a natural ecosystem, and they can be copied by humans in order to blend human developments with the natural landscape. By doing this, we can meet human needs with regenerating life-support systems. The regenerative capacity of the landscape is affected by these processes, which influence the flow of water, nutrients, and energy within an ecosystem:

Processes of Regeneration

1. Conversion
2. Distribution
3. Filtration
4. Assimilation
5. Storage

These five processes maintain an ecosystem in a healthy, self-renewing condition.

1. *Conversion.* Conversion is the process of converting from one thing to another. A great example of conversion is what happens with the light from the sun. The sun's rays are collected by plants, and through photosynthesis the sun's energy is converted into food for the plant, and food for whatever eats the plant. Once the sun's energy is converted to plants and the plants are eaten, the plants are then converted into the biomass of animals. Milk and meat produced to feed people are examples of conversion. When plants are harvested for creating ethanol, a natural substitute for gasoline, they are converted from one form to another—a further example.

2. *Distribution.* Nature provides many ways for energy and materials to get to all the users in the ecosystem. Wind, water, and traveling animals distribute materials naturally to the users. Human transportation systems have impacted natural distribution patterns by transporting materials beyond the places to which they would have been moved naturally. Notably disastrous human distributions include transporting various pathogenic viruses and bacteria, fire ants, and invasive plants that thrive outside their natural ecosystems and take over the habitats of native plants and animals.

3. *Filtration.* Nature's air and water purification system is composed of plants, microbes, humus, soil, and rock. As air moves over and through the landscape, organic and inorganic matter is removed through filtration by plant leaves and consumption by bacteria located on plant leaves and stems and within decaying plant matter. Water is filtered, removing organic and inorganic matter, by plant detritus or organic matter on the forest floor, in our planting beds, and in freshwater wetlands and saltwater marshes. Grass, for example, filters water as it slows down sediment-laden runoff and retains the sediment so that it does not enter the stream system. Soil and fragmented rock perform the last filtration step before the water joins a larger reservoir of pure underground water.

4. *Assimilation.* To be assimilated means to be absorbed and incorporated. When animals consume plant biomass, the plants are assimilated into the living tissue of animals. As plants shed their leaves and die, plant matter is consumed by microorganisms, or decomposers, who assimilate the matter and transform it into soil minerals for eventual use by living plants. Decomposers include insects, worms, bacteria, and fungi. When animals create waste or die, they undergo the same decomposition by microbes as do the plants, and their waste or dead bodies are transformed into soil minerals. A popular newsmagazine calls microbes "the New Emperors" in honor of the important role they play in health, cleanliness, and productivity (Charles W. Petit and Laura Tangley, "The Invisible Emperors," *U.S. News and World Report,* November 1999.). Microbes are largely responsible for assimilating waste and generating minerals for plant use. They assist in closing the loop of the continuous flow of energy and materials in the natural ecological system. When nutrient-enriched treated sewage biosolids and liquid effluent are placed on hay fields, the grasses assimilate both the nutrients and the liquid effluent, which also contains nutrients. When chicken manure is spread on a vegetable garden for fertilizer, the nutrients in the manure will be assimilated by the plants and incorporated into new plant biomass.

5. *Storage.* In the natural system materials are usually stored for a period of time before they are reused. The humus on the forest floor is stored plant food, awaiting further decomposition before being made available following mineralization. The nutrients from human sewage can be stored in human-made lagoons and wetlands for eventual land application. Both aquifers and cisterns store water, and even fossil fuels are stored underground, sometimes for millions of years. Storage is essential for meeting the needs of the natural plant and animal community, which includes human beings.

Human Influence and the Ecosystem

Because human activities affect all life on earth, it is important to include human thought in the process of design and management of natural systems. Natural systems are not machines and therefore require constant observation and evaluation in order for managers to remain aware of their health and performance. It is important for us to understand the processes of nature and to consider them in the management of natural preserves, in the design of new human landscapes, and in the redesign or retrofitting of existing and unsustainable human landscapes. Table 2-1 relates the processing characteristics of the ecosystem to human activities.

That human development must become a harmonious partner with nature is the challenge. If a healthy earth is to be maintained, then human needs and natural processes must be considered together. The survival of natural, wild preserves where nature can evolve without human influence is an essential part of the challenge. Landscape architect John Lyle said that it is the garden that will eventually sustain humankind. Human thought

Table 2-1 Relating Ecosystem Processing Characteristics to Activities Within the Human Ecosystem

Flows of Energy, Water, and Materials	*Ecosystem Processing Characteristics*
Gardens are planned according to the seasons for provision of food for the family.	Human thought
Plantings receive sunlight, water, and nutrients, which stimulate growth.	Assimilation/conversion
Food is produced from the plantings.	Conversion
Food is harvested and taken to the kitchen.	Distribution
Meals are created and consumed by the family.	Assimilation/conversion
Food is processed and preserved for future use.	Conversion/storage
Kitchen food waste is taken to a compost pile.	Distribution
Food scraps break down into nutrients in the compost pile.	Assimilation/conversion
Cured compost is placed on the garden.	Distribution
Plants use compost for nourishment.	Assimilation
Human sewage created by the family travels to the septic tank.	Distribution
Sewage biosolids are consumed by microbes in the septic tank.	Conversion/storage
Nutrients from biosolids are co-composted with plant biomass.	Distribution/assimilation
Sewage effluent is treated by microbes in a rock-reed (plant-reed) biological sewage treatment system.	Conversion
Nutrient-enriched sewage effluent is stored for irrigation use and applied to the gardens when needed.	Storage/assimilation
Sunlight is captured by regenerative technologies for use in the shelter.	Conversion
Solar radiation (sun heat) is stockpiled in the thermal mass during the heating season to be used for space heating when interior temperatures become too cold.	Storage
Solar radiation is captured by solar collectors for water and space heating.	Conversion
Solar radiation is used to make electricity through the use of photovoltaics.	Conversion
Trees capture solar radiation and combine it with water and nutrients to create wood biomass.	Assimilation/conversion
Wood biomass is used for cooking and heating.	Conversion
Wood ashes (potash) are spread on the garden for plant nourishment.	Assimilation
Rain that falls on the shelter roof is harvested and stored for future use.	Storage
Stored water is used for irrigation, cleaning, flushing.	Distribution/assimilation
Runoff water is detained to remove suspended sediments, pathogens, and nutrients before being released into the natural drainage system.	Storage/filtration

will be essential for continuous evaluation of the performance of the garden and other regenerative technologies used in the human ecosystem to sustain human developments and landscapes.

Human Life-Support System

People have basic needs that must be met. The following are the various components of the human life-support system:

Components of the Human Life-Support System

1. Food
2. Water
3. Shelter
4. Energy
5. Waste processing
6. Landscape management

The provision of these needs often results in the creation of waste, pollution, and the indiscriminate use of fossil fuels. Life-support system needs must be planned for up front when creating sustainable landscapes, in order to blend with the natural ecological system and not be a burden on the already strained environment.

Regenerative Technologies

When a technology that supports human developments has the ability to occur over and over without using nonrenewable resources, it is said to be regenerative. Examples of regenerative technologies include storing rainwater in cisterns, using constructed wetlands for sewage treatment, applying sewage effluent (the liquid part) and biosolids (the solid part) on land for plant growth, using solar collectors for heating water and photovoltaics for making electricity, designing shelters that use thermal mass for heat storage, creating overhangs for sun control, and siting shelters with a south-facing orientation for optimizing solar heat gain in the heating season and minimizing solar heat gain during the cooling season. Regenerative technologies also include using wind to pump water and generate electricity, gardening in an intensive and organically based manner for food production, composting, using a bicycle for transportation, and creating meadows and forests to replace grassed lawn areas. Note that all of these regenerative technologies use renewable resources, such as sun, wind, soil, water, plants, animals, and insects, rather than depending heavily on nonrenewable resources.

Blending Humans with Nature

The human ecosystem should be the blending of humans with nature in such a manner that human life support needs are met through regenerative processes characteristic of the natural ecological system. In the human ecosystem, the necessity for food, water, shelter, waste processing, energy, and landscape management can be met by modeling those

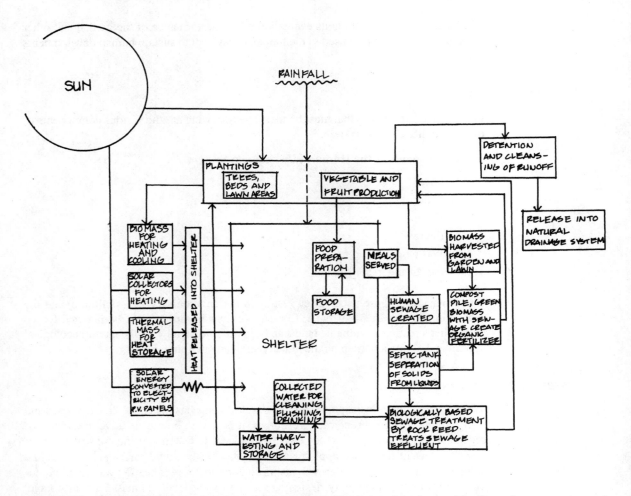

Figure 2-4 Flow of energy, water, and waste in the sustainably designed landscape. The flow of energy, water, and materials or nutrients is shown in this human ecosystem flow diagram. The lines with arrows illustrate the paths of flow for the sun's energy, rainfall, and materials or nutrients necessary for survival and growth. Note that the paths of flow form loops where all waste is reused and no waste is created.

needs on the regenerative processes of conversion, distribution, filtration, assimilation, storage, and human thought. Let us define *human ecosystem*.

The human ecosystem is a human-made landscape created to accommodate people and their needs in a sustainable manner. In this well-conceived landscape, the life support systems of the people are modeled on the regenerative processes of the natural ecological system.

The Human Landscape of Today

The human landscape of today is a result of design and planning modes that evolved during the Renaissance, which placed people as central and dominant in the design and development of all landscapes. Land existed primarily for the benefit of humankind. There was little care or concern for the health of the natural landscape. The old ways of planning, design, and management do not work with the natural processes of the world. Observe, if you will, the many resulting impacts of humans on nature, including the hole in the ozone layer, global warming, the impending rise in sea level, dwindling natural wild areas, loss of biodiversity, growing extinction of species, polluted runoff, groundwater depletion and pollution, air pollution, and chemically tainted food products.

CONCLUSION

The purpose of this discussion on how we can blend human developments with the natural ecological system is to provide an understanding of a landscape, an ecosystem, renewable resources, nonrenewable resources, sustainability, regenerative processes in the ecosystem, human life support needs, regenerative technologies, and human ecosystems.

By being aware of how natural systems work, we can design human life support systems without relying heavily on nonrenewable resources, and without creating wastes that are not assimilated and reused (Figure 2-4). The natural ecosystem can become the model for redevelopment of human landscapes and for basing new designs and management processes on the indefinitely sustainable natural ecological system. This natural model will keep human landscapes healthy and productive, without damaging and destroying the environment in which we live.

Chapter 3

Estimating Costs in the Sustainable Landscape

Cost Savings: By computing costs based on factors such as the initial outlay of capital, the longer-term costs of operation and management, and the cost of environmental impacts, enough information will be available to make intelligent and sound choices that can save enormous amounts of money over the life of a material, technology, or development. By making cost estimates inclusive of environmental impacts, regenerative technologies can be equitably compared with more conventional ways of meeting human needs.

In estimating costs, there are several different ways to compute expenditures, such as determining the first costs of a purchase and identifying the long-term operation and management costs. These latter costs will provide the investor with a more accurate view of true costs throughout the life of a material, technology, or development. Another category of cost is the value of adverse environmental impacts of a facility or project. Someone or some group will eventually have to pay for these adverse impacts. When a land developer builds a project, detrimental or adverse impacts may include increased storm drainage; pollution of runoff; increased traffic and the need for more and bigger roadways; demand for sewage treatment facilities, water supply facilities, electricity and power generation facilities; and increased pollution of air. Other effects may even include disturbance of wildlife habitat and disruption of the migrating corridors of larger mammals like the bobcat. Mitigating all of these impacts will cost money, and it is usually the taxpayers who collectively bear these expenses produced by private land development and by inferior first-cost material and technology choices. If all of these costs can be determined, wouldn't it be more equitable for the developer who creates the impacts and the need for these changes to finance the abatement of the impending impacts? In estimating costs, should more than just the initial costs be considered? Maybe public policy should charge such predictable impacts to the developer. Knowing that these costs will occur, a developer can then pass the charges along to buyers.

WHAT COSTS ARE BASED ON

In estimating expenditures, it is important to define the full breadth of costs to be incurred. Let us evaluate an example of the costs that can accrue beyond the purchase of a new lawn mower for $400. Although repair costs should be limited for the first few years, there will be fuel and oil costs, as well as the cost of transportation and time needed to purchase these products. Time will also be expended to keep the air filter and sparkplug clean, the underside of the mower cleared of grass, and the mower blade sharpened (about every eight cuttings). When the mower needs repair, the cost of labor for evaluation and repair and the purchase price of parts will be a portion of the ongoing costs. Transportation and time for dropping the mower off at a repair shop, and picking it up when finished, should be added to the overall expenditure. When not being used, the mower will have to be stored and protected from the weather; will a special shelter be needed for this storage? It will also have to be winterized when the growing season is over, and checked for readiness at the beginning of the spring mowing season. The impact on air quality of a gasoline-powered lawn mower is significant and, collectively, can be a very serious problem in many urban areas. The state of California is seeking to make traditional gasoline-powered lawn mowers more efficient and has established a program whereby it will exchange an electric-powered mower for one that is gas-powered. Finally, when the mower is worn out, what is the cost of depositing it in a landfill? Or should the mower be disassembled and its components and materials reused and recycled? It is clear that the $400 cost of the mower can expand to be much greater than the initial cost. Added expenses can include the costs of operation and management, the impacts associated with air pollution, and the expense of either placing the mower in a landfill or disassembling it and recycling and reusing the parts.

Because the list of hidden costs can vary, we are going to define several ways to compute costs. An understanding of the different ways expenditures can be classified may help to convince people of the value of regenerative technologies and sustainable development methods that have lower life cycle and long-term environmental degradation costs.

First Costs

The $400 cost of the mower in this example is a first cost. When equipment or materials are purchased, the money paid for the commodities is the first cost. If a contractor gives a price to construct a project, it will be a first cost and will include the labor and materials needed to get the project built. In buying a mower or creating a land development project, first costs are usually the only costs considered by owners and contractors. A developer of a "speculation project," once the property sells, has no further interest in it, as that builder's first costs and profit have been met. The initial costs and all future costs are then passed on to the next owner. The label "first costs" implies that there will be additional costs to come.

Life Cycle Costs

As in the case of costs incurred after purchase of a mower, the next property owner will pay not only the initial costs, but also life cycle costs, which will include the expenses of operation and management over the entire life of a material, technology, or development. For example, an installed landscape composed of grassed areas, mulched shrub and flower beds, tree plantings, and walkways will cost about 20% of its original, installed price to be professionally maintained each year. After five years, the life cycle expenditures will equal the original installed costs of the landscape. The owner will be buying that landscape every five years by paying the operation and management, or life cycle, costs.

Often, when first costs are low, the life cycle costs can be high because of the inefficiency or less durable construction of a material or technology, which usually consume more energy and materials. Heaters and air conditioners are good examples. Lower first costs usually mean that the unit is less efficient and will require more energy and more frequent replacement of parts. The more expensive units with higher efficiency ratings will have increased longevity and lower energy requirements for the provision of heating and cooling. In creating a sustainable development, it is important to be aware not only of first costs, but also of life cycle or the long-term costs of facility operation and management.

Regenerative technologies and sustainable developments usually have lower life cycle costs because of a decreased consumption of energy and materials. For example, a constructed wetland sewage treatment facility will have significantly lower construction costs, and operation and management costs will be a fraction of those at an energy-intensive conventional concrete and steel facility. For The Woodlands, a planned unit development in Texas, landscape architects designed an aboveground storm drainage system composed of swales and detention pools instead of one composed of underground pipes and catch basins. The first costs of the aboveground system, which was based on the natural model of how nature would catch and release water, were 75% less than a belowground system of pipes would have been. In addition, life cycle costs are lower and runoff water quality has been improved. Impending federal regulations will require communities, by 2008, to clean up the quality of their storm drainage to reduce impacts on rivers and other receiving waters like bays, estuaries, and gulfs. This is an example of environmental impact costs that have been saved through relying on a regenerative technology.

When deciding on whether to select a conventional convection heating and cooling system or an earth-coupled heat pump for the landscape architecture design studios, Mississippi State University administrators chose to invest a greater amount of up-front money (first costs) for a ground source (earth-coupled) heat pump system and thus pay up to 50% lower energy bills (life cycle costs) throughout the life of the more energy-efficient system. This decision was made after studying the life cycle costs of the two systems. The electrically powered ground source heat pump system also produced about 30% less CO_2 than the conventional system, even considering the energy it took to produce the electricity at the power plant. This forward thinking by university administrators demonstrates the value of considering life cycle costs as a way of accounting for costs that also promotes energy conservation and reduced environmental impacts.

Total Costs Including Impacts on the Environment

There is an inclusive way of figuring costs that embraces all of the expenditures of a project, technology, or material. Total costs can include the expense of reducing air pollution, water pollution, storm water runoff, the disruption of wildlife migration corridors, and degradation of the environment caused by increased traffic. An interesting example

Figure 3-1 Land development that completely covers the land and creates large amounts of runoff.

of management costs that are known but not included with first costs paid by the American consumer is the approximately $80 cost per barrel of oil for military protection of Middle East oil fields and the safeguarding of shipping lanes. These costs are not passed on to oil companies and added to the $35 cost per barrel of oil to be made into heating oil and gasoline, but instead are absorbed as a military expense. When all measurable costs are considered, the true impact to the environment becomes apparent. As in the case of problems caused by the use of asbestos or fiberglass materials, someone at some time is going to have to pay for the problems caused by a land development project that completely covers a site with impermeable paving, creating great quantities of water runoff and smothering biotic communities that once were a part of the biodiversity of the area. Figure 3-1 shows an example of a development that impacts the environment by covering a large part of a landscape and creating massive amounts of storm water runoff.

In convincing users and government officials of the need for regenerative technologies, a project's first costs, life cycle costs, and total costs, including environmental impacts, should be developed and presented as measurable project costs so as to allow a full and fair comparison of all of the costs of the project.

PART II

Water in the Sustainable Landscape

Chapter 4

Water Quality

A basic understanding of water quality is an essential component in the overall understanding of sustainable living and regenerative systems.

We cannot survive without clean high-quality water. If we do not have it to drink, we die in three to four days. Water is essential for food production, as well as for many commercial activities. Yet we frequently treat our water as though it has no value. We pay little for it, and we sometimes waste a great deal of it.

Like other resources, our water is not limitless. Although our supply of water is continually renewed by rains, the amount of surface water plus groundwater available for our use at any one time is finite. In many parts of the world (including places within the United States) there are predictions of water shortages in the next 20 years. The Johns Hopkins Population Information Program says that by 2025, the probability of wars being fought over water sources is high, unless prompt and concerted action is taken.

Many of the sustainable approaches presented in this book are based on a working knowledge of "water quality." This is a general term that can mean many things, but all aspects of water quality refer to a central theme: the effect that the constituents or characteristics of water have on the organisms or communities of organisms that depend on water for survival.

People can harm water quality in a multitude of ways. We divide types of human-induced water pollution into two categories: point source and non-point source. In its most general sense, a point source is a concentrated and identifiable source of pollutants added to water. Discharges from sewage treatment plants, factories, and animal feedlots are obvious examples of concentrated discharge sites. *Non-point source* (NPS) pollution, in its most general sense, includes all the diffuse and not easily defined ways that pollutants can enter receiving waters (nonconcentrated storm water runoff, deposition from combustion exhausts, wind blown deposits, etc.). Legally, in the United States, a point source is defined by the Water Quality Act of 1987. National Pollutant Discharge Elimination System (NPDES) permits are required for city and town sewage treatment plants, industries, storm water runoff from cities of more than 100,000 population, storm water runoff from certain industries, and animal feedlots with more than 1,000 animal units. Everything else is considered part of non-point pollution. This definition is changing, however, as Phase II of the Clean Water Act begins to take effect. Under Phase II, the preceding definitions will become considerably more stringent.

This book focuses on the impacts that individuals can make on the quality of their environment in their daily lives. The ways in which we affect water quality as individuals fall mostly in the non-point source category. It's important to realize, though, that there are indirect collective effects of the things we do that can diminish or improve the quality of our streams, rivers, lakes, and coastal waters. By conserving energy in transportation, we can also reduce a variety of pollutants that enter water via deposition and runoff. Power plant combustion can cause significant damage to natural systems. By incorporating methods to conserve energy (many of which are presented in this book), we can decrease the emissions from fossil-fuel-powered electrical generating plants.

EUTROPHICATION—TOO MUCH OF A GOOD THING

We touched on eutrophication in Chapter 1, "Introduction to Sustainability." Many of the problems that we call pollution in bodies of water are caused by constituents of runoff that, in smaller concentrations, are essential to the organisms and communities of organisms that live there. Plants and bacteria, which form much of the bottom of the food chain in aquatic systems, depend on nutrients that runoff carries from land. In addition, bacteria require organic molecules and, in certain cases (see nitrification, as discussed in a later section under "Nutrients"), nutrient compounds for their energy metabolism. Without these resources, the organisms that feed further up the chain (including many commercially important species) would starve.

Problems arise, however, when any of these "good" constituents in runoff become so abundant that they damage or alter the biological communities that use them. Eutrophication is the process by which a body of water becomes overenriched with nutrients and organic compounds. This happens when the rate at which organic materials are transported into the water, or are produced in the water via photosynthesis, exceeds the capacity of the water to process them without major physical or biological alterations. The dissolved oxygen concentration in an eutrophic body of water may be depleted when microorganisms consume the dead organic material. This can result in fish (and other organism) kills, the production of noxious odors, and a site suitable for pathogenic microorganisms. When re-aeration is sufficient to prevent anoxia (low oxygen), the perturbed conditions may upset the species composition in the body of water, causing a new or existing species to become dominant by out-competing other species that may be essential for the existing community. The dominant photosynthetic organisms in most bodies of water are phytoplankton, which are small single-celled plants. Certain species of phytoplankton (e.g., blue-green algae) thrive in low-oxygen, nutrient-laden conditions and are capable of shading out desirable plants. Chronic low oxygen has been a problem in many areas, including a 7,000 mi^2 (18,000 km^2) region of the Gulf of Mexico. Competitive exclusion of important species due to nutrient enrichment is also an important problem. The Chesapeake Bay is currently a prominent example of this process.

Before we go any further, let's take a closer look at the materials that lead to eutrophication: organic molecules and nutrients.

Organic Molecules

Most commonly occurring organic molecules are created by living creatures (we're excluding manufactured or modified organics for the moment). With the exception of those in a few unusual habitats, only plants and photosynthetic bacteria can create organic molecules from inorganic components, so most other organisms, such as people, are made of material that can be traced back to photosynthesis. Organic molecules always contain carbon atoms that are joined to each other, and to other types of atoms, by bonds that can be created and broken biochemically. The organisms use energy to connect the atoms in organic molecules, and much of this energy is retained in the bonds that connect them. When an organism consumes an organic molecule for food, these bonds can be broken in the process of digestion, releasing energy that is then used by the organism to sustain life.

The aerobic digestion of organic molecules consumes oxygen. The following is a "model" organic molecule (simple carbohydrate):

$$CH_2O + O_2 \rightarrow H_2O + CO_2$$
(carbohydrate + oxygen yields water + carbon dioxide)

The most dramatic effect of adding too much organic material to a body of water is a marked decline in the dissolved oxygen (DO) concentration. A moderate drop in DO can cause stress in aquatic communities. A DO "crash" can wipe out the oxygen-breathing species that cannot escape.

Although it is possible to measure organic carbon in a water sample directly, the most commonly used and reported method is to determine biochemical oxygen demand (BOD). The BOD test measures the oxygen consumed by microorganisms in a sample of water over a specified period of time (usually 5 or 120 days) at a standard temperature (68°F, 20°C). The BOD test directly measures the amount of oxygen required to biologically digest the organic material in the water sample. For a 5-day period, the test measures the amount of oxygen required to consume the readily digestible (most quickly decomposed) fraction of the organic material. For the 120-day test, it is the amount required to digest nearly all of the organic material. Indirectly, BOD is an indicator of the concentration of biodegradable material in the water (primarily organic molecules). The units of BOD are mg/l (milligrams per liter) or ppm (parts per million). Because there are roughly 1 million milligrams in a liter of water, the terms can be used interchangeably.

Nutrients

A nutrient is any type of material necessary for the routine metabolic function of a living organism. Using this definition, organic molecules can be considered nutrients because the energy they release upon digestion is necessary for life. More commonly, though, nutrients include the host of organic and inorganic materials that are necessary to construct specialized types of organic molecules without which the organism would be seriously compromised. Organisms require many nutrients to exist, grow, and reproduce.

Nutrients cycle regeneratively in natural systems. The two nutrients that usually receive most attention in a discussion of environmental issues are nitrogen and phosphorus. The nitrogen cycle is illustrated in Figure 4-1. Organic molecules containing nitrogen are digested by bacteria (ammonifiers), which release ammonia (NH_3). Nitrifying bacteria (species of the genera *Nitrosomonas* and *Nitrobacter*) convert the ammonia to nitrite (NO_2) and then to nitrate (NO_3) in the two-step aerobic process called nitrification. Denitrifying bacteria convert nitrate to gaseous forms of nitrogen in the anaerobic process called denitrification. The gaseous nitrogen then diffuses into the atmosphere. Certain plants and bacteria are able to use ("fix") nitrogen gas (N_2) in the atmosphere (the most common gaseous form) to meet their nitrogen needs. Other plants must get nitrogen from ammonia and/or nitrate. Organically bound nitrogen (in plants and animals) becomes available when the organisms die and are degraded or (in the case of animals) through excretion and feces.

Like nitrogen, phosphorus cycles back and forth between organic and inorganic forms. The most common inorganic form is phosphate (PO_4^{3-}), also commonly referred to as orthophosphorus or reactive phosphorus.

Although there are forms of nitrogen that can be toxic to fish and other organisms in aquatic systems (ammonia and nitrite), the main reason that nitrogen and phosphorus receive so much attention is their effect on species composition and abundance in aquatic systems. Usually, one or the other of them is the "limiting nutrient" for the system. A nutrient is limiting if a small increase in its concentration causes a relatively large increase (a "bloom") in the population of photosynthetic organisms. Other nutrients, although necessary, are sufficiently abundant that small increases in their concentrations have little effect on the population.

Nitrogen and phosphorus are measured with a variety of tests. Like BOD, they are reported in units of mg/l or ppm.

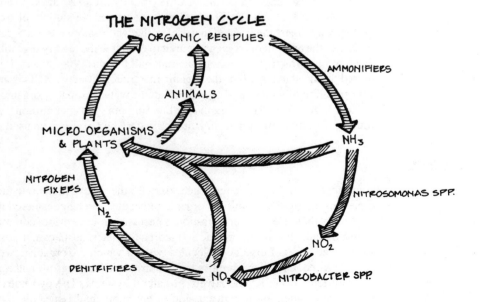

Figure 4-1 The nitrogen cycle.

Primary and Secondary BOD

Eutrophication, and depressed DO concentrations, can result from the effects of organic materials added directly to the water or from organic material produced during increased rates of photosynthesis. Often both will occur. The elevated BODs caused by inflowing organic materials will be followed by a secondary BOD in which nutrients released by the microbial decay of the organic material join with the free inorganic nutrients to drive an increased rate of photosynthesis. Because photosynthesis converts inorganic carbon (CO_2) to organic molecules, the amount of organic material in the water increases, which ultimately increases the BOD of the water.

Seasonal phytoplankton blooms are natural features in many waters. If the blooms are unnaturally large or unnaturally sustained as a result of nutrients added to the water by human activity, undesirable effects may follow. If relatively modest in size, an enhanced or extended bloom can alter the species composition of the habitat. If larger, a subsequent die-off by the population of phytoplankton (a "crash" often follows a "bloom") can lead to oxygen depletion in the water as microorganisms digest the dead phytoplankton. Problems caused by secondary BOD can occur far from the points where the nutrients entered the receiving waters.

EFFECTS OF EROSION ON WATER QUALITY

Human activities frequently cause the turbidity of receiving waters to increase as a result of the transport of eroded soil and other inorganic solids from land to water. Usually, this transport accompanies storm water runoff. In urban and suburban settings, erosion can increase when protective ground cover is removed during construction. After construction, if permeable surfaces are covered with impermeable materials, there is an increase in the volume and velocity of storm water runoff into receiving waters, resulting in further erosion along stream banks (see "Effects of Storm Water Runoff from Impermeable Surfaces" later in this chapter).

The direct effects of erosion are most commonly seen in an increase in the quantity of material suspended in the water column. The method most commonly used to estimate the quantity of this material is a test for "total suspended solids" (TSS). This technique is also sometimes called a determination of "total filterable solids" because, traditionally, TSS was measured by passing water through a filter to capture the solid material. An increase in TSS, if caused by erosion, will result in decreased light penetration into the water, which will inhibit photosynthesis. Increased TSS can also lead to changes in the character of the bottom, as sediment settles out, and a change in species composition, because certain organisms cannot tolerate high TSS.

Humans have had a profound, and mainly detrimental, effect on the solids content of many waterways. There are numerous observations of rivers and streams that ran very clear in the last century that are highly turbid today.

INDICATORS OF SEWAGE CONTAMINATION

Another aspect of water quality is its potential as a source of disease. A number of serious illnesses can be contracted from drinking, or simply coming in contact with, contaminated water. Many human illnesses are transmitted via contact with sewage, and contaminated water can be a vehicle for such contact.

Water quality tests are available to determine whether water has been contaminated with sewage and the degree of contamination. Typically, water samples are screened for contamination by looking for coliform bacteria. Coliform bacteria are mostly non-pathogenic, but they occur in the intestines of all warm-blooded animals (including humans). For this reason, their occurrence in water is used as an indicator of possible sewage contamination. Two tests are routinely performed to determine the presence of coliform bacteria. The total coliform test is simple to perform but indicates only the presence or absence of the bacteria. The fecal coliform test is somewhat more difficult and is used to measure the number of coliform bacteria per 100 ml sample. Often, the total coliform test is used to screen samples, with the fecal coliform test then used to provide quantitative results on samples that tested positive. Water that tests positive for coliform may also be tested for pathogenic bacteria, specific internal parasites, and viruses, depending on need.

Although standards vary somewhat by location, in general:

- Water having any coliform bacteria per 100 ml of water is not generally considered suitable for drinking.
- Water having counts of the bacteria in excess of 200 per 100 ml is usually considered unsafe for swimming.
- Water with counts greater than 1000 per 100 ml is considered unsafe for any contact, and such bodies of water are officially closed.

EFFECTS OF COMBUSTION PRODUCTS FROM FOSSIL FUELS

Combustion products from fossil fuels can have a number of harmful effects if not efficiently "scrubbed" from the exhaust gases. The most dramatic effect, however, appears to be acid deposition.

Acid deposition (frequently referred to as "acid rain") comes about as a result of sulfur dioxide (SO_2) and nitrogen oxides (NO_2 and NO, usually grouped as NO_x) in combustion emissions. The sulfur is a component of burned fossil fuels and other industrial processes. Much of the nitrogen comes from atmospheric nitrogen that reacts with the fuel during the combustion process. Both sulfur and nitrogen oxides readily convert to sulfuric, nitric, and nitrous acids in the atmosphere:

$$2SO_2 + O_2 \rightarrow 2SO_3$$
$$SO_3 + H_2O \rightarrow H_2SO_4$$

(conversion of sulfur dioxide to sulfuric acid)

$$2NO_2 + H_2O \rightarrow HNO_3 + HNO_2$$

(conversion of nitrogen dioxide to nitric and nitrous acids)

The acids do not have to combine with water before they can drop to earth. They can also be deposited as dry acid "salts," hence the term *acid deposition* instead of *acid rain*.

Before going further, let's take a moment to talk about acids, bases, and pH. The degree of acidity of a liquid is determined by testing the "pH." The pH scale runs from 0 to 14. A solution with a pH of less than 7 is acidic; with a pH above 7, it is basic. The definition of pH, and its calculation, are as follows:

$$pH = -\log_{10}[H_3O^+]$$

or minus the base 10 log of the hydronium concentration. Hydronium is a prototypical acid, based on the dissociation of water into an acidic part (hydronium) and a basic part (hydroxide, OH^-):

$$2\,H_2O = H_3O^+ + OH^-$$

The relative proportions of hydronium and hydroxide in water vary, but the product of their molar concentrations will always be 10^{-14}.

EXAMPLE 1. Find the hydronium and hydroxide concentrations and the pH of neutral (neither acidic nor basic) water.

If the water is neutral, then hydroxide and hydronium concentrations must be equal. If the product of the two concentrations is 10^{-14}, then they must each be 10^{-7}. (Remember that when you multiply two exponential numbers, the exponents are added: $10^3 \times 10^3 = 10^6$).

$$[H_3O^+] \times [OH^-] = 10^{14} = [10^{-7}] \times [10^{-7}]$$

The pH is $-\log_{10}[10^{-7}] = 7$.

Now, back to acid deposition. Rain is naturally a weak acid. Water in the atmosphere combines with carbon dioxide to give rain a pH of about 5.6. Rainwater is such a weak acid that it does not affect the buffering capacity of the surfaces it strikes when it hits the earth. *Buffering capacity* refers to the resistance of soil or water to a change in pH. A well-buffered lake won't change pH very much when moderate amounts of acid are added to it.

Most natural waters and soils are well buffered (they have a reasonably high alkalinity, which is a measure of buffering capacity). Their buffering capacity is not, however, unlimited. Adding a sufficient quantity of an acid will eventually drive the pH down to a level that will damage the system. An acid raindrop typically has a pH of less than 4. At the minimum, this means that it is 40 times more acidic than normal rain.

Significant damage has been attributed to acid deposition in extensive regions downwind from sources of sulfur and nitrogen oxides. Not all soils and water bodies are equally well buffered. Waters and soils of low alkalinity suffer most when exposed to acid deposition. Table 4-1 summarizes the effects in lakes.

EFFECTS OF STORM WATER RUNOFF FROM IMPERMEABLE SURFACES

Human development inevitably results in the covering of permeable soil with impermeable materials (asphalt, cement, building covers, etc.). In addition to decreasing the

Table 4-1   Effects of Acid Deposition in Lakes

pH	Effect
6	Decline of some crustacean, insect, and phytoplankton populations
5–6	Alterations in plankton communities; proliferation of less desirable species of algae; likely decline in fish populations
< 5	Virtual elimination of fish species; decline of bacteria population; proliferation of near shore undesirable species

Source: http://www.ec.gc.ca/acidrain/acidwater.html.

recharge of aquifers, this can have severe effects on the quality of the receiving surface waters.

Increased Runoff Volume and Rate

Impermeable surfaces greatly increase both the total volume of runoff from a storm and the maximum flow rate of the runoff, as illustrated in Figure 4-2. The increased runoff volume can contribute to flooding and erosion in receiving streams. The increased velocity and flow rate of the water, as compared with predevelopment rates, exacerbates the flooding and erosion that result from the increased volume. In extreme cases, the increased volume and energy of flow can lead to scouring and channeling of the stream bed.

Flow volumes and velocities can be measured with the use of standard U.S. Geological Survey (USGS) gauging stations or stage recorders mounted in flumes. The methodology for predicting runoff rates and volumes is also well established and produces storm water hydrographs, such as shown in Figure 4-2.

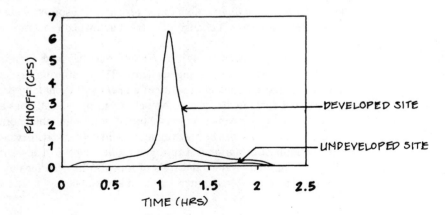

Figure 4-2   Runoff rate for an undeveloped 1 ac (0.4 ha) site, and the same site following coverage with an impermeable surface material (2 in. [5 cm], 2 hour storm). Runoff given in cubic feet per second (CFS).

Bacteria Concentration

Impermeable surfaces do not provide the opportunities for entrapment and filtration that occur in vegetated permeable surfaces. Runoff from impermeable surfaces invariably contains excrement from pets and other animals and can show positive results in tests for coliform bacteria.

Contribution to Eutrophication

Intensively fertilized property (lawns, parks, golf courses) are frequently adjacent to impermeable surfaces. Because there are few opportunities for entrapment or filtration, runoff from such impermeable surfaces may contain measurable nutrient concentrations in addition to bacteria. Moreover, grass and shrub clippings may contribute organic material to the runoff. See an earlier section of this chapter for details pertaining to eutrophication.

Pesticides

Adjacent planted property is also a source of herbicides and insecticides in runoff. Many pesticides are manufactured organic chemicals. A myriad of different chemicals are used, and the long-term effects of low-level exposure have frequently not been determined. Measurement is difficult unless a specific type or class of pesticides is suspected. Units of measurement are generally $\mu g/l$ (microgram per liter) or ppb (parts per billion).

Roadway Contaminants

A variety of organic and inorganic materials are contributed by automobiles. These include gasoline, oil, antifreeze, heavy metals from tires and brakes, rubber, and assorted exhaust products. The toxicities of some of these materials (e.g., petroleum products, heavy metals) are well established.

CONCLUSION

There are many types of pollutants that can enter water. Some are pollutants only because they are added in quantities beyond the capacity of the aquatic system to process or assimilate them.

There are not many avenues by which pollutants enter the water. We can pollute water by contaminating groundwater, by allowing pollutants to enter via storm water runoff, by discharging them from point sources, and by depositing them in the air and letting them drop down later.

Avoiding the addition of pollutants to our waters and protecting the integrity of aquatic systems is partly a matter of attitude, partly a matter of design, and partly a matter of knowledge. It is the latter area that this chapter has, we hope, helped to address.

Chapter 5

Rainwater Harvesting

A properly designed rainwater harvesting system can supply up to 100% of household water needs.

Rainwater harvesting is the practice of capturing and storing rain to provide water for human use. Simple rainwater harvesting systems can be used to supply landscape needs. Systems incorporating more rigorous filtration and treatment processes can be used to meet indoor and potable water needs as well. This chapter addresses residential rainwater harvesting. Regulations for commercial application are more rigorous and beyond the scope of this book.

In many parts of the world, water supply is, or may soon be, inadequate for the needs of the people who live there. Water is continually replenished through the hydrologic cycle so, on a global scale, we are not in danger of running out of this essential resource. But rain does not always arrive where and when we want it. As our population expands, the need to manage this resource in a sustainable manner will become more critical (it is already critical in many locations; see Figure 5-1). Water harvesting, a technology once common but now rarely seen in most places, is a method that allows individuals to play a role in the intelligent management of rainfall. This practice allows the capture and later use of rainwater for a variety of purposes. In addition to taking the pressure off local aquifers and municipal water systems, and providing a measure of independence to water users, rainwater harvesting is useful for other reasons. In terms of our use of energy and resources, it makes little sense to pump and treat water for drinking only to have it applied to grass, gardens, and dirty automobiles. For gardeners, rainwater is a better source of water than treated municipal water because it does not contain residual chlorine that can harm plants. Rainwater harvesting can also help to reduce storm water runoff by intercepting and sequestering it for later use. For all of these reasons, rainwater harvesting can be considered a sustainable practice.

RAINWATER HARVESTING SYSTEMS

Rainwater harvesting systems most frequently collect water from building roofs and store it in tanks, called cisterns. These systems can be divided into two broad groups:

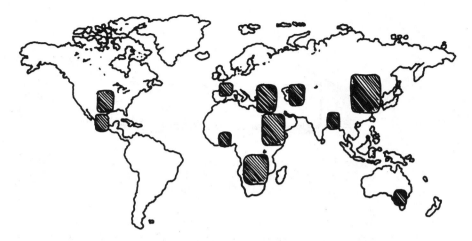

Figure 5-1 Parts of the world experiencing chronic or potentially chronic water supply problems. (*Source:* BBC News Service.)

- *Outdoor-use systems* are systems used strictly to meet outdoor (nonpotable water) needs. Outdoor residential water use in the United States varies from about 7% of the total domestic use (Pennsylvania) to about 44% (California). Outdoor-use-only systems are relatively simple to construct and manage.
- *Indoor-/outdoor-use systems (including potable water)* can be used to meet all domestic water requirements. Of necessity, they are larger and must include a more thorough filtration component than outdoor-only systems. They must also make provision for treating the water to meet drinking water standards.

Because the outdoor-use-only systems are relatively simple in their design, we will begin with these.

Outdoor-Use systems

Outdoor (nonpotable) systems, such as shown in Figure 5-2, usually include the following components:

- *Catchment area*—usually a roof that acts as a surface to collect and direct rainfall
- *Conveyance*—usually a gutter/downspout to transport the collected water to the cistern
- *Filtration*—a method to remove unwanted material from the collected water
- *Cistern (tank)*—used to store collected rainwater
- *Delivery system*—used to transport stored water to the locations where it is used

Systems designed to serve outdoor (nonpotable) water needs range in size from small rain-barrel-sized units to larger systems designed to meet all outdoor needs for an

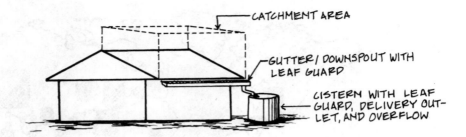

Figure 5-2 Components of a rainwater harvesting system designed for nonpotable (outdoor) uses. Note that the collection area (catchment) is the planar area of the roof. Only one side of the roof is used for collection in the illustration.

extended period of time. All systems reduce the consumption of city and well water. Larger systems can have an impact on storm water runoff during periods of use.

Catchment Area

Most residential rainwater harvesting systems use building roofs as their catchment surfaces. It is also possible to use gullies, drains, and swales to collect and channel water, but these are less common means.

Metal, tile, and slate roofs allow virtually all rainfall to run off. Other materials (such as asphalt shingles) will retain an average of 10 to 15% of incident rainfall.

All roof area is potentially useful as a catchment area. Sections not shaded by trees are preferable, however, because of the increased maintenance associated with debris from trees and its effect on water quality.

The amount of rainwater you can collect in a particular storm depends on the capacity of the catchment area. The catchment is the planar area, rather than the sloped area of a roof (length times width), that has flow routed to a cistern (Figure 5-3).

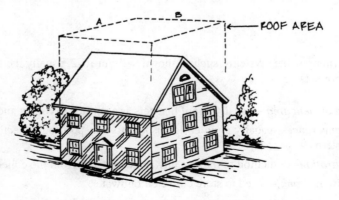

Figure 5-3 The catchment for a rainwater harvesting system is the planar roof area (not the actual area of the covered surface).

EXAMPLE 1. Calculate catchment area for a section of roof. Only one side of a slanted roof is being used for catchment. The planar dimensions of that side are illustrated in Figure 5-4. Compute the area.

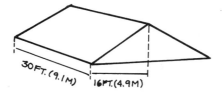

Figure 5-4 Roof from Example 1.

Solution:

$$\text{Area} = 30 \text{ ft} \times 16 \text{ ft} = 480 \text{ ft}^2 (45 \text{ m}^2)$$

The volume of water that will run off the catchment in a particular storm depends on the amount of rain that strikes the catchment, the amount of water retained on the roof, and the amount of water that overshoots the gutters.

The amount of water striking the catchment, in ft^3, is calculated as the amount of rain (converted to feet) times the catchment planar area.

EXAMPLE 2. Calculate the volume of water that lands on the catchment in Example 1 during an 0.8 in. storm.

Solution:

$$\text{Volume of water} = (0.8/12) \text{ ft} \times 480 \text{ ft}^2 = 32 \text{ ft}^3 (0.9 \text{ m}^3)$$

Notice the conversion of inches of rain to feet of rain. Because each cubic foot of rain equals 7.48 gal, the volume of rain calculated here is equal to approximately 239 gal.

A convenient rule of thumb for the volume of water that strikes a catchment is 600 gal per 1000 ft^2 of catchment area for every 1 in. of rain (970 l per 100 m^2 for each 1 cm of rain).

EXAMPLE 3. Resolve Example 2 using the preceding rule of thumb.

Solution:

$$\text{Volume of water} = 0.8 \times (480/1000) \times 600 = 230 \text{ gal (approximate) (885 l)}$$

The fraction of water that runs off the roof and can be stored (i.e., is not lost to retention, overshooting the gutters, leaks, or spillage) varies with the size of the storm, the material and slope of the roof, and the type of system used. For sloped metal, ceramic, or slate roofs, a reasonable rule of thumb is that 90% (0.9) of the volume of rain that strikes the catchment surface can be captured and stored. For sloped shingle roofs, 75% (0.75) is commonly used. For flat roofs, the amount captured may be as little as 50% (0.50).

EXAMPLE 4. Estimate the volume of water that can be captured from a 2 in. rain event on a 700 ft^2 catchment roof. The roof is made of sloped asphalt shingles.

Solution:

Volume captured = (the fraction of water captured) × (the amount of rainfall) × (roof area) × (runoff rule of thumb)

$$V = 0.75 \times 2 \text{ in. } \times 700 \text{ ft}^2 \times (600 \text{ gal}/1000 \text{ ft}^2) = 525 \text{ gal } (2000 \text{ l})$$

Water Conveyance

Gutters, downspouts, and supplemental pipes are usually used to carry rainwater from the roof catchment to the cistern (Figure 5-5). Gutters and downspouts made of aluminum, vinyl, or steel provide the greatest strength and durability, although plastic gutters can be used for short roof runs. Gutters should have a slope of 1/4 to 5/8 in. per 10 ft run. Hangers should be spaced 3 ft (0.9 m) apart. The outer edge of a gutter should be slightly lower than the edge facing the roof. This will direct overflow, should it occur, away from the building. The gutter should be placed slightly below the slope of the roof to protect it from large pieces of debris.

Downspouts should have at least 1 in.^{2} of opening for each 100 ft^2 (7 cm^2 per 10 m^2) of roof area, and there should be at least one downspout per 50 ft (15 m) of run. Although rigorous filtration is not required for an outdoor-use-only system, it is necessary to prevent large objects (leaves, sticks, etc.) from plugging the gutters. Preventing their entry also minimizes other aspects of maintenance (such as cistern cleaning) and helps to keep the stored water aesthetically appealing. There are several types of leaf and debris guards available (Figure 5-5). Traditional leaf guards can be screwed into the gutters. Leaf baskets can be placed at the tops of downspouts. A screen can also be placed at the entrance to the cistern itself.

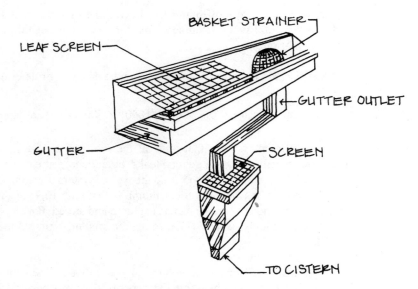

Figure 5-5 Principal features of a conveyance system from the roof to the cistern.

Downspouts often drain directly into the cistern. When the cistern location makes this impractical, pipes can be used to transport water from the downspouts to the tank. Pipes to the tank may be elevated and then turned down into the tank. Alternately, the conveyance structure shown in Figure 5-6 may be used. The vertical pipe will fill up to the elevation (pressure head) that is required to transport the water the required distance and height. Provided that the rigid vertical pipe conveying water to ground level, as shown in Figure 5-6, is taller than the tank, water will flow from the gutters to the tank. It is desirable to make the vertical pipe 2 to 3 ft (60 to 90 cm) taller than the tank to allow the buildup of a pressure head in the event of a partial blockage of the conduit. This configuration is easy to construct and requires minimal support, as most of the weight of the water in the pipe is supported by the ground. A threaded cap on a "tee" at the bottom of the vertical allows water to be manually drained for mosquito control and water quality maintenance.

Water Storage

Storage tanks, or cisterns, come in many sizes and shapes. They can vary from a bucket placed under a downspout to a tank large enough to meet all family needs during extended dry periods. For most rainwater harvesting systems, the tank is the costliest component.

All storage tanks have certain features in common:

- Access that allows periodic cleaning
- A method to exclude mosquitoes
- A method to manage overflow
- A method to withdraw water for use or for emptying

Small Tanks Small tanks have volumes of less than 75 gal (290 l) or so. Small tanks were once common residential features. They were usually "rain barrels," which

Figure 5-6 The height to which water can be lifted depends on the length and width of the pipe used, the number of elbows, and the required flow rate.

provided water usable for a variety of purposes. In a number of forms, small tanks are again becoming popular.

The most commonly used small tanks are 55 gal (200 l) polyethylene drums, although other small containers have been used. They are most often used seasonally in gardens but are useful for other purposes as well (such as washing the car or garden implements and watering indoor plants).

Small cisterns provide an inexpensive and relatively convenient way to try out water harvesting. They can provide high-quality nonchlorinated water in modest volumes. Small cisterns, many of which resemble the traditional rain barrel, are commercially available. Polyethylene drums from food-processing plants are also available and may be adapted for this purpose.

Typically, a small cistern costs relatively little to construct or purchase, is relatively easy to implement, and can produce high-quality water for outdoor uses. The disadvantages are that the volume of water actually captured is not great enough to substantially replace city or well water use or reduce storm water runoff. A small cistern will be quickly exhausted during dry periods and will be quickly filled by runoff from even a modest-sized roof during a heavy rain.

Many people who have larger rainwater harvesting systems started small. The changes that have to be made to the gutters and downspouts to accommodate a rain barrel are easy to do and easy to reverse, so the effort is nearly risk free. It's a great way to try out the concept and gain experience in its implementation.

Small Tank 1—The Simplest Approach   The smallest containers are buckets or small trash barrels. The downspout to be used must generally be shortened so that the spout empties at the bucket height. Alternately, a retractable diversion spout can be installed that can be opened for collection and closed for conventional draining (Figure 5-7). The downspout is shortened, or the diversion spout installed, to accommodate a particular bucket/barrel height.

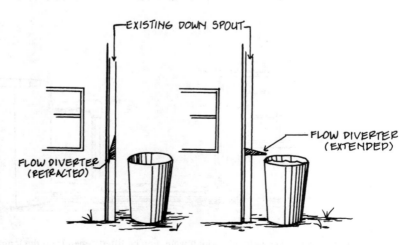

Figure 5-7 A small cistern used with a flow diverter.

Small containers are easy to clean between uses. Many trash barrels come with removable lids that can be used to cover the water surface after collection to prevent contamination with assorted leaves, debris, and insects. If the barrel is too heavy to carry, the water can be dipped or siphoned. Mosquitoes will not be a problem as long as the container is kept covered. Overflow will be over the top of the sides. This may not be a problem, provided the barrel is placed at a location where spillage can be tolerated. A tapered container, such as shown in Figure 5-7, may become top-heavy when full. This may be a consideration if small children are present. To minimize messiness and limit the height of the water in the container, you can drill a hole at the desired height to let the water out. A hose or tube can then be attached to direct the overflow to a desired location.

Small Tank 2—The Rain Barrel   Commercially produced rain barrels come in a variety of shapes and sizes (Figure 5-8). Prices for commercially manufactured containers vary, but are usually about $100. Polyethylene plastic and metal are the predominant materials. Sizes range from 45 to 100 gal (170 to 385 l). Some are made directly from recycled food container drums.

Although the commercially produced containers have a more "finished" appearance, many users make their own, as the process is neither complicated nor difficult. Figure 5-9 shows the necessary components. The screen top is removable for washing. The screen and the tight seal around the inlet prevent entry of mosquitoes and debris. The overflow directs outflow when maximum volume is exceeded. Users sometimes direct the overflow into other containers for additional storage. Delivery is via a faucet and hose. The concrete blocks help to provide a stable base and make it easier to fill containers and empty the barrel.

Medium- to Large-Sized Tanks   Small tanks allow beginners to start collecting water. Medium and large tanks require a greater investment of resources. For this reason, it is useful to consider the size (volume) of the storage system in additional detail.

Figure 5-8   Commercially produced "rain barrels" come in a variety of shapes and sizes.

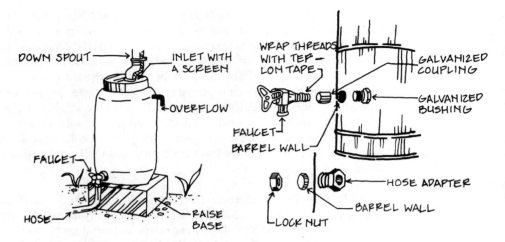

Figure 5-9 Components of a rain barrel. The entire container (top left). Details of the outflow faucet delivery (top right). Details of the overflow (bottom right).

The best tank size for a particular outdoor-use-only application depends on:

- The area of the proposed collection surface
- The amount and frequency of precipitation expected at your location
- How water will be used and delivered
- Financial resources available

Tank Size and Patterns of Precipitation

The area of the collection surface and local patterns of precipitation work together to determine the maximum amount of water that you may reasonably expect to collect at your site (Figure 5-10). If average precipitation in a month is 4 in. (10 cm), then a 1000 ft^2 (93 m^2) collecting surface covered with asphalt shingles will (under average conditions) produce about 1800 gal (7000 l) of water that month (4 in. × 600 gal per 1000 ft^2 × 0.75). If monthly precipitation is 2 in. (5 cm), then average production under the same conditions will be about 900 gal (3400 l).

How much of this maximum amount you actually capture depends on the size of your tank. Precipitation for a month may occur over multiple days or may arrive all at once during one large storm. Distribution of rainfall, as any gardener knows, can vary a great deal.

Water Use and Method of Delivery

Most outdoor-only systems use captured rainwater to water gardens. Flowers, shrubs, and vegetables are the usual recipients. It is possible to irrigate lawns, but the amount of water required makes this application less attractive to many users (roughly 1250 gal

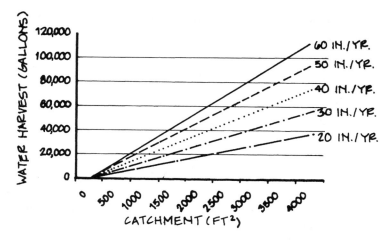

Figure 5-10 Potential rainwater collection as a function of catchment area and annual rainfall (assumes 25% loss due to spillage, leakage, etc.).

(4800 l) per application to provide a 2000 ft² (185 m²) lawn an in. (2.5 cm) of water per week).

The method you will use to apply the water to the garden also has an influence on how much you will use your system. Gravity flow is attractively simple, but requires that all sites of application be lower than the storage tank. Extended distances through hoses can result in very slow water delivery if the elevation differences are not great (friction from the inner surface of the hose slows the velocity of the water to the point of use). Direct filling of water cans from the tank is also a simple approach, but can be a time-consuming and strenuous task if you wish to use a lot of water (30 gal per day in a 2 gal can means 15 trips to the tank). Although this approach does supply healthful exercise (and has been adopted by some), it is not attractive to all users. A third alternative, if an outdoor electrical outlet is near the tank, is a small pump. The pump can be contained in a weather-resistant box, then connected to the pump outlet with a small section of garden hose or PVC, to pump water through a garden hose to sites both above and below the tank location. Small and inexpensive pumps do not provide high pressure or high flow rates, but do allow the water to be applied with a minimum of effort. Convenience of use appears to have a substantial effect on how much these systems are actually used once installed.

Available Tanks

Unless you have a very large garden or plan to irrigate grass, medium-sized tanks (200 to 1000 gal, 770 to 3850 l) work well for outdoor-use-only rainwater harvesting systems. Tanks in this size range are available in metal, polyethylene, and fiberglass.

Table 5-1 shows typical dimensions of aboveground tanks in this size range. Although belowground tanks are available, they are harder to install, harder to repair or replace, and do not allow gravity flow to the site of use. Aboveground tanks take up

Table 5-1 Circular Water Storage Tanks (Polypropylene)

Capacity (gal)	Diameter (in.)	Height (in.)	Fill Opening (in.)	Outlet Drain (in.)
165	31	55	16	2
300	36	78	16	2
305	46	49	16	2
500	48	72	16	2
550	67	42	16	2
750	48	102	16	2
1000	64	79	16	2

space on the surface and are considered unsightly by some. They should be opaque, so as to inhibit growth of algae in the tank, and, if plastic, should be coated to prevent damage from exposure to sunlight.

Installing the Tank

You will want to place your tank reasonably near the downspout of your system to minimize pipe run. A shady spot is preferable, to minimize bacteria growth in the tank (lower water temperature decreases growth rate of bacteria). A relatively high location is a good idea if you plan to rely on gravity to distribute your water. The soil should be flat and stable. If your favorite site is not quite level, you can build a simple concrete and earth pad (use pressure-treated 2×4's for the frame, fill with sand or gravel, spread dry concrete over the top, and saturate the mixture with water).

Mosquito Control

Female mosquitoes each lay 100 to 400 eggs at a time. The eggs take about three days to hatch, seven to ten days to get through their larval stage, and another two to three days for a "pupal" stage. So, in about two weeks, your water tank can become a fully functional mosquito factory. It is important that mosquitoes be prevented from getting into the tank. For larger tanks, as we shall see later, closed (attached) connections are generally used. For small to midsized tanks, however, it is often necessary to wrap the downspout and opening with mosquito netting or some other material to prevent the mosquitoes from gaining entry.

Potable and Indoor-Use Systems

Rainwater harvesting systems intended to supply all water needs for a home require more careful design than the outdoor-use-only systems described earlier.

- These systems tend to be the main water source for homes that use them (there are some systems connected to city water as well, but they are relatively rare). If they fail or run out of water, alternatives can be inconvenient.

- The system should provide more extensive filtering prior to entry into the water tank.

- The system must treat the water to ensure that potable water standards are being met.

- The system must be pressurized for certain in-house functions.

Prefiltration and Diversion

Organic material (including everything from leaves and sticks to insects and bird droppings) that make it into your water storage tank can compromise the quality of your collected water and increase the amount and frequency of tank cleaning. There are an assortment of strategies to intercept organic materials.

Double screening (using leaf guards or downspout baskets in conjunction with a screen closer to your tank) is one such method. Large objects are intercepted at the gutters or downspouts, with smaller objects being captured by a finer-mesh screen farther along the conveyance.

Finer-mesh screens are sometimes sold with removable mesh filters. An innovative design (Figure 5-11a) diverts debris away from the water stream while providing a measure of supplemental filtration by means of a removable foam mesh. Another approach to accomplish the same purpose is shown in Figure 5-11b. In this design, the separation of debris from rainwater is based on the mass difference between water and debris and the surface tension of the water.

Regular cleaning of all screens (unless they are self-cleaning) is essential. Organic

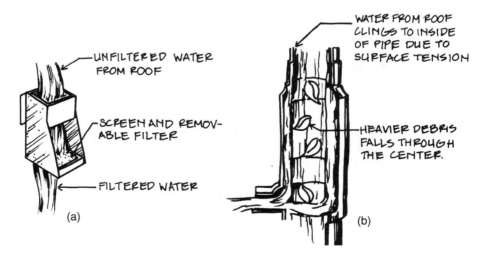

Figure 5-11 Commercially available screen and filtration devices between the roof and the cistern (a). Debris is removed mechanically by filter and screen. Most of the water passes through to the cistern (b). Surface tension of water causes it to cling to inner surface of pipe. Contaminants fall through the center.

material allowed to remain on screens will undergo microbial decay and/or breakage, which will reduce particle size and allow more material to pass through the screens.

Although screens and prefiltration are helpful, very small particles, such as pollen, suspended fecal material, and insect parts, will often get through. Much of the organic material that lands on roofs accumulates between rainstorms. When a rainstorm occurs, the "first flush" off of the roof is too contaminated to use, so it is generally diverted out of the conveyance in some manner. The device that diverts the dirty first flush is called a roof washer. The generally accepted rule is that 10 gal (38 l) of first-flush runoff should be diverted per 1000 ft^2 (10 m^2) of collection surface.

There are a variety of roof washer designs, some of which are homemade and others commercially available. The simplest roof washer (Figure 5-12a) is a standpipe connected to the rain gutter. The standpipe (which may be extended via one or more elbows) must fill with water before water can pass to the tank. The roof washer can be emptied between storms with the use of a threaded cap mounted at the end or the lowest point of the roof washer. Some users have drilled a $1/8$ in. [0.3 cm] hole through the threaded cap so that the roof washer will self empty. The cap is then removed only for flushing and cleaning the washer. This type of roof washer allows some mixing of the diverted water with water passing to the tank (although the $1/8$ in. [0.3 cm] hole maintains some positive flow away from the stream of clean water).

EXAMPLE 5.   Determine the length of 4 in. (10 cm) inner diameter pipe required to capture 10 gal (38 l) of first-flush roof runoff.

Solution:
   1 ft^3 is equal to 7.48 gal, so the volume of the roof washer must be 10 gal/7.48 gal per ft^3 = 1.33 ft^3 (38 l).

Four inches is equal to $1/3$ of a foot (0.33 ft). The cross-sectional area of a 4 in. diameter pipe is about 0.087 ft^2 (A = $\pi D^2/4$, where π = 3.14 and D is diameter). The volume of the washer is pipe length times cross-sectional area (V = Length$_{pipe}$ × A), so the required length is 1.33 ft^3/0.087 ft^2 = 15.3 ft (call it 16 ft, because the inner diameter of 4 in. pipe is not quite 4 in).

Another version of this design is shown in Figure 5-12b. The box must sit above the level of the tank and drains into the tank only after the storage volume causes the water level to reach the height of the drain. A number of variations of these designs have been used, including a multicompartment version of Figure 5-12b (to minimize mixing) and a commercially available system that includes a disposable cartridge filter between the outlet and the storage tank. All roof washing systems require regular maintenance to make sure that they are functioning properly. Debris will inevitably accumulate in the washer, and care must be taken to avoid obstructions in both the entrance and the small hole that allows it to self-drain.

Storage Tank (Cistern)

Other than the catchment surface (which is usually an existing roof), the storage tank is the largest component of a potable rainwater harvesting system. There are a number of requirements for tanks used in such systems:

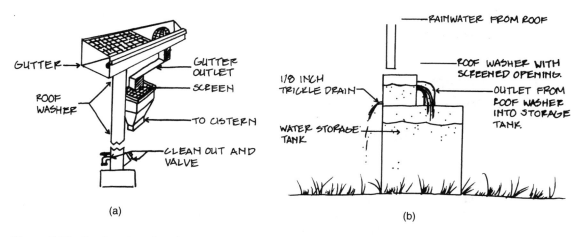

Figure 5-12 Roof washers for rainwater harvesting systems (a). Vertical PVC can be extended using tees or elbows to capture required volume of water. Valve at base can be replaced with a 1/8 in. drain hole to allow roof washer to drain itself (b). Box must fill to outlet height before water reaches the tank. Small (1/8 in.) drain hole allows roof washer to self-drain.

- The tank should conform to the published specifications of the American Waterworks Association for potable water storage and be made of materials that are approved by the Food and Drug Administration (FDA).
- The tank should be sited at least 50 ft (15 m) from sources of contamination (animal holding facilities, septic tank leach fields, etc.).
- If this is the sole source of domestic water, the tank should be sited within reach of a water transport vehicle to supply water should the cistern run dry.
- If possible, site an aboveground tank in the shade to inhibit growth of bacteria.
- The tank should have a sealable opening sufficiently large to allow entry for cleaning and maintenance.
- Outlets and inlets should be reinforced.
- The tank should have an overflow to a nonflooding area.
- If above the surface of the ground, the tank should be located on a stable surface.
- The tank should be opaque, to inhibit algae growth.

Tanks used for potable water supplies have been made from many materials, including galvanized steel, fiberglass, polyethelene, polypropylene, ferrocement, stone, concrete, and mortared block. Concrete, galvanized steel, fiberglass, and the plastics have seen the most use. Metal and concrete were very common in the recent past, but fiberglass and the plastics are becoming more common because of their light weight and lower cost. Note, however, that polyethelene and polypropylene degrade in sunlight, so it is important that tanks made of these materials have protective coatings.

The use of multiple storage tanks is more expensive than using a single tank, even when total volume remains the same, but there is an advantage to having multiple tanks.

They allow you to perform maintenance and repairs on one tank without taking the entire system off-line.

Pumps, Pressure Tanks, and Line Pressure

Water line pressure is usually in the range of 40 to 60 psi (275 to 412 kPa). This provides us with water at the rate we expect to get it (from taps and showers). A significant line pressure (greater than 20 psi, 140 kPa) is also required to open the valves used by a variety of household appliances (dishwashers, clothes washers). If line pressures are below this limit, the appliances will not fill.

In towns, line pressure is provided by water towers that are 90 ft (27 m) high or higher. In well water systems, the expected water pressures are produced by a combination of pumps and water pressure tanks. The pumps supply the pressure and the tanks "store" the pressure so that the pumps do not have to run continuously.

When it comes to the pump, a rainwater harvesting system is equivalent to using an extremely shallow aquifer in a well water system. This means that a shallow well pump (as compared with a deep well pump) will adequately serve your purpose.

The pump and the pressure tank work together to provide line pressure. The pressure tank includes a sensor connected to a switch. The switch turns the pump on and off. The sensor will allow you to select two pressure values, one to turn the pump on and the other to turn it off. Generally, to avoid overrunning your pump, you should set these pressures at least 10 psi (70 kPa) apart. For example, for a target line pressure of 40 psi (275 kPa), the pump should go on when line pressure drops below 35 psi (240 kPa) and go off when pressure goes above 45 psi (310 kPa).

The pump and pressure tank, as in conventional well water systems, should be sheltered and in reasonably close proximity to each other. Usually this means placing them in the same room in the house or locating the pump in a "pump house" close to the tank. The pump, tank, and all exposed piping should be protected from freezing. In temperate environments, enough supplemental heat can come from a 60 to 100 W incandescent lightbulb to prevent freezing.

For an aboveground tank at an elevation greater than that of the pump, there will always be positive pressure to the pump as long as water is in the tank. If tank and pump are at the same level, or if a subsurface tank is being used, a one-way ("foot") valve should be installed to maintain the pump prime (self-priming pumps are also available, but they cost more). The opening from the tank to the pump should be screened. "Floating outlets" from the tank to the pump are available. These draw water from about a foot below the water surface in the tank and avoid both floating debris and debris collected at the tank bottom. There should also be a float switch installed in the tank that prevents the pump from running dry should water be exhausted.

The pump (in particular) and the tank should be well anchored. The vibration and torque generated by a running pump can cause the pump to move enough to stress or fracture pipes.

For a rainwater harvesting system such as described here, a $1/2$ to $3/4$ hp (375 to 560 W) shallow well pump is adequate ($1/2$ hp works well for many systems). The pump and tank can be purchased in many hardware and home improvement centers.

Filtration Between the Tank and the House

Potable water systems require treatment to ensure that harmful chemicals and pathogens do not create health risks. Treatment systems commonly used for indoor-use rainwater harvesting systems perform better if small organic and inorganic particulates are removed.

Cartridge type filters (Figure 5-13) work well to remove particulate material. Particulate filters are generally rated by the size of particle they will capture. Using filters in series, with a coarse (20 micron) filter followed by a fine (5 micron) filter, will provide good removal of suspended particles. Progressive in-line cartridge filters are the most common type of filtration systems used in rainwater harvesting systems. Cartridges must be periodically changed, based on manufacturer's recommendations.

Activated charcoal filters can be used to remove very small particles (1.0 to 0.5 microns). Some authors contend that because activated charcoal is readily colonized by bacteria, it should not be used on the tap side of the disinfection system (see the following section). There is, however, some disagreement about whether this is a significant concern. Like cartridge filters, activated charcoal media must be periodically replaced.

Reverse osmosis systems remove practically all particulate matter from water by forcing the water through "semipermeable" membranes that are extremely fine. In general, these systems are used at individual water faucets.

Water Disinfection

Water disinfection, as used here, refers to the part of the treatment process specifically designed to kill bacteria, parasites, or viruses that may be in water. In our municipal

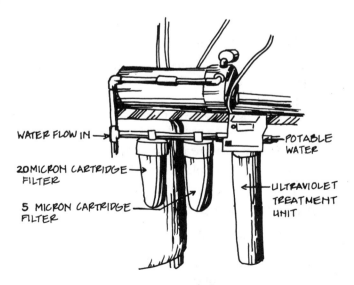

Figure 5-13 Cartridge filters in line with a UV water treatment unit prior to use in a potable water harvesting system.

systems, chlorine is generally used for this purpose. Although chlorine (and occasionally other chemicals) have been used for disinfection in some rainwater harvesting systems, ultraviolet light or ozone treatment systems are more frequently used.

Ultraviolet (UV) "light" consists of radiation that is just outside the range of radiation wavelengths we can see. It has higher energy than visible light and, under sufficient intensity, kills bacteria and viruses that are exposed to it. Because particles of matter can block or reflect this light, the filtration step described previously enhances the effectiveness of UV treatment. The UV bulb in the treatment unit is powered by electricity. Ultraviolet disinfection systems should be calibrated and tested prior to use and should include a light sensor to warn when bulb intensity drops below minimum performance standards. In addition, bulbs should be replaced per manufacturers' recommendations.

Ozone is a molecule that has an extra oxygen atom (O_3 instead of O_2). Ozone is a strong oxidant, meaning that it will readily react with organic materials, converting them to harmless by-products. Because bacteria and viruses are organic, ozone in sufficient concentration kills both. Filtration, as described earlier, removes organic materials from the incoming water that would otherwise be oxidized by the ozone. By removing organic particles, the filtration increases the effectiveness of ozone disinfection. Like UV, ozone is generated from electricity. It has been a more popular option in Europe than in the United States for rainwater harvesting systems, but now appears to be catching on here. Unlike UV (but like chlorine), ozone supplies some residual protection beyond the treatment unit itself. Transport of ozone through the pipes to the faucet is considered an advantage by some and a disadvantage by others.

Both UV and ozone disinfection are effective for treating rainwater prior to use. Both types of systems come in a variety of rated capacities. In general, 12 to 24 gal per minute (45 to 90 l/m) capacities are advisable for whole-house systems.

System Maintenance

Maintenance is an essential element of rainwater harvesting systems used for potable and high-contact water. There are a number of requirements:

- Periodic tests of water quality should be conducted. Basic tests include those for fecal coliform bacteria and pH. These should be performed at least once per year.
- System components should be inspected regularly and cleaned as required.
- Cartridges, bulbs, etc., should be replaced per manufacturers' recommendations.

Additional Components and Considerations

There are other features and considerations in using a rainwater harvesting system:

- *Tank pump and collection tank.* At times, logistics at your site will dictate that you simply cannot gravity-fill the main storage tank. In this case, a smaller tank can be used to provide collection adjacent to the collection surface and a small pump used to move the water from the collection tank to the storage tank. Small tanks and pumps are relatively inexpensive and have the advantage of providing water in the event of problems with the main system.

- *Valves.* Valves should be installed at virtually every point between segments of the system between the tank and the tap. When pipes crack, filters plug, or any other problem arises, it is nice to be able to isolate the problem section from the rest of the system.

- *Conservation.* Average per capita water use in the United States is approximately 100 gallons per day (gpd) per person. A family of four, at this rate, would require 146,000 gal (560 m^3) per year. Experiences with cutting waste suggest that per capita use can be reduced 40 to 50% with minimal inconvenience. Clearly, a commitment to reducing water waste provides incentive for getting by on a "water budget."

CONCLUSION

Rainwater harvesting as a practice is not new. It was discarded in the past partly because we thought our supplies of water were unlimited. It was also left behind because it was truly unsafe as compared with using the municipally treated water and the pure deep wells that had become accessible. We have found, and are finding, that our supplies of water are not unlimited. Luckily for us though, the technologies associated with this old practice have been greatly improved. With proper design and maintenance, the quality of harvested rainwater can be truly excellent.

Chapter 6

Using Domestic Gray Water

Gray water can replace treated drinking water in a number of applications. This can be a valuable method to reduce water use in areas experiencing water shortages and can also reduce the energy and expense required to treat and pump water from aquifers and reservoirs.

Gray water is domestic wastewater that does not have an inordinately large concentration of organic material or bacteria and so is suitable for reuse. Water from showers, baths, clothes washers, and bathroom sinks most commonly falls within the conventional definition of gray water. Gray water can replace treated drinking water for applications such as landscape irrigation, toilet flushing, and the first wash cycle in a clothes washer.

Pumping and treating water only to use it for flushing toilets and landscape irrigation is wasteful of energy and resources. In areas having low or diminishing water availability, gray water can be substituted for these and other uses. In this way per capita water usage can be reduced. Practices such as gray water use may help people reduce water demands to levels sustainable in particular locations.

GRAY WATER AND BLACK WATER

Until recently, gray water has received little attention because water availability and prices were not problems. Growing populations, the stresses of urban and suburban development, and persistent droughts appear to be changing this picture. In light of these factors, it is prudent to reuse water when appropriate.

Water from showers, baths, clothes washers, and bathroom sinks most commonly falls within the conventional definition of gray water. Water containing sewage (urine and feces) is always considered black water and is never reused without treatment. Kitchen water (from dishwashers and kitchen sinks) elicits divergent opinions. The more conservative opinion is that kitchens tend to produce water that has a high organic waste and grease/oil content. Because of potential health and nuisance issues, waters from these sources are conservatively regarded as "black." An alternate opinion contends that a biologically active surface soil layer is a robust and efficient treatment system. Adherents to this opinion say that an intelligently designed and managed gray water system allows kitchen water use without problems. The volume of water from dishwashers and kitchen sinks tends to be small relative to that of other water uses (clothes washers, baths, showers, other sinks), so there is little disadvantage from the standpoint of water quantity, in taking the conservative approach. State regulations vary on this issue.

Potential Uses of Gray Water

Gray water can be used both indoors and outdoors. Indoor uses include the following:

- *Water for house plants.* Most gray water is appropriate for this use, with the possible exception of wash cycle water from a clothes washer (very high detergent content).
- *Flush water for toilets.* All gray water is appropriate for this use if added directly to the bowl. Gray water cannot be added to the tank unless safeguards are in place to prevent backflow into the clean water supply.
- *First cycle water for a clothes washer.* The rinse water from a previous load can be used to supply the wash water of the next load. Alternately, dilute bath/shower water can be used.

Outdoors, gray water is mainly used for landscape irrigation. All gray waters are appropriate for this purpose, provided that the basic rules of gray water use are observed (see "Rules and Suggestions" later in this chapter).

Practical Issues in the Use of Gray Water

Gray water use is currently in a very dynamic period of development. On one hand, there are very good reasons for adopting gray water use. In areas experiencing water shortages due to drought or explosive development, gray water is a valuable resource. During the growing season, more than half of residential water use may be outdoors in some areas. Gray water is appropriate for much of this need. It could supply up to half of the water used in clothes washers and all of the water used for toilet flushing. Gray water could greatly reduce per capita water use. For families considering rainwater harvesting as a water source (see Chapter 5), gray water could make the difference between adequate and inadequate quantities of domestic water.

On the other hand, gray water use has been, and continues to be in many places, an alien concept. A truly integrated gray water system requires parallel drainage systems: one for black water and the other for gray. The black water system is routed to the sanitary sewer system or septic tank. Gray water drainage is routed to a distribution system. This is not hard to achieve in new construction. In existing housing, though, it is difficult to impossible. It requires replumbing, with many of the existing pipe junctions located behind walls or in otherwise inaccessible locations.

Actual implementation of gray water use in existing homes often appears to be an opportunistic and somewhat jury-rigged affair. Clothes washers located near access to the outside get used for gray water; washers in the center of the house do not. Exposed pipes in basements are replumbed; those behind walls are avoided. Indoor delivery also requires additional water supply pipes to be installed.

Newly constructed homes are not, in general, including provision for gray water recycling, so the outlook for convenient integrated gray water use anytime in the near future appears bleak. Using only gray water sources that are particularly accessible limits the impact of this practice. The use of all, or nearly all, gray water produced in the home appears to be limited, for the time being, to those areas that have acute needs to conserve drinking water and to those who are otherwise committed to water conservation.

Legal Status of Gray Water

Many states have regulations that define the acceptable sources of gray water and the manner in which it must be treated and applied. Definitions of acceptable sources usually either include or exclude kitchen water. Methods of treatment and application usually specify the following:

- *Whether a holding (septic) tank is required for initial treatment.* Some states require that gray water be treated in exactly the same manner as sewage in a septic tank system. A few states allow the direct application of gray water without a holding tank.

- *The size of the holding (septic) tank, if it is required.* The majority of states require a septic/holding tank that provides some fraction of the holding time required for sewage. This is tacit recognition that gray water requires less treatment than black water but still assumes that it is "too harmful" to allow application without treatment.

- *The allowed method of application.* The majority of states require subsurface application of treated gray water. A few allow subsurface application of untreated water. An even smaller number allow surface application, but specify that pooling cannot occur.

There are still some states that have no regulations regarding gray water systems at all. There are others that are in the process of altering their regulations (usually relaxing them somewhat). For the majority of states, the greatest difference between conventional septic tank regulations and those for gray water pertain to tank capacity (treatment/holding time) and allowed release depth (allowing application shallow enough for water to get into the root zone of plants; septic tank systems typically release deeper than the root zone).

Health Concerns

Normal constituents of gray water include soaps and detergents. The water will contain elevated concentrations of nutrients (nitrogen or phosphorus) and elevated salt concentrations (mainly sodium and chloride). The amounts of these constituents present will be highly variable, depending on the amount of water used (amount of dilution) and the specific practices of residents (soap/detergent type, amounts, water use in bathing, etc.).

The nutrient and organic content of gray water make it a marvelous medium for bacteria growth. In warm summer conditions, gray water can noticeably degrade in as little as three hours. If the water is directly applied to the landscape (i.e., not stored), this is not an issue, provided that standing puddles are not created and the soil is not highly granular and porous (drainage through highly porous soils may contaminate groundwater). If stored aboveground in a container, all of the water should be applied within 24 hours. After that, it will become noxious, anaerobic, and a potential source of human pathogens. Longer storage is possible, but the container should be sealed and a subsurface delivery system should (and in most areas must) be used for application to the landscape. Ideally, extended storage tanks should be installed below ground level to keep the contents as cool as possible and minimize the possibility of large spills.

Gray water may sometimes cross the line and become black water. We have already mentioned kitchen water, which we consider "black" because of its high organic content. Clothes wash water from loads containing soiled diapers is also black water and should not be used in a gray water system. Children's bath water may, at times, contain urine. Urine is not a source of disease when it originates in a healthy person. For this reason, all bath and shower water can probably be used, provided residents (particularly children) are healthy. If issues such as the use of diapers are relevant in a particular residence, then either clothes washing water should not be used in the system or else the system should allow for optional use (water going to the gray water system or to sewage treatment at the discretion of the user).

Effect on Plants

Under normal conditions, gray water will not damage trees, shrubs, or plants if it is applied directly to the soil. Gray water does not appear to damage soils, provided that harsh chemical content is avoided (see "Rules and Suggestions" in the following section).

Availability

All of the water used in baths/showers, clothes washers, and bathroom sinks is potentially available for gray water use. Table 6.1 summarizes the average "per use" volumes of gray water produced from these sources.

The actual amount of gray water generated in a particular household depends on many factors: the number of persons in the household, their habits, and the types of fixtures used (older fixtures use more water; newer fixtures are frequently designed to use less water).

Table 6-1 Average Volumes of Water Generated Per Use from Acceptable Gray Water Sources

Bathtub/shower	24–29 gal (91–110 l)
Clothes washer	34–53 gal (129–200 l)
Bathroom sink	0.5 gal (1.9 l)
Kitchen sink	Varies with use
Dishwasher	5–7 gal (19–26 l)

Average domestic per capita water use in the United States is approximately 100 gal per person per day. Because relatively little of this water is lost via evaporation, total wastewater production should be very nearly that amount. On average, about 65% of wastewater generated is gray water. These figures, plus knowledge of your personal habits, will help you to estimate your gray water production rate.

RULES AND SUGGESTIONS REGARDING GRAY WATER USE

Because gray water is, in fact, wastewater, it is important to be diligent and responsible in the way you use it. The following is a fairly extensive set of "do's and don'ts" that may help you to develop good practice habits. They are organized according the various aspects and considerations pertaining to gray water use. They also, on occasion, address things "to do" that may be illegal in your state (such as surface application). Be aware that these suggestions are directed to areas where such actions are legal and, perhaps, to others that may alter regulations in the future.

Gray Water Content

- Do not use gray water that contains harsh detergents, ammonia cleaners, or special-use chemicals (e.g., drain cleaners).
- If using washing machine water, do not use bleach or water softeners. Try to use only biodegradable detergents. Never use a product that contains borax (borax can harm plants).
- Do not use gray water from a water softener. Water softeners replace calcium and magnesium with sodium. High-sodium water can damage soil.
- Do not use water from your swimming pool. It has chloride and bromide salts that are harmful to plants and soil.
- Liquid detergents rather than powdered detergents are a better choice for gray water. Liquid detergents have a lower sodium content.

Gray Water Land Application

- Do not apply gray water with a garden sprinkler, as direct leaf contact can be damaging to plants.
- Do not apply gray water to areas near a well or near a ditch that runs into a stream. Do not allow gray water to drain into curbside gutters or storm sewers. Gray water can contribute to eutrophication if it collects in receiving waters.
- Do not use gray water directly on edible plants. Application to the roots of fruit trees is okay.
- Direct application onto a well-mulched bed maximizes the benefits of gray water while enhancing microbial digestion of gray water constituents.
- Do not apply gray water onto saturated soils. Allow previous applications to drain thoroughly before the next application. Distribute the applications, if possible.

- It is best to avoid using gray water on acid-loving plants, as the alkali portion of soaps will raise soil pH. If application on such plants is unavoidable, it should be accompanied by pH control (e.g., an elemental sulphur additive).

Gray Water Storage

- Tanks for surface storage should be small and emptied completely between fillings. Otherwise, the bacteria-laden remainder will effectively inoculate the new water.

- Only septic tanks should be used for extended storage. Ideally, the tank should be installed like any other septic tank. Effluent release from the tank should be subsurface to a leach field or root delivery system.

Gray Water Delivery System

- Keep your system simple and inexpensive. Sophisticated systems may be more prone to failure or require more maintenance than you are willing to deliver. All manufactured items and all energy usage have environmental consequences. These environmental trade-offs should be considered.

- Avoid pumps if possible. They add to cost and are unreliable without filtration.

- A gray water system does not necessarily have to have piped delivery to the point of use. Using buckets or a gravity-fed hose to distribute the water is a viable approach. This becomes impractical with systems that generate hundreds of gallons (liters) per day.

Health Concerns

- Mark gray water garden hoses, and do not use them for other purposes.

- Do not apply gray water with a sprinkler. Very small droplets containing contaminants and bacteria may be harmful if inhaled.

- Do not use gray water from the laundering of soiled diapers or from clothing/bath water of someone who has a contagious illness.

- Do not apply gray water to lawn areas that receive significant use.

SAMPLE SYSTEM DESIGNS

Figures 6.1 and 6.2 show sample gray water distribution systems. Be aware that there are many ways to successfully distribute gray water. The samples shown do not conform to regulations in some states (consult standard septic tank designs for these systems; only the tank size and the pipe depth will change).

You should also be aware that there are many ways that gray water distribution systems can fail (we strongly recommend that you look at "A Compendium of Greywater Mistakes and Misinformation on the Web" available at *http://www.oasisdesign.net/ books/misinfo.htm*).

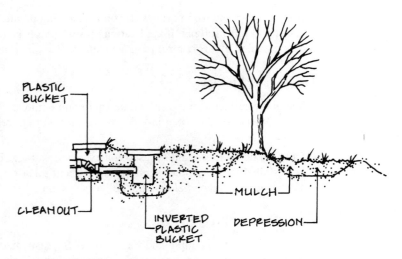

Figure 6-1   Subsurface gray water delivery system. Flow is driven by gravity alone.

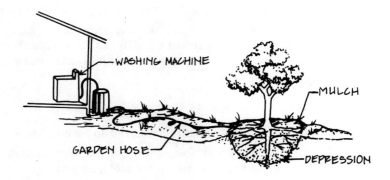

Figure 6-2   Surface flow gravity driven gray water delivery.

The systems shown in Figures 6-1 and 6-2 rely on gravity to distribute water. Although pumps can and have been used in these systems, their use increases the probability of failure.

Figure 6-1 shows a subsurface delivery system. Notice that the design incorporates locations for cleanout and uses relatively simple materials. The flow is strictly through mulch and the distribution is based on avoiding water collection at low points.

Figure 6-2 shows an even simpler system than that illustrated in Figure 6-1. Gray water is collected in a 55 gal (200 l) drum to temporarily hold the excess volume while the flow is passed through a garden hose. Application is at the surface through a well-mulched layer. Note that in this sort of system, it is important to continually shift the point of application. By doing so, you distribute the gray water onto a greater volume of mulch and subsoil, minimizing possible problems and maximizing treatment.

CONCLUSION

Gray water systems offer the hope that per capita water use can be greatly reduced by appropriately recycling our water. The technology for retrofitting existing construction is largely lacking, however. Achieving large-scale reductions in our water use will have to wait until the need for water recycling becomes generally accepted. In the meantime, those who recognize the need now and are willing to go to some inconvenience can begin to make better use of our water resources.

PART III

Shelters and the Sustainable Landscape

Chapter 7

Shelter Design

Energy savings: *Properly designed, a shelter should be able to adequately serve its occupants with little or no energy for heating, cooling, and daylighting in most climate zones in the United States. This can result in a savings of 20 to 100% of the energy used for heating, cooling, and lighting.*

It would be easy to dwell on the environmental and social problems caused by the current state of shelters, such as their wasteful use of energy and consumption of materials and their impact on the immediate landscape through the smothering of biotic communities and creation of excessive water runoff. The way shelters and human settlements have evolved has apparently contributed to social fragmentation and disruption of the sense of community, and to the environmental crises we are experiencing—global warming, urban heat islands, and ground and surface water degradation. Shelter performance over the last 100 years might receive an evaluation of "ecological dysfunction and gross adverse environmental effects." Given the obvious out-of-balance nature of current environmental conditions, we will dwell on what shelters should and could be and how they can become a harmonious part of the natural ecological system.

IN HARMONY WITH THE ENVIRONMENT

Landscape is used by geographers, political scientists, and many writers to mean the land and everything on it, including trees, hills, meadows, buildings, roadways, walks, and recreational play spaces. As a part of this landscape, a shelter cannot exist harmoniously with the land without being considered an integral and productive component. Just as the living and nonliving parts of the ecosystem play important roles in its health and function, so should the shelter be a participating, nonliving component. It should adapt to natural processes without interrupting them and should contribute to human health, productivity, and happiness. Natural processes include photosynthesis, organic growth, heat absorption and reflection, storage of thermal energy, building of soil, the absorption, storage, and filtration of water, and provision of habitat for plants, animals, insects, and microbes.

Figure 7-1 Two views from the windows to the gardens.

A sustainably designed shelter can provide a safe, healthful, and comfortable human habitat that is also attractive to its users. By attractive, we mean that the design of the shelter should have unity versus chaos and possibly reflect the interests and character of its users. Its outward appearance does not have to be patterned after a set building fashion like a pueblo, colonial, or ranch style, but instead could be designed to be visually subordinate to the landscape, to blend with or reflect the character of the land, and to be considerate of the climate zone. Many have been personally influenced by the story of the Japanese family that invited guests to experience their new home. The visitors came to see not the edifice, but the views from the windows to the outdoor spaces and gardens. This is a more meaningful experience than looking at a building, and it gives the domicile a greater sense of importance and affects the well-being of the inhabitants. The owners of a home in central Mississippi have tried to create the same experience. Where possible, the spaces and gardens seen in views from the windows are interesting and diverse. Some of the scenes give the family a feeling of accomplishment and make them smile, and other views are of artistically designed spaces. Figure 7-1 illustrates views from the windows of the house. A shelter should positively influence people and contribute to their mental and physical health by having good views from windows, meaningful spaces that have positive effects on the users, and good relationships between indoor and outdoor spaces.

The shelters designed and built around the South Rim of the Grand Canyon in Arizona by Mary Colter are exemplary. Colter was a schoolteacher who studied the people and the geography of the Southwest, and she was so good at designing buildings that reflected the people and the character of the land that she spent most of her career creating great shelters for people. She was guided by the thoughts of landscape architect

Figure 7-2 Shelters designed by Mary Colter that reflect the character of the land and local culture.

Frederick Law Olmsted, who said that a building should be subordinate to the landscape in which it is located and should reflect the character of the people who reside there. Figure 7-2 illustrates several shelters of the early 1900s designed by Colter that blend with the land and influence the users of the spaces. Figure 7-3 illustrates other attractive shelters that reflect their climate and region.

Considering the Climate

Buildings consume 75% of the electricity used in the United States, and of that amount 50% or more is used for heating and cooling interior spaces (Figure 7-4). In designing and building shelters to be as energy-efficient as possible, in the United States, the broadside of a shelter should almost always be sited to face south toward the low angle and

Figure 7-3 Shelters that consider the local climate and region.

limited solar azimuth of the winter sun. This simple siting effort will enable a rectangle-shaped shelter to passively capture as much winter sun heat as possible, thereby reducing energy use by about 33%. When a south-facing orientation is used, only the narrow sides of a rectangular structure are then exposed to the early morning and late afternoon summer sun, thereby reducing heat gain in the summer. Because of the lower sun angles in the morning and evening, it is difficult to shade the eastern and western walls with building overhangs or awnings; however, plantings of either deciduous or evergreen trees will block this potential source of heat gain. Keeping the sun off a shelter during the summer is of paramount importance in reducing the need for cooling. South sides of shelters can be protected with overhangs, awnings, and first-floor setbacks that block the high midday sun angle during the summer season.

In addition to considering the seasonal movement of the sun, there are other climatic factors that should influence the design of shelters:

- Cold winter winds
- Hot summer sunshine
- The warming effects of the low angle of the winter sun

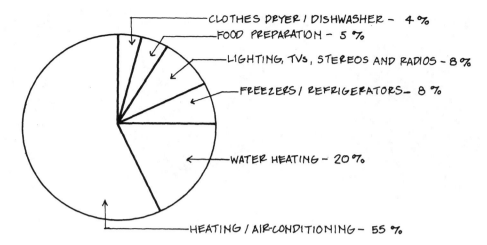

CLOTHES DRYER / DISHWASHER - 4 %
FOOD PREPARATION - 5 %
LIGHTING, TVs, STEREOS AND RADIOS - 8 %
FREEZERS / REFRIGERATORS - 8 %
WATER HEATING - 20 %
HEATING / AIR-CONDITIONING - 55 %

Figure 7-4 Typical energy use for a residence. (*Source: The Power of Conservation,* Entergy Corporation.)

Vernacularly designed shelters and landscapes have often considered climate effects and incorporated physical features responding to these factors. To combat cold winter winds, a wind ramp can be planted for deflection of the wind. A *wind ramp* is created by locating increasingly taller evergreen plants in a grouping so they can direct wind up and over a structure of outdoor space in order to reduce heat loss. The ramp of plants will also keep the air still around the shelter and reduce heat loss through convection. To further reduce the effects of cold winds, New England shelters were (and sometimes still are) designed to be compact, decreasing the amount of exterior surface area of the shelter exposed to the cold outdoor temperatures and winds. The New England saltbox is a classically designed structure allowing comfortable habitation within a very challenging climate zone. The saltbox house was usually two stories in height and had spaces compactly laid out around interior fireplaces. It had few to no windows on the north side, and its roof was sloped to deflect cold winter winds.

To combat the warming effect of the summer sun, shelters can be shaded with building overhangs and/or trees. To keep temperatures 8° to 10°F (4° to 6°C) cooler, summertime sun should be kept off the shelter and outdoor use areas. In the dogtrot pioneer home (in which two parts of the shelter were connected with a roofed passage) comfortable spaces were created with overhangs and tree plantings. In the West Indian and pioneer home style, comfortable spaces were created with overhangs and tree plantings. Figure 7-5 illustrates these summer-sun-conscious building styles.

Capturing winter sun and using it for heating enables winter heating demands to be met passively. Winter sunshine allowed to enter shelters and strike thermal mass floors and walls will be converted to thermal energy and released when interior spaces become cool. Through implementing these low-tech processes, very little energy will be needed for heating. We should resolve to shape the shelter to join with the earth and its natural processes. To that end, we should thoroughly consider the materials used and the form

Figure 7-5 Pioneer stagecoach stop (*left*) and West Indian style shelter (*right*).

of the facility as related to the sun, the wind, and the hot and cold seasons within our climate zones.

Windows and Their Location

Windows serve many purposes within a shelter; providing views, air circulation, transmission of solar radiation for absorption and storage of thermal energy, light, and cross-ventilation of air within the structure. In the development of site plans for a shelter, views to existing and proposed landscape features should be defined for consideration in the location of windows. In the design phase, the location of windows for transmission of light into the shelter should also consider the further utilization of natural light. Not only can light be admitted from the outside perimeter of shelters, it can also be captured for use within interior spaces by locating skylights on roofs and creating clerestories. Care must be exercised in locating skylights and clerestories, as solar heat gain during the cooling season may compound the challenge of keeping interior spaces cool. See Figure 7-6 for a clerestory design that prevents direct sun gain during the summer but allows both light and solar radiation during the winter heating season.

The location of windows can affect the natural air movement within a shelter. If windows are located on opposite sides of a building (and with no wind-impeding walls separating the space), the difference in air pressure caused by outdoor winds striking the building will cause a buildup of pressure on the side receiving the wind and a lower pressure zone on the opposite wall where there is no wind, thereby causing air to flow from the high pressure zone to the lower pressure zone (see Figure 7-7). Another way to capture the natural movement of air to ventilate and cool interior spaces is through the use of natural convection, whereby warmer and less dense air will rise and be displaced with cooler and heavier air. This principle is well illustrated at Waverly Plantation, a nineteenth-century home along the Tombigbee River. The designer located the rooms and windows around a three-story open space in the center of the house. When cooling is desired, windows on the first floor and third floor are opened to induce air movement through the interior spaces, resulting in more pleasant conditions for the occupants. There is no mechanical air-conditioning of the home, but the interior spaces

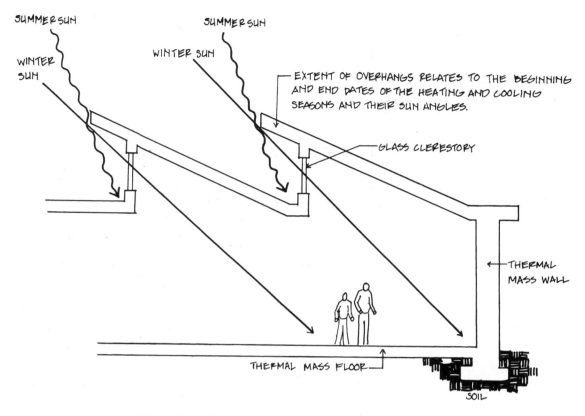

Figure 7-6 Clerestory design that protects from summer sun.

feel cool even on a hot day. The home (Figure 7-8) is constructed of 10 in. (254 mm) thick masonry walls that act as a thermal sink, absorbing heat from the air during the predominant summer cooling season. During the winter, sun streaming in through windows in the south-facing façade is transformed into thermal energy and stored in the thick masonry thermal mass for release when interior temperatures become cool. Windows in the three-story interior open space are closed to retain warmth during the heating season.

Shading for Creation of Cooler Temperatures

Where the cooling need is greater than the heating need, the creation of shaded areas will produce more comfortable temperatures both within and around a shelter. In the shade, it is 8° to 15°F (4° to 8°C) cooler than in the sun. Shelter overhangs, either roof overhangs or building setbacks (in the case of two-story buildings), will block nearly all incoming solar radiation that creates heat. In selecting trees, note that deciduous trees will block 60 to 90% of solar radiation during the summer and 20 to 50% of solar radiation during the winter (when they are leafless and when heat from the sun is desired). It is apparent

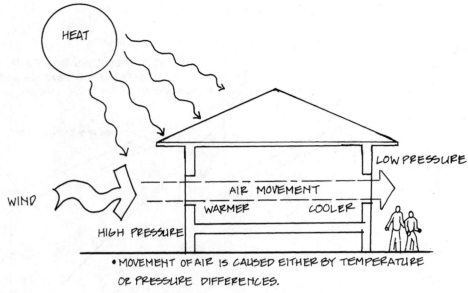

HEAT

WIND

HIGH PRESSURE

AIR MOVEMENT

WARMER   COOLER

LOW PRESSURE

- MOVEMENT OF AIR IS CAUSED EITHER BY TEMPERATURE OR PRESSURE DIFFERENCES.
- THE AIR WILL HEAT UP ON THE SUNNY SIDE, RISE AND MOVE TOWARD THE COOLER SIDE.
- WHEN WINDOW OPENINGS ARE LOCATED ON OPPOSITE SIDES, THE DIFFERENCES IN AIR PRESSURE CAUSES MOVEMENT OF AIR BETWEEN THEM. WIND CREATES A ZONE OF HIGHER PRESSURE ON THE SIDE OF THE SHELTER IT STRIKES, AND A LOW PRESSURE ZONE ON THE OPPOSITE SIDE, CAUSING AIR TO FLOW THROUGH WINDOWS FROM THE WINDWARD SIDE TO THE LOW PRESSURE SIDE.

Figure 7-7 Creating an opportunity for cross ventilation.

that deciduous trees will block solar energy radiation, but they will not perform as well as constructed overhangs.

A shelter built off the ground on raised foundations will benefit from the 8° to 15°F (4° to 8°C) cooler shaded space it covers. Interior heat buildup will move through the floor to the cooler shaded space beneath, leaving cooler conditions within the shelter. When a shelter is built on a slab on top of the earth, heat in the interior of the shelter is conducted through the slab into the ground when the ground temperature is lower than that of the interior air. The same movement of heat can happen even during the winter, when we are trying to retain warm interior conditions, unless polystyrene insulation is placed between the earth and the concrete slab to prevent conduction of heat. Even using mulch over the soil next to a shelter can create cooler conditions, as the mulch will act as an insulation barrier to heat seeking to move into the cooler soil.

Figure 7-8   The central open space at Waverly Plantation enhances natural cooling through convection.

EMBEDDED ENERGY WITHIN MATERIALS

For a regeneratively designed shelter, consider using materials available locally rather than relying on materials that have to be shipped to the site from long distances. Embedded energy contained within a material is the energy it takes to grow or produce, shape, manufacture, and ship that material. Conscientious shelter designers will use materials with low embedded energy ratings to reduce the impact of the shelter on the landscape. Materials with low embedded energy content tend to be naturally occurring materials available in the local area that don't need large amounts of energy for processing. To compare the embedded energy within various materials, let us look at the results of a study that computed the embedded energy in wood (yard lumber) at 639 kWh per ton of material. The embedded energy within other building materials as compared with locally grown wood is shown in Table 7-1.

Materials used by the National Park Service are evaluated for the energy used to produce the material, adverse impacts to the environment, and waste produced during manufacture of the material. A material is traced from its source availability and extraction, to refinement, fabrication, treatment with additives, transportation, use, and eventual reuse or disposal. This evaluation of the life cycle, or "cradle-to-grave" analysis, ensures that the materials being used will have the least impact on the environment as possible. Table 7-2 shows the factors considered in analyzing the life cycle of a material.

Table 7-1 Embedded Energy Comparison
(Units are in kilowatt hours per ton.)

Wood	639 kWh	Energy it takes to produce a ton of wood
Brick	2,556 kWh	4 times the energy it takes to produce wood
Concrete	3,195 kWh	5 times the energy it takes to produce wood
Plastic	3,834 kWh	6 times the energy it takes to produce wood
Glass	8,946 kWh	14 times the energy it takes to produce wood
Steel	15,336 kWh	24 times the energy it takes to produce wood
Aluminum	80,514 kWh	126 times the energy it takes to produce wood

Source: John Lyle, *Regenerative Design for Sustainable Development* (New York: John Wiley & Sons, Inc., 1993).

Table 7-2 Material Life Cycle Evaluation

Source of raw ingredients—Are they renewable, sustainable, locally available, nontoxic?
Raw material extraction—Energy required, habitat destruction, topsoil erosion, siltation and pollution from runoff?
Transportation—Local source, fuel consumption, air pollution?
Processing and/or manufacturing—Energy input, air-water-noise pollution, waste generation and disposal?
Treatments and additives—Use of petrochemicals, exposure to and disposal of hazardous materials?
Use and operation—Energy requirements, longevity of products used, indoor air quality, waste generation?
Resource recovery/disposal—Potential for recycling/reusing materials, disposal of solid/toxic wastes?

Source: Guiding Principles of Sustainable Design (National Park Service, 1993).

RENEWABLE MATERIALS

When selecting building materials, consider choosing those that are renewable rather than materials that are not produced naturally. Renewable materials, like wood, should come from sources where they are being cultivated for renewal, such as wood from tree farms, as opposed to rare and exotic woods from rain forests where there is no sustainable reproduction or cultivation occurring. A material will probably be sustainable when it is natural and does not require large amounts of energy to produce, and does not outgas volatile organic compounds that contribute to indoor air pollution. When sustainable materials are acquired from local producers, air and water runoff pollution associated with transportation is reduced and the local economy benefits. Sustainable resources are also durable materials that will have reduced energy costs for maintenance.

MODULAR MATERIALS AND FUTURE REUSE

Another option in choosing materials is to select and design with modular materials that can be reused when the shelter and landscape are demolished. There are alternatives to

Figure 7-9 Sandstone patio placed over a thick mortar bed.

using large expanses of asphalt and concrete paving that have to be broken up and hauled away to landfills when they are no longer useful. For instance, in the construction of a sandstone patio around a pool (Figure 7-9), the sandstone was placed on a thick mortar bed over gravel instead of over a steel-reinforced 4 in. (102 mm) concrete slab. Filter fabric was placed under the 2 in. (51 mm) of well-graded gravel to maintain the strength of the gravel layer and prevent it from working into the soil. A thick mortar bed over the gravel created a level surface and kept the sandstone stable, as it would be if placed over a concrete slab. When it is time for the patio to be removed one day, the sandstone can be lifted up with a pry bar, the mortar removed, and the sandstone reused on another surface. The gravel beneath can also be raked up and reused along with the filter fabric.

Instead of using poured-in-place concrete for a driveway, consider using modular materials that can be recycled and reused. Place a 3 in. (76 mm) layer of river gravel over an excavated area covered with filter fabric to keep the gravel from working into the soil. Gravel or sand can be as strong as concrete if it is contained. Use wood edging to hold the gravel in place and keep the edge neat looking. Next, place precast squares of concrete in the drive space over the gravel, and sweep crushed gravel fines between the cracks to keep the squares in place. The driveway shown in Figure 7-10 was constructed in this manner. It was built entirely by hand with hand tools, and it can be completely disassembled by hand and reused. Voids in the gravel beneath the drive hold and slowly release runoff as it percolates into the soil. The use of materials that can be disassembled and reused is an important sustainable practice. The entire drive construction process is composed of modular units that can be replaced by hand and disassembled by hand later on if needed. The cost of labor and materials to build this modular driveway was $3.52 per ft^2 and if it had been built with poured-in-place concrete the cost would have been $3.00 per ft^2.

Figure 7-10 Modular driveway construction sequence.

RUNOFF AND SHELTER DESIGN

Shelters and their developed landscapes produce large amounts of runoff from precipitation. A 2000 ft^2 (610 m^2) home in the hot-humid climate zone where 58 in. (1473 mm) of precipitation per year is received will shed 72,247 gal (273,454 l) of water per year.

Computing Runoff from the Roof Structure
58 in. rainfall/12 in. = 4.83 ft of rain per year in the region
2000 ft^2 roof area × 4.83 ft of rain per year = 9660 ft^3 of water hits the roof each year
1 ft^3 of water = 7.48 gal
9660 ft^3 of water × 7.48 gal = 72,257 gal of water the roof will shed each year

Metric version:
1473 mm rainfall/1000 mm = 1.47 m of rain per year in the region
186 m^2 roof area × 1.47 m of rain per year = 274 m^3 of water hits the roof each year
1 m^3 = 1000 l
274 m^3 of water × 1000 l = 274,000 l of water the roof will shed each year

This unnatural amount of runoff scours the ground, gathering sediment as it runs off. There are also high rates of runoff from paved patios and driveways and from grassed lawn areas. Once the water reaches a swale, it is mixed with other water running off the land and even more sediment gathers in the water as a result of erosion and sloughing off of ditch banks. When the large volume of soil-laden runoff water reaches a creek, the creek becomes filled with sediment and organic matter and the delicate balance of aquatic life and water quality is upset. The aquatic habitat is affected and the water quality is changed, perhaps even impaired to the point that it becomes depleted of oxygen, suffocating the creek life that depends on oxygen and transforming the water body to a habitat that will support only anaerobic bacteria.

Runoff from areas covered with roofs and built landscapes used to soak into a layer of dead plant and animal matter on the forest or prairie floor. This detrital layer, composed of plant leaves, twigs, branches, and animal waste, constituted a 6 to 9 in. (152 to 229 mm) deep natural mulch layer, which served as an important habitat, nutrient storage media, and filter for runoff water. In fact, the natural woodland and prairie or meadow landscape had very little natural runoff. The detrital layer soaked up and stored as much as 90% of the water that fell on it. Water that did escape the sponge of the detrital layer was cleansed by microbes in the mulch and slowly released, suspended sediment was filtered, and clean and clear runoff was produced. Understanding this natural model for storing, cleansing, and slowly releasing water should provide direction for the collection, cleansing, and slow release of runoff water in all built landscapes. Water runoff is a very important burgeoning problem, but can be solved through observing and following the natural model.

BASIC SHELTER FORMS RELATED TO ENERGY FLOW

Controlling the energy balance within a shelter can be accomplished through reflection, absorption, and storage of heat, and through movement of air by natural convection and cross ventilation. The three basic building forms that help with the control of heat are the raised structure, the earth shelter, and the sunspace shelter.

Raised Structure

A raised shelter is built off the ground, creating a cool, shaded space beneath that contributes to the cooling of interior spaces. This type of structure is generally used in hot tropical and subtropical climates where more energy is expended for cooling than for heating. Overhangs are also used to increase the shaded zone. Cross ventilation helps with moving air, especially when there is prevailing and frequent wind movement. Because the shelter is raised off the ground and has overhangs, most of the air around the shelter is 8° to 15°F (4° to 8°C) cooler than nearby sunny areas.

Earth Shelter

An earth shelter is usually dug into the earth or has soil pulled up over its sides for insulation from weather extremes. Below the ground in the United States the earth's temperature is 54° to 60°F (12° to 16°C). When a shelter is connected to this zone of coolness during the summer and warmth during the winter, interior temperatures can benefit. During the summer, interior heat will move through conduction to the cooler environs of the adjacent soil. During the winter, the soil protects the skin (or walls) of the building from cold outside temperatures, thus slowing conduction of heat from inside to the outside. This building form is best used where there are extremes of very hot or very cold weather. In the Southwest, Native Americans have used earth shelters in the form of cliff dwellings for protection from the 104° to 110°F (40° to 43°C) daytime desert temperatures.

Sunspace Shelter

A sunspace shelter allows solar radiation to enter or to be transmitted through glass and strike a thermal mass. The solar radiation is then transformed into thermal energy and stored until temperatures drop within the shelter. Then the heat moves from the thermal mass into the interior space to passively provide warmth. All of this happens because heat energy naturally moves from regions of high temperatures to regions of low temperatures. Short-wave solar radiation is easily transmitted through glass. When converted into thermal energy, it becomes long-wave radiation, which no longer moves easily through glass, and is trapped or detained within the space. Because glass can also allow unwanted solar radiation into the shelter during the cooling season, south-facing windows need to be protected by overhangs during the summer when the sun is higher in the sky.

SUSTAINABLE BUILDING DESIGN

Generally, in order for a shelter to be sustainable, resource degradation and consumption should be minimized. Experience with a sustainably designed shelter should raise a person's awareness of the environment and demonstrate its importance in sustaining a healthy environment. The facility should connect people to the environment for the spiritual, emotional, and therapeutic benefits provided by nature. The natural and cultural history of a site should be shared with site users and inhabitants. The National Park Service has a well-composed checklist (Table 7-3) for sustainable building design that can serve as a model for creating sustainable shelters. It includes general design directions and natural factors to consider in designing a shelter.

Table 7-3   Checklist for Sustainable Shelter Design

General Design Direction

- Be subordinate to the ecosystem and cultural context; respect the natural and cultural resources of the site and minimize impacts of any development.
- Use the resource as the primary experience of the site and as the primary design determinant.
- Enhance the appreciation of the natural environment.
- Use the simplest technology to meet building and site needs, and incorporate passive energy-conserving technologies that are responsive to the local climate.
- Avoid the use of nonrenewable resources, and use renewable and locally grown and produced building materials.
- Use the cradle-to-grave analysis of materials for selection, and avoid the use of hazardous and environmentally damaging materials.
- Strive to create the smallest facility possible that also optimizes the flexibility and multiuse of indoor and outdoor spaces.
- Identify opportunities for construction waste reuse.
- Provide equal access to people with physical and sensory impairments.
- Build facilities in phases in order to sequentially evaluate their impact.
- Plan for future expansion with minimum demolition and waste.
- Incorporate recycling of daily waste production into the design and management of the facility.

Natural Factors for Consideration

Climate

- Apply natural and passive air-conditioning techniques to create human comfort levels, making sure human experiences are not isolated from the environment.
- Avoid overdependence on mechanical heating and cooling systems to alter the climate, as overdependency connotes an inappropriate shelter design.

Temperature

- Areas that are very dry or at high elevations typically have large temperature swings from day to night, which can be reduced with heavy/massive construction to yield more constant indoor temperatures.
- In climates too hot for comfort, minimize solid enclosures and thermal mass in shelters that will collect and store heat, maximize ventilation of roof structures, and use elongated and/or segmented floor plans to minimize internal heat gain and maximize exposure for ventilation of warm air.
- In predominantly hot climates, separate rooms and functions with covered breezeways to maximize wall shading and ventilation, isolate heat-generating functions such as kitchens and laundries from living areas, provide plenty of shaded outdoor living areas such as porches and decks, in order to make use of cooler nighttime temperatures.

(**Table 7-3** *continued*)

- In climates too cold for comfort, consolidate interior functions into compact configurations, insulate to minimize heat loss, minimize air infiltration and exfiltration through the use of barrier sheeting, weatherstripping, sealants, and airlock entries, and minimize all openings not oriented toward the low angle of the winter sun.

Sun

When solar gain causes conditions too hot for comfort:

- Use overhangs to shade walls and openings.
- Use vegetation to provide shading on east- and west-facing walls and outdoor-use areas.
- Shade the southern exposure during the summer with building overhangs that will allow lower winter sun angles to provide warmth.
- Use shading devices such as louvers, covered porches, and trellises with vines to block the sun.
- Orient large surfaces of shelters away from hot afternoon western sun.
- Use light-colored wall and roofing materials to reflect solar radiation.

When solar gain is desired to offset conditions too cold for comfort:

- Maximize building exposure and openings facing south.
- Increase thermal mass and envelope insulation.
- Use dark-colored building exteriors to absorb solar radiation and promote heat gain.

Wind

- Because wind strips away heat from shelter envelopes through the process of convection, screen shelters with windbreaks or wind ramps to deflect cold winter winds and create pockets of still air near shelters.
- In hot climates, use natural ventilation when possible, limit air-conditioning to areas requiring special humidity and temperature control, maximize exposure to the ventilating effects of wind through the location and number of wall and roof openings, and use wind turbines to induce ventilation in attic spaces on sites with limited wind movement.

Moisture

- High humidity does not allow people to evaporatively cool through perspiring, therefore minimize humidity through maximizing ventilation, inducing air flow around facilities, and venting or moving moisture-producing uses such as kitchens, bathrooms, and laundries to outside areas.
- In hot, dry climates, air can be cooled and humidified by locating water features in front of areas where breezes will blow onto facilities, thereby cooling the moving air through the process of evaporative cooling.
- Harvest rainfall from all roofs and paved areas for irrigation and other shelter uses.
- Collect water that runs off lawn areas, detain and filter the runoff, and slowly release the water into the natural system.

Source: Guiding Principles of Sustainable Design (National Park Service, 1993).

Chapter 8

Earth Sheltering

It is possible to save 50 to 100% on energy heating bills through the use of earth-sheltered structures. Soil can be mounded on the sides and roofs of shelters, allowing one elevation to be exposed to the south, to eliminate or dramatically reduce the amount of energy used for heating and cooling.

Earth sheltering is a practice whereby a shelter is placed either partly or wholly in the ground, or soil is mounded up around the sides and roof of the shelter, for energy-saving benefits. Researchers at the Underground Space Center at the University of Minnesota have studied the advantages and disadvantages of earth sheltering for housing. They have concluded that using earth sheltering can save 50 to 100% on heating bills in their state and can significantly reduce or eliminate the need for mechanical cooling during the summer. Earth sheltering also creates very quiet interior spaces because of the sound-reduction properties of the thick soil covers on the exterior. The techniques and value of using the earth in planning and designing shelters in the sustainable landscape are discussed in this chapter.

TYPES OF EARTH SHELTERS

Some earth shelters are above grade, and some are below. The three basic types of earth shelters are the fully recessed on a flat site shelter, the fully recessed into a hillside shelter, and the bermed-up shelter. See Figure 8-1 for illustrations of these basic earth shelter types. Based on window layouts, there are three concepts for laying out rooms in an earth shelter: the layout with windows on one elevation, the courtyard layout, and the layout with multiple window perforations (see Figure 8-2).

Windows Along One Elevation

The first layout type concentrates all of the windows along one elevation, usually in a south-facing wall, with the goal of using the sun for heating. Direct sunlight enters only the rooms along that elevation. With a normal room height of 8 or 9 ft (2.4 or

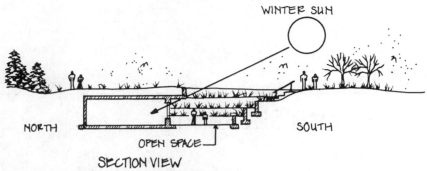

WINTER SUN

NORTH

OPEN SPACE

SOUTH

SECTION VIEW
FULLY RECESSED ON A FLAT SITE.

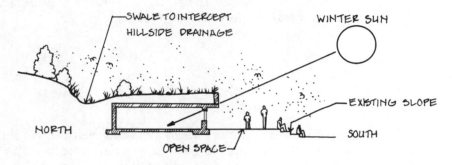

SWALE TO INTERCEPT
HILLSIDE DRAINAGE

WINTER SUN

EXISTING SLOPE

NORTH

OPEN SPACE

SOUTH

SECTION VIEW
FULLY RECESSED INTO A HILLSIDE.

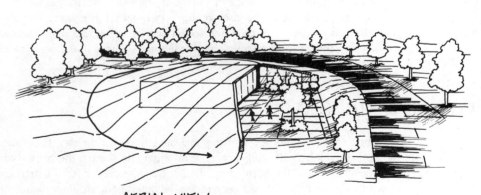

AERIAL VIEW
BERMED UP OVER THE SHELTER

Figure 8-1   Basic types of earth shelters.

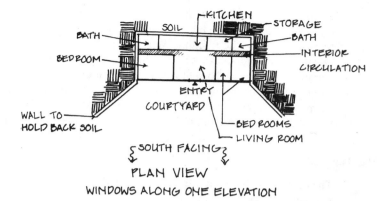

PLAN VIEW
WINDOWS ALONG ONE ELEVATION

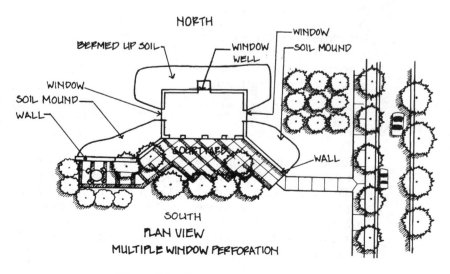

PLAN VIEW
COURTYARD LAYOUT

PLAN VIEW
MULTIPLE WINDOW PERFORATION

Figure 8-2 Concepts for laying out rooms.

2.7 m), winter sunlight will extend about 16 ft (4.9 m) into the space. Skylights that face south can allow both natural lighting and direct solar radiation heat gain into more recessed areas of the building. When all the windows are on one side, it is possible to maximize the amount of soil around the structure, which is the best arrangement for energy conservation. To get fresh air from natural cross ventilation, vents will be needed along the side or through the roof structure opposite the windows. It is best to arrange living and sleeping spaces along the window side of the house, and lesser-used rooms, like utility rooms and bathrooms, toward the earth-sheltered side.

Courtyard Layout

The courtyard layout clusters rooms around an exterior central open space (if located in a warm climate) or an interior atrium court (in a colder climate). The courtyard can be faced with rooms on all four sides, or on three sides with the fourth side being open. It can also be constructed as a covered court for use in any climate. In temperate or cold climates, the covered court can be used as a thermal mass to capture heat during the day to be used by the rooms along the court, thereby increasing energy savings for the shelter.

Multiple Window Perforation

The layout with multiple window perforations is used when the earth shelter is bermed up with soil; the windows become portals through the earth, located to allow light and views. In this layout, it is best to mass most windows along the south side for passive solar heating. Living spaces should also be located along this bright side of the shelter. Other windows can be located wherever they are desired. The disadvantage of locating multiple windows on sides other than the south side is the loss of the continuous blanket of earth that warms the building in the winter and protects it from solar heat gain during the summer. When that continuous blanket of earth is broken, large areas of soil near window openings will be cooled and warmed by the weather. The more window openings there are, the less the earth can act as a large, continuous insulation blanket and the greater the area that is exposed to cold winter air and hot summer sun. Interior heat passes through glass by conduction at a greater rate than through a wall. Using insulated shutters on windows will help to reduce heat flow to the outside during the winter, and into the shelter during the summer.

SITE PLANNING

There are a number of important siting considerations in locating an earth shelter: should the shelter be located to face south? Can it be located where it can be recessed into the soil or can be bermed up with soil? Can cold winds be deflected away from the shelter to prevent heat loss during the winter? Can good views on the site be seen? Can outdoor use areas be located near the shelter? In addition, are the geologic conditions and soil of the site suitable? Will the water table be a problem? Does the site drain well? All of these concerns must be addressed in developing site plans for an earth shelter landscape.

Facing South

In regard to energy savings, a south-facing earth shelter will have the advantage of direct sun gain on the front of the structure and through its glazing in the wintertime. Solar radiation provides direct heat gain for shelters with a large amount of thermal mass. South-facing windows that are double-glazed will receive and transmit more heat than they lose. Any heat lost from the windows will be the result of conduction and infiltration. Structures located on slopes other than those that are facing south may not receive the benefit of passive solar heat gain through south-facing glass, but they can still benefit from the blanket of soil that helps to keep the structure warm in the winter and acts as an insulated wrap for cooling in the summer.

Covering the Shelter with Soil

The best solution for protecting earth-sheltered structures is to cover the east, west, and north sides and the roof of the structure with soil. When land conditions permit, a sloping site that faces south is best for creating a fully recessed earth-sheltered structure. Place the structure into a slope so that one side, or elevation, is exposed and faces outward for access to outdoor areas and for maximum views. Develop the space around the southern exposure so that it remains open to the warming benefits of the low-angle winter sun. An earth shelter that is tucked into a hillside and fully recessed is only about 5% more energy efficient than a shelter that has soil mounded up on the walls and roof.

Planning for Wind Control

Not only does a south-facing earth shelter take advantage of the warming benefits of winter sun regimes, but it is also protected from north and northwesterly winter winds. Winter winds cannot strike the shelter walls and roof and remove heat by convection from the building envelope, as happens with above-grade or surface shelters. For maximum conservation of energy, avoid locating doors and windows on the north and west sides of the shelter. Winter winds striking these surfaces cause heat loss by convection and infiltration. South-facing glass, and vents on the opposite or northern side of the structure, will be needed in order to get natural air ventilation through the house. South-facing skylights that also have vents can be used to get cross ventilation. If the slope on which you are building also faces south, ideal site conditions will exist for passive solar heating.

Plants can be arranged to create a windbreak to deflect winter winds over the structure and nearby outdoor-use areas. Plant a wind ramp composed of evergreen trees and shrubs on the north, northwest, and northeast sides of the shelter for maximum wind deflection. A ramp works best and does not create wind turbulence as a line of evergreen trees might. Winds can be deflected up to five times the height of the windbreak. This can greatly reduce energy loss from the shelter and extend the use of outdoor areas beyond their normal season.

Considering Geologic Conditions

Site soil conditions, water table conditions, and drainage conditions must be suitable for an earth shelter. In the northern parts of the United States frost can penetrate soil up to 3 ft

(0.9 m) deep. In the South the frost line is 6 in. (152 mm) deep. Foundations, according to federal specification guidelines, should be placed 18 in. (457 mm) below the frost line to prevent upheaval during prolonged freezes. Soil conditions should be investigated to determine whether there are clay soils that expand when wet and contract when dry. These soils can be removed when creating a foundation and replaced with soils that are not expansive. In designing a waterproofing system for an earth shelter, it is important to know the water table level and how it fluctuates seasonally. For example, in Starkville, Mississippi, the water table in some soils is 18 in. (457 mm) below the surface of the ground in January and February, and more than 3 ft (0.9 m) deep the rest of the year. How water drains around the shelter is important. Surface water should be drained away from the earth shelter so as to eliminate drainage and leakage problems.

THERMAL ENERGY AND THE EARTH-SHELTERED STRUCTURE

Let us examine how an earth-sheltered structure can store heat for use in the winter and how it can remove heat from interior spaces during the summer. Having these passive heating and cooling qualities is what makes an earth shelter desirable for use in the sustainable landscape.

Historical Shelter Design

Historically, in temperate and cold climates of the world, structures were medium- to dark-colored, compact, and had as little exposed surface area as possible. The use of darker colors enhanced absorption of heat during the winter. The shelter's compactness reduced surface area and the amount of heat that would be lost by conduction, convection, and infiltration during the cold winters. Two-storied structures were commonly used in cold climates. Structures with two stories have less surface area—in fact, about 35% less—than the same-sized structure laid out as a single story. Windows were usually small and were not numerous. Historically, builders were trying to design with the climate, and being able to retain heat inside a structure during the winter might mean being alive in the springtime. This is often a consideration even today in the northernmost parts of the United States, where a blizzard and extreme freezing temperatures can sever power sources for four or five days. In an earth shelter that is without power for supplemental heating, indoor temperatures will drop about 1.8°F (1°C) per day, but they will not drop below freezing in most cases. In considering energy conservation plans, first determine cooling and heating needs, then decide where to put the emphasis—will it be on maximizing cooling or on minimizing heating losses?

Influence of Sun Angles

Two sun angle extremes can affect the design of the south elevation of an earth-sheltered structure. The winter sun angle on December 22 is the lowest noon sun angle of the year, and that of June 22 is the highest noon sun angle of the year. In designing the south elevation of an earth structure, your objective should be to allow sun into the shelter during the heating season and to block sun during the cooling season. First, identify the heating, cooling, and transition seasons, then plot sun angles to determine the extent of the roof overhang that will allow sun during the winter and block it during the summer. In addition to roof overhangs, arbors and movable awnings can be used to block the sun. Deciduous trees can effectively block summer sun gain, but when they lose their leaves the branching and trunk structure can block 50 to 75% of solar radiation. This denies the earth shelter solar radiation that can be converted to thermal energy and stored in thermal mass, waiting for release when needed for heating.

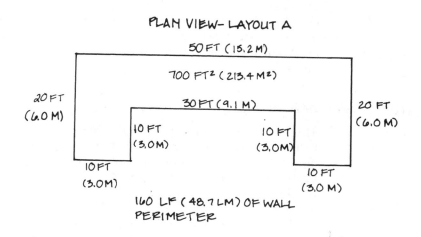

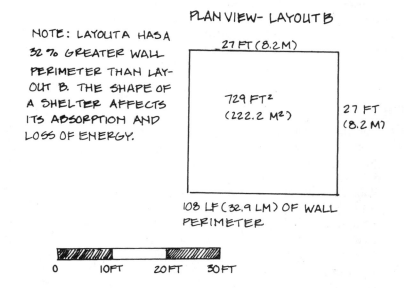

Figure 8-3 Shape related to the area of shelter sides.

Shelter Surface and Energy Loss

Energy loss in any shelter is directly related to the area of the building surface through which heat energy can be conducted to the outside. The larger the surface area, the more heat can be transmitted by conduction from the inside to the outside. A structure of the same square footage but with more surface area due to creating a longer layout, or a layout with offsets and jogs in the building design, will lose more heat than a structure with a compact square or rectangular layout that has a smaller surface area (Figure 8-3). The larger surface area works best with the climate in the hot-humid and hot-arid parts of the world where getting rid of heat is a priority, but it does not work in the temperate and cold climates of the world where retaining heat is of primary concern. In the hot-humid climate zone, thick masonry walls absorb heat within a shelter during the daytime and release it to the cooler out-of-doors during the cooler evening. Throughout the summer of 2001 in Mississippi, for instance, it was always 78°F (26°C) or cooler during the late evenings.

Transmission of Heat

The wintertime energy goal for earth-sheltered structures is to reduce the transfer of heat. Transmission of heat in surface structures is primarily caused by conduction of heat through the walls and roof and by infiltration of cold air into and out of the structure. The transmission of heat in an earth-sheltered structure is primarily caused by conduction of heat through the walls. Infiltration of cold air into and out of the structure is usually insignificant in earth-sheltered conditions because soil is covering most of the building envelope. Along with heat loss through conduction, heat loss (or gain) also occurs when the structure is ventilated with fresh air. In residences, most ventilation takes place when outside air infiltrates through cracks around windows, vents, and doors and during the opening and closing of doors and windows. In public facilities, ventilation or fresh air exchanges also occur mechanically, according to codes and heating and cooling guidelines. Fresh air brought in from the outside in the wintertime is humidified and heated, and in the summer it is dehumidified and cooled.

Soil Temperature

The soil around an earth-sheltered structure acts as insulation to reduce temperature fluctuations. Two meters (6.6 ft) below ground in the northernmost parts of the United States, the temperature is a constant 50°F (10°C), and in the southern part of the country it is 58°F (14°C). Those temperatures are relatively constant and do not vary much from winter to summer. In the winter the soil mass around an earth shelter buffers the shelter walls against low outside temperatures and helps to reduce transmission of heat to the air by convection. As temperatures rise during the day and fall during the night, even as little as 8 in. (200 mm) of soil over a structure will help to buffer temperature fluctuations. During very cold weather, temperatures in the interior of an earth-sheltered structure do not usually fall below freezing, and if they do, it will take a period of days for that to occur. This protects the interior of the structure, and in emergencies when there is a loss of power, the residents of an earth shelter will be protected from freezing.

In summer, the cool temperature from the surrounding earth can make the inside of the shelter cool, just as it does in a cave. For visitors to a cave, tour guides recommend wearing jackets because of the cold temperatures. What is actually happening in the cave—and in the shelter—is that the heat in the warm interior air moves through the walls to the cooler earth, where there is a low concentration of energy. The earth is acting as a heat sink, or storage place, for the energy in the warm air.

Thermal Mass

When there is a thermal mass composed of concrete, rock, brick, or water within a structure, solar radiation transmitted through south-facing windows will slowly and gently warm the interior of the space. Most of the heat, though, will be absorbed by the thermal mass. Heat energy will be conducted to the interior of the thermal mass, then released back into the space at night when the room cools, causing temperatures to fall slowly rather than drop quickly. Large amounts of thermal mass in a space absorbs sun heat during the day and prevents temperatures from dropping at night. If a shelter does not have a significant amount of thermal mass, temperatures resulting from the sunlight during the day can get uncomfortably hot and the space will probably need to be cooled. If there is little thermal mass to store solar radiation, the space can get cold very quickly at night, probably requiring supplemental heating.

Roof Systems

The roof is where the greatest amount of heat is lost during the winter and gained during the summer. In considering soil depths and the use of polystyrene insulation over concrete roofs, keep in mind that a roof that has a 10 ft (3 m) layer of soil will be only 2.4% more energy efficient than a roof that has a 1.5 ft (46 m) soil layer and a .33 ft (.10 m) layer of polystyrene insulation. The use of insulation and soil together is the best approach for roof insulation. In seeking to create an energy-efficient roof, it is best to increase insulation thickness rather than increase soil depth. Heavier roofs will require larger structural members to support increased loads, and costs will become extreme.

Planting for Thermal Energy Control

When grass is planted on the bermed-up walls or on the roof of a shelter to create a green area, energy efficiency increases because the grass shades the soil mass, it reflects heat, and evapotranspiration helps to cool the berm or roof environment. If we compare summer temperatures on a sunny concrete sidewalk and an adjacent grassed area, the sidewalk will be up to 15°F (8°C) warmer than the air, and the grassed area will be cooler than the air by 1° to 7°F (0.5° to 4°C). Summer temperature differences between the two materials do not exist during the winter because of the low angle of the sun and the reduced amount of solar energy available. Soil depth over a roof should be sufficient to sustain the growth of ground covers. Grass tends to be a suitable ground cover on roofs because certain species are very tolerant of dry and stressful environmental conditions. Consider the extreme environment of grasses on a sand dune. The sand dune is in the sun all day long, conditions are usually windy, and water drains through the sand quickly.

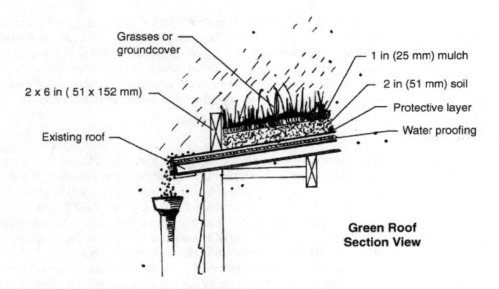

Grasses or groundcover

2 x 6 in (51 x 152 mm)

Existing roof

1 in (25 mm) mulch

2 in (51 mm) soil

Protective layer

Water proofing

**Green Roof
Section View**

Figure 8-4   Green roof components—section view.

Grasses are among the healthiest and best-performing native plants that grow on dunes and hold the sand together. In fact, grasses are nature's choice for protecting sand dunes. Grasses also do a good job of holding the soil on the sides and roof of an earth shelter. Figure 8-4 illustrates the components of a green roof.

HEATING AND COOLING THE STRUCTURE

Although earth-sheltered structures provide reasonably comfortable interior temperatures year-round, there will be times when temperatures have to be modified for maximum comfort. Supplemental heating and cooling systems and control of humidity levels will need to be considered.

Heating

Earth-sheltered structures can be heated with conventional fossil-fueled systems where oil, natural gas, liquid propane gas, or electricity can be used. Most electricity is provided through the burning of coal, natural gas, or oil. Fossil fuels are used to produce the electricity, and CO_2 is produced just as in the direct burning of oil- or gas-derived fossil fuels. Heat pumps are fueled by electricity, and for each unit of electricity used they provide 2.5 to 4.0 units of heat energy to interior spaces (2.5 to 4.0 is the coefficient of performance [COP] figure for a heat pump). Heat pumps will produce less CO_2 than conventional fossil-fueled systems. Wood-burning stoves and flat plate solar heating systems can also be used to provide heat. Flat plate solar heating systems capture solar radiation in an enclosed panel and transfer the heat to a storage medium like water or rock and eventually release it into the interior space. In addition to using flat plate collectors, capturing solar radiation passively with large thermal masses can be an effective choice in providing most of the heat needed.

Cooling

Although an earth shelter will probably have to be heated in the winter, it may not need supplemental cooling in the summer. Conduction of the heat in warm interior air through the walls and into the soil mass surrounding the building walls and roof will produce cool air. The large thermal masses of the concrete and masonry materials used in the earth shelter will absorb large amounts of heat from the air during the daytime and protect interior spaces from becoming uncomfortably hot. Heat is conducted through the walls and into the cooler soil. Ventilation of cool air into the structure at night can enhance the exchange of warm air for cool air during the summer. Earth-sheltered structures in regions of hot-arid and hot-humid climates will probably need mechanical cooling. In a hot-humid climate, dehumidification of the moisture-laden air will be necessary. In most climates in the summer, nighttime temperatures drop to levels that are cooler than daytime temperatures. Even in a hot-humid region, nighttime temperatures usually drop to 78°F (26°C) during the summer. Earth-sheltered structures can be cooled by ventilating the interior spaces with cooler night air. The thermal mass of concrete or brick that has been cooled will be able once again to receive heat during the warmer daytime hours. Some more conventional surface style structures with large thermal masses often use this strategy of cooling the interior at night with air-conditioning or night air so that the interior spaces will be cool throughout the daytime and mechanical systems will not have to rely on peak-use electricity.

Internal Heat Gain

For an earth shelter, heating loads are dramatically reduced and supplemental heating systems do not have to provide as much heat as they do for aboveground or surface structures. The amount of heat generated by people and machines indoors can contribute significantly to the heat gain within the interior of a structure. See Table 8-1 for an estimate of the amount of heat provided by people and machines. You can see that the internal heat load produced by a family of four plus the use of various machines will contribute nearly 30 kWh of heat to the daily heat load in the home during the winter. Rates for summer will be lower because people will be involved in more outdoor activities.

Interior Air Ventilation

The air within a structure must be exchanged with outside air periodically to provide fresh air to the occupants. In many homes, outgasing of volatile organic compounds (VOC) from synthetic materials in the home, such as vinyl tile, nylon carpet, and the glues in plywood, will get into the air and, for health reasons, have to be removed by ventilation from the interior. See Table 8-2 for chemicals often found within structures and their sources. It is always best to use materials indoors that do not outgas VOCs.

Table 8-1   Internal Heat Gains

(Computed in kilowatt hours per day for winter use.)

Refrigerator	7.20 kWh	(24,000 Btu)
Television	0.60 kWh	(2,000 Btu)
Computer	1.90 kWh	(6,500 Btu)
Cooking	4.0 kWh	(13,600 Btu)
Clothes dryer (vent indoors)	5.0 kWh	(17,000 Btu)
Water heater	3.6 kWh	(12,000 Btu)
Lights	3.4 kWh	(11,600 Btu)
People (4)	4.0 kWh	(13,600 Btu)
	29.7 kWh per day	(100,300 Btu)

Source: Underground Space Center at the University of Minneosta, *Earth Sheltered Housing Design*, (New York: Van Nostrand Reinhold, 1979).

Table 8-2   Chemicals Found in Shelters and Their Sources

Chemicals	*Sources in the Home*
Formaldehyde	Adhesives
	Caulking
	Draperies
	Fabrics
	Paints
	Plywood
Xylene/toluene	Ceiling tiles
	Computer screens
	Floor coverings
	Wall coverings
Benzene	Floor coverings
	Paints
	Tobacco smoke
	Wall coverings
Chloroform	Chlorinated tap water
Ammonia	Cleaning products
	Photocopiers
Alcohols	Carpeting
	Cosmetics
	Floor coverings
	Paints
	Stains and varnishes
Acetone	Nail polish remover
	Preprinted paper forms

Source: B. C. Wolverton, *EcoFriendly Houseplants* (Weidenfeld and Nicholson, 1996).

Ventilation also helps in exchanging cooler air for warmer interior air. Older homes usually experience significant air infiltration around doors and windows, whereas some newer homes and many earth shelters have been constructed to eliminate most air infiltration. A residence with tight construction that allows some infiltration needs two complete air exchanges per day, according to the Minnesota Energy Code. If fireplaces or stoves are used, more ventilation is needed, or outside air should be brought to the combustion unit. Considering a 32 ft × 46 ft × 8 ft (10 m × 14 m × 2.5 m) house that has 11,776 ft^3 (350 m^3) of air, the code recommends a minimum ventilation rate of 28,783 ft^3 (815 m^3) of fresh air per day. For maximum energy performance, it is best to ventilate summertime air during the night and wintertime air during the daytime, thereby taking advantage of the varying amounts of energy in the air during the different seasons and during the day and night.

Humidity

The amount of humidity in the air will affect how warm or cool you feel in a space. The more humidity in the air during the winter, the warmer the air will feel. High humidity in the air during the summer will also make the air feel warmer. When there is low humidity, normally produced body moisture on skin will evaporate more readily, making you feel cooler.

Evaporation occurs when water goes from a liquid to a gas state. The amount of evaporation that can occur depends largely on humidity (the lower the humidity, the greater the evaporation). When the moisture on your skin evaporates, your body is getting rid of heat and you will feel cooler. When humidity is controlled in an interior space, the result is a more comfortable environment and a reduction in the use of energy for providing heating and cooling.

The term *relative humidity* is frequently used in referring to humidity levels. Relative humidity is the percentage of moisture in the air that can be in the air. If the relative humidity is 50%, which is a comfortable humidity level for the springtime, it means that the air is capable of holding twice as much moisture as it is presently holding. As the air temperature changes, though, the ability of that air to hold moisture changes. Warm air holds more moisture than cold air. In the winter when the relative humidity is 100%, there is actually very little moisture in the air. Steel will rust when the relative humidity is greater than 40%. Wood furniture will crack when the relative humidity drops below 30%. Besides the humidity in fresh air that is brought into a shelter, other sources of humidification of interior air are running a shower, washing dishes, boiling food, watering indoor plants, human perspiration and respiration (breathing), and washing clothes (recall the warm, moist smell of a laundry room on wash day).

Dew Point

Dew point is another term that is important to understand. Related to humidity, the dew-point is the temperature at which moisture in the air will begin to condense. In an earth shelter, as with basement walls or the walls of a cave, the surface temperature of the walls may be cooler than the air, and it may be at or below the dew point of the air. When the air is cooled by the wall, moisture in the air will condense on the wall surface, potentially causing problems like water damage and mold growth. As long as surface temperatures are at the temperature of the air, there is no moisture problem. When wall surface temperatures are considerably cooler than the air, the warm air and warm moisture in the air will seek to move from warm to cool and moisture beads will form on the wall surface.

ENERGY ADVANTAGES OF AN EARTH-SHELTERED STRUCTURE

Just how energy efficient is an earth-sheltered home? The University of Minnesota Underground Space Center compared energy use in underground shelters and surface or aboveground shelters. The 1507 ft^2 (140 m^2) shelters the investigators compared were rectangular with the long side facing south. The southern exposure was composed of 35% double-insulated glass windows for passive solar radiation gain. Indoor temperatures were maintained at 68°F (20°C) during the winter and 78°F (26°C) during the summer. They found that transmission of heat in an earth shelter during the winter from walls, windows, and doors was far less than that of a surface house. It is interesting to note that heat gained from the internal heat load of people and machines, coupled with passive solar radiation gain, was greater than the amount of heat people needed to be comfortable, and greater than that which was lost by conduction through the walls. For winter conditions, it was found that the 1507 ft^2 (140 m^2) earth-sheltered structure had slightly more heat energy than it needed. Researchers' data showed that the home would not need supplemental heating to combat the Minnesota winters. In reality, the earth shelter would probably need a small supplemental heating unit for uninterrupted comfort. The surface structure shelter required 8579 kWh for heating during the winter, whereas the earth-sheltered home required no supplemental heating. At $.10 per kWh, the energy cost for the surface shelter during the winter was $858.

In considering safety from blizzard conditions during the winter, the research team found that the temperature of an earth shelter shell will drop only 1.8°F (1°C) per day during January temperature conditions for Minnesota. This is a comforting feature of an earth shelter for those living where power outages can occur during extremely cold times in the winter.

During the summer, the walls and earth around earth shelters help to cool the interiors. Cooling loads for the surface structures were six to eight times greater than for the earth shelter. The masonry walls of an earth-sheltered home assist in cooling by moving interior heat (thermal energy) through conduction into the thermal mass of the walls and soil. The Minnesota home would probably not need supplemental cooling. The walls of the surface house gained heat through convection and radiation, and heat was transferred through the walls through conduction. This house had six to eight times more heat gain by being exposed to the sun and warm summer air than the earth shelter house. Supplemental cooling will probably be necessary for maximum comfort. In comparing an earth-covered roof and a conventional roof for a single-story earth shelter, the winter heating requirement of the conventional roof is only slightly higher. But the summer heat gain from direct solar radiation on the exposed roof nearly doubles the cooling load. Use of a green roof on a conventional structure can dramatically reduce transmission of heat.

In regard to the placement of windows and their impact on energy loads, it was found that window openings on the east, west, and north sides of the earth-sheltered house will reduce the energy efficiency of the structure. The research team found that the transmission of heat loss by south-facing windows was half that of shelters in which the windows faced east or west. The positive effect of solar radiation gain during the heating season was very important and contributed to low overall energy needs. When windows could face only north, transmission losses were 2½ times greater than when facing south. Moreover, the north-facing windows did not get the heating benefit of solar radiation in the southern sky. Where a small window that was only 5% of the area of the north wall was placed on the north side of the earth shelter, overall shelter heat loss was increased by 10%, and the cooling effect provided by the wall was reduced by 15%. Where a small unshaded window (5% of the wall) was placed on the west side of the shelter, the summer cooling load increased by 23%. When 10% of the west wall was converted into an unshaded window, the cooling load of the earth shelter increased by 45%. Location of windows in an earth shelter on elevations other than the south wall should be thoroughly considered before implementation.

WATERPROOFING EARTH SHELTERS

There are three situations to consider regarding water in planning an earth shelter. The designer should make sure that the shelter is not in a floodplain, that it is not in a swale or an area where flowing water collects, and that the groundwater table and its seasonal variation are known and planned for when waterproofing the earth shelter. In addition, it is necessary to understand how dampness on interior walls can occur and how to prevent it.

Floodplains

When selecting a site for building an earth shelter, consider the site physiography, or physical form of the land. Is the site on a hillside, stream terrace, hilltop, or plateau, or is it in a floodplain that is subject to periodic flooding? Do not build on a site that floods, even if flooding occurs only once every 30 years.

Drainage Swales

When examining the physical form of a site, note where drainage swales are located and mark the site drainage patterns. When making a preliminary site analysis, consult a U.S. Geological Survey map to locate drainage trends. Such maps are available at libraries and for purchase in digital formats from commercial sources. Note the locations of swales and ridges, and be sure to site an earth shelter outside drainage swales. It is best to locate a shelter on a hilltop or hillside where water can drain away from the structure.

Water Tables

Next, explore the site for seasonally high water tables. Consult a Natural Resources Conservation Service (NRCS) soil survey for information on water table depths for the soil types on your site. In the winter season when there is significant rainfall, water tables can be higher than they are in the summer. If more information than a soil survey will supply is desired, a soil analysis from a geologic exploration company can predict seasonal depths for the water table in your area. If a site has a high water table, it may be best to relocate the earth shelter. If the shelter must be built where there is a high water table, locate drainage pipes at the bases of wall footings and beneath the structure to intercept and drain away water before it can get into the structure. Waterproof walls with either proven protective coatings or a continuous wall drain, located flat against the wall, that creates an air space between the wall and the adjacent soil. Waterproofing can prevent water from entering the wall. Drainpipes at the bottom of the wall will collect and drain water to a low point on the site. Although soil water from a high water table can be drained away from an earth shelter, an effective drainage system for an earth shelter located in an area with a high water table will probably be expensive.

Damp-proofing

Most of the dampness within an earth shelter is caused by moisture in the air condensing on cool walls. Dampness can also be caused by capillary movement of water in adjacent soils through shelter walls. Moisture in the air within the interior of an earth shelter will condense on walls if the temperature of the surface of the wall is at the dew point of the air. Air, and the water vapor inside an earth shelter, are usually at a higher temperature than the temperature of the surrounding earth. Recall that soil temperatures about 6.5 ft (2 m) below grade are 50°F (10°C) in the northern parts of the United States and about 58°F (14°C) in the deep South. Because of the warm indoor air and the cooler outside soil, heat in the air is transported to the solid surface by conduction. The heat energy in the water vapor is released during condensation, and the heat then passes into the wall through convection and conduction. When the air and water vapor meet a cool surface that is at the dew point of the air, the water in the air will condense on the surface, possibly causing moisture damage. Moisture on interior walls will likely evaporate into the interior air, increasing humidity within the space and taking heat from the cool wall to the interior air. When nighttime temperatures drop to the dew point of the air, the result is condensation of water or dew on plant leaves. This is the same event that happens within the earth shelter.

In an above-grade structure, a vapor barrier such as Visqueen plastic is stapled between the sheet rock and wood stud walls so that indoor water vapor cannot travel through walls to reach a cooler surface where it can condense into water droplets. If condensation becomes a problem in an earth shelter, it will probably occur during the summer when humidity levels are high. The use of a dehumidifier will help to lower interior moisture levels and reduce dampness.

Besides being caused by moisture condensing on cool wall surfaces, dampness also results from moisture being drawn through masonry walls to inside surfaces from cool, moist soils belowground. This movement of moisture through the wall is called capillary movement. It is similar to what happens when a cookie is dunked into a cup of coffee. Recall how the liquid moves upward into the cookie. The movement of moisture from the ground into the wall is the same process. After moving through the wall, the moisture will collect on the wall surface and, through convection, evaporate into the air and raise the humidity of the interior space. To prevent this movement of ground moisture into the earth shelter, install a damp-proof barrier outside the shelter masonry wall. A moisture barrier will stop the transfer of dampness into the shelter. The barrier can be either a wall waterproofing membrane, such as layers or membranes of waterproof sheets and asphaltic coatings, or a plastic barrier with a filter fabric covering that creates an air space between the wall and the egg-carton-shaped plastic barrier. Both of these construction methods will prevent capillary movement of water into and through a wall. Under the shelter flooring, a water vapor barrier can be placed between the gravel subbase and the concrete floor of the shelter. The plastic vapor barrier will prevent the movement of moisture through the soil and concrete floor into the shelter. Drains at the outside bases of exterior walls are essential in order to remove water.

Chapter 9

Computing Overhangs for Solar Energy Control

Blocking the sun during the cooling season and allowing sunlight to warm the south-facing building sides and penetrate south-facing windows during the heating season can save 20 to 100% of fossil fuel energy used for heating and cooling purposes. By keeping the sun off the walls of a shelter and out of its windows during the summertime, temperatures inside the shelter can be 8° to 15°F (4° to 8°C) cooler than in a structure exposed to direct sunlight.

THE NEED FOR CONTROLLING SUNLIGHT

Throughout history, we have considered the sun and its effect on our places of habitation. Many nineteenth-century homes were located to face the south, to be passively warmed by winter sunlight. The shelters had long overhangs to control the hot summer sun, and trees were liberally planted around the homesteads to keep inside and outside spaces as cool as possible. For instance, in the 1950s a Missouri family planted a sweetgum tree to keep the summer afternoon sun from hitting the back side of their house and coming through a bedroom window. This western-facing window was where a big box window fan was located, and this was the means of cooling the home during the intensely hot summers in St. Louis. At night the breeze created by the window fan made sleeping comfortable for the family as the air moving over the sweat beads on their skin helped to evaporate moisture and keep them feeling cool. It has been determined that moving air can make people feel up to 8° to 10°F (4° to 6°C) cooler. Before the use of the window fan, people moved to sleeping porches during the summer to seek sleeping spaces that were as cool and comfortable as possible, relying on the forces of nature during the evenings to provide some relief from the heat that had built up during the day. When mechanical air-conditioning systems became available, many shelters were located and designed without concern for natural climate conditions.

RELATED ECONOMIC AND ENVIRONMENTAL HEALTH ISSUES

In our shelters today, there is a need for interior space heating during the winter and a desire for no heat gain and at least some cooling of interior spaces during the summer. Energy costs for providing these requirements are becoming considerable, and families and businesses are seeking alternative ways of meeting such needs less expensively. Related to the growth in energy consumption is the increased production of carbon dioxide through burning fossil fuels, which is contributing to large excesses of carbon in the atmosphere. The earth's plants cannot sequester this carbon fast enough, resulting in a warming of the atmosphere and an impending change in climate patterns and rise in sea level. Because sunlight is a renewable resource, technologies that rely on the sun are sustainable and will never run out of power for operation. Regenerative technologies using solar power are nonpolluting.

APPROACHES TO SUNLIGHT CONTROL

There are various ways to prevent the sun from hitting the sides and windows of buildings during the cooling season. Roof overhangs, first-floor setbacks, awnings, and trees can all keep the sun off the south-facing walls of a structure. Of these sun-control devices, roof overhangs and setbacks are the most effective means to control solar heat gain. Where the addition of building overhangs and setbacks is not possible, awnings or trees can help prevent solar heat gain during the summer. Movable awnings can block sunlight from reaching the window or wall surface of a shelter and prevent thermal mass from absorbing heat and conducting it to cooler spaces within. In retrofitting a shelter for control of the sun, use trees to shade south-facing exposures. When placing deciduous trees on the south side to block summer sunshine, be aware that they will also block the low angle of the winter sun and reduce solar heat gain possibilities by 55 to 80%. The more branching and twig structure in a deciduous tree, the more sun heat (solar energy) that will be blocked during the wintertime. Locate trees close to structures and remove limbs and branches to prevent branch structures from blocking winter sunlight. See Figure 9-1 for examples of sun blocking devices.

Determining Sun Angles

Calculating and plotting sun angles related to a proposed shelter or outdoor use area will help in figuring the location of facilities and land uses that involve passive use of the sun. It can also help in determining the actual physical form of a shelter, including location of overhangs, first-floor setbacks, awnings, and windows. In planning to use the sun to warm a shelter and site, it is essential to be able to compute sun angles for any time during the day, and any day during the year. Sunlight can be absorbed through direct exposure to a shelter's sides and by beaming through windows and being absorbed in a thermal mass. When sunlight strikes a strategically located thermal mass, it is absorbed into the mass throughout the day and released when interior spaces become cooler, thus maintaining comfortable interior spaces with only passive use of the sun. The thermal mass is usually a concrete, brick, or rock floor or wall that will absorb and store heat from the sun.

AWNINGS — AWNINGS ARE MOVABLE SUN BLOCKING DEVICES THAT PREVENT DIRECT SOLAR GAIN TO THE WINDOW. THESE AWNINGS PROTECT THE WEST FACING WINDOWS DURING THE SUMMER. IN THE WINTER THE AWNINGS ARE PULLED UP TO ALLOW LIGHT AND HEAT FROM THE SUN TO WARM INTERIOR SPACES.

OVERHANGS — THESE 19TH CENTURY HOMES IN SAVANNAH, GEORGIA HAVE OVERHANGS TO CONTROL THE HEAT GAIN POTENTIAL FROM THE SUMMER SUN.

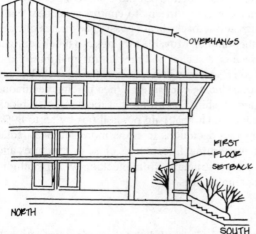

OVERHANGS

FIRST FLOOR SETBACK

NORTH

SOUTH

FIRST FLOOR SETBACKS — THE SOUTH FACING NEW LANDSCAPE ARCHITECTURE FACILITY AT MISSISSIPPI STATE UNIVERSITY HAS BOTH ROOF OVERHANGS AND FIRST-FLOOR SETBACKS TO PREVENT SUN FROM HITTING THE BUILDING AND BEAMING THROUGH WINDOWS UNTIL NEEDED DURING THE WINTER HEATING SEASON WHEN THE SUN IS AT A LOW ANGLE IN THE SKY.

SUN

SHELTER

SOUTH

NORTH

USE OF TREES — TREES CAN BE PLANTED NEAR SHELTERS TO BLOCK THE HIGH-IN-THE-SKY SUMMER SUN AND ALLOW THE LOWER ANGLE WINTER SUNSHINE DURING THE HEATING SEASON. LIMB UP TREES TO REDUCE BLOCKING OF LOW ANGLE SUNSHINE.

Figure 9-1 Examples of sun-blocking devices.

A recently designed classroom facility at Mississippi State University employed many elements of passive solar design. At that latitude and location in the hot-humid climate of the Deep South, it was determined that classroom/design studio buildings full of people and computers, and having a concrete floor that was also a thermal mass, were going to be more difficult to cool than to heat. Therefore, it was decided that the emphasis would be on keeping the facility cool most of the year by preventing all sun from hitting the walls and windows of the building from May 1 through October 1, but allowing the sun to strike and warm the shelter during a three-month heating season. Because of the changing azimuths and lower altitude of the sun before 10:00 A.M. and after 2:00 P.M., sunlight will hit the north, south, east, and west sides of the building during summer, but will not transmit as much heat as when the sun is higher in the sky and its rays are more intense. In determining sun angles for the facility, the planners calculated a need for 7 ft 3 in. (2.2 m) overhangs to keep the sun out of the building and off its south side from 10:00 A.M. through 2:00 P.M. during the entire cooling season. During the heating season, the 7 ft 3 in. (2.2 m) overhang will allow sun to hit the south side of the building and begin coming through the south-facing windows by November 7. The entire south side of the building will receive sunlight, and sunlight will penetrate into south-facing windows by December 1 through January 11. By February 6, as the sun moves higher in the sky, the south side of the building will still receive sunlight but the sun will no longer penetrate very far into the windows. The placement of overhangs controlling the amount of heat being absorbed by the shelter is based on the determination of when heat is needed, according to historical temperature regimes. Solar radiation thus blocked during the cooling season does not have to be removed with an air conditioner.

Determining Heating and Cooling Seasons

Historically, in the hot-humid climate of Mississippi, there are warm to hot summer days from May 1 through September 30. October and November are usually very pleasant fall months, with daytime temperatures in the 50° to 60°F (10° to 16°C) range and nighttime temperatures in the 43° to 51°F (6° to 11°C) range. Interior heating is needed from December 1 through February 28, when day temperatures are 40° to 45°F (4° to 7°C) and night temperatures average 30° to 34°F (−2° to 1°C). March and April are like October and November. They are pleasant springtime months with daytime temperatures in the 54° to 63°F (12° to 17°C) range and nighttime temperatures in the 43° to 52°F (6° to 11°C) range. Temperatures and humidity begin to become uncomfortable about May 1 and persist through the end of September. See Table 9-1 for a comparison of average daily temperatures throughout the year for the Mississippi State University campus.

Through an evaluation of existing climate information, the year can be divided into seasons during which a shelter will need cooling and dehumidification, heating and humidification, or neither cooling nor heating. Transition seasons, the periods between the cooling and heating seasons, are the times when neither cooling nor heating is absolutely necessary. See Table 9-2 for the cooling and heating seasons determined for the new landscape architecture facility.

Table 9-1   Comparison of Daily and Nightly Average Temperatures Throughout the Year for Mississippi State University Campus (1930–1999)

In Degrees Fahrenheit

	J	F	M	A	M	J	J	A	S	O	N	D
Day	54	59	65	75	83	88	91	92	87	76	65	56
Night	33	36	44	51	60	68	71	70	64	52	44	35

In Degrees Celcius

	J	F	M	A	M	J	J	A	S	O	N	D
Day	12	15	18	24	28	31	33	33	31	24	18	13
Night	1	2	8	11	16	20	22	21	18	11	7	2

Table 9-2   Interior Space Cooling and Heating Need Seasons for Mississippi State University Campus (33½° NL)

Interior Comfort	Duration	Time of Year	Temperatures	Condition
Cooling Need	5 months	May 1–Sept. 30	84–90°F (29–32°C) days 78–80°F (26–27°C) nights	Warm-hot days Warm nights
Transition Season	2 months	Oct. 1–Nov. 30	50–60°F (10–16°C) days 43–51°F (6–11°C) nights	Pleasant fall months
Heating Need	3 months	Dec. 1–Feb. 28	40–45°F (4–7°C) days 30–34°F (−2–1°C) nights	Cold days Cold nights
Transition Season	2 months	March 1–April 30	54–63°F (12–17°C) days 43–52°F (6–11°C) nights	Pleasant spring months

Energy Availability and Costs

In the hot-humid climate of the Mississippi State University, costs for cooling are generally greater than costs for heating. Of the total yearly energy costs for a typical residence, electrical cooling costs are 66% and natural gas heating costs are 34%. Researchers evaluated a residence that used electricity for cooling and natural gas for heating. Natural gas also supplied the heat for two hot water heaters and a stove. Figure 9-2 shows the amount of electricity and natural gas used for this residence in one year. You can see from the figures how to estimate costs related to interior space heating and cooling. This can be helpful information in figuring energy savings resulting from the application of

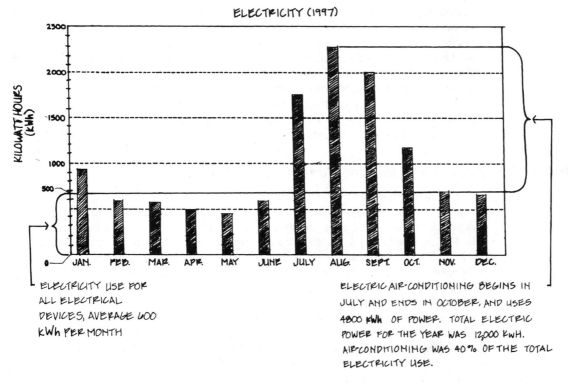

ELECTRICITY USE FOR ALL ELECTRICAL DEVICES, AVERAGE 600 kWh PER MONTH

ELECTRIC AIR-CONDITIONING BEGINS IN JULY AND ENDS IN OCTOBER, AND USES 4800 kWh OF POWER. TOTAL ELECTRIC POWER FOR THE YEAR WAS 12,000 kWH. AIR-CONDITIONING WAS 40% OF THE TOTAL ELECTRICITY USE.

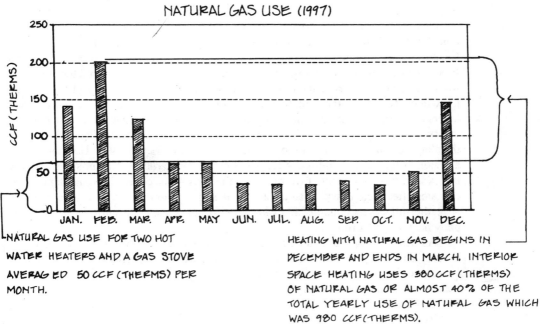

NATURAL GAS USE FOR TWO HOT WATER HEATERS AND A GAS STOVE AVERAGED 50 CCF (THERMS) PER MONTH.

HEATING WITH NATURAL GAS BEGINS IN DECEMBER AND ENDS IN MARCH. INTERIOR SPACE HEATING USES 380 CCF (THERMS) OF NATURAL GAS OR ALMOST 40% OF THE TOTAL YEARLY USE OF NATURAL GAS WHICH WAS 980 CCF (THERMS).

Figure 9-2 Electricity and natural gas use for a residence for one year.

various regenerative technologies that rely on renewable resources. In comparing costs of two different types of energy, it must be realized that the cost for different types of energy can fluctuate on a seasonal basis. Natural gas has historically been less expensive for heating as compared with electricity, but this can change as the availability of fuel fluctuates. Designers and managers should be aware not only of energy costs and the total amount of energy used, but also the quantity of CO_2 produced by burning different fuels, because additional CO_2 contributes to the total global warming load. Production of CO_2 in the world will soon be regulated, and there will be costs associated with sequestering carbon produced by fossil fuels.

Indoor Air Temperatures and the Human Comfort Level

The human comfort level affects the determination of cooling and heating seasons. During the Arab oil embargo in the late 1970s, President Carter had a fireside chat with the American public about using energy. He was wearing a sweater, and a fire was burning in the fireplace behind him. He noted that because so much money in the United States was going out of the country to pay for oil, the economic health of the country was being threatened. Moreover, the scarcity of oil had driven its price to an all-time high. The president was asking people to lower their thermostats to a maximum of 65°F (18°C) during the day in winter and a minimum of 78°F (26°C) during the day in summer. This effort was envisioned to help conserve fossil fuels and keep our country economically healthy. In fact, the effort paid off and we had a tremendous growth in gross national product for a three-year period, with an actual national decrease in the use of fossil fuels.

Indoor air temperatures and their effect on the human comfort range is, of course, variable. It seems that larger people need more cooling and less heat and smaller people don't like temperatures too cool and enjoy warmer indoor temperatures during the winter. Larger people probably have more fat insulation and are therefore warmer when it is cold and hot when it is warm. The Eskimos traditionally consumed a large amount of fat for storing on their bodies as protection from the cold and as a ready energy supply when food became scarce. Canadians, because of their long winter season and the cost of fuel for heating, generally keep their thermostats no higher than 65° to 68°F (18° to 20°C) in the winter. To combat the cold, they wear multiple layers of clothing for warmth. More layers are warmer than one thick layer of clothing, because the air spaces between the layers reduce the conduction of cold into the body, and of body heat to the cold air beyond the clothing. The second law of thermodynamics applies here as well: Heat moves from a region of high temperature to a region of colder temperature. The air spaces between layers slow this movement of warmth from the body to the cooler air. Inhabitants of cold climates often wear down vests throughout the day in the winter to conserve body heat. A feather-filled vest contains a large number of air spaces, preventing conductance of body heat to colder room air.

A further example of human comfort level draws on home-life conditions of a family in rural Mississippi. Their home had two wood-burning fireplaces and a wood-burning cookstove for heat in winter. In central Mississippi, temperatures frequently fall below freezing in December, January, and part of February. The family ate, did homework, and read near the fireplace. Their bedtime ritual was to get thoroughly warm beside the fireplace before running to the bedrooms and jumping into their beds, which were usually piled high with homemade quilts. The number of quilts was based on how cold it was.

There were always enough quilts to contain body heat, so those in beds would remain warm all through the night. Near freezing conditions occurred nightly in the bedrooms away from the fireplace.

Another family's home has a fireplace with glass doors that heats by a natural convection draft, as well as through radiant heating, like most traditional fireplaces. When a fire is lit, it might be 80°F (27°C) near the fireplace while in the next room the temperature is 65° to 70°F (18° to 21°C). Because the rooms away from the fireplace are cooler, when family members settle down to read, visit, or do a project, they usually land somewhere close to the fireplace. When they have to be away from the fireplace, they dress for the 10° to 15°F (6° to 8°C) cooler temperatures in the other rooms.

Regarding human comfort level averages and the need to conserve fossil fuels, it appears that during the winter people can tolerate 65°F (18°C) air temperatures in the daytime, and as low as 55°F (13°C) at night without significant discomfort. Providing moisture in the air indoors during the winter will make the temperature feel warmer than it is. One way to accomplish this is to cultivate plants indoors that need only low levels of light. As part of their transpiration process, plants give off both oxygen and moisture, which combats the dryness normally found indoors due to the drying of the air by heating systems. During the summer, a temperature of 80°F (27°C) is acceptable to many, but a temperature of 78°F (26°C) is more comfortable to more people. Many people keep their homes at 80°F (27°C) during the summer, except when they have visitors who are uncomfortable at this temperature; then they turn the cooling down to 75° to 78°F (24° to 26°C). Ceiling fans in the rooms where people are congregating evaporate skin moisture and make them feel about 8° to 10°F (4° to 6°C) cooler than the actual room temperature.

In the new facility mentioned earlier, the plan is for interior temperatures no warmer than 68°F (20°C) in winter and no cooler than 78°F (26°C) in summer. To make these temperatures feel more comfortable, the relative humidity in the interior air is to be lowered during the summer and moisture added during the winter.

DETERMINING THE LENGTH OF OVERHANGS

As the sun rises and moves through the sky, it changes azimuths (compass directions) throughout the day, and its angle or altitude in relation to the earth continuously changes, reaching a maximum angle at noon. To understand the impact of the location of the sun, it is helpful to plot sun angles in an elevation or section drawing, and azimuths in plan view throughout the day, as fully explained in Chapter 16, "Determining Sun Path." Pick the dates for which you want to evaluate the sun's path and locate sun path lines on a solar altitude and azimuth chart, as shown in Figure 9-3. This process is explained in Table 9-3. If you are selecting dates not listed on the solar altitude and azimuth chart, either estimate where your date would fall or use an analemma chart to get the specific declination for the date you want. Relate that declination to the declinations on the solar altitude and azimuth chart, and draw a light sun path line on the chart. Note that you must use a chart that is made for your latitude. Once sun path lines have been penciled in for the dates selected (Figure 9-3), note the sun angles where the sun path line crosses the time-of-day lines on the chart's concentric degree rings. Plot these in a section view drawing, as shown in Figure 9-4, so that the physical sun control components of the shelter can be accurately designed, and trees selected and located for sun control. We

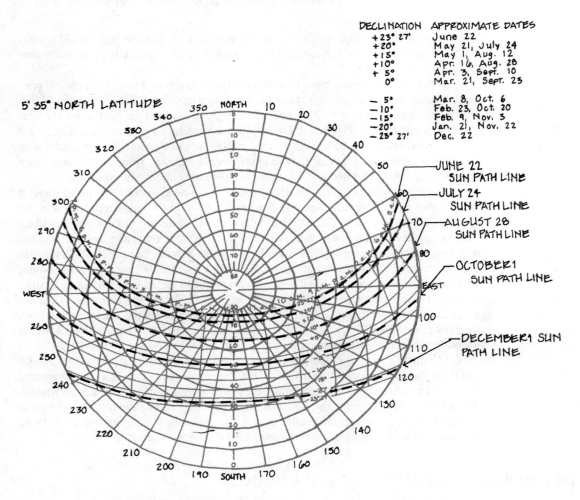

Figure 9-3 Penciled-in sun path lines for computing hourly sun angles.

have shown hourly sun movement for five dates during the year to fully illustrate the sun's daily path related to different seasons.

The cooling season for Mississippi State University has been defined in Table 9-2 from May 1 through September 30 (May-June-July-August-September). In plotting sun angles for the proposed facility, October 1 was selected as the end of the cooling season and the extreme date to determine how far to extend a roof overhang to make sure the sun's heat was kept completely off and out of the buildings. October 1, the end of the cooling season, is also the beginning of the transition season. This is the period when the sun is gradually allowed to strike and warm building walls and come into the windows so that enough solar heat will be available during the heating season, which begins December 1. See Figure 9-5 for comparisons of the overhang lengths and their effects on the sun path during cooling and heating seasons. On December 1, sunlight will strike nearly two-thirds of the south-facing building wall and extend up to 7½ ft (2.3 m) into interior spaces. This exposure to the south-facing wall and into interior spaces

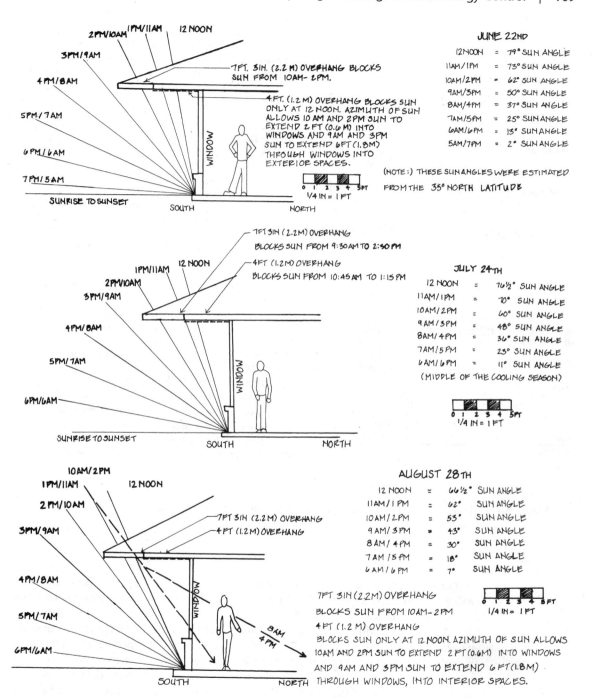

JUNE 22ND

12NOON	=	79° SUN ANGLE
11AM/1PM	=	73° SUN ANGLE
10AM/2PM	=	62° SUN ANGLE
9AM/3PM	=	50° SUN ANGLE
8AM/4PM	=	37° SUN ANGLE
7AM/5PM	=	25° SUN ANGLE
6AM/6PM	=	13° SUN ANGLE
5AM/7PM	=	2° SUN ANGLE

(NOTE:) THESE SUN ANGLES WERE ESTIMATED FROM THE 35° NORTH LATITUDE

7FT. 3IN. (2.2 M) OVERHANG BLOCKS SUN FROM 10AM- 2PM.

4FT. (1.2 M) OVERHANG BLOCKS SUN ONLY AT 12 NOON. AZIMUTH OF SUN ALLOWS 10 AM AND 2PM SUN TO EXTEND 2 FT (0.6 M) INTO WINDOWS AND 9AM AND 3PM SUN TO EXTEND 6FT (1.8M) THROUGH WINDOWS INTO EXTERIOR SPACES.

JULY 24TH

12 NOON	=	76½° SUN ANGLE
11AM/1PM	=	70° SUN ANGLE
10AM/2PM	=	60° SUN ANGLE
9AM/3PM	=	48° SUN ANGLE
8AM/4PM	=	36° SUN ANGLE
7AM/5PM	=	23° SUN ANGLE
6AM/6PM	=	11° SUN ANGLE

(MIDDLE OF THE COOLING SEASON)

7FT 3IN (2.2M) OVERHANG BLOCKS SUN FROM 9:30AM TO 2:30PM

4FT (1.2M) OVERHANG BLOCKS SUN FROM 10:45AM TO 1:15PM

AUGUST 28TH

12 NOON	=	66½° SUN ANGLE
11AM/1PM	=	62° SUN ANGLE
10AM/2PM	=	53° SUN ANGLE
9AM/3PM	=	43° SUN ANGLE
8AM/4PM	=	30° SUN ANGLE
7AM/5PM	=	18° SUN ANGLE
6AM/6PM	=	7° SUN ANGLE

7FT 3IN (2.2M) OVERHANG BLOCKS SUN FROM 10AM-2PM

4FT (1.2 M) OVERHANG BLOCKS SUN ONLY AT 12 NOON. AZIMUTH OF SUN ALLOWS 10AM AND 2PM SUN TO EXTEND 2 FT (0.6M) INTO WINDOWS AND 9AM AND 3PM SUN TO EXTEND 6 FT (1.8M) THROUGH WINDOWS, INTO INTERIOR SPACES.

Figure 9-4 Determining overhangs with hourly sun angles.

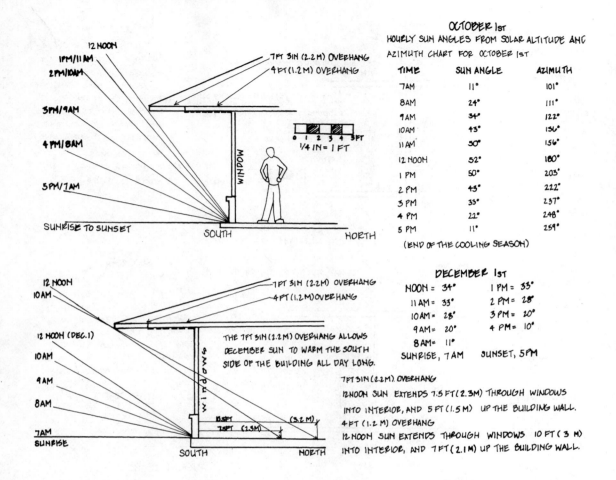

OCTOBER 1st

HOURLY SUN ANGLES FROM SOLAR ALTITUDE AND AZIMUTH CHART FOR OCTOBER 1st

TIME	SUN ANGLE	AZIMUTH
7 AM	11°	101°
8 AM	24°	111°
9 AM	34°	122°
10 AM	43°	136°
11 AM	50°	156°
12 NOON	52°	180°
1 PM	50°	203°
2 PM	43°	222°
3 PM	33°	237°
4 PM	22°	248°
5 PM	11°	259°

(END OF THE COOLING SEASON)

DECEMBER 1st

NOON = 34°	1 PM = 33°
11 AM = 33°	2 PM = 28°
10 AM = 28°	3 PM = 20°
9 AM = 20°	4 PM = 10°
8 AM = 11°	

SUNRISE, 7 AM   SUNSET, 5 PM

7 FT 3 IN (2.2 M) OVERHANG

12 NOON SUN EXTENDS 7.5 FT (2.3 M) THROUGH WINDOWS INTO INTERIOR, AND 5 FT (1.5 M) UP THE BUILDING WALL.

4 FT (1.2 M) OVERHANG

12 NOON SUN EXTENDS THROUGH WINDOWS 10 FT (3 M) INTO INTERIOR, AND 7 FT (2.1 M) UP THE BUILDING WALL.

Figure 9-4 *continued* Using hourly sun angles for Oct. 1, end of cooling season—33 1/2° North Latitude

will increase until December 22, which is the winter solstice. Beyond this date, the sun will gradually move higher in the sky and there will be less solar heat gain on the walls and within the space.

As compared with a residential structure, a classroom building has a great deal more internal heat gain, caused by machines and the presence of many people. Managing heat is critically important to creating comfortable interior spaces so they do not have to be cooled during the wintertime. Sun should be kept out of similar nonresidential structures until the coldest part of the winter. If the sun is kept off and out of a building during the cooling season, then interior spaces will not accumulate heat from direct solar gain and will be significantly cooler. To begin to accomplish this, planners at Mississippi State

Table 9-3 Process for Finding Sun Angles on the Solar Altitude and Azimuth Chart

1. Go to the analemma chart (Figure 16-6 in Chapter 16, "Determining Sun Path") or look in the approximate dates and declinations table in Figure 9-3 to find the declination of the sun (where the sun is at 90° to the earth) on June 22. It will be +23½° (the noon sun on this date makes a 90° angle at the Tropic of Cancer line). Table 9-4 shows how to use the analemma chart to find declinations and then how to compute noon sun angles.

2. Plot the sun path line on the solar altitude and azimuth chart (it is already drawn on the charts for June 22).

3. For approximate sun angles for June 22, note where the sun path line crosses the time of day lines and then, for the times of day you select, read the approximate sun angles on the concentric degree rings.

4. For June 22, we discovered the following approximate sun angles and azimuths:

Sun Angle	Time of Day	Azimuth
13°	6:00 A.M.	71°
37°	8:00 A.M.	86°
62°	10:00 A.M.	107°
78°	12:00 noon	180°
62°	2:00 P.M.	253°
37°	4:00 P.M.	274°
13°	6:00 P.M.	288°

Table 9-4 Using the Analemma for Computing Specific Noon Sun Angles

Sun Date	Declination		Latitude		Equation		Sun Angle
May 1/Aug. 12	+14½°	−	(+33½°)	=	−19 + 90	=	71°
June 1/July 13	+22°	−	(+33½°)	=	−11.5 + 90	=	78.5°
July 1/June 12	+23½°	−	(+33½°)	=	−10 + 90	=	80°
Aug. 1/May 14	+18½°	−	(+33½°)	=	−15 + 90	=	75°
Sept. 1/April 12	+ 8½°	−	(+33½°)	=	−25 + 90	=	65°
Oct. 1/March 14	− 3°	−	(+33½°)	=	−36.5 + 90	=	53.5°

Note: The latitude will always be subtracted from the declination because the sun angle for areas above and below the equator will always be less than a 90° angle with the earth.

University envisioned that the east and west sides of the structure would be planted to block direct solar heat gain from low morning and late afternoon sun angles. North sides of shelters should be planted to create windbreaks for deflection of cold winter winds, as shown in Figure 9-6. This planting will also block early morning and late afternoon summer sunshine on the east and west sides. Winter sun should be allowed to heat the south side of a shelter (the south side is the only side of the building that low winter sunlight will strike anyway). Building with materials composed of brick, concrete block,

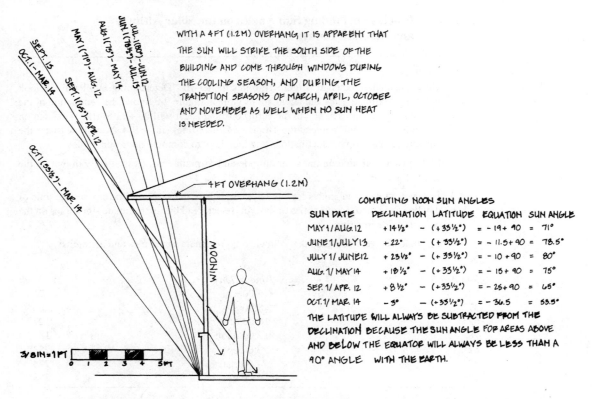

WITH A 4 FT (1.2 M) OVERHANG, IT IS APPARENT THAT THE SUN WILL STRIKE THE SOUTH SIDE OF THE BUILDING AND COME THROUGH WINDOWS DURING THE COOLING SEASON, AND DURING THE TRANSITION SEASONS OF MARCH, APRIL, OCTOBER AND NOVEMBER AS WELL WHEN NO SUN HEAT IS NEEDED.

COMPUTING NOON SUN ANGLES

SUN DATE	DECLINATION	LATITUDE	EQUATION	SUN ANGLE
MAY 1/ AUG. 12	+14½°	– (+33½°)	= –19+ 90	= 71°
JUNE 1/JULY 13	+22°	– (+33½°)	= –11.5+90	= 78.5°
JULY 1/ JUNE 12	+23½°	– (+33½°)	= –10 +90	= 80°
AUG. 1/ MAY 14	+18½°	– (+33½°)	= –15+ 90	= 75°
SEP. 1/ APR. 12	+8½°	– (+33½°)	= –25+90	= 65°
OCT. 1/ MAR. 14	–3°	– (+33½°)	= –36.5	= 53.5°

THE LATITUDE WILL ALWAYS BE SUBTRACTED FROM THE DECLINATION BECAUSE THE SUN ANGLE FOR AREAS ABOVE AND BELOW THE EQUATOR WILL ALWAYS BE LESS THAN A 90° ANGLE WITH THE EARTH.

Figure 9-5 Noon sun angles and the effect of overhangs during heating and cooling seasons.

and steel will create a good thermal mass that will absorb solar insolation and release stored energy as the temperatures cool within the structure.

During the cooling season, the sun angle will vary from an altitude (noon sun angle) of 53½° to 80°. To prevent most of the sun from hitting the south facing building sides during the hottest part of the day, between 10:00 A.M. and 2:00 P.M., an overhang of 7 ft 3 in. (2.2 m) is desired. Compare the following effects of the 7 ft 3 in. (2.2 m) overhang and the 4 ft (1.2 m) overhang, as shown in Table 9-5. During the heating season, the objective in planning the classroom facility was to permit passive solar heating of the shelter through allowing direct solar gain on the building from December 1 through February 28. Overhangs and plantings should be designed to allow the warming benefit of the sun during this period of time.

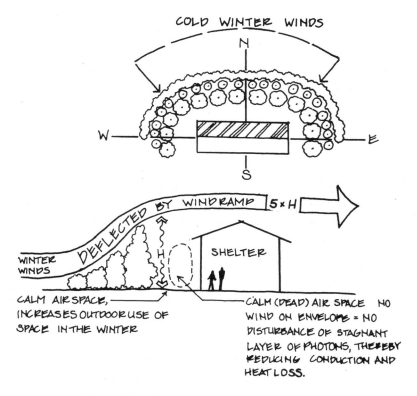

Figure 9-6 Winter wind control with wind ramps.

Table 9-5 Comparing the Effectiveness of Overhangs in Preventing the Sun from Hitting the South Side of a Building

	7 ft 3 in. (2.2 m) Overhang	*4 ft (1.2 m) Overhang*
June 22	Blocks sun from 9:15 A.M. until 2:45 P.M.	Blocks sun from 10:30 A.M. until 1:30 P.M.
July 24	Blocks sun from 9:30 A.M until 2:30 P.M.	Blocks sun from 10:45 A.M. until 1:15 P.M.
August 28	Blocks sun from 10:00 A.M. until 2:00 P.M.	Blocks sun only at 12:00. Azimuth of sun allows 10 A.M. and 2:00 P.M. sun to extend 2 ft (0.6 m) into the building, and 9:00 A.M. and 3:00 P.M. sun to extend 6 ft (1.8 m) through windows into interior spaces.
October 1	Blocks sun at 12:00 noon.	12:00 noon sun hits halfway up building wall and beams 3 ft (0.9 m) through windows into interior spaces.
December 1	12:00 noon sun extends 7.5 ft (2.3 m) through windows into the interior, and 5 ft (1.5 m) up the building wall.	12:00 noon sun extends through windows 10 ft (3 m) into interior, and 7 ft (2.1 m) up the building wall.

Chapter 10

Heating Shelters with the Sun

Energy from the sun is sufficiently available nearly everywhere to provide 30 to 100% of interior space heating needs. Use of the sun's renewable resource potential will save fuel costs, maintain reserves of nonrenewable resources, and significantly reduce the production of carbon dioxide that results from the combustion of fossil fuels.

Human settlements were once influenced and shaped by climatic factors. People lived as part of the ecological system, settling where they had access to food and water and where they could sustain themselves. They settled where they could live within the climate zone using renewable resources like the sun and wood biomass for heating and shade for cooling. Passive or inactive methods of heating, cooling, and air movement that did not require mechanical means were relied on for comfort. In contrast, shelters today are heated and cooled with mechanical systems fueled with nonrenewable resources, including coal, oil, and natural gas. Mechanical means of providing heat, cooling, and air movement are called active systems. As fossil fuels dwindle and the carbon dioxide that results from their combustion is added to the overabundance of carbon dioxide in the air, we are compelled to seek alternatives to energy-intensive active heating and cooling systems. A large portion of heating needs can be met by using the renewable energy of the sun. Cooling needs can be reduced or eliminated through the use of insulation, sun blocking devices, and ground source cooling.

PASSIVE SOLAR HEATING

In order to have a successful passive solar heating system, it is best for a shelter to be sited with its long side oriented toward the south and to have south-facing glass for transmission of solar radiation into interior spaces. Thermal mass within spaces is needed for the absorption, storage, and, then, radiation of heat back into the spaces. To effectively collect solar radiation, the building materials used must have sufficient capacity to store the needed amount of heat. The following discussion of terms and processes will enable you to begin incorporating passive solar energy use into shelter design. Figure 10-1 graphically depicts the siting requirements and components.

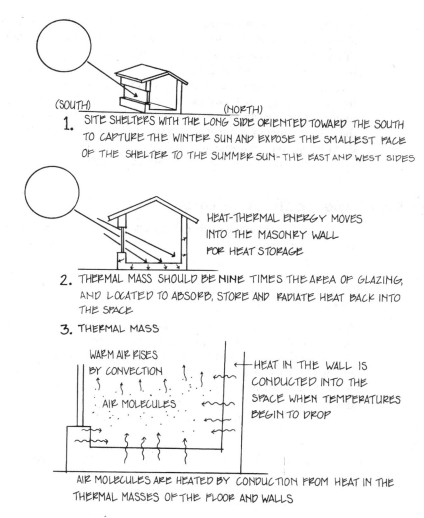

1. SITE SHELTERS WITH THE LONG SIDE ORIENTED TOWARD THE SOUTH TO CAPTURE THE WINTER SUN AND EXPOSE THE SMALLEST FACE OF THE SHELTER TO THE SUMMER SUN - THE EAST AND WEST SIDES

(SOUTH)   (NORTH)

HEAT-THERMAL ENERGY MOVES INTO THE MASONRY WALL FOR HEAT STORAGE

2. THERMAL MASS SHOULD BE NINE TIMES THE AREA OF GLAZING, AND LOCATED TO ABSORB, STORE AND RADIATE HEAT BACK INTO THE SPACE

3. THERMAL MASS

WARM AIR RISES BY CONVECTION

AIR MOLECULES

HEAT IN THE WALL IS CONDUCTED INTO THE SPACE WHEN TEMPERATURES BEGIN TO DROP

AIR MOLECULES ARE HEATED BY CONDUCTION FROM HEAT IN THE THERMAL MASSES OF THE FLOOR AND WALLS

Figure 10-1   Components of a passive solar heating system.

Amount of Energy Available from the Sun

Scientists tell us that when the sun's rays hit the earth's atmosphere at a 90° angle they provide 429.2 Btu of heat per square foot per hour. Because the outer extremity of the atmosphere is about 6 miles above the surface of the earth, the amount of sun heat or solar radiation that gets through the atmosphere and makes it to the surface of the earth is less, about 250 to 300 Btu per square foot per hour. Factors that affect the amount of energy that gets to the earth include cloud cover and the tilt of the earth toward and away from the sun (the seasons). The most solar radiation occurs where the sun strikes the earth at a 90° angle. That happens only within the tropics of Cancer and Capricorn, which are at 23½° north latitude (NL) and 23½° south latitude (SL). These two lines above and below the equator are the boundaries of the 90° sun angle. Sun angles outside this area will always be less than 90°, and the energy received will always be less than that received at the equator. The closer the angle of incidence of the sun is to 90°, the greater the intensity of solar radiation on the earth's surface. The angle of incidence is the angle sun rays make with a line that is perpendicular to the earth, and this angle of incidence controls the degree of sunshine that is received on a surface. See Table 10-1 for the daily amount of sun that gets to the earth at Fort Worth, Texas, and New York City. Solar insolation is the amount of solar energy striking the earth's surface. It is expressed in units per area and per time, as shown in this table.

When Solar Radiation Strikes the Earth

When the sun strikes the earth and objects on the earth, it is either reflected, transmitted, or absorbed. Let us define these terms to better understand how the solar radiation is distributed.

Reflection

Most materials that receive sunlight reflect some of the light (Figure 10-2). When a material with a smooth surface like a mirror or polished metal surface reflects sunshine, the reflected sun rays can be seen forming a distinct pattern, on a floor or on a wall, that is the shape of the reflecting material. Rough-textured building materials like rock or brick will reflect sunlight too, but because of their rough surfaces, sun rays will be diffused or scattered and a defined reflection pattern will not be apparent as it is with a polished surface. Both surfaces, however, reflect sunlight.

Table 10-1 Daily Solar Insolation for Fort Worth, Texas (32°50' NL) and New York City (40°46' NL)

(Units are in Btu per square foot [0.09 m²] per day.)

	Fort Worth	New York
January	936	540
February	1198	791
March	1597	1180
April	1829	1426
May	2105	1738
June	2438	1994
July	2293	1939
August	2216	1606
September	1880	1349
October	1476	978
November	1148	598
December	913	476

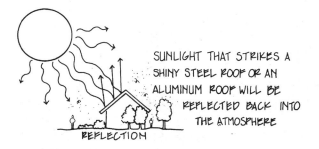

Figure 10-2 Reflection of solar radiation.

Transmission

Sunlight that is not reflected can move through (or transmit through) a material. Glass is an example of a material that transmits sunlight. Not all of the solar radiation will go through the glass. Some will be absorbed by the glass itself and the glass will become warm, as shown in Figure 10-3, and some will be reflected by the glass. Windows with double and triple panes of glass will reduce the transmittance of solar radiation by about 10 to 20%. Solar radiation is energy from the sun that strikes objects on earth without warming the air between. Clear glass will transmit visible solar radiation in a pattern without distorting the sun's rays, whereas translucent glass, or glass that is not clear, will let sunlight pass through, diffusing or scattering the sun's rays (photons) rather than concentrating them. The word *translucent* comes from the Latin *trans,* which means "through," and *lucere,* which means "to shine." Together they refer to a surface that allows light to shine through but is not transparent.

Absorption

When sunlight hits most materials, heat is absorbed and conducted or moved into the interior of the material, as shown in Figure 10-4. The second law of thermodynamics states that energy (heat) will move from areas of high concentration to areas of low concentration. When the sunlit surface of a material begins to heat up, the heat energy moves toward the inside of the material where there is less energy and it is cooler. Let us examine the way this "heating up" actually works. The sun's energy in the form of heat hits the surface of a brick wall. The molecules in the brick begin to oscillate more because of this heat. As movement of the heated molecules increases at the surface of the brick wall, the increased energy of the molecules is passed on to the molecules farther within the wall until the molecules in the entire wall mass are heated to the same energy level, due to the absorption of sun energy. Heat energy always moves from warm to cool areas. Note in Table 10-2, for instance, that flat black paint absorbs 95% of the solar radiation that strikes it and glossy white paint absorbs only 25%.

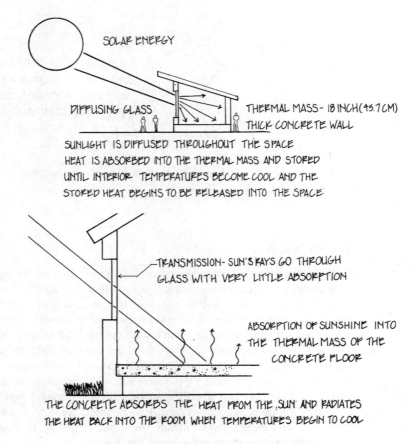

SOLAR ENERGY

DIFFUSING GLASS

THERMAL MASS- 18 INCH (45.7 CM) THICK CONCRETE WALL

SUNLIGHT IS DIFFUSED THROUGHOUT THE SPACE HEAT IS ABSORBED INTO THE THERMAL MASS AND STORED UNTIL INTERIOR TEMPERATURES BECOME COOL AND THE STORED HEAT BEGINS TO BE RELEASED INTO THE SPACE.

TRANSMISSION- SUN'S RAYS GO THROUGH GLASS WITH VERY LITTLE ABSORPTION

ABSORPTION OF SUNSHINE INTO THE THERMAL MASS OF THE CONCRETE FLOOR

THE CONCRETE ABSORBS THE HEAT FROM THE SUN AND RADIATES THE HEAT BACK INTO THE ROOM WHEN TEMPERATURES BEGIN TO COOL

Figure 10-3 Transmission of solar radiation.

Heat Supplied by Solar Energy for Warming Shelters

There is enough solar radiation in most of North and South America to provide 30 to 100% of the heating for shelters. Energy used for interior space heating is 50% of the total energy used in the United States. Table 10-3 presents an estimate of the amount of heating the sun could provide in a south-facing structure using an 18 in. (457 mm) thick passive thermal wall constructed of concrete. The percentages of yearly heating needs that could be provided are for various areas in the United States, Canada, and Japan.

IMPACTS OF USING FOSSIL FUELS FOR HEATING

Most people's first concern in regard to heating is how much fuel is going to cost next month or next season. The economic impact on home, civic, and commercial budgets

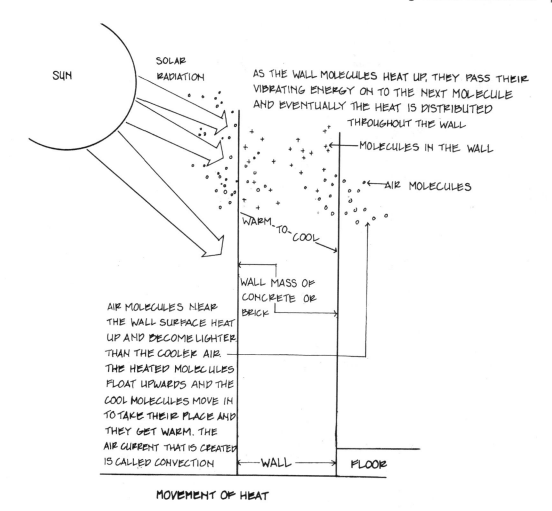

SUN

SOLAR RADIATION

AS THE WALL MOLECULES HEAT UP, THEY PASS THEIR VIBRATING ENERGY ON TO THE NEXT MOLECULE AND EVENTUALLY THE HEAT IS DISTRIBUTED THROUGHOUT THE WALL

MOLECULES IN THE WALL

AIR MOLECULES

WARM-TO-COOL

WALL MASS OF CONCRETE OR BRICK

AIR MOLECULES NEAR THE WALL SURFACE HEAT UP AND BECOME LIGHTER THAN THE COOLER AIR. THE HEATED MOLECULES FLOAT UPWARDS AND THE COOL MOLECULES MOVE IN TO TAKE THEIR PLACE AND THEY GET WARM. THE AIR CURRENT THAT IS CREATED IS CALLED CONVECTION

WALL

FLOOR

MOVEMENT OF HEAT

Figure 10-4   Absorption and conduction of thermal energy.

is significant and merits consideration. But there are global concerns that are important to consider as well. World oil reserves are estimated to be depleted by about 2060. Depletion of oil would deny future generations the use of oil in a variety of applications, including medicines and research. When fossil fuels are burned to release their stored energy, not only is heat generated, but carbon dioxide gas is also released. This gas is added to an already overburdened twenty-first-century atmosphere containing enough carbon dioxide that the earth's climate is becoming affected. Trees just cannot sequester enough carbon dioxide from the atmosphere. The overabundance of this gas has been caused by the worldwide burning of ancient reserves of carbon (coal, gas, oil) for the past 150 years. If only wood biomass (a renewable resource) from sustainable forests were burned, the trees on the earth would keep the amount of carbon dioxide in the atmosphere balanced and global warming would not be a worldwide threat.

Table 10-2   Absorptive Characteristics of Materials

(Expressed in the amount of solar radiation a material can absorb.)

Flat black paint	.98
Dark gray paint	.91
Black concrete	.91
Dark olive drab paint	.89
Dark brown paint	.88
Brown concrete	.85
Medium brown paint	.84
Light gray oil paint	.75
Red oil paint	.74
Red brick	.70
Regular concrete	.65
Light buff-colored brick	.60
Medium dull green paint	.59
Medium orange paint	.58
Medium yellow paint	.57
Medium blue paint	.51
Light green paint	.47
White semigloss paint	.30
White gloss paint	.25
Silver paint	.25
Polished aluminum sheet	.12

Source: Steven Winter Associates, *The Passive Solar Design and Construction Handbook* (New York: John Wiley & Sons, Inc., 1998).

Table 10-3   Percentage of Heat Supplied by a South-Facing, 18 in. (457 mm) Thick Concrete Thermal Wall

Los Angeles, CA	99.9%
Fort Worth, TX	80.8%
Nashville, TN	65.2%
Seattle, WA	52.2%
New York, NY	60.2%
Madison, WI	42.6%
Tokyo, Japan	85.8%
Ottawa, Canada	31.9%

Source: "Passive Solar Energy Evaluated," *Solar Age* (August 1977).

The buildup of carbon dioxide contributing to the greenhouse effect occurs when long-wave (thermal) radiation is re-radiated from the earth back toward outer space. The radiated long-wave energy is trapped by the excess carbon dioxide in the atmosphere, causing air temperatures to heat up. A major U.S. newsmagazine cover has proclaimed that we are experiencing "arctic meltdown," a condition causing the freshwater polar ice caps to begin to melt. Contributing further evidence that global warming is real, the U.S. government has released a publication entitled *Sea Level Rise,* providing instructions to people in the coastal zones on how to prepare for this impending global event. It is estimated that the seas could rise from 1 to 2 ft (0.3 to 0.6 m) over a 50-year period.

UNDERSTANDING THE HEAT TRANSFER PROCESS

Let us review the terminology, processes, and technologies that will enable us to incorporate passive solar heating systems into shelter designs. In planning to use the sun for interior space heating or extending wintertime use in outdoor spaces, it is essential to understand how heat moves into a material for storage and then back into a space for heating. To begin, some of the sunlight that strikes a material will be absorbed, and that heat will be transported into or away from the surface through conduction, convection, or radiation. Understanding these processes will enable us to direct, store, and use energy from the sun.

Conduction

When sunlight (solar radiation) strikes the surface of a material, like a brick wall, heat is absorbed by the material (brick). Because the material on the inside of the wall is cooler, the heat predictably moves from the warmer surface of the wall to the cooler interior. This movement of heat through a solid material is called *conduction*. Conduction of heat occurs in all materials but is mainly important in solids as opposed to liquids and gases (in which energy is also transferred by convection). Another example of conduction is the movement of heat from the air within a basement space through the wall into the adjacent ground, which results in a cool belowground basement space. The same movement of heat occurs in caves, which are also cool because of the cool temperature of the surrounding ground. In areas at 35° north latitude, the ground temperatures 7 ft (2 m) below the surface are about 58° to 62°F (14° to 17°C). See Table 10-4 for average yearly ground temperatures for different parts of the United States.

It is essential to consider storage and conduction, as they relate to thermal energy, in selecting materials for a heat storage mass. To be suitable for passive heating, a material must be able to transfer heat from its surface to its interior for storage. Brick and concrete both have a high capacity for storing heat, and both materials can conduct heat effectively. Wood has a high capacity to store heat, but it conducts heat slowly. The *thermal conductivity* of a material is the term used to indicate how much heat the material is able to transfer. When thermal conductivity is multiplied by the temperature difference and divided by the material width, the actual amount of conduction heat transfer is computed (in Btu/hr). Recall that as the surface molecules of a material are heated by solar energy, their vibration affects adjacent molecules and heat is passed on to the cooler molecules within the material. Conductivity of a material is also important because shelters lose heat in winter by conduction through walls, floors, roofs, and windows. Table 10-5 shows conduction per unit width and per degree temperature difference for a number of building materials.

Table 10-4   Average Ground Temperatures, 10 ft (3 m) Deep

Location	Average Temperature	
	°F	°C
Alabama	62	17
Arizona	72	22
California	72	22
Colorado	50	10
Idaho	47	8
Illinois	53	12
Indiana	52	11
Kansas	55	13
Kentucky	58	14
Maryland	56	13
Michigan	50	10
Minnesota	49	9
Montana	47	8
New Jersey	54	12
North Carolina	61	16
Oklahoma	53	12
South Dakota	47	8
Vermont	49	9

Source: Richard Montgomery, *The Solar Decision Book of Homes* (New York: John Wiley & Sons, 1982).

Table 10-5   Thermal Conduction Rates of Common Building Materials

Conductivity rates are given in Btu per hour that will pass through a 1 in. thick, 1 ft^2 [25 mm, 0.09 m^2] area of material.

Material	Conduction
Brick, common	5.0 Btu/hr
Brick, face	9.0
Concrete	12.0
Gypsum plaster	5.5
Plywood	0.8
Sandstone	12.5
Sand	12.5
Softwoods	0.8
Expanded Polystyrene	0.20

Source: Richard Montgomery, *The Solar Decision Book of Homes* (New York: John Wiley & Sons, 1982).

Convection

When a solid material, such as a wall, becomes heated with energy from the sun, the air adjacent to the material (wall) becomes heated. As heat transfers from the warm wall to the cool interior air, the cool air molecules become less dense and they begin to rise or float upward. See Figure 10-4 for a graphic example of this process. As the heated air rises, it is replaced with cooler and heavier air from below, and the air molecule heating process begins all over. This exchange and movement of heat between the solid wall and the air is called *convection*. An air conditioner cools a room by convection as cold air is blown into a space, making the objects in the space cooler. An example of convection between two fluids (air and water) can be perceived seasonally at Raccoon Lake near Centralia, Illinois. Here, warm summer breezes blowing across the lake are cooled by the colder lake water, resulting in cooler summer temperatures for those living along the edge of the lake. In fact, temperatures during the warm season are 8° to 10°F (4° to 6° C) cooler, because the heat in the air moves into the cooler water in summer. Conversely, temperatures around the lake are warmer during the winter because of the solar heat in the lake water that moves into the cooler air, keeping the lakeside warmer than areas farther away from the lake. By reducing temperature extremes, convection contributes to the desirability of lakeside living. This cooling and warming process occurs around nearly all lakes.

Radiation

All materials are emitting, or sending out, small amounts of energy at all times. Some materials emit a lot of heat (as in thermal radiation), and some emit very little. Solar radiation is converted to thermal energy, or heat, when it strikes an object. The object will reemit some of the thermal radiation. Most of the solar radiation that strikes a material with high emissivity will be emitted, or sent back, into the atmosphere. *Emittance* refers to that property of a material whereby it absorbs and sends out thermal or long-wave (infrared) radiation rather than just absorbing and storing energy for later use. Ideally, for passive heating, a material would have high absorption characteristics and low emissivity. Brick, concrete, and rock have both high emissivity and high absorption characteristics (Figure 10-5). Flat black paint has high emissivity, and shiny aluminum has very low emissivity. Most building materials have high emissivity rates, which basically means that they will radiate much of the thermal radiation they absorb from solar radiation. Flat black paint's 0.96 emissivity means it will radiate 96% of the maximum possible thermal energy it absorbs (at a given temperature).

When choosing materials for heating a shelter with a direct solar heat gain system, you will want to know how much energy a material will absorb and emit in order to develop a successful solar heating system. For example, a concrete block storage wall whose cores are filled with concrete should be designed to absorb the maximum solar radiation on the sun collector side, and emit the maximum thermal radiation (long-wave or infrared radiation) on the interior of the space needing heat. How much radiant energy or energy from the sun a material can potentially give off will depend on the actual amount of heat or solar radiation that was absorbed and the level of warmth in the material. Note the building materials and their capacity as emitters of thermal radiation in Table 10-6. An emissivity of 0.93 means that building brick will radiate 93% of the thermal energy possible (at a given temperature).

EMISSIVITY- IS THE ABILITY OF A MATERIAL
TO GIVE OFF THERMAL RADIATION.

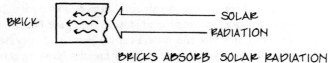

BRICKS ABSORB SOLAR RADIATION

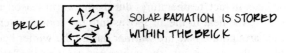

SOLAR RADIATION IS STORED
WITHIN THE BRICK

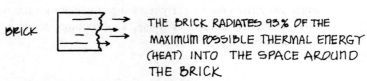

THE BRICK RADIATES 93% OF THE
MAXIMUM POSSIBLE THERMAL ENERGY
(HEAT) INTO THE SPACE AROUND
THE BRICK

MOST NONMETAL BUILDING MATERIALS HAVE HIGH
EMISSIVITY RATES- MOST METALS- ESPECIALLY THOSE
WITH POLISHED SURFACES- HAVE POOR EMISSIVITY RATES.

Figure 10-5 Emissivity of materials.

Table 10-6   Building Materials and Emissivities

Paint—flat black lacquer	0.96
Marble	0.931
Brick, building	0.93
Paint—white enamel	0.91
Gypsum	0.903
White oak wood	0.90
Paint—aluminum lacquer	0.39
Steel	0.12
Aluminum	0.09
Red brass	0.030
Gold	0.02

Source: American Society of Heating, Refrigerating, and Air-Conditioning Engineers (ASHRAE) *Handbook of Fundamentals* (1997).

MATERIALS AND THEIR SUITABILITY FOR STORING HEAT

Our objective for heating a shelter passively is to provide human comfort through the use of a renewable resource, the sun. To this end, the shelter is designed so that solar radiation heats a wall or other interior physical feature, and the wall releases the heat when the space becomes cool.

Heat Capacity

Because building materials have weight and volume, when comparing the heat-absorbing capabilities of a material it is best to consider their heat capacity in cubic feet (cubic meters). Looking at Table 10-7, you can see that water and scrap iron can store the most heat per cubic foot (cubic meter) of material. Commonly used building materials such as brick and concrete can store approximately one-half the amount held by water and scrap iron per degree temperature change. But because brick and concrete are frequently used building materials and they have acceptable embedded energy levels, they are ideal for incorporation into passive thermal heating systems.

METHODS OF COLLECTING SOLAR RADIATION TO BE USED FOR HEATING

There are three means of including passive solar energy heating: the direct sun gain living space, the thermal storage wall, and the attached sunroom space. In a direct sun gain living space, the interior space of the shelter is constructed so that it is the sun heat collector. Walls, floors, and even ceilings can be used to collect and store solar radiation for use when interior spaces become cold. A thermal storage wall is composed of a thick wall located within the south side of a shelter, whose purpose is to collect solar radiation during the winter, store the heat within the wall, and warm the adjacent interior spaces behind the wall when they become cool. In the third passive heating system, an attached sunroom space is located on the south side of a shelter to collect heat for interior use.

Direct Sun Gain Living Space

In an appropriately considered interior space designed for passive solar heating, the sun will provide enough solar heat for use on a cold January day, and throughout the winter with little additional heating. If the space is properly designed, room temperatures should

Table 10-7   Heat Capacity of Building Materials

	$Btu/ft^3 \, °F$ when temperature is raised $1°F$
Water	62.4
Brick, common	25.0
Brick, face	25.4
Adobe	24.0
Concrete	30.0
Sand	18.0
Wood (pine)	20.8
Limestone	22.4
Granite	31.8
Scrap iron	58.8

vary from about 60°F (16°C) at night to 75°F (24°C) during the day. Within this passive heating system, south-facing glass allows sunlight into the shelter, which directly strikes the floors and walls of the interior living spaces, as shown in Figure 10-6. The entire space then becomes the collector for absorbing and storing heat. Once solar radiation is collected and converted to heat, the heat is then released when indoor temperatures drop below human comfort levels. Temperatures for human comfort levels range from 65° to 80°F (18° to 27°C). Many people prefer indoor temperatures no lower than 68°F (20°C) and no higher than 78°F (26°C). The transfer of stored heat to interior spaces as they become cool follows the second law of thermodynamics, which says that the movement of energy is always from areas of high concentration to areas of low concentration, or warm to cool. Adequate sunlight is available in most of North and South America to provide enough energy to heat shelters or to supplement or replace conventional fossil-fueled heating systems.

In designing direct gain systems, it is essential that the correct amount of glass and thermal mass be located within the space for heat storage in order to provide enough heat to keep a space comfortable during cold winter nights. It is also important to allow the maximum amount of sun to be transmitted through south-facing glass in the heating season, and to prevent sunlight from reaching the glass and being transmitted into a space that does not need heat during the cooling season. The extent of roof overhangs can be determined through defining the heating and cooling seasons and plotting sun angles. See Chapter 9, "Computing Overhangs for Solar Energy Control," for more on this subject. Shutters, awnings, and curtains can also be used to block summer sun intrusion into interior spaces.

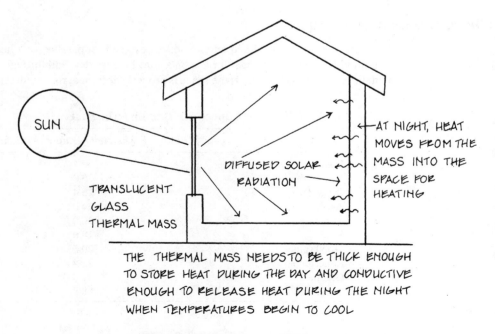

THE THERMAL MASS NEEDS TO BE THICK ENOUGH TO STORE HEAT DURING THE DAY AND CONDUCTIVE ENOUGH TO RELEASE HEAT DURING THE NIGHT WHEN TEMPERATURES BEGIN TO COOL

Figure 10-6 Direct sun gain living space.

The ideal building materials for direct gain thermal walls are concrete, concrete block with grout-filled cores, brick, adobe, and rock, all commonly available materials traditionally used in building construction. Their thermal properties have potential to capture solar radiation, convert it to heat, store it, and release it when interior temperatures begin to cool. For there to be enough storage within a direct gain system using only masonry construction, one-half to two-thirds of the surface area of a space must be constructed of masonry materials. It is advisable to create storage mass throughout the interior direct sun gain space. Make masonry walls and floors 4 in. (102 mm) thick for best distribution of stored heat. An evenly distributed storage mass spread throughout the space outperforms a thicker and concentrated storage mass. A large, thick masonry mass receiving direct sun gain in a space will probably heat up too quickly and make the living space uncomfortably warm. Design the interior spaces and windows so that as much as possible of the masonry mass within the space can receive direct sunlight. Mass in the space that does not receive sunlight will still absorb heat from the air and help prevent overheating. A mass that is struck directly by sunlight will absorb about four times more heat than a mass that absorbs only heat from the air. To enhance absorption of heat by masonry wall and floor areas that do not receive direct sun, light-colored reflector walls or sloped paved areas can be located to reflect solar radiation to these areas. These masses can also be warmed through the use of translucent glazings that diffuse or scatter solar radiation. For best absorption of solar radiation, use a dark color for the thermal storage masses of the living spaces that receive direct sunlight. When sizing the masonry thermal storage masses, use 3 ft^2 (0.3 m^2) of 4 in. (102 mm) thick masonry mass for each square foot of south-facing solar collector. When properly sized, the direct sun gain heating system can provide enough or almost enough heat for a living space to meet the needs of most users. Research has shown that an interior space with 4 in. (102 mm) thick concrete and masonry walls and floors, where there was nine times more thermal mass surface area than glazing, resulted in daily temperature fluctuations of only 13°F (7°C). This study considered either using translucent glass for diffusing the sun's rays, or allowing sunlight to strike a light-colored wall and diffuse the sun (heat). The 24-hour temperature fluctuation for the same space with wood frame and sheet rock construction was 38°F (21°C).

Consider a typical home with a mechanical heating system, in which wintertime night temperatures are allowed to drop to 55°F (13°C) and which is heated mechanically to as warm as 68°F (20°C) during the day. Many families would not think that this 13°F (7°C) fluctuation is uncomfortable.

Water is also a good material for storing heat, and it can be used within interior spaces for directly soaking up sunlight during the day and releasing it in the evening as temperatures drop. When water is used for direct gain heat storage, it is usually maintained in metal tubes or drums placed somewhere in the space so that sun can hit the containers and transfer heat to the fluid (water). The heat in the water then moves to the room air by convection and radiation as temperatures drop. If the whole interior of a space is being designed to be a thermal mass, temperature fluctuations will not be extreme.

Windows or solar collectors for the direct sun gain living spaces should face due south but may be oriented 20° on either side of due south without significantly reducing passive heating. An azimuth of 160° should be the maximum easterly orientation from a due south azimuth of 180°. The azimuth of the sun is like a compass reading and refers to the horizontal angle of the sun. Angles can range from 0° to 360° with 0° and 360° being at true north and 180° being true south. Schools and other facilities that depend on early-in-the-day use of interior space will actually benefit from a more southeasterly orientation as opposed to a due south orientation. Using clerestory windows, as shown in Figure 10-7, for areas deeper within shelters that cannot be reached by sunlight from the south-facing wall, will allow the lower angle of the wintertime sun to bathe the masonry walls with sunlight. These clerestories can reduce heating and lighting needs through the distribution, collection, and absorption of naturally available sunlight. See Table 10-8 to compute the size of the south-facing solar collector (windows) needed to allow enough solar radiation into a direct sun gain living space to adequately warm the space during the winter heating season.

Sizing the Solar Collector and Masonry Storage Mass for a Direct Sun Gain Living Space

Let us use the information in Table 10-8 to determine the amount of glazing required for a shelter at Mississippi State University, located at 33½°NL and having an average January temperature of 40°F (4°C). We will select the .13 ft² (0.012 m²) of glazing needed per square foot (0.092 m²) of floor area to be heated passively.

Room size to be heated = 20 × 40 ft = 800 ft² (6.09 × 12.19 m = 74 m²)
800 ft² × .13 ft² (74 m² × 0.012 m²) of glazing needed = 104 ft² (9.66 m²) of south-facing glazing required
This could be a double glazed window 8 ft tall by 14 ft long (2.4 × 4.26 m²)

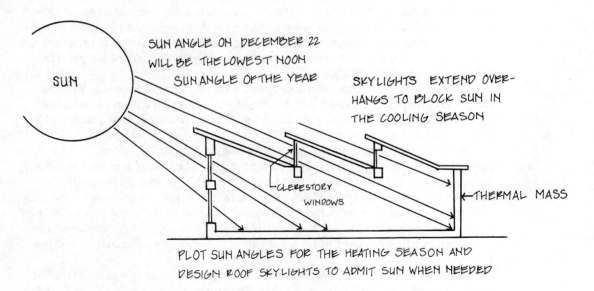

PLOT SUN ANGLES FOR THE HEATING SEASON AND DESIGN ROOF SKYLIGHTS TO ADMIT SUN WHEN NEEDED

Figure 10-7 Uses of clerestory windows.

Table 10-8   Glazing Required for Direct Sun Gain Living Spaces

Average January/February Outdoor Temperature on a Clear Day	Square Feet of Glazing Needed per Square Foot of Floor Area			
	36°NL	40°NL	44°NL	48°NL
Cold Climates				
20°F	.24	.25	.29	.31 (w/NI)
25°F	.22	.23	.25	.28 (w/NI)
30°F	.19	.20	.22	.24
Temperate Climates				
35°F	.16	.17	.19	.21
40°F	.13	.14	.16	.17
45°F	.10	.11	.12	.13

Source: Steven Winter Associates, *The Passive Solar Design and Construction Handbook* (New York: John Wiley & Sons, Inc., 1998).

Note: NI is nighttime insulation, which refers to the need for having insulation over the collector at night.

Now, in order to size the amount of masonry thermal mass to store the needed amount of solar radiation to keep the spaces warm, use 3 ft^2 (0.28 m^2) of 4 in. (101 mm) thick masonry mass for each 1 ft^2 (0.092 m^2) of south-facing solar collector required.

104 ft^2 (9.7 m^2) of glazing required $\times$ 3 ft^2 (0.28 m^2) of 4 in. (101 mm) thick masonry mass = 312 ft^2 (29 m^2) of masonry storage mass within the direct solar gain living space

Because the floor area of the space is 800 ft^2 (74.3 m^2), a 312 ft^2 (29 m^2) portion of the floor space could be built as a masonry thermal storage mass, or a combination of part of the back wall and part of the 800 ft^2 (74.3 m^2) floor could become the masonry thermal storage mass. The entire floor space could be built as masonry thermal storage.

Thermal Storage Wall

The thermal storage wall system is best for mild to severe winters. In this indirect sun gain system, sunlight first warms a wall of concrete, unit masonry, concrete block with cells filled with concrete or grout, or water, and then releases heat into the living spaces located on the other side of the wall (Figure 10-8). Figure 10-9 is an example of a thermal storage wall composed of tubes of water. If a concrete or concrete block wall is used, two coatings of a dark plaster on the south-facing side will help to increase absorption of solar radiation. Concrete block with cores filled with concrete has a very high emissivity rate of 0.97. This material will emit, or send out, 97% of the thermal energy possible, at a given temperature. The collection and storage of heat happens outside the living space. As indoor temperatures drop, heat is transferred into interior living spaces by convection and radiation. It is best if the wall faces south or 20° on either side of due south. Double glazed glass should be used for the wall collector not only to transmit sunlight, but also

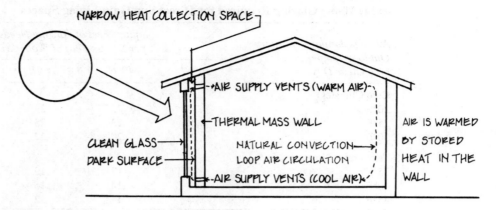

Figure 10-8 Thermal storage wall.

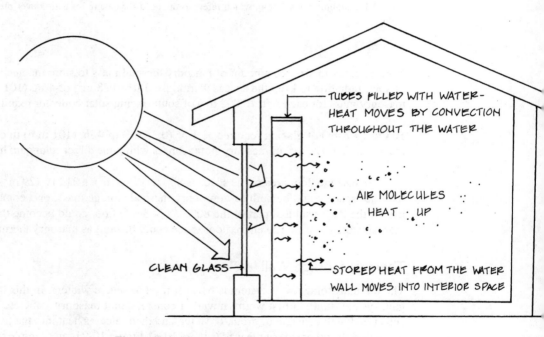

Figure 10-9 Thermal storage waterwall.

to keep outdoor temperatures and wind from removing heat collected in the thermal wall. The wall is separated from the double glazed collector by a 2 to 4 in. (51 to 102 mm) air space, which serves to warm the air via the thermal energy collected in the wall.

In designing thermal walls, the building materials used should have optimum thicknesses for absorbing and radiating heat. Edward Mazria, in his *Passive Solar Energy Book,* recommends the thicknesses shown in Table 10-9 as a guide for determining wall depths. Note the wall thicknesses and temperature fluctuations in Table 10-10. As a gen-

Table 10-9   Thermal Wall Thicknesses

Adobe	8–12 in. (203–305 mm) thick
Brick	10–14 in. (254–356 mm) thick
Concrete	12–18 in. (305–457 mm) thick
Water	≥ 6 in. (152 mm) thick (A water wall less than 6 in. [152 mm] thick will get too warm and overheat a space.)

Source: Edward Mazria, *The Passive Solar Energy Book* (Emmaus, PA: Rodale Press, 1979).

Table 10-10   Effect of Thermal Wall Thickness on Temperature Fluctuations Within a Space

Material	Recommended Thickness	Temperature Fluctuation (°F) Related to Wall Thickness					
		4 in.	8 in.	12 in.	16 in.	20 in.	24 in.
Adobe	8–12 in.	. . .	18°	7°	7°	6°	. . .
Brick—red	10–14 in.	. . .	24°	11°	7°	. . .	. . .
Concrete	12–18 in.	. . .	28°	16°	10°	6°	5°
Brick—dark	16–24 in.	. . .	35°	24°	17°	12°	9°
Water	6 in. or more	31°	18°	13°	11°	10°	9°

Source: Edward Mazria, *The Passive Solar Energy Book* (Emmaus, PA: Rodale Press, 1979).
Note: These figures assume the use of double glazing, and clear January days.

eral rule, the greater the thicknesses of the thermal wall, the less indoor temperatures will vary over a 24-hour period.

If operable vents are integrated along the top and bottom of the wall, greater control of the thermal energy system will result. When interior living spaces become cool, the vents can be opened, allowing warm air from the wall space to enter into the adjacent space and cool air from the floor area of the space to move into the thermal wall space and become filled with heat (energy). When this happens, the cooler air is warmed and floats upward by natural convection to the top of the heated air space through the vents and into the living space. This movement of air is called *convection loop circulation.* Air is heated by the thermal energy wall to about 90°F (32°C) and is vented into living spaces by convection loop circulation; alternately, fans can be used to circulate the heated air throughout interior spaces.

If a thermal wall is constructed without vents, the thermal energy in the sun-heated wall will radiate slowly into living spaces as they become cooler throughout the night. Concrete and masonry construction conducts heat slowly; it takes five hours for heat to conduct through an 8 in. (203 mm) concrete wall. Air temperatures within the narrow air space between the wall and the collector can get as high as 150° to 180°F (65° to 82°C). Shelters in cold climates with severe winters will need larger thermal storage walls than those in milder, more moderate winter climate zones. Solar collectors will have to be the same size as the thermal wall. See Table 10-11 for information used in sizing a thermal storage wall.

Table 10-11   Glazing Required for a Thermal Storage Wall

Average January/February Outdoor Temperature on a Clear Day	Square Feet of Glazing Needed per Square Foot of Floor Area			
	36°NL	40°NL	44°NL	48°NL
Cold Climates				
20°F	.71	.75	.85	.98 (w/NI)
25°F	.59	.63	.75	.84 (w/NI)
30°F	.50	.53	.60	.70
Temperate Climates				
35°F	.40	.43	.50	.55
40°F	.32	.35	.40	.44
45°F	.25	.26	.30	.33

Source: Steven Winter Associates, *The Passive Solar Design and Construction Handbook* (New York: John Wiley & Sons, Inc., 1998).

Note: NI is nighttime insulation, which refers to the need for having insulation over the collector at night.

Sizing the Solar Collector and Thermal Storage Wall

Let us use the information in Table 10-11 to determine the amount of thermal storage wall required for a shelter at Mississippi State University, located at 33½°NL and having an average January temperature of 40°F (4°C).

Size of space to be heated = 20 × 40 ft (6 × 12 m) = 800 ft² (74 m²)
800 ft² × .32 ft² (74 m² × 0.03 m²) of glazing needed = 256 ft² (23.8 m²) of south-facing glazing required

This could be a wall that is 10 ft (3 m) tall by 26 ft (8 m) long. The solar collector would be the same size as the wall and would consist of double glazed glass.

To increase the amount of solar radiation directed to the thermal energy wall, a reflector outside the shelter's south-facing wall at ground level, sloped 5% away from the building, could increase the amount of solar radiation reaching the collector and thermal energy wall. The reflector may be a light-colored patio or terrace. Insulation placed over south-facing windows each night will reduce the need for thermal mass by 15%. If insulated curtains or shutters are used, the required square footage of the thermal mass wall could be reduced by 15%. For further information for computing the size of a thermal storage wall, see Table 10-12, from Edward Mazria's *The Passive Solar Energy Book*.

Passive thermal heating systems have proven to be reliable providers of heat. Mazria reports that a properly sized thermal storage wall heating system in a New Jersey location (40°NL) provided 76% of the shelter's heat from the sun. Daily temperatures in the residence fluctuated only 10°F (°C). The low temperature inside at night was 58°F (14°C), and the high temperature during the day was 68°F (20°C). You can see that even in cold winter climates thermal energy heating systems can be effective in supplying all

Table 10-12 **Determining Sizes of Thermal Storage Walls to Maintain Indoor Spaces at 65°–75°F (18°–24°C) for a 24-Hour Period**

December/January Average Temperatures	Square Foot of Thermal Wall Area per Square Foot of Floor Area	
	Masonry Wall	Water Wall
Very Cold Climates		
15°F	0.72–1.0	0.55–1.0
20°F	0.60–1.0	0.45–0.85
Cold Climates		
25°F	0.51–0.93	0.38–0.70
30°F	0.43–0.78	0.31–0.55
Temperate Climates		
35°F	0.35–0.60	0.25–0.43
40°F	0.28–0.46	0.20–0.34
45°F	0.22–0.35	0.16–0.25

Source: Edward Mazria, *The Passive Solar Energy Book* (Emmaus, PA: Rodale Press, 1979).

Note: For southern latitudes, such as 35° NL, use lower ratios; for northern latitudes, such as 48°NL, use higher ratios.

or almost all of the cold season heating by using the sun as a continuously renewable resource.

Attached Greenhouse Sun Space

Another passive solar heating system utilizes an attached greenhouse-type structure located on the south side of a shelter for collecting and storing solar radiation. Like the direct sun gain living space system, attached greenhouses absorb solar radiation and convert it to heat. Some heat is stored in the thermal mass of the space, and some heat moves into adjacent living spaces. Although this system loses heat at night, it gains significantly more heat in the daytime than it loses. Heat loss can be reduced by using double glazing and insulated solar collector covers. The collectors are composed of vertical and sloped sections of glass. The sloped sections should be at a 45° to 60° angle. Where the winter climate is predominantly overcast and foggy, collectors should be at 45° angles. Where the winter season is clear and sunny, use the 60° angle tilt. The attached greenhouse sun space should face due south or up to 20° on either side of south. Its end walls, which face east and west, should be wrapped with the shelter's wall material because those sides do not assist in the collection of solar radiation. In fact, if left uninsulated, they can contribute to significant heat loss.

There are four variations of the attached greenhouse sun spaces: the open wall space, the direct sun gain space, the air exchange space, and the thermal wall space. The open wall sun space opens up to the interior living space, as shown in Figure 10-10. The space collects, stores, and distributes thermal radiation to the interior living space as it begins to cool. Solar radiation is primarily stored in the floor and end walls of the sun space but may be stored in water containers located in the space. If winter sun reaches into the interior living space, sun heat can be stored in masonry composition floors as well. During the summer, provisions for covering the glass collector will be necessary because of the potential for solar heat gain.

In the direct sun gain space, the greenhouse is separated by a movable glass wall from the interior living space (Figure 10-11). The greenhouse structure provides heat and light from the sun to the living space. Solar radiation is primarily stored in the floor and end walls of the sun space but may also be stored in water containers located in the space. Movable glass in the wall helps to reduce heat loss at night and to gain heat during the day in interior spaces. Movable insulation along the glass wall can further reduce the heat loss.

The air exchange space, shown in Figure 10-12, incorporates a vented thermal storage wall at the rear of the greenhouse space to store solar radiation. Interior spaces get no direct solar radiation because of the wall separating the greenhouse space from the interior living space. The operable vents in the top and bottom of the wall can be opened and closed to use the warmed air within the greenhouse. The wall can be from 8 to 18 in. (203 to 457 mm) thick and will radiate heat during the nighttime into the interior space. Insulation over the collector windows will be necessary to prevent the heating of the thermal storage wall and the transfer of unwanted heat into interior spaces.

The thermal storage wall space is similar to the air exchange space, except that there are no vents (Figure 10-13). Heating of the interior spaces depends on the conduction of

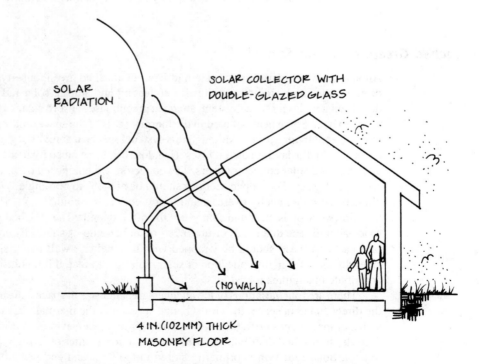

Figure 10-10 Shelter with translucent glass and a thermal storage wall.

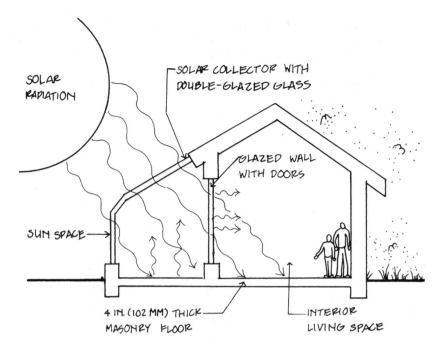

Figure 10-11 Thermal storage wall separating sun space from living space.

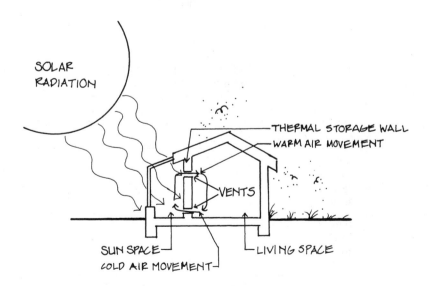

Figure 10-12 Air exchange space.

heat through the thermal storage wall and the heating of interior air through convection and radiation. The wall can be 8 to 18 in. (203 to 457 mm) thick. As with all of the variations of the greenhouse sun space, it is best to be able to cover the sun space collector to conserve heat during the winter and prevent heat gain during the summer. The information in Table 10-13 can help in determining the amount of sun space collector area necessary for heating a given area of interior living space.

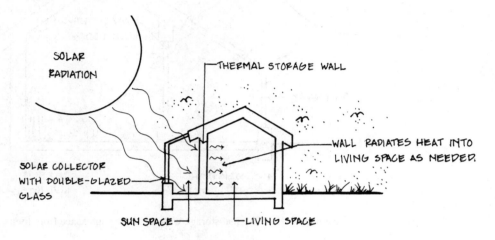

Figure 10-13 Thermal storage wall.

Table 10-13 **Glazing Area Required per Square Foot of Floor Area for Greenhouse Sun Spaces**

Average January/February Outdoor Temperature on a Clear Day	Square Feet of Glazing Needed per Square Foot of Floor Area
Cold Climates	
20°F	0.90–1.50
25°F	0.78–1.30
30°F	0.65–1.17
Temperate Climates	
35°F	0.53–0.90
40°F	0.42–0.69
45°F	0.33–0.53

Source: Steven Winter Associates, *The Passive Solar Design and Construction Handbook* (New York: John Wiley & Sons, Inc., 1998).

Note: For southern latitudes use the lower figures, and for northern latitudes use the higher figures. Figures provided are for insulated spaces.

Sizing the Solar Collector and Masonry Storage Mass

Let us use the information in Table 10-13 to determine the amount of thermal storage wall required for a shelter at Mississippi State University, having an average January temperature of 40°F (4°C) and being located in a very southernly latitude (33½° NL).

Size of space to be heated = 20 × 40 ft (6 × 12 m) = 800 ft² (74 m²)
800 ft² × 0.42 ft² (74 m² × 0.04 m²) of glazing needed = 336 ft² (31.2 m²) of south-facing glazing required

This could be a double glazed collector that is composed of 16 ft (5 m) of vertical and sloped glass, 22 ft (6.7 m) long. The size of the sun space would be the same size as the glazing.

Chapter 11

Surface Reflectivity

Energy Savings: According to the EPA's guidebook for creating cooler communities, as much as 22% in energy savings can result from the use of reflective surfaces on the roofs and walls of smaller, residential-scaled shelters. Large shelters can realize cost reductions as well, but the savings will not be as large because these buildings have smaller ratios of outside surface to indoor volume and they tend to generate large amounts of internal heat. With the use of reflective materials in the landscape, outdoor temperatures can be up to 5°F (3°C) cooler.

CLIMATE ZONES AND HUMAN COMFORT

Every part of the world is part of a climate zone that affects the extent to which people can live comfortably without relying on huge amounts of fossil fuels. Currently, people use fossil fuel energy to make even the most extreme climates in the world comfortable. How the human environment is designed to absorb and reflect the sun can significantly affect how much energy is used to keep the home and work environments comfortable. The four climate regions in the United States shown in Figure 11-1 are the cold, temperate, hot-arid, and hot-humid environments. The northern cold climate zone has long, cold winters and short, mild summers. The temperate zone has a moderately cold winter and mild to hot summers. The hot-arid zone has short but mild winters and long, hot summers. The low humidity of this zone enables people to withstand warm temperatures and remain generally comfortable. The hot-humid zone has short and mild winters and long, hot summers with high humidity. The high humidity in the warm season can cause people to be uncomfortable because evaporation of normally occurring body perspiration from the skin is reduced, slowing the body's natural function for controlling heat.

ALBEDO AND SURFACE REFLECTION

Temperatures are generally 8° to 15°F (4° to 8°C) warmer in built-up city and suburban areas, as compared with rural, country areas, because of the amount of hard construction materials and use of colors that absorb heat from the sun. This phenomenon, called the

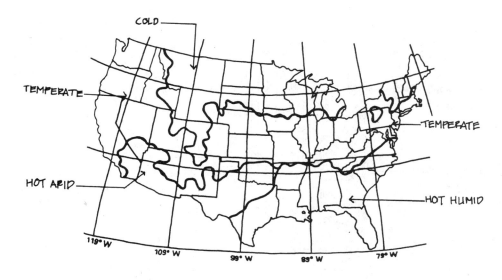

Figure 11-1 The four climate regions in the United States (based on heating and cooling requirements from *Cooling Our Communities*).

"heat island effect," has caused some cities like Los Angeles and Atlanta to even create their own weather. If building materials are dark in color, they absorb a lot of heat. If they are light and reflective, they absorb relatively little heat. The ability of a surface to reflect incoming solar radiation is called the *albedo*. See Table 11-1 for albedo values of materials commonly used in the landscape. White paint on a structure has a surface albedo of up to .90. This means that the white paint reflects 90% of the incoming solar radiation. An asphalt roadway has an albedo as low as .05, meaning that it reflects only 5% of the incoming solar radiation. This ability of a surface to reflect the heat of the sun (albedo) is measured from 0, the lowest reflectivity value, to 1.0, the highest reflectivity value. Figure 11-2 illustrates the albedo of materials used in the landscape.

Heat Island Effect

Temperatures in urban areas are 8° to 15°F (5° to 8°C) hotter than those in rural areas where the landscape is not built up and there are no large concentrations of hardscape materials. What causes this increase in temperature in the urban human landscapes is all of the paving, including concrete and asphalt, the use of brick, rock, and steel for our shelters, and the elimination of trees and the perennially cool, moist forest floor humus layer. The paving, masonry, and metal materials absorb heat and release it when the air temperatures begin to cool in the afternoon, thereby increasing the air temperature and extending the hot temperatures that existed during the middle of the day. Generally, the darker the color of a material, the more sun heat it absorbs. When our urban areas were forests and meadows, shade was everywhere and plants were transpiring water as part of their metabolism. This evaporating water from plant leaves helped to cool the air.

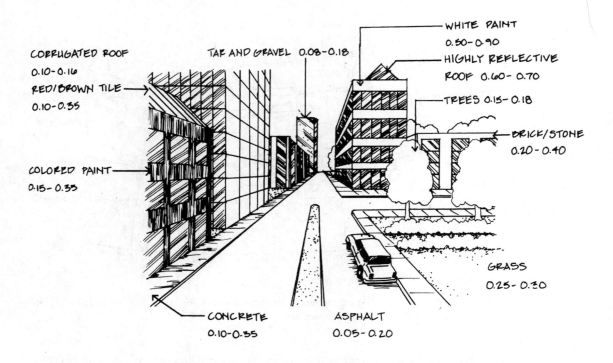

Figure 11-2 Surface albedo in the built landscape.

Contributing to the urban heat island effect is the banishment of creeks, streams, and rivers to underground drainage tunnels.

Surface Reflection and Energy Use

Generally, light-colored surfaces have high albedo values and reflect most of the sun's energy, and dark-colored surfaces have low albedo values and absorb most of the sun's energy, as a black asphalt road does. In relation to heat gain in shelters, dark-colored structures with low albedo surface ratings will have higher interior temperatures and cooling loads because the heat from the hot exterior walls and roofs will be transferred into the interior spaces through conduction. Conduction is the movement of heat (high energy) through the building walls to the areas of low energy, or cooler spaces, within the building. Only a thick layer of insulation will stop the conduction of warm air to cool air. A study in Sacramento, California, showed that by changing the roof and wall color of a home from an albedo of 0.30 to 0.90, the cooling bill was reduced by 20%.

Another study in Sacramento showed that by changing roof shingles from a dark to a light color, and changing walls from a gray color to white, surface values were changed from an albedo of 0.20 to 0.60 and cooling bills could be reduced by 22%. An acquaintance had a jarring experience with albedo recently. He and his wife bought a white

Table 11-1   Surface Albedo Values of Materials in the Human Landscape

Material	Albedo Value
Asphalt paving	0.05–0.20
Concrete paving	0.10–0.35
Aluminum foil	0.92–0.97
Aluminum sheet	0.80–0.95
Lawns	0.25–0.30
Trees	0.15–0.18
Masonry materials (brick and stone)	0.20–0.40
White paint	0.50–0.90
Colored paint	0.15–0.35
Corrugated roof	0.10–0.16
Tar and gravel roof	0.08–0.18
Red-brown tile roof	0.10–0.35

Source: Environmental Protection Agency, *Cooling Our Communities: A Guidebook on Tree Planting and Light-Colored Surfacing* (1992).

frame home that was adequately cooled with two window air-conditioning units. They decided to paint the home a gray color, and when they did they had to buy an additional window unit to keep the house cool. The two window units that cooled the house when it was painted white could no longer keep the darker-colored house cool. Interestingly, a computer study simulating the use of energy for a Sacramento, California, one-story ranch style house painted gray (0.25 albedo) showed that by painting the walls an off-white color, the amount of cooling energy used dropped by 19%. The study was carried out by researchers at the Lawrence Berkeley Laboratory in Berkeley, California.

Computer studies have also shown, in pre-1970s houses where insulation was at low levels, that by increasing the outside surface (roofs and walls) albedo from 0.30 to 0.40, 11 to 22% less cooling energy was required. For well-insulated houses, the same treatment resulted in an energy savings of 8 to 13%. Considering energy savings at a citywide scale, increasing albedo by 0.15 can save nearly 40% citywide and reduce ambient air temperatures by 5°F (3°C). The built landscape of cities in many Mediterranean countries, such as Greece, have been light in color for centuries to help cool the environment.

Making a residential or small commercial building's wall and roof surfaces reflective will lower cooling costs. Although albedo is important in a larger structure, such as an office or school, there are other factors to consider. Larger buildings have higher internal heat loads, caused by more electrical equipment and larger numbers of people than would be the case in a residence. Moreover, the surface area of the building exterior in relation to the volume of the interior is much greater for a residence than for a larger office type building. Energy savings in larger shelters will probably not be as dramatic as in residential structures, but reflective surfaces can help to lower costs. Another advantage of reducing the amount of energy used is a decrease in the production of carbon dioxide and a reduction in its effect on global warming.

Energy use and human comfort are affected in the out-of-doors by reflectivity as well. On a 90°F (32°C) day when the asphalt paving heats up to 140°F (60°C), the surrounding air temperature is about 5°F (3°C) warmer than the air temperature over a grassed area. During warm summer days, light-colored surfaces in the built landscape that have higher albedo values are about 15°F (8°C) cooler than dark-colored surfaces with lower albedo values. Table 11-2 shows the temperatures of different materials used in the landscape.

Table 11-2   Temperatures of Materials on a Warm Day, 86°F (30°C)

Material	Temperature
Asphalt paving	103°F (39°C)
Dark asphalt shingle roof	135°F (57°C)
Light gray asphalt shingle roof	126°F (52°C)
Red brick wall	92°F (33°C)
Light-colored wood fence, sunny side	97°F (36°C)
Light-colored wood fence, shaded side	92°F (33°C)
Rock paving	102°F (39°C)
Concrete paving	107°F (42°C)
Grassed lawn	88°F (31°C)
Surface of tree leaves	85°F (29°C)
Pine straw mulch bed	121°F (49°C)
Chipped pine bark mulch bed	107°F (42°C)

Chapter 12

Indoor Air Quality

Air is produced and cleaned by the living processes of plants, resulting in clean air that is relatively free from toxins and healthful for the users of the indoor space.

The air inside some buildings is polluted with poisonous chemicals that can affect human health. Those airborne poisons come from three sources, the chemicals in building materials and home furnishings, and the air we exhale. When chemicals build up to certain concentrations as they do, for instance, within sealed buildings, human health can be impaired. A worldwide oil shortage in the 1970s prompted the construction of shelters that were more energy efficient. The world saw the price of electricity jump from $.02 a kilowatt hour to about $.07 a kilowatt hour. As energy costs surged and shelters were built to use less energy, construction strategies included the use of increased insulation, the use of more reflective building materials in hot climates, and sealing buildings to hold in heated and cooled air. Some of these energy efficiency techniques trapped toxic gases inside shelters, often creating conditions that were intolerable to building users and causing buildings to be abandoned: The effect was labeled "sick building syndrome." Studies at the National Aeronautic and Space Administration (NASA) by Bill Wolverton and his staff have proven that plants used indoors can dramatically reduce toxic vapors and make living in a tightly sealed house less harmful to people.

EFFECTS OF POLLUTED INDOOR AIR

People spend a lot of time indoors, more now than they have ever spent inside buildings. Long-term exposure to indoor toxic vapors has probably contributed to an increase in a host of human health problems including asthma, allergies, other upper respiratory problems, and cancer. Additional symptoms associated with poor indoor air quality are eye, ear, nose, and throat irritations, sinus problems, headaches, weakness, and nervous system problems. There are many who say that sudden infant death syndrome (SIDS), the unexpected death of infants and children under age four months, may be caused by indoor air pollution. The Environmental Protection Agency (EPA) ranks indoor air pollution as one of the top five threats to human health.

SOURCES OF INDOOR AIR POLLUTION

We have been experiencing airtight shelters since about 1975, and since that time there has been a dramatic increase in allergy and asthma problems, in addition to the aforementioned associated health problems. Let us now look at the toxic vapor components that are contributing to the many health problems associated with sick building syndrome. We know that more energy-efficient and tightly sealed buildings are trapping gases eminating from synthetic materials. Furnishings for buildings, which used to be made from natural materials such as wood, steel, stone, cotton, and wool, are now generally made from synthetic materials, many of which are held together with manufactured glues. Particleboard and plywood now often replace the use of solid wood. Carpeting made from synthetic materials has been an integral part of nearly all shelters since the 1960s. In addition to outgasing various chemicals, carpeting also harbors dust, dirt, dust mites, and other microbes. The toxic vapors released by these synthetic materials are generally listed under the heading of volatile organic compounds (VOCs). Manufacturers are required to label the VOCs of the materials and furnishings they produce.

Chemical Emissions

The chemical formaldehyde is found in adhesives, caulking, ceiling tiles, permanent press fabrics, draperies, floor coverings, paints, chipboard, plywood, and paper towels. Formaldehyde causes irritation of the eyes, the throat, and the nose. Exposure to formaldehyde is also generally thought to cause asthma, other chronic upper respiratory diseases, and different types of cancer. Benzene is found in all of the aforementioned materials and in computer printers, photocopiers, and wall coverings. Chloroform comes from chlorine-treated drinking water. Ammonia is emitted from blueprint machines, cleaning products, and film developers. Duplicating machines, nail polish remover, and preprinted paper forms are sources of acetone. Xylene and toluene come from computer screens, floor coverings, paints, stains and varnishes, and wall coverings. Alcohol vapor is emitted from carpeting glue, ceiling tiles, floor coverings, paints, permanent press clothing, and wall coverings.

Bioeffluents

People confined in a space for a prolonged period of time will produce chemicals that, in quantities, can be harmful to others. In addition to exhaling carbon dioxide, people also produce carbon monoxide, hydrogen, methane, alcohols, phenols, methyl indole, aldehydes, ammonia, hydrogen sulfide, and nitrogen oxides. Each of us has a personal breathing space from which we get our air to breathe. Scientists define this space as an area of about 6 to 8 ft^3 (0.17 to 0.23 m^3). A personal breathing zone is the space in which an individual remains for several hours at a time, breathing the air from that space. When plants are located within a personal breathing zone, they add humidity and remove bioeffluents and VOCs. Plants also filter airborne microbes with their leaves and root systems. These airborne molds, bacteria, and viruses are trapped and consumed by the plants.

THE EARTH'S NATURAL SYSTEMS AS A MODEL FOR CLEAN AIR

Air is produced and cleaned by the living processes of plants. Plants are integral to the development of sustainable life support systems for humans on earth. Bill Wolverton, in his excellent book *Eco-Friendly House Plants* (Weidenfeld and Nicolson, Ltd., 1996), describes the cleansing processes of the earth's natural systems like this:

> In its simplest form, the earth can be viewed as a living organism. Rainforests act as the earth's lungs, producing oxygen and removing carbon dioxide—the opposite process of human and animal lungs. Wetlands function as the earth's kidneys. Aquatic plants filter nutrients and environmental toxins from the water as it flows back into streams, rivers and oceans in much the same way as kidneys filter impurities from our blood.

USING PLANTS TO REDUCE INDOOR AIR POLLUTION

How do people begin to solve the problems created by outgasing of VOCs in today's tightly sealed shelters? First, because material and furnishing manufacturers publish their products' VOCs, manufactured materials can be selected that have very low VOC rates and natural materials can be selected that don't outgas VOCs.

In a shelter that has existing VOCs, plants can be used profusely to combat indoor air pollution. Plants will absorb airborne chemicals and convert them into organic substances that can be used for plant food. Many types of indoor house plant leaves will absorb airborne chemicals and transport them to the root zone for consumption and assimilation. This system simulates the way nature cleans the earth's atmosphere. Studies have shown that each plant has an ecosystem around its leaves and root system. An abundance of healthy plants indoors will ensure that the air will be healthy to breathe. The presence of microbes on plant leaves and in the root zone helps a plant to persist and to grow. The soil near the plant's roots has vigorous biological activity that helps protect the plant and converts organic matter into plant food. Plants secrete substances in the root zone that encourage the microbes they need to survive. They also emit substances that suppress the microbes that can be harmful.

Plants also add moisture to the air. In fact, they play an important role in controlling indoor humidity levels. As part of a plant's daily life cycle, it produces oxygen, converts carbon dioxide and hydrogen into plant sugars, and transpires or gives off water through its leaves. The ideal relative humidity level for human comfort is between 35 and 65%. During the wintertime, when forced-air convection heating systems are used, the air dries as it is heated. People feel warmer during the winter when the humidity is high, and cooler during the summer when humidity is low. People nearly always have perspiration (moisture) on their skin; in fact, they will perspire about 2000 ml of moisture per day during the summer. This moisture will evaporate when indoor air is dry, causing people to feel cooler. When evaporation occurs heat is carried away from the skin. This condition is ideal when cooling indoor air during the summertime. In winter, making indoor spaces humid and warm will reduce the evaporation of this moisture on skin and the cooling effect caused by the evaporation. As a result, people will perceive the indoor spaces to be warmer, and this will help reduce heating loads.

It is important to consider human health and air quality when planning interior spaces. Dry air irritates nasal and throat membranes and makes people more vulnerable to viruses, allergies, and toxic vapors in the air. People tend to be more susceptible to colds and asthma during the dry winter months. In summer, if indoor humidity is too high, human skin will not be able to sweat and thereby feel cooler as the water evaporates. When relative humidity levels are above 70%, mold and mildew begin to grow and can damage furniture and equipment and cause health problems. Conventional air-conditioning systems reduce humidity and create precise indoor temperature levels. In studies performed by Wolverton, it was found that there were three times as many airborne microbes in a bedroom of a house that had no indoor plants, as compared with a plant-filled sunroom. Interestingly, because of the presence of the plants, the relative humidity of a sunroom was found to be 72%, as compared with a relative humidity of 56% in a bedroom that had no plants. In a room with a relative humidity level of 50%, a fig tree emitted 2 liters (l) (2.1 qt) of water in a 24-hour period, and an areca palm emitted 5 l (5½ qt) of water during the same period. When the humidity level was lower, such as during the wintertime, the fig tree emitted 5 l of water in the 24-hour period and the areca palm emitted 10 l (10½ qt) of water vapor. The finding that plant-filled rooms had 50 to 60% fewer airborne mold spores and bacteria than rooms with no plants is fairly compelling evidence, making a strong case for the inclusion of plants in our shelters as a matter of regular and healthful design.

Interestingly, plants do release small amounts of VOCs. In fact, the small amounts of VOCs released by plants are important in protecting the plant from invasion or infection by airborne microbes and mold spores. That plants improve the quality of the air we breathe is well known and generally accepted. They are important in considering air quality when designing the indoor spaces of shelters to provide maximum healthful conditions for people.

Part IV

Energy in the Sustainable Landscape

Chapter 13

Energy Conservation as
a Sustainable Practice

By conserving energy, it is possible to make a substantial difference in our use of non-renewable energy sources and the amount of pollution (particularly carbon dioxide) we add to our environment.

ENERGY CONSERVATION

Energy conservation includes any of the myriad things we can do to reduce the amount of energy we use in our daily activities. Many of the chapters of this book look closely at practices that, if implemented, will reduce energy consumption, such as planting trees to decrease heating and cooling loads, passive solar heating, and the use of overhangs, among others. There are, however, many relatively simple things we can do that can make a difference in the amount of energy we consume. Often, it is hard to determine what the impact of these practices might be and whether it is worth going to the trouble to adopt them. In this chapter, we examine a variety of practices that are well worth consideration.

THE NEED FOR A SUSTAINABLE ENERGY SOURCE

If we all had access to an unlimited source of sustainable energy (energy that wouldn't be used up or lead to other types of problems), then energy conservation would be unimportant. The advances being made in photovoltaics and other renewable sources of energy suggest that we may someday have this luxury, but we are not there yet. For the most part, we continue to rely mainly on fossil fuels (coal, oil, natural gas), which we burn to release energy for useful work. But, clearly, there are problems with using fossil fuels.

The Depletion of Fossil Fuels

Ultimately, we will run out of fossil fuels. They constitute a finite resource, and once they are fully depleted, they will be gone. How quickly will this occur? It depends on the fuel—and the accuracy of the prediction. It is fairly likely that petroleum will be depleted, or become prohibitively expensive, in the next 50 to 100 years. Natural gas will last longer, perhaps 100 to 200 years. Coal will probably last half a millennium. It is probable that these resources can last long enough for us to find other energy sources. However, there may be severe hardships and instability as we close in on the last of the petroleum reserves (petroleum is such a convenient and portable energy source that it's hard to imagine a painless replacement). Five hundred years from now, when the last of the coal goes up in smoke, we will probably have mastered fusion, cheap solar power, or some other energy source. Trying to make our petroleum last will be a kindness to our children and grandchildren (and should be undertaken for that reason alone), but its exhaustion probably will not disrupt the regenerative cycles upon which we depend.

Pollution by Fossil Fuels

By *polluting* we mean putting toxic constituents into our environment. Minor constituents in fossil fuels, such as sulfur, can create compounds that pollute, harming natural systems directly and indirectly. Combustion products that include nitrogen, partly combusted particulates, and volatile organic compounds (VOCs) can also be harmful. We have learned, and continue to learn, how to prevent the formation of these compounds and to "scrub" them out of the exhaust when they do occur. It is possible to argue that the pollution caused by fossil fuel combustion is just a technical problem that is partly solved now and will be completely solved soon. We are not making light of the problems people are currently experiencing because of pollution (their suffering is and will continue to be real, and there is some doubt about the willingness of regulators to institute controls), but the argument that our technology can "handle" this before irreparable harm to regenerative cycles occurs is plausible. Technology can sometimes make nonsustainable practices sustainable.

Energy Conservation

Yet after making the arguments proposed in the preceding paragraphs (and alienating most of our environmentalist friends), there is still a problem with burning fossil fuels at the present rates: the emission of carbon dioxide (CO_2). This is the product of burning fossil fuels that we cannot prevent or sequester after the fact (in adequate amounts).

Carbon dioxide is a "greenhouse gas." As described earlier, this means that it allows most short-wave solar radiation to reach the earth's surface but absorbs a part of the long-wave (infrared) radiation that the earth radiates back toward space. By absorbing the long-wave radiation, carbon dioxide helps to hold some of the sun's heat within our atmosphere. The carbon dioxide in the earth's atmosphere has always done this (and helped to maintain earth's comfortable temperature). Carbon dioxide goes in and out of the atmosphere as part of various regenerative cycles (Figure 13-1).

Fossil fuels consist of organic molecules (molecules created directly or indirectly via photosynthesis) that have been chemically altered in a way that preserved the solar energy originally captured by plants. By burning these fuels (coal, oil, natural gas), we

Figure 13-1 Carbon dioxide cycles in and out of the atmosphere through a number of different types of cycles.

release the trapped energy for our own purposes. Recall the model organic molecule from the introduction of this book (see p. 4):

$$CH_2O + O_2 \rightarrow H_2O + CO_2 + \text{ energy}$$
(carbohydrate + oxygen   yields   water + carbon dioxide + energy)

We initiate this oxidation reaction when we light a fire.

The large-scale use of fossil fuels has put carbon dioxide into the atmosphere at a rate that greatly exceeds the removal rates of existing cycles. As a result, carbon dioxide has accumulated in the earth's atmosphere. The increased carbon dioxide content (along with increases in other greenhouse gases) has contributed to what has been called "global warming." Global warming, for reasons discussed in Chapter 1, has the potential to seriously disrupt essential regenerative cycles as they currently exist. For this reason, any practice that prevents or diminishes the magnitude of the disruption can be said to be "sustainable." Energy conservation, in most parts of the world, reduces the amount of fossil fuels that are combusted and so decreases the amount of carbon dioxide that is released. Hence, energy conservation is a sustainable practice.

CARBON DIOXIDE—THE DIFFERENCE ONE PERSON (OR FAMILY) CAN MAKE

In 1998 more than 24 billion metric tons (52 trillion lb) of carbon dioxide entered the atmosphere as a result of human activities. World emissions per capita were about 4 metric tons (8800 lb). Is it somehow possible to reduce these numbers to an appreciable extent, or should we throw our hands up in despair?

Consider the case of workers trying to shore up a riverbank when the river threatens to flood a town. Everyone who works there knows that the 50 or so sandbags one person can carry in several hours won't prevent a flood, but that doesn't stop hundreds of people from filling, carrying, and placing sandbags to save their town.

It is clear that many small differences can make a big difference. Now we're talking about 6 billion people working to solve a problem that some refuse even to acknowledge. This is a daunting task. Yet, considering the per capita production of CO_2 in the United States, it is also clear that we, as a nation, have an opportunity to make a big difference in carbon dioxide emissions if we can work to lower our per person production rate to that of other industrialized nations (Figure 13-2).

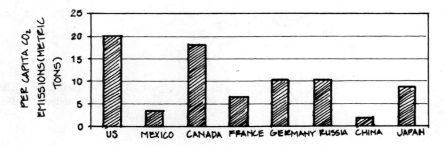

Figure 13-2 Per capita carbon dioxide emissions for a sampling of countries. (*Source:* U.S. Department of Energy.)

PRODUCTION OF CARBON DIOXIDE

Before we can determine how to make reductions in CO_2 emissions, we have to be able to estimate rates of CO_2 production caused by various human activities. To do this, we start with the energy contained in different fossil fuels.

Energy in Fuels

When we talk about energy of any sort, we generally use one of several energy "units." In the metric system, we use joules (J). In the English system, we use British thermal units (Btu). In both systems (mainly when talking about electricity), we use kilowatt hours (kWh). They all describe exactly the same physical quantity and can be converted back and forth, as needed:

$$1 \text{Btu} = 1{,}054.8 \text{ J}$$
$$1 \text{kWh} = 3{,}600{,}000 \text{ J} = 3{,}413 \text{ Btu}$$

Table 13-1 shows the typical energy contents of an assortment of fuels. This is the total energy that is potentially available when the fuel is burned.

EXAMPLE 1. Calculate the mass of kerosene, anthracite, and hardwood required to provide 1500 W of heat for 10 hours.

A watt (W) is equal to one joule per second (1 J/s). For the moment, assume that our heaters are 100% efficient (all the energy is converted to useful heat).

First determine how much energy is used when a 1500 W heater is run for 10 hours.

$$1500 \text{ W} = 1500 \text{ J/s}$$
$$1500 \text{ J/s} \times 3600 \text{ s} / 1 \text{ hr} \times 10 \text{ hrs} = 54{,}000{,}000 \text{ J}$$

Because energy in Table 13-1 is expressed as Btu, convert the energy in the preceding equation to Btu:

Table 13-1 Energy Content of Various Fossil Fuels

Fuel Type	Average Energy Btu / Commonly Used Unit	Btu / kg
Gasoline (winter)	112,500/gal	43,700
Gasoline (summer)	114,500/gal	44,400
Kerosene	135,000/gal	44,500
No. 2 fuel oil	140,000/gal	41,000
Natural gas	1,028,000/1000 ft^3	55,000
Propane	91,333/gal	47,100
Bituminous coal	23,000,000/ton	25,300
Anthracite coal	24,800,000/ton	27,300
Lignite coal	14,000,000/ton	15,000
Hardwood	24,000,000/cord	9,400
Pine	18,000,000/128 ft^3 (1 cord)	8,400

Sources: The Energy Efficiency and Renewable Energy Clearinghouse and the U.S. Environmental Protection Agency.

$$\text{Energy in Btu} = 54,000,000 \text{ J} \times 1 \text{ Btu} / 1054.8 \text{ J} = 51,195 \text{ Btu}$$

Then, the masses of the various fuels are:

$$\text{Kerosene} = 51,195 \text{ Btu} \times 1 \text{ kg} / 44,500 \text{ Btu} = 1.15 \text{ kg} (0.379 \text{ gal})$$
$$\text{Anthracite} = 51,195 \text{ Btu} \times 1 \text{ kg} / 27,300 \text{ Btu} = 1.88 \text{ kg} (4 \text{ lb})$$
$$\text{Hardwood} = 51,195 \text{ Btu} \times 1 \text{ kg} / 9,400 \text{ Btu} = 5.4 \text{ kg} (0.27 \text{ ft}^3)$$

Efficiency

Next, we have to introduce efficiency into our calculations. We rarely get the full benefit of the energy that is released with the combustion of any fuel. Incandescent lightbulbs produce heat when we want light. Furnaces lose heat up chimneys. Energy used in motors is lost because of friction.

Efficiency is the quantity of useful energy output from a device divided by the energy input to run the device. Table 13-2 lists the efficiencies of many devices we use each day. The devices in Table 13-2 can be divided into two groups. The first includes those that release energy (burn the fuel) at the point of use: gas- and oil-burning heaters and appliances. The other group includes electrical devices. Utility power plants produce electricity at other locations and transport it to the place where it is used. In the United States, 70% of our electrical power comes from the burning of fossil fuels (Figure 13-3). More than half of the total comes from the burning of coal.

The fossil fuel utility power generators have efficiencies that range from less than 30% to about 40%. The lowest efficiencies are characteristics of older coal-fired units. The best efficiencies are achieved primarily by newer gas-fired power generators. The rightmost column in Table 13-2 includes the efficiency of the electric generation process

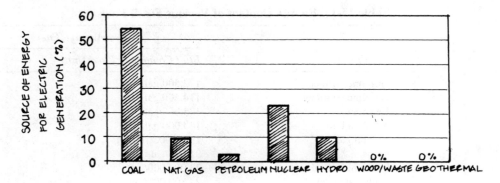

Figure 13-3 Electrical energy production by source in the U.S. (*Source:* U.S. Department of Energy.)

to better compare the performance of energy-using devices in our household (we have assumed 33% efficiency for combined utility generators and line losses due to transport of the energy to the location of use).

EXAMPLE 2. Calculate the mass of natural gas required to provide 1500 W of heat for 10 hours with an efficiency of 75%.

In Example 1, we found that a 1500 W heater running for 10 hours used 51,195 Btu. This is the useful energy out of the system. We want to find the energy that went

Table 13-2   Appliance and Household Device Efficiencies

Device	Percent of Efficiency (excludes efficiency of power generation)	Percent of Efficiency (includes efficiency of power generation—33%)
Heating		
Gas (natural gas, propane)		
High efficiency (new)	80–96	80–96
Mid efficiency (new)	78–80	78–80
Older	60	60
Electric (resistive)	100	33
Electric (heat pump)	200	66
Oil	65	65
Lighting		
Incandescent bulb (60 W)	10	3.3
(produces ∼ 6 W of visible light)		
Compact fluorescent (13 W)	45	15
(produces ∼ 6 W of visible light)		
Mechanical		
Automobile engine	25	25
Electric motor (refrigerator)	90	30

into the heater to get this heat. The efficiency is 0.75 (75%). This corresponds to a fairly inefficient vented natural gas heater.

$$0.75 = 51{,}195 \text{ / energy in}$$

Solving for "energy in":

$$\text{Energy in} = 51{,}195 / 0.75 = 68{,}260 \text{ Btu}$$

According to Table 13-1, natural gas has an average energy content of 55,000 Btu / kg. The mass of natural gas used is then:

$$\text{Mass natural gas} = 68{,}260 \times 1 \text{ kg} / 55{,}000 = 1.24 \text{ kg}$$

or a little more than 66 ft^3 of natural gas.

Estimating CO_2 Production

Fossil fuels are chemically different enough from one another that the amount of CO_2 each produces varies. Table 13-3 gives the average CO_2 emission from each fossil fuel source per million Btu of energy released.

EXAMPLE 3. Compare the carbon dioxide production of the fossil-fuel-powered heaters in Examples 1 and 2.

All are functioning with an efficiency of 75% (we found that this was 68,260 Btu in Example 2).

$$\text{Kerosene} = 71.57 \times 68{,}260/1{,}000{,}000 = 4.9 \text{ kg } CO_2$$
$$\text{Anthracite} = 103.4 \times 68{,}260/1{,}000{,}000 = 7.1 \text{ kg } CO_2$$
$$\text{Natural gas} = 53.10 \times 68{,}260/1{,}000{,}000 = 3.6 \text{ kg } CO_2$$

Table 13-3   Carbon Dioxide Emissions from Fossil Fuels

Fuel	Emissions (kg CO_2 per 1 million Btu)
Coal	
Anthracite	103.4
Bituminous	93.3
Lignite	98.3
Gasoline	70.29
Kerosene	71.57
Natural gas (includes propane)	53.10
Fuel oil	73.33

Source: U.S. Department of Energy.

Notice that we left hardwood out of Example 3. Burning hardwood (or any other non-fossilized bio-fuel) does not contribute to atmospheric changes. Bio-fuels cycle CO_2 over such a short time period (6 months to 50 years) that their effect on atmospheric CO_2 content is negligible. Bio-fuels (also called "biomass") are a sustainable source of energy in relation to carbon dioxide.

NUCLEAR AND HYDROELECTRIC POWER PRODUCTION

Power plants fueled by nuclear energy and water-driven turbines produce little or no carbon dioxide. At present, 20% of power in the United States comes from nuclear and 10% from hydroelectric plants. If you are in an area serviced by either of these power sources, then your use of electricity does not produce carbon dioxide emissions. The percentage of power contributed by nuclear plants has probably reached its peak in the this country. New plants are not being built, and older plants are being decommissioned as they reach the end of their service lives. Hydroelectric utility power production has also probably peaked. Most suitable sites have already been developed, and there is a growing awareness of the environmental damage caused by the large-scale damming of watersheds.

Table 13-4 shows the combined contribution of nuclear and hydroelectric power production in each state. In addition, California uses renewable energy sources (wind, solar, biomass) to generate approximately 11% of its total power. Connecticut, Iowa, Maine, Massachusetts, Minnesota, New Hampshire, Rhode Island, Vermont, and Wisconsin each produce about 1% of their needs from renewable sources.

Table 13-4 Contribution of Nuclear and Large-Scale Hydroelectric Power Production to Total

	%		%		%
Alabama	33	Louisiana	33	Ohio	19
Alaska	22	Maine	28	Oklahoma	14
Arizona	24	Maryland	40	Oregon	75
Arkansas	33	Massachusetts	28	Pennsylvania	40
California	38	Michigan	19	Rhode Island	28
Colorado	24	Minnesota	18	South Carolina	33
Connecticut	28	Mississippi	33	South Dakota	33
Delaware	18	Missouri	14	Tennessee	33
Florida	16	Montana	75	Texas	14
Georgia	33	Nebraska	33	Utah	24
Hawaii	0	Nevada	24	Vermont	28
Idaho	75	New Hampshire	28	Virginia	18
Illinois	19	New Jersey	40	Washington	75
Indiana	19	New Mexico	24	West Virginia	18
Iowa	18	New York	54	Wisconsin	18
Kansas	14	North Carolina	33	Wyoming	75
Kentucky	33	North Dakota	33		

"INTERMITTENT-USE" DEVICES

As you can see from the preceding sections, if you know the power demand of a device, the number of hours per day you use it, and its efficiency, it is possible to estimate the energy consumption of the device and (if the utility is fossil-fuel powered) the amount of carbon dioxide produced to generate that amount of energy. Some devices complicate matters by running only part of the time. Most refrigerators, air conditioners, furnaces, and central heating fans run only when a sensor indicates that they are needed. Some appliances, such as vacuum cleaners, are operated for varying periods, depending on needs. Other appliances may not be used each day.

Energy consumption estimates for these types of devices and situations are derived from actual measurements of existing systems and surveys of users. Table 13-5 provides monthly estimates of energy consumption for a variety of uses.

LOWERING CO$_2$ EMISSIONS

In considering the energy used at a residence (the energy use that you would read from a meter), it appears that natural gas is the principal source of energy used in American homes (Figure 13-4a). It is easy to miss the fact that electricity is energy that has come

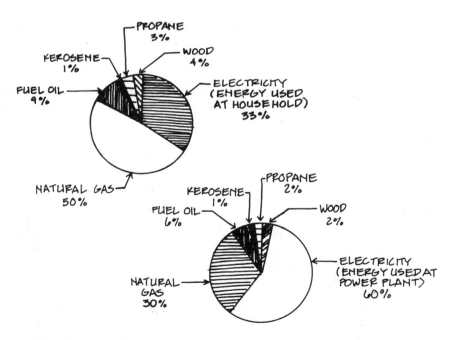

Figure 13-4 Energy use by source in the home (top). Metered use in the home (the amount of energy that actually arrives and is used in the home) (bottom). Energy use by source when electrical line losses and power plant efficiency are taken into account.

from another energy source, usually a fossil fuel. The process of creating and delivering electricity is usually only 30 to 40% efficient, meaning that the actual energy used is 2½ to 3 times that which has gone through the meter. Figure 13-4 (bottom) illustrates actual residential energy use by source. When line losses (the energy loss due to the friction of high-voltage cables used to transport the electricity) are taken into account, an overall efficiency of about 33% becomes a good estimate.

In the following sections, we first consider some of the relatively easy things you can do to reduce energy consumption and carbon dioxide emissions.

Dishwasher Drying Cycle

According to Table 13-5, avoiding the heated drying cycle in a dishwasher will reduce power consumption by approximately 60 kWh per month. For households that consistently use this cycle, it is possible to realize a significant decrease in CO_2 emission.

EXAMPLE 4. Calculate carbon dioxide reduction per year for a household that routinely uses the dishwasher drying cycle, if it eliminates this function.

First, compute energy savings for the year on the household electric meter:

$$\text{Energy savings on-site} = 12 \text{ months} \times 60 \text{ kWh} = 720 \text{ kWh}$$

The energy use avoided at the power plant is approximately three times that on the meter:

$$\text{Energy use avoided at the power plant} = 720 \text{ kWh} \times 3 = 2160 \text{ kWh}$$
$$1 \text{ kWh} = 3413 \text{ Btu; therefore, } 2160 \text{ kWh} = 7{,}370{,}000 \text{ Btu}$$

Coal-fired power plants make up nearly 80% of the fossil-fuel-powered generation segment; we will use coal as our benchmark for CO_2 production. As shown in Table 13-3, 1 million Btu from bituminous coal leads to 93.3 kg of carbon dioxide emission (somewhat more from other coal sources).

$$CO_2 \text{ emission prevented} = 7{,}370{,}000 \text{ Btu/yr} \times 93.3 \text{ kg } CO_2 \text{ / } 1{,}000{,}000 \text{ Btu}$$
$$= 687 \text{ kg } CO_2 \text{ per year}$$

Lighting

The amount of energy used each month for lighting in an average household, 60 kWh (Table 13-5), is primarily used by incandescent lightbulbs. This corresponds to approximately four 60 W bulbs being used eight hours per day each day of the month (this is a fairly conservative estimate). Compact fluorescent bulbs are much more efficient than incandescent: A 13 W compact fluorescent bulb generates about the same light as a 60 W incandescent bulb (the fluorescent bulb has 60 W/13 W = 4.6 times the efficiency of the incandescent bulb). The life span of compact fluorescent bulbs is much longer than that of the incandescents, their size and convenience are similar, and their prices have come down greatly. They more than pay for themselves during their lifetimes, so they are economically attractive as well.

Table 13-5 Monthly Energy Consumption for Typical Household Appliances and Uses

(Electric use is metered and does not include losses due to the process of power generation.)

	kWh/month
Clothes washer (30 loads per month)	
Heated water (electric heater)	120
Power for motor	20
Clothes dryer	
Electric	80
Gas	93
Dishwasher	
Hot water (electric heater)	70
Dry cycle off	10
Dry cycle on	70
Electric blanket	40
Heater (1500 W, resistive, 12 hr/day)	558
Freezer	
24 ft^3 (upright/chest)	200/124
18 ft^3 (upright/chest)	185/115
15 ft^3 (upright/chest)	170/95
Hair dryer	5
Lighting	60
Iron	5
Microwave oven	25
PC with printer (4 hr/day)	20
Stove (oven plus cooktop)	
Electric	50
Gas	90
Refrigerator	
24 ft^3 (frost free, side by side)	210
20 ft^3 (frost free, side by side)	180
17 ft^3 (frost free, top-bottom)	140
14 ft^3 (manual defrost)	95
Toaster	4
TV	
Color (4 hr/day)	40
Black and white (4 hr/day)	12
Water heater	
Electric	420
Gas	700
VCR	4

EXAMPLE 5. Calculate carbon dioxide reduction per year if incandescent bulbs used for household lighting are replaced by compact fluorescent bulbs.

From Example 4, we know that saving 60 kWh per month prevents the emission of 687 kg CO_2 per year. By replacing incandescent bulbs with compact fluorescent bulbs for household lighting, we will see a reduction in energy use equal to $(60\ W - 13\ W)/60\ W = 78\%$. The energy savings are proportional to the percent reduction in power use.

Energy savings per year on the meter = 12 months $\times$ 0.78 $\times$ 60 kWh = 562 kWh

Energy saved at the power plant = 562 kWh $\times$ 3 = 1686 kWh = 5.75 million Btu

One million Btu from bituminous coal produces 93.3 kg of carbon dioxide emission.

CO_2 emission prevented = 5,750,000 Btu/yr $\times$ 93.3 kg CO_2 / 1,000,000 BTU
= 536 kg CO_2 per year.

Clothes Washing

Notice, in Table 13-5, that the energy used to heat the wash water greatly exceeded the power required to work the spinner or agitator. In Table 13-5 the heating value included an assortment of "warm" and "hot" washes. For most washing purposes, cold water washing works about as well as warm water washing. This is especially true if you soak the wash (hold the wash with the tank full of water for a period of time before starting agitation). For a family that consistently washes in warm or hot water, it is possible to reduce monthly electrical use by 120 kWh (Table 13-5).

EXAMPLE 6. Determine CO_2 reduction if only cold water washes are used.
From Example 4, we know that a 60 kWh reduction in energy use can reduce CO_2 emission by 687 kg. The reduction expected from a 120 kWh savings is proportional to this:

Reduction = (120 kWh / 60 kWh) $\times$ 687 kg CO_2 = 1374 kg CO_2

For the household of Examples 4 through 6, the total decrease in carbon dioxide emission would be more than 2600 kg. If this is a household of four, that would amount to a per capita decrease of nearly 0.65 metric tons of CO_2.

ADJUSTING THE THERMOSTAT

Heating and cooling are significant components of residential energy consumption. Table 13-6 shows estimates of heating and cooling energy requirements for a typical two-story, 2400 ft^2 home at three locations in the contiguous United States. In the southeast, cooling dominates the energy mix. Because all forms of air-conditioning are powered by electrical energy, a system driven by coal-fired utility power can be a huge producer of carbon dioxide. In the north (Chicago), heating is the principal energy consumer. The low air-conditioning values in the southwest (Phoenix) are due to the use of evaporators ("swamp coolers") that require relatively little energy to operate. These devices also require relatively low relative humidity to work effectively, precluding their efficient use elsewhere.

Table 13-6 Projected Heating and Cooling Energy Use and Carbon Dioxide Emissions

Figures are for two-story, 2400 ft^2 houses at three different locations. Heating is done with natural gas (with a small electrical component for fans). Cooling is electric central air-conditioning in Atlanta and Chicago and evaporative cooling in Phoenix. "Percent of total" refers to the total heating, cooling, or CO_2 emission load at each location. Electrical energy use is the energy used at the power plant, not metered electricity.

		Million Btu	*% of Total*	*kg CO_2**	*% of Total*
Atlanta, GA	Heating	79	28.9	4309	20.4
	Cooling	90	32.6	8365	39.6
Chicago, IL	Heating	170	53.6	9228	43.1
	Cooling	47	14.8	4389	20.5
Phoenix, AZ	Heating	29	19.8	1554	14.2
	Cooling	15	10.4	1410	12.9

*CO_2 emission is based on natural gas (53.1 kg CO_2 per million Btu) or bituminous coal (93.3 kg CO_2 per million Btu) power generation.
Source: Nexus Energy Software.

The estimates of Table 13-6 are based on indoor temperatures deemed comfortable. Adjusting your thermostat lower during the heating season and higher during times of cooling reduces both energy use and CO_2 emissions. During the winter, each degree (F) change results in a 2 to 3% reduction in heating energy use. During the cooling season, the reductions are even greater: 3 to 5% per degree F. Let's see how big a difference this can make.

EXAMPLE 7. Estimate annual energy use and CO_2 emission reductions that result from decreasing the furnace set point 4° in the model house in Chicago.
    Assuming a 2.5% per degree savings:

$$\text{Heating energy decrease} = 4° \times 0.025 \text{ / degree} \times 170{,}000{,}000 \text{ Btu}$$
$$= 17{,}000{,}000 \text{ Btu}$$

Estimating CO_2 emission reductions corresponding to this energy drop (natural gas, 53.1 kg CO_2 / million Btu):

$$\text{Reduction in } CO_2 \text{ emission} = 17{,}000{,}000 \text{ Btu} \times 53.1 \text{ kg } CO_2 \text{ / million Btu}$$
$$= 900 \text{ kg } CO_2$$

EXAMPLE 8. Repeat Example 7 for a 4° set point increase in Atlanta.
    Assuming a 4% per degree savings:

$$\text{Cooling energy decrease} = 4° \times 0.04 \text{ / degree} \times 90{,}000{,}000 \text{ Btu}$$
$$= 14{,}400{,}000 \text{ Btu}$$

Estimating CO_2 emission reductions corresponding to this energy drop (coal-fired power generation, 93.3 kg CO_2 / million Btu for bituminous):

$$\text{Reduction in } CO_2 \text{ emission} = 14,400,000 \text{ Btu} \times 93.3 \text{ kg } CO_2 \text{ / million Btu}$$
$$= 1340 \text{ kg } CO_2$$

These calculations are, of course, estimates based on simplifying assumptions. It is clear, however, that we can make meaningful decreases in energy use and CO_2 emissions by changing our thermostat set points.

DECIDING ON AN ENERGY SOURCE

When building or remodeling, it is often possible to decide on the type of energy you will use in your residence. Careful design, including elements found elsewhere in this book, can reduce your energy needs and, consequently, your residential carbon dioxide emissions. Renewable energy sources (solar, wind, biomass) are "CO_2 free": They result in no net carbon dioxide increase in the atmosphere. See the relevant chapters in this book on these topics.

The decision about energy sources should, at least in part, be based on carbon dioxide emissions. Table 13-7 gives projected total CO_2 emissions for the same houses shown in Table 13-6. The metered energies in the "all electric" and "electric plus gas" houses are comparable. The differences are due to the relatively low efficiency of power generation and the high CO_2 emission rate of coal.

DECIDING ON APPLIANCES

The decisions you make when purchasing appliances can affect the amount of energy your household consumes and your carbon dioxide emissions. There is a big difference in efficiencies of many appliances, and the differences in energy requirements of comparably sized devices can be considerable. Table 13-8 lists typical annual energy use for a number of appliances.

Table 13-7   Projected Carbon Dioxide Emissions (in metric tons per year)

The figures are for the same house in Table 13-6, in three different locations. Carbon dioxide emissions are based on natural gas (53.1 kg CO_2 per million Btu) in the "gas plus electricity" house and coal-fired electric generation (bituminous coal, 93.3 kg CO_2 per million Btu; delivery efficiency of 33%).

	All Electric	Gas Heat, Hot Water, Clothes Dryer, and Stove
Atlanta, GA	32	21
Chicago, IL	42	21
Phoenix, AZ	30	17

Table 13-8 Projected Energy Use for Household Appliances Under Typical Operating Conditions

Energy Star is a government designed labeling system for devices that meet conservation criteria.

Item	kWh/yr[1]
Refrigerator	
Typical	746
20.5 ft^3 Energy Star[2] (top mount)	620
20.5 ft^3 best available (top mount)[3]	472
20.5 ft^3 Energy Star[2] (side/side)	770
20.5 ft^3 best available (side/side)[3]	606
16 ft^3 super-low energy[4]	285
Dishwasher	
Typical (energy factor = 0.46)[5]	700
Energy Star[2] (energy factor = 0.58)[5]	555
Best available[3] (energy factor = 1.16)[5]	277
Clothes washer	
Typical (energy factor = 1.18)[5]	880
Energy Star[2] (energy factor = 2.50)[5]	315
Front-loading best available[3] (energy factor = 4)[5]	176
Room air conditioner (10,000 Btu)	
Typical (EER = 9.8)[6]	765
Energy Star[2] (EER = 10.7)[6]	700
Best available[3] (EER = 11.7)[6]	640
Central air conditioner (36,000 Btu)	
Typical (SEER = 10)[7]	3,600
Energy Star[2] (SEER = 12)[7]	3,000
Best available[3] (SEER = 18)[7]	2,000
Hot water heater (50 gal, electric)	
Typical (energy factor = 0.86)[5]	5,106
Energy Star[2] (energy factor = 0.92)[5]	4,773
Best available[3] (Energy Factor = 0.95)[5]	4,622
Hot water heater (50 gal, gas)	
Typical (energy factor = 0.54)[5]	8,116
Energy Star[2] (energy factor = 0.61)[5]	7,207
Best available[3] (energy factor = 0.65)[5]	6,739
Furnace (70,000 Btu/hr, gas)	
Typical (78% efficiency)	23,150
Energy Star[2] (90% efficiency)	20,070
Best Available[3] (97% efficiency)	18,610
Heat pump (36,000 Btu, air source)	
Typical (HSPF/SEER = 6.8/10)[7,8]	12,500
Energy Star[2] (HSPF/SEER = 7.6/12)[7,8]	10,800
Best available[3] (HSPF/SEER = 9.9/17)[7,8]	8,000

[1]Metered energy (not energy used at power plant)
[2]U.S. Department of Energy (DOE) recommended
[3]Among best-known manufacturers
[4]Mainly used in alternate energy homes
[5]Energy factor = energy supplied or jobs completed by the appliance divided by the total energy used
[6]EER = Energy Efficiency Ratio = cooling capacity (Btu/hr) divided by power input (W).
[7]SEER = Seasonal Energy Efficiency Ratio = heating or cooling output (in Btu) divided by total energy input (in Wh)
[8]HSPF = Heating Seasonal Performance Factor = heating output (in Btu) divided by total energy input (in Wh)

EXAMPLE 9. Compute annual reduction in carbon dioxide emissions if a "typical" refrigerator is replaced by a "best available" top-mount refrigerator. Assume electrical power production from a bituminous coal-fired plant.

As given in Table 13-8, the reduction in annual energy use would be $746 - 472 = 274$ kWh/yr. At the power plant, this represents $274 \times 3 = 822$ kWh/yr (2.8 million Btu) in energy use reduction. Emissions from a bituminous coal power plant are 93.3 kg CO_2 per million Btu, so:

$$CO_2 \text{ reduction} = 2.8 \text{ million Btu} \times 93.3 \text{ kg } CO_2 \text{ / million Btu}$$
$$= 261 \text{ kg } CO_2$$

Table 13-9 represents the approach of Example 9 applied to the appliances in Table 13-8.

The estimated reduction in carbon dioxide emission achieved by replacing all of the listed electrical devices (except the room air conditioner) listed in Table 13-9 would be approximately 7.6 metric tons per year.

PHANTOM LOADS

Many electrical devices are always drawing power, even when they are "off." If you have a remote control TV, there must always be power to the TV in order for the remote "on" button to work. The same is true for other remote-driven devices (stereo receivers). The clock on your VCR and microwave oven draw power, and any device that has a "box" on the electrical cord is using electricity (the box converts 120 V AC to low-voltage DC current). The amount of power being used is actually small, perhaps less than 1 W. Unfortunately, the circuitry used to regulate or convert the current is usually fairly

Table 13-9 Reduction in Carbon Dioxide Emissions

Reductions result from replacing "typical" appliances (Table 13-8) with "best available" appliances. Calculations for electrical devices are based on power from a coal-fired plant (bituminous, 93.3 kg CO_2/million Btu) having an overall efficiency of 33%. Calculations for gas appliances are based on on-site natural gas use (53.1 kg CO_2/million Btu).

Device	CO_2 Reduction (kg/yr)
Refrigerator	262
Dishwasher	404
Clothes washer	673
Room AC	119
Central AC	1528
Hot water (electric)	462
Hot water (gas)	250
Furnace (gas)	823
Heat pump	4299

Source: U.S. Department of Energy.

cheap and inefficient, so the amount of AC power going in (the phantom load) may be surprisingly large.

Table 13-10 lists devices having phantom loads and the magnitude of the power being consumed.

Many houses contain multiple devices, so the household total in Table 13-10 is probably conservative. The carbon dioxide emission due to phantom loads (bituminous coal power source) is 675 kWh/yr × 3 × 3413 Btu/kWh × 93.3 kg CO_2 / million Btu = 645 kg CO_2 per year.

TRANSPORTATION

So far, we have concentrated on household energy consumption and CO_2 emission. We would be remiss if we left out automobiles. Currently, new vehicles sold in the United States have a combined fuel mileage of approximately 25 miles per gallon (mpg). Older cars, of course, do not do as well as that. The average car in the United States travels 11,400 mi each year.

EXAMPLE 10. Compute annual carbon dioxide emission from an average car.
First, calculate gallons of gasoline used in a year:

$$\text{Fuel used} = 11,400 \text{ mi}/25 \text{ mpg} = 456 \text{ gal}$$

Next, determine the energy that this volume of gasoline represents (energy from 1 gal of gas is given in Table 13-1; we'll average summer and winter energy contents):

$$\text{Energy from gas} = 456 \text{ gal} \times 113,500 \text{ Btu / gal} = 51,756,000 \text{ Btu}$$

The carbon dioxide emission rate (Table 13-3) is 70.29 kg CO_2 per million Btu. Total carbon dioxide emission is:

$$51,756,000 \text{ Btu} \times 70.29 \text{ kg } CO_2 / 1,000,000 \text{ Btu} = 3,640 \text{ kg } CO_2 \text{ per year.}$$

Table 13-10   Phantom Loads

Device	Power (W)	Annual Energy Use (kWh)
Color television	28	245
Stove auto-lighter	14	123
VCR clock	14	123
Microwave oven clock	8	70
Stereo receiver	8	70
"Box" on printer cord	5	44
Total		675

Source: R. Perez, "The Phantom Loads," *Home Power Magazine,* 38(1993): 46–48.

Hybrid automobiles (vehicles that combine electric and some other power source) are just now becoming available. Mileage figures on these vehicles indicate that they offer approximately twice the fuel mileage of the average car sold in the United States (50 versus 25 mpg). This means that a carbon dioxide reduction of approximately 1,820 kg CO_2 per vehicle per year could be realized by switching to hybrid vehicles.

There are other ways to improve mileage and reduce carbon dioxide emissions. One of the easiest is simply going more slowly on highways. Gas mileage for vehicles traveling at 55 mph is about 15% better than at 65 mph.

EXAMPLE 11. A minivan traveled 200 miles at 65 mph and used 10 gal of gasoline. How much would carbon dioxide emission have been reduced if the van had traveled at 55 mph?

Fifteen percent of 10 gal is 1.5 gal.

Energy from 1.5 gal $= 1.5$ gal $\times$ 113,500 Btu / gal $= 170,250$ Btu

CO_2 emission $= 170,250$ Btu $\times$ 70.29 kg CO_2 /1,000,000 Btu $= 12$ kg CO_2

CONCLUSION

We started this chapter wondering whether meaningful reductions in carbon dioxide emissions could be made by individuals in their daily lives. The examples offered illustrate that there are many ways we can make such reductions. All we have to do is decide to make them.

Chapter 14

Heat Value of the Sun

Being aware of how much heat or solar radiation is available from the sun can enable a designer or engineer to provide useful thermal energy to meet human needs. Using solar radiation can save 20 to 100% of fossil fuels used for both space heating and domestic hot water heating.

Of just how much value is the sun as a heat source for use on earth? Only about 5% of the solar insolation, or the sun's heat, is absorbed and used on earth. *Insolation* is the amount of solar radiation that strikes a surface on the earth. Most solar radiation is reflected back into the atmosphere. The potential for using this renewable resource to perform heating tasks in the human ecosystem is great. Let us examine just how much heat can be absorbed from the sun to perform the task of heating water. Suppose, for example, we are interested in seeing whether there is enough sun heat to warm water either for a swimming pool, in order to extend the outdoor swimming season, or for domestic hot water use. We know water is comfortable to swim in as long as it is about 80°F (27°C). Some prefer water at about 83°F (28°C), and for them, 78°F (26°C) is cold! Others may even heat their pools to 88°F (31°C), but that seems too much like bathwater for most people. On March 28, in Starkville, Mississippi, the water in one resident's pool was found to be 65°F (18°C). Trout and sea cod probably like water that cold.

SOLAR ENERGY AND HEAT VALUE

Each day the sun bathes the earth with solar energy. That energy is used by plants to carry out photosynthesis, and some of the heat is absorbed by the earth and influences climate. The amount of solar energy, or heat from the sun, is quantified and available from many sources for areas all over the world. In Table 14-1 it can be seen that Jackson, Mississippi, for example, gets the least heat from the sun in December and January, and the most heat in May, June, July, and August. The varying amounts of energy received coincide with the different seasons, especially with the winter and summer seasons. The table shows the number of joules (J) from the sun's heat hitting 1 m^2 of the earth in this region. The daily figure is an average of the amount of energy received in a month; this includes sunny days, cloudy days, and days when it rained.

Table 14-1 Average Daily Solar Energy for Jackson, Mississippi

(Figures are in millions of joules per square meter per day— MJ/m²/day.)

Month	MJ/m2/day
January	8.6
February	11.7
March	15.6
April	19.4
May	22
June	23
July	21.7
August	20.2
September	17.1
October	14.4
November	10.2
December	8.1

To determine the amount of heat from the sun striking the earth, it is important to understand the units of energy being discussed. A joule is a very small amount of energy: a joule's worth of energy is about the amount of heat you would feel if someone came up to you and puffed a small amount of air on your cheek. See Table 14-2 for energy conversion factors related to joules. Now the question is, How much heat is the 19.4 million joules received daily during April, and is that enough heat to try to capture and use, thereby possibly reducing dependence on fossil fuels?

Determining the Value of the Sun for Heating Water

To resolve the question of just what 19.4 million joules of heat can do, let us create an equation. In the equation, let us compare the temperature of the water before and after receiving the warming benefits of the sun. The equation will be set up to determine the amount of heat received by the water and how much the water temperature will increase.

$$T_{after} = T_{before} + Q/MC$$

Table 14-2 Energy Conversion Factors

1 kilowatt hour = 3,412 Btu
1 Btu = 1,055.6 joules
1 kilowatt hour = 3,601,707 joules
1 cubic foot of natural gas = 1,000 Btu
100 cubic feet (CCF) of natural gas = 100,000 Btu
1 therm = 100,000 Btu

Note: The heat from a match is about one Btu (British thermal unit). A Btu is a measure of the amount of heat it takes to raise the temperature of 1 lb (453 g) of water 1°F (0.6°C).

T_{after} is the temperature of the water after being heated by the sun. This is what we are seeking to find.

T_{before} is the temperature of the water before being heated.

Q is the quantity of heat being absorbed from the sun. In April, Jackson receives a daily average of 19.4 million joules.

M is the mass (for everyday purposes, mass means weight) of water in the metric unit of kilograms.

C is the heat capacity of the material you are using to collect and store heat.

Heat Capacity

We are using water to absorb and store solar radiation in our example, and the heat capacity of water is 4200 joules/kilogram per degree Celcius (J/K/°C). The "rate" of receiving the heat is per day. That means that if 4200 joules of heat are transferred into a liter of water, the temperature of the water will rise 1°C (1.8°F). If it takes all day for the 19.4 million J to move into the water, then by the end of the day the water will be as warm as it can be from solar radiation. Every material type has a capacity for absorbing and storing energy. See Table 14-3 for examples of materials and their capacity for storing a certain amount of heat. Heat storage capacities are expressed in joules per kilogram per degree Celcius (J/K/°C).

Effectiveness of Solar Radiation for Heating Water

In Jackson, Mississippi, people normally begin using their swimming pools in May, but with the potential for solar heating, it may be interesting to see whether the pool water can be heated a month early in the year so that people can begin using their pools in April. Now, let us determine how much the water will heat up by capturing the solar energy available in April. We begin by setting up our equation and then looking at the solar energy chart to determine the daily average solar heat gain. In Jackson, Mississippi, in April, it is 19.4 million J/m^2/day. The configuration of the body of water to collect the sun's heat is 1 m^2 of water (10.8 ft^2), 2 m deep (6.6 ft). Note the shape we are evaluating in Figure 14-1.

Next, let us work through the equation to see how warm the 2 m^3 (70 ft^3) of water will get by the end of the day after absorbing the 19.4 million of energy available in April. The components of the following equation are explained in Figure 14-2.

$$T_{after} = T_{before} + \frac{(19.4 \times 10^6 \text{ J/M})(1\text{m}^2)}{1000 \text{ K/m}^3 (2 \text{ m}^3)(4200 \text{ J/K°C})}$$

Table 14-3   Heat Capacity of Different Materials

Aluminum	900 J/K/°C
Granite	1017 J/K/°C
Wood	1760 J/K/°C
Water	4200 J/K/°C

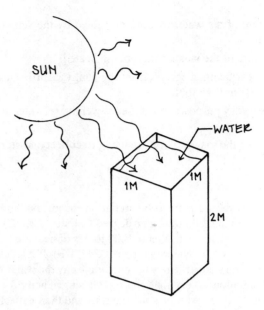

SUN

WATER

1M

1M

2M

Figure 14-1 Two cubic meters of water, one meter square and two meters high.

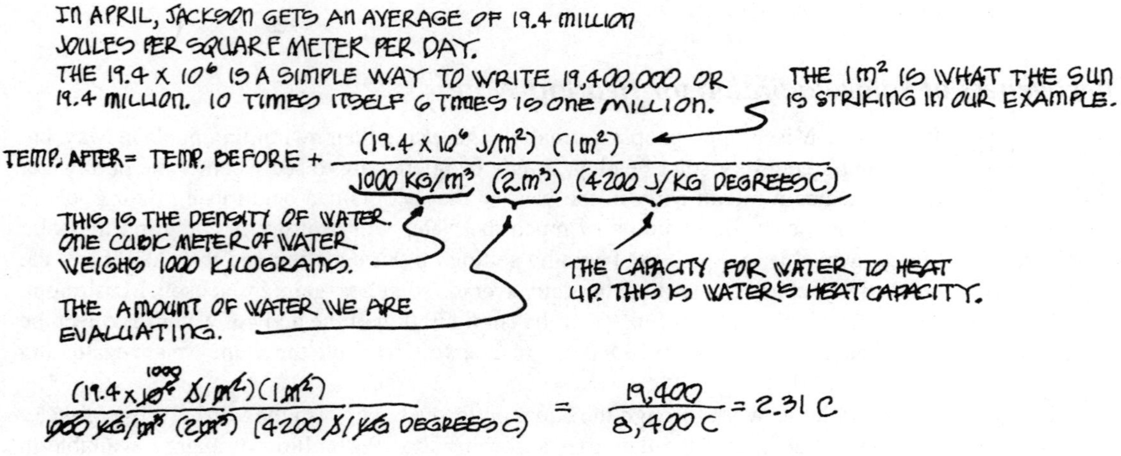

IN APRIL, JACKSON GETS AN AVERAGE OF 19.4 MILLION JOULES PER SQUARE METER PER DAY.

THE 19.4 X 10⁶ IS A SIMPLE WAY TO WRITE 19,400,000 OR 19.4 MILLION. 10 TIMES ITSELF 6 TIMES IS ONE MILLION.

THE 1M² IS WHAT THE SUN IS STRIKING IN OUR EXAMPLE.

$$\text{TEMP. AFTER} = \text{TEMP. BEFORE} + \frac{(19.4 \times 10^6 \text{ J/m}^2)(1 \text{ m}^2)}{1000 \text{ KG/m}^3 (2 \text{ m}^3)(4200 \text{ J/KG DEGREES C})}$$

THIS IS THE DENSITY OF WATER. ONE CUBIC METER OF WATER WEIGHS 1000 KILOGRAMS.

THE AMOUNT OF WATER WE ARE EVALUATING.

THE CAPACITY FOR WATER TO HEAT UP. THIS IS WATER'S HEAT CAPACITY.

$$\frac{(19.4 \times 10^6 \text{ J/m}^2)(1 \text{ m}^2)}{1000 \text{ KG/m}^3 (2 \text{ m}^3)(4200 \text{ J/KG DEGREES C})} = \frac{19,400}{8,400 \text{ C}} = 2.31 \text{ C}$$

Figure 14-2 Explanation of the equation.

Through the equation it can be deduced that a day's worth of sun in April will increase the heat in the 2 m³ of water by 2.31°C (3.6°F). The 2.31°C (36°F) is not a lot of heat gain, especially when considering that the existing water temperature in March was 65°F (18°C) and how much it needed to be increased to be comfortable for swimming. Consider, too, that the swimming pool will be exposed to the air and that heat loss from the pool water through convection, evaporation, and radiation will be occurring in the cooler springtime.

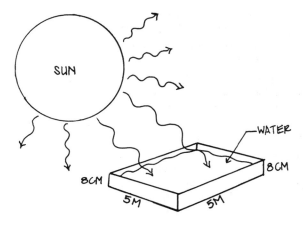

Figure 14-3 Two cubic meters of water, but flatter layout five meters square and eight centimeters high.

Now, let us see whether there is a difference in how much heat is absorbed if we change the shape of our collection medium by spreading out the water, rather than having a large cube of water with a surface area of only 1 m² (10.8 ft²). Let us take the 1 m² (10.8 ft²) surface area of the water and spread it out to a 5 m² (53.8 ft²) configuration. Spreading it out in a thinner layer, as shown in Figure 14-3, will expose five times more surface area of the water to the sun. We still have a total of 2 m³ (70.6 ft³) of water, but it is now only 8 cm (20 in.) deep. The 2 m³ (70.6 ft³) in the new configuration is computed like this:

$$5m \times 5m \times 8m^3 \quad \text{or} \quad 0.08m = 2m^3 \ (16 \text{ ft} \times 16 \text{ ft} \times 0.26 \text{ ft} = 70.6 \text{ ft}^3)$$

We will use the same equation to solve the problem. Only the surface expanse of the collection area will change, and it changes from 1 m² to 25 m² (10.8 ft² to 269 ft²).

$$T_{\text{after}} = T_{\text{before}} + \frac{(19.4 \times 10^6 \text{ J/M}^2)(25 \text{ M}^2)}{1000 \text{ K/m}^3 \ (2m^3) \ (4200 \text{ J/K °C})}$$

$$= \frac{485,000}{8400} = T_{\text{before}} + 57.74°C$$

CONCLUSION

By spreading the water from 1 m² (10.8 ft²) surface area to a 25 m² (269 ft²) surface area, the temperature of the water is raised by 57.74°C (136°F), an increase in 55°C (99°F) over the first solar collection configuration. That is quite a jump in heat absorption, and it tells us that the amount of surface area exposed to the sun is what created the greater absorption of heat. Recalling our intent to warm the pool earlier in the year so that people can swim comfortably, the pool was 65°F (18°C) in March, and an ideal temperature for swimming was 83°F (28°C). By creating solar panels where the shallow layers of water can absorb more heat, the pool water can be heated with the sun earlier in the year than when it would normally be ready for swimming. The solar panel can be an enclosed flat plate solar collector that protects the surface of the water from winds, evaporation, and cool springtime temperatures, and retains most of the sun's heat striking the panel. It can be concluded that there is a good chance that the sun can provide enough heat to sufficiently heat the pool water and extend the swimming season.

Other variables that influence how much water can be heated and how much heat will be retained in the water include whether the water is exposed to the air, the existing air temperature, exposure to winds, and evaporation. The heat that is waiting to be used in the water is being stored in its top layer, near the surface, where it is also easily lost. These issues must be considered in designing any solar energy capture system.

The example was offered to illustrate the amount of energy available in a day of sunshine. In an actual system, the temperature rise would be less than 57.74°C. Part of the solar radiation would be reflected both at the water surface and from the bottom of the pool. In addition, convection, evaporation, and radiation would remove heat from the pool. Nevertheless, it can be seen from the example that a useful amount of heat can be derived from the sun. The sun is a renewable and abundant energy resource that is waiting to be used.

Chapter 15

Controlling Heat Transfer
In and Out of Buildings

Transfer of heat in and out of buildings is, in most locations, the largest component of domestic energy consumption. Understanding and controlling heat transfer can substantially reduce energy use in most buildings.

Heat transfer refers to the ways in which heat moves from one place to another in the environment. Heat is transferred in a variety of ways. In regard to buildings, the mechanisms of heat transfer that matter to us are conduction, convection, radiation, and infiltration.

CONTROLLING HEAT TRANSFER IN BUILDINGS

By controlling the rate at which heat leaves our buildings during the heating season, and controlling the rate in which it enters during the cooling season, we can minimize both the amount of energy required to keep us comfortable and the quantity of waste products produced through the combustion of fossil fuels to extract the energy. The world in general and North America in particular are using energy (and producing combustion waste products) at a rate that is probably not sustainable (Figure 15-1). Controlling heat transfer in buildings is a logical way to decrease our use of this energy.

UNITS OF HEAT TRANSFER

In the following sections, we will be using two different unit systems to describe and predict heat transfer in buildings: the English and the metric. It is tempting to use just one system, but both are common for different applications and in different areas. Trying to replicate all calculations and specifications in both systems also has its disadvantages. Use of both unnecessarily complicates example calculations and obscures the concepts that are, in reality, more important than the numbers themselves. As a result, we use both unit systems but offer Table 15-1 to facilitate conversions between them.

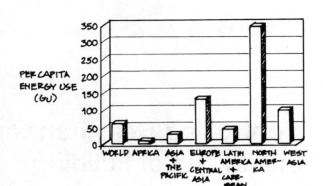

Figure 15-1 Per capita energy use in different parts of the world.

Table 15-1 Units of Common Heat Transfer Quantities and Factors Used for Interconversion

Name of Quantity	Metric	Conversion to English
Area	m^2	$ft^2 = m^2 / 10.76$
Conductance	$W/(m^2°C)$	$Btu/(hr\ ft^2°F) = 0.176\ (\ W/(m^2°C))$
Conduction coefficient	$W/(m°C)$	$Btu/(hr\ ft^2°F) = 0.578\ (\ W/(m°C))$
Convection coefficient	$W/(m^2°C)$	$Btu/(hr\ ft^2°F) = 0.176\ (\ W/(m^2°C))$
Density	$kg\ /\ m^3$	$lb\ /\ ft^3 = 0.062\ (kg\ /\ m^3)$
Length	m	$ft = m\ /\ 3.28$
Resistance	$m^2°C\ /\ W$	$hr\ ft^2°F\ /\ Btu = 5.68\ (m^2°C\ /\ W)$
Specific heat	$kJ\ /\ (kg°C)$	$Btu/(lb°F) = 0.239\ (kJ\ /\ (kg°C))$
Temperature	$°C$	$°F = (1.8°C) + 32$
Temperature difference	$°C$	$°F = 1.8°C$
Volume	m^3	$ft^3 = 35.3\ m^3$

THE BASICS OF HEAT TRANSFER

Heat moves in, out, and through buildings in a variety of ways. In trying to control this movement, it is helpful to understand the basic mechanisms by which it occurs. This section discusses the four mechanisms that matter the most in buildings: conduction, convection, radiation, and infiltration.

Thermal Energy

Thermal energy is energy that we perceive as "heat." All molecules in a solid material are in constant motion. Because they are in a solid, they can't go very far. Instead, they oscillate, or vibrate, more or less in place. The faster they oscillate, the hotter they feel to us. Molecules in a fluid, such as air or water, behave in a similar manner, except that their motion is less constrained. They can move about more, but because they are always bouncing off each other, their motion is quite erratic. Molecules of a warm fluid move with greater force and velocity than those of a cooler fluid, which is why the pressure increases in an air-filled container when you heat it. Molecules having a high thermal energy content feel "hot" because thermoreceptors in our bodies send signals to our brain that we interpret as warmth (hot) or coolness (cold). We measure thermal energy using instruments that change physically as the thermal energy content changes. The mercury in a thermometer expands as thermal energy increases. Temperature is the scale we have created to measure thermal energy.

The Second Law of Thermodynamics

The law of nature called the second law of thermodynamics can be stated in a number of ways. For our purposes, we will simply say that the direction of energy flow or transport is from a region of high energy toward a region of lower energy. Because temperature is our measuring scale for thermal energy, we can also say that thermal energy transport occurs from a region of higher temperature to a region of lower temperature. The amount of heat transferred will be directly proportional to the size of the temperature difference (i.e., larger temperature differences lead to higher rates of heat transfer within a particular object). This is important because it describes what will happen when there are differences in temperature within a space or an environment. In the summertime, a cool room in the morning may be warm by the afternoon because the higher thermal energy of the outdoor air will be transported indoors. When you walk into a cold house, your body becomes chilled because you lose heat (thermal energy) to your surroundings, including the cold air, cold walls and floor, and cold furniture.

Conduction

Conduction is the way heat is transferred in a solid. Heat transfer through a brick or a piece of wood is via conduction. As mentioned earlier, all molecules are in some form of motion as a result of their thermal energy content. The warmer molecules in a solid have a more vigorous oscillatory motion than cooler molecules. The warmer molecules "bump" the cooler molecules adjacent to them, increasing their rate of motion. In the process, the warmer molecules lose thermal energy and the cooler molecules gain it. In winter, the temperature of the inner side of the walls and roof of your house is greater than the temperature of the outer side; hence, heat is lost to the environment through the wall and roof material via conduction. In summer, the situation is reversed.

The amount of thermal energy transferred by conduction depends on the temperature difference across the solid, the width of the solid (measured along the direction of heat transfer), and the nature of the solid material. The temperature difference divided by the object width is called the temperature gradient. Increasing the temperature gradient increases heat transfer. As shown in Figure 15-2, you can decrease heat transfer by making the difference between the inner surface temperature and outer surface temperature $(T_{in} - T_{out})$ smaller or making the width (W) larger. The direction of heat transfer is from T_{in} to T_{out} if "$T_{in} - T_{out}$" is positive, and in the opposite direction if "$T_{in} - T_{out}$" is negative.

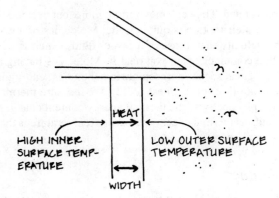

Figure 15-2 Heat conduction through a solid wall during the heating season.

The "nature of the material" referred to earlier is the intrinsic heat conducting capability of the material. For conduction, we can use a conduction coefficient, "k," to describe the ability of the material to conduct heat. The larger the k, the better the material conducts. In the metric system, the units of the conduction coefficient are W/(m°C) (watts per meter degree Celsius). If we factor the width of the material (w) into this, we have a commonly used descriptor called "conductance" (usually called U in product information). Conductance is just k/w and has units of W/(m²°C).

We can calculate the amount of heat transferred by conduction using the conduction coefficient and the temperature gradient (or conductance and the temperature difference):

$$q = k(T_{in} - T_{out})/w = U(T_{in} - T_{out})$$
$$Q = qA$$

where
- q = heat transfer per unit area (W/m²)
- k = conduction coefficient (W/(m°C))
- T = temperature (°C)
- w = width in the direction of heat transfer (m)
- U = conductance W/(m²°C)
- Q = total heat transfer (W)
- A = area (m²)

EXAMPLE 1. Glass conducts heat very readily: k = 5 W/(m°C). For a 0.5 cm (¹/₅ in.) pane of solid glass having an inside surface temperature (T_{in}) of 20°C and an outside surface temperature (T_{out}) of 5°C, find the heat transfer by conduction.

$$q = 5 \times (20 - 5)/0.005 = 15,000 \text{ W/m}^2$$

Notice that the glass width was converted to meters to keep units consistent. According to this solution, for every square meter of glass surface, 15,000 W will be transferred via conduction. *Note:* Actual heat transfer through single-pane glass in a home is actually much less than this. You will see why shortly.

The conduction equation can be rewritten to incorporate a useful concept; resistance (R):

$$q = (T_{in} - T_{out})/R, \text{ where } R = w/k$$

Notice that resistance is the inverse of conductance, $R = 1/U$. Resistance comes in handy when you have more than one kind of material in series, because resistances of individual materials in series can be added together to get the total resistance.

$$q = (T_1 - T_2)/(R_a + R_b + \ldots R_n)$$

where the subscripts $a, b, \ldots n$ refer to different materials. Note that although resistances can be added to get total resistance, conductances cannot be added to get total conductance.

EXAMPLE 2. Say we had a 10 cm (4 in.) wide brick butted up against a 2.5 cm (1 in.) piece of wood (Figure 15-3). The inside temperature, T_{in}, is still 20°C. The outside temperature, T_{out}, is still 5°C. Calculate conduction through this wall.

$$k_{brick} = 0.7 \text{ W}/(\text{m°C}) \qquad k_{wood} = 0.14 \text{ W}/(\text{m°C})$$
$$w_{brick} = 0.10 \qquad mw_{wood} = 0.025 \text{ m}$$
$$R_{brick} = 0.10/0.7 = 0.14(\text{m}^2\text{°C})/\text{W}$$
$$R_{wood} = 0.025/0.14 = 0.18(\text{m}^2\text{°C})/\text{W}$$
$$R_{total} = 0.14 + 0.18 = 0.32(\text{m}^2\text{°C})/\text{W}$$
$$q = (T_{in} - T_{out})/R_{total}$$
$$q = (20 - 5)/0.32 = 47 \text{ W/m}^2$$

This equation indicates that for each square meter of wall surface, 47 watts of power (47 joules of energy per second) will be lost to the outside.

Resistance (R) values are commonly used when discussing and comparing the insulating properties of materials. A material having a high R is a good insulator.

EXAMPLE 3. We have a 12 m² (129 ft²) wall made up of the board and brick from Example 2. We add 7.5 cm (3 in.) of fiberglass blanket insulation to the composite wall. Indoor and outdoor temperatures are as in Example 2. Calculate conduction heat transfer

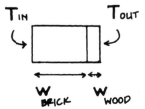

Figure 15-3 Conduction through a composite wall.

through this modified wall. The conduction coefficient of fiberglass insulation is about 0.045 W/(m°C).

$$R_{fiberglass} = 0.075 \text{ m}/0.045 \text{ W}/(m°C) = 1.67(m^2°C)/W$$
$$R_{total} = 1.67 + 0.14 + 0.18 = 1.99(m^2°C)/W$$
$$q = (20 - 5)/1.99 = 7.5 \text{ W}/m^2$$
$$Q = qA = 7.5 \times 12 = 90 \text{ W}$$

Notice that total heat transfer (Q) is just the transfer per square meter multiplied by the area of the wall. Adding 7.5 cm (3 in.) of insulation decreased conduction from 47 to 7.5 W/m² (or 84%).

Convection

The second mechanism of heat transfer that we will discuss is convection. Convection is a way that thermal energy can be transferred between a solid and a fluid (from the inside air to the inner wall surface of a house; from the outer wall surface to the outside air) or between two fluids (water and air). It differs from conduction in that one (or both) fluids are in motion over and above that which is caused by the thermal energy content of individual molecules.

Let's use the outside of a house in winter as an example (Figure 15-4). Air molecules that are in contact with the outer wall of the house are warmed by the heat that has been conducted through the walls. The warmed molecules are removed by the wind and replaced by colder molecules. The actual method by which thermal energy is transferred from the outer wall surface to the air molecules touching the wall is still conduction. The fact that there is a constantly renewed supply of "cold" molecules coming into position to receive the heat speeds the transfer process by keeping the temperature gradient greater than it would be in the absence of wind. This is convection.

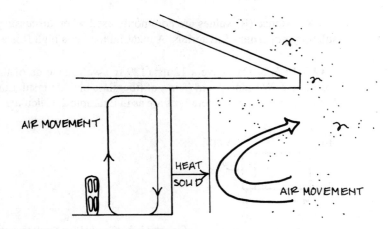

Figure 15-4 "Free" convection inside a house and "forced" convection outside a house.

When an external agency, like the wind, is moving the fluid molecules, the process is called "forced" convection. Another example of forced convection occurs when we use fans to cool (or warm) ourselves.

The movement of the fluid can also be caused by the heating or cooling process itself. Most fluids (air, water) change density as their heat content changes. They will become more or less buoyant than the surrounding fluid, depending on whether they are getter hotter (in most cases, less dense) or colder (in most cases, more dense). The air inside your house in winter is cooled by contact with an outer wall. It becomes denser than the air in the rest of the room, and so drops toward the floor, allowing warmer air to take its place next to the wall. This convective motion, caused by the density changes brought about by cooling (or heating) is especially noticeable near windows. It is intrinsically different from forced convection, because the energy to move the fluid does not have an external source. This is called "free" convection.

The amount of heat transferred via convection depends on the temperature difference between the solid and the fluid, the velocity of the moving fluid, and the kind of fluid involved. Free convection tends to transfer less heat than forced convection because of the relatively lower velocity of the fluid moved by buoyancy differences.

Convection heat transfer between a solid and a fluid can be calculated using a convection coefficient, "h":

$$q = h(T_{surface} - T_{fluid})$$
$$Q = qA$$

where q = convection heat transfer per unit area (W/m^2)

   h = convection coefficient (W/(m^2°C))

   $T_{surface}$ = temperature of the surface of the solid (°C)

   T_{fluid} = temperature of the fluid (°C)

   Q = total convection heat transfer (W)

   A = area of the surface experiencing convection (m^2)

Like the conduction equation, convection can be calculated using resistance:

$$R = 1/h$$

where R = the resistance to heat transfer at the convecting surface (m^2°C / W). All resistances, whether from conduction or convection, are additive. This is very helpful in solving practical problems.

In Example 1 we solved for heat transfer through a single-pane window using just conduction and the inner and outer air temperatures. The heat loss through the window was correct for the conditions given, but much larger than would be the case in a real home. In the following example, you will see how this problem can be made more realistic.

EXAMPLE 4. The room air temperature in a house is 20°C (68°F). The outdoor air temperature is 5°C (41°F). As in Example 1 of the previous section, heat is passing through a window having the following characteristics:

$$k_{window} = 5 \text{ W}/(\text{m}°\text{C}) \quad w_{window} = 0.005 \text{ m}$$

The convection coefficient on the inside of the window is 5.7 W/(m^2°C) and 34.0 W/(m^2°C) on the outside of the window (both of these are typical values). Calculate heat transfer from the room to the outside.

Solution:

$$R_{window} = 0.005/5 = 0.001 \text{ m}^2°\text{C/W}$$
$$R_{inside} = 1/5.7 = 0.175 \text{ m}^2°\text{C/W}$$
$$R_{outside} = 1/34 = 0.029 \text{ m}^2°\text{C/W}$$
$$R_{total} = 0.205$$
$$q = (20 - 5)/0.205 = 73 \text{ W/m}^2$$

This is a much lower transfer rate than we found in Example 1. Does this mean that the conduction equation we used in Example 1 is wrong? No, we just used the wrong numbers: We used air temperatures in Example 1 instead of the temperatures of the solid surfaces. We can determine the inner surface temperature of the glass:

$$(T_{inside \ air} - T_{inner \ surface})/R_{inside} = 73 \text{ W/m}^2 = (20 - T_{inner \ surface})/0.175$$

Solving for the inner surface temperature, we find that the temperature of the inner surface of the glass is about 7.2°C. Doing the same thing for the outside temperature, we find that the outer surface temperature is slightly more than 7.1°C . The surface temperatures are really quite a bit different from the air temperatures, and this is because of convection. You can see that ignoring convection in this problem leads to huge errors.

Radiation

Radiation refers to the transport of energy in small "packets" called photons. All objects in the universe (with the exception of black holes) continually radiate photons. A photon is radiated (released) whenever an electron drops from a higher energy position in an atom to a lower energy position (Figure 15-5).

Photons do not all carry the same amount of energy. Some photons transport smaller quantities of energy; some transport larger quantities. In general, the energy range (or

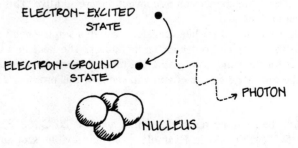

Figure 15-5 Radiation of a photon from an atom.

GAMMA RAYS	ULTRA-VIOLET	INFRARED
RADIO	XRAYS	VISIBLE MICROWAVE

HIGH ENERGY————————→LOW ENERGY

Figure 15-6 Photons are grouped according to energy.

spectrum) of the radiated photons depends on the temperature of the object doing the radiating. Photons from our sun, and other stars, radiate a spectrum of photons that include very high energy photons, such as gamma rays and X rays, to very low energies, such as infrared waves and radio waves (Figure 15-6). About half the photons from our sun fall into the range of energies that we can detect with our eyes (e.g., visible light—red through violet). A wood fire, having a much lower temperature than the sun, radiates mostly in the infrared (IR) range, with a smaller percentage of photons in the visible range and no high-energy photons at all (e.g., ultraviolet, X ray). We humans and most of our surroundings are relatively cool and radiate in the IR range and below (which is why we, and our surroundings, don't glow).

As mentioned earlier, the energy range of radiated photons and the total amount of energy radiated depend mainly on the temperature of the radiating body. Temperature, however, is not the only factor that influences the amount of energy transported this way. The characteristics of the radiating (and absorbing) material play a big part in the quantity of energy lost or received.

All photons that strike an object are reflected, absorbed, or pass through the object (Figure 15-7). There are many illustrations of this in the world. We see the objects in our room because at least some of the photons that hit the objects are reflected. We see that the objects have colors because only a portion of the "visible light" photons are reflected. An object is red because most of the photons in the red color range that hit it are reflected while most of the photons in other color ranges are absorbed. Only the photons that are absorbed can cause an object to get hotter. Photons that are reflected or pass through a material add no thermal energy to that material. We see objects through a window because most of the photons in the visible energy range pass through the glass.

When estimating radiation heat transfer for design and analysis, we can include the characteristics of the radiating/absorbing bodies by using *transmittance, absorbance, emittance,* and *reflectance* (*albedo* is another term for reflectance).

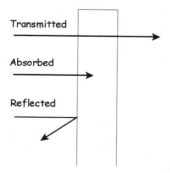

Transmitted

Absorbed

Reflected

Figure 15-7 Photons that strike an object can pass through, be absorbed, or be reflected.

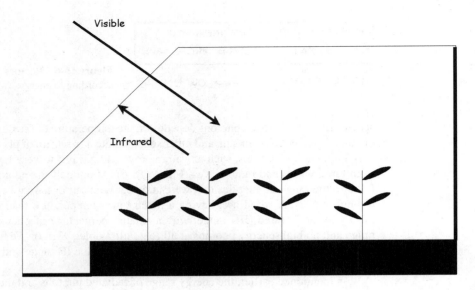

Figure 15-8 Differing transmittances and absorbances in the visible and IR ranges cause the "greenhouse effect."

Conventional window glass has a high transmittance for photons in the visible energy range. Reflectance and absorbance are relatively low. In the IR range, however, absorbance is high and transmittance low (i.e., most photons in the IR range are absorbed by the glass and do not pass through it). This is the origin of the phrase "greenhouse effect" (Figure 15-8). More than half of the solar radiation energy that reaches the earth's surface is in the visible range. Most of these photons pass through the glass. If the material under the glass has a high absorbance, then many of the photons will be absorbed. The absorbing material will radiate relatively low-energy IR photons, which cannot pass through the glass. A portion of this "trapped" thermal energy will escape via conduction through the glass to the outside, but a sizable portion will be reradiated back inside. In this way, the inside of a greenhouse, or a windowed room, will experience and maintain a higher thermal energy than would otherwise be the case.

Emittance is a measure of the ability of a material to radiate photons. Most shingles used on the roofs of houses have a high absorbance for light in the visible range and a low emittance in the IR range. These characteristics enhance the collection of solar radiation and impede its reradiation to the surroundings. This is helpful in cooler regions, where heating load is greater than cooling load. It is a disadvantage in warmer regions, where cooling load predominates. Summer roof temperature in the southern United States may be 30°C (85°F) warmer than air temperature.

Like roof shingles, low emissivity ("low-e") glass has a low emittance in the IR range. This helps to conserve heat in a home during winter by decreasing the heat loss to the outside by radiation. Low emissivity in a particular wavelength range also corresponds to low absorbance in that range as well. Therefore, low-e glass also prevents outside long wave radiation from being absorbed by the window (it's reflected). This is particularly helpful in summer, when heated surroundings radiate a great deal of IR.

Infiltration

Infiltration refers to air exchange with the outdoors in a building. Whenever a door to the outside of a building is opened, some indoor air escapes and is replaced by outdoor air. Infiltration can come through in many places: windows, openings between the floor and doors, fireplaces, electrical outlets, and unsealed seams in walls. Infiltration always increases heating and cooling loads because of the necessity of either heating or cooling the outdoor air to indoor conditions.

Ventilation refers to infiltration rates that have been designed into the structure for health reasons. Some air exchange is necessary for the well-being of inhabitants. *Leakage* refers to inadvertent air exchanges due to normal activities (opening windows and doors) and poorly sealed seams in the building envelope (e.g., openings around the edges of doors, windows, etc.).

Infiltration rates are most frequently expressed as air changes per hour (ACH). The term is usually applied to the volume of the entire house. An infiltration rate of 1 ACH means that a volume equivalent to the entire house volume has been exchanged with the outdoors in a period of an hour. For new construction, typical residential infiltration rates are about 0.25 to 0.35 ACH. Very well sealed homes have a rate of 0.20 ACH or less. Estimates of average infiltration rates of U.S. homes fall between 0.6 and 1.1 ACH. In summer, infiltration can be the single largest load placed on cooling systems. It should be noted that older homes and low-income housing can have infiltration rates that are three or more times the national average.

It is possible to estimate the heating or cooling load caused by infiltration:

$$Q_{infil} = ACH \times V \times \rho \times Cp \times \Delta T$$

where
$$
\begin{aligned}
Q_{infil} &= \text{energy to be removed (in Btu or kJ)} \\
V &= \text{volume of interior (heated or cooled; in ft}^3 \text{ or m}^3) \\
\rho &= \text{density of air (in lbm/ft}^3 \text{ or kg/m}^3) \\
Cp &= \text{specific heat of air (Btu/(lbm} \times °F) \text{ or kJ/(kg} \times °C)) \\
\Delta T &= \text{temperature difference between outside and indoor air}
\end{aligned}
$$

EXAMPLE 5. A house has an infiltration rate of 1 ACH. Calculate the infiltration cooling load of this house if its volume is 283 m³ (about 10,000 ft³), the outside air temperature is 35°C (95°F), and the indoor temperature is held at 22°C (72°F). The density and specific heat of air at room temperature are 1.18 kg/m³ and 1.01 kJ/(kg × °C).

$$Q = 1 \text{ ACH} \times 283 \text{ m}^3 \times 1.18 \text{ kg/m}^3 \times 1.01 \text{ kJ/(kg} \times °C) \times (35 \text{ C} - 22 \text{ C}) = 4400 \text{ kJ/hr}$$

In English units, this value is about 4250 Btu/hr, which is roughly equivalent to dedicating a window unit air conditioner to infiltration alone.

INSULATION

In the section of this chapter on conduction, you saw that every material has some thermal insulating properties. The resistance of a material to conduction heat transfer (R) was equal to w/k, where w was the thickness of the material (in the direction of heat flow) and k was its thermal conductivity. By putting any material in series with the other materials in a wall (as in Examples 2 and 3), it was possible to increase the total resistance of the wall and, consequently, its resistance to heat transfer.

Certain materials are manufactured and used in walls, roofs, and floors solely because their thermal conductivities are so low (and their resistances are so great). Such materials are thermal insulators. In most cases, these insulators work by creating still pockets of air that impede heat transfer. Air has a very low thermal conductivity when it is held in place (when it is not held in place, the air transfers heat via convection, which increases heat transfer). In some advanced insulators, inert gases, such as argon, replace air as the main insulator. The inert gases have thermal conductivities even lower than that of air and so provide even greater resistance to conduction.

We can compare the performance of thermal insulators by looking at their resistances. The R value for a particular insulator is the same R that we have been talking about (w/k). In the United States, where the English system of units is still widely used, R has units of $°F \times ft^2 \times h / Btu$ (degrees Fahrenheit times square feet times hour over Btu). In areas where the metric system predominates, R is expressed as $°C \times m^2/W$. The two can be converted back and forth according to the following:

$$R_{metric} = R_{English} \times 0.176$$

The R values of insulators are usually given for specific thicknesses (3 in., 6 in., etc.) or per inch of thickness.

Insulating Ceilings, Floors, and Walls

Insulation comes in many forms, including batts, blankets, rolls, rigid board, loose fill, sprayed foam, and reflective insulators.

- Batts (Figure 15-9a) are precut, with multiple batts packaged together.

- Rolls (Figure 15-9b) are not precut but, as implied by the name, are sold rolled up. Batts and rolls are designed (and sized) to be installed between studs (vertical 2 × 4s or 2 × 6s in walls) and joists (horizontal 2 × 6s or 2 × 8s in ceilings and floors). They usually have a facing that acts as a vapor barrier.

- Blankets, like batts, are precut but do not have a facing. Their purpose is to sit over existing insulation, mainly in attic floors.

- Rigid board insulation (Figure 15-9c) can be used in many parts of a building. It is used below and on the sides of slabs and along basement walls. It can be used under siding and can be placed on the inside of studs, beneath the wallboard.

- Loose-fill insulation is poured or blown into open spaces in walls, floors, or ceilings. There is a wet spray technique that combines the loose insulation fill with a binder. This promotes adhesion at the location of use and makes the entire application process less dusty and difficult.

(a)   BATT INSULATION   (b)   ROLL INSULATION

(c)   RIGID BOARD INSULATION   (d)   FOAM INSULATION

Figure 15-9   Some of the different types of insulation used in buildings.

- Spray foam (Figure 15-9d) is often used in combination with batts and blankets to enhance the overall insulation, or it can be used by itself (it is the best of the insulators but is also the most expensive to use).
- Reflective insulation differs from the aforementioned types in that it has little effect on conduction heat transfer. As implied by the name, reflective insulation has one or two reflective surfaces and a low emissivity (low tendency to radiate heat when warm). It is usually placed just inside the outer shell of the building and creates a "radiant barrier." If the reflective surface is directed away from the house interior, it reduces radiation heat transfer from the heated outer shell of the building during periods of warm weather. If directed toward the interior of the

building, it helps to prevent heat loss due to radiation in winter. If the insulator has two reflective faces, it does both. Reflective insulators appear to be most effective in areas where cooling makes up a large part of energy usage. Tests indicate that they can reduce cooling load by 2 to 15% in such areas.

These insulation materials are available in a range of thicknesses. The thickness actually used is often dictated by building design. A fiberglass batt for 2 × 4 studs cannot be much thicker than 3.5 in. (you cannot compress insulators without decreasing their insulation properties). Rigid boards to be used under wallboards cannot be much more than an inch or so, because nails must be able to adequately penetrate the underlying wood.

Table 15-2 provides resistance values per inch for many insulating materials currently available.

Recommended R Values for Walls and Roofs

The U.S. Department of Energy has recommendations for insulation for ceilings, walls, and floors, based on the heating requirements for different parts of the country. The recommendations are quite uniform for most locations:

Attics	R49
Cathedral ceilings	R38
Walls	R18
Floors	R25

Heat Transfer Through Windows

Windows are a weak link in our building envelope. We want to allow daylight into our homes, we want to be able to see what is outside, and we want to be able to conveniently allow fresh air in on a nice day. A window does all this for us. On the other hand, there is no way that a thin piece of glass can thermally perform like an R18 wall. The resistance of single-pane clear glass can be less than 1 h °F ft^2/Btu. By having windows, we deliberately design heat leaks into our buildings. These leaks can be large, accounting for as much as 30% of the heating and cooling energy use in residences.

Over the last 20 years or so, a lot of work has been done to find ways to reduce unwanted heat loss or gain through windows. Heat passes through windows in almost every possible way:

- Heated air can pass through gaps in the window frames (contributing to infiltration).

- Heat can pass through the glass and frame via conduction.

- Heat can pass through the glass via radiation (longer wavelength infrared and shorter wavelength visible light). Some of the infrared spectrum is absorbed on the outside and reradiated inside (or vice versa). Other wavelengths in the infrared range simply pass right through (glass is not a perfect absorber of IR).

Table 15-2 Insulating Values of Various Materials

Material	R Value per Inch (h °F ft² / Btu)
Loose Fill	
Cellulose	3.5
Fiberglass	2.2
Rock wool	2.9
Batts, Blankets, and Roll	
Fiberglass	3.2
Rock wool	3.6
Boards	
Cellular glass	2.6
Mineral fiber with binder	3.5
Polyurethane, Polyisocyanurate	
No facing	6.0
With facing	7.4
Fiberglass	4.3
Expanded Polystyrene	
Extruded	5.0
Molded	4.2
Wood fiber	2.3
Foam (Polyurethane or polyisocynurate, applied at site)	6.0

Source: University of Florida Extension.

Window performance in all of these areas has been improved. Conduction heat transfer has been reduced by the introduction of thermal-pane glass. By using two or three panes of glass separated by insulated air spaces (space size 1/2 to 5/8 in. for best performance), the window's R value has been increased. Moreover, this system has been refined by adding an inert gas to the air space that further reduces conduction between the panes (space size 1/2 in. for argon, 1/4 in. for krypton). When multiple panes are used, spacers must be employed at the edges to separate the panes. Aluminum has commonly been used for this purpose. Because aluminum is a poor insulator, the spacers have allowed additional heat transfer at the window edges and have promoted condensation between the panes (which can harm window performance). Manufacturers have begun to produce windows that use spacers made from materials with insulating properties.

A number of film coatings and tintings have been attempted so as to reduce radiant heat transfer through the glass. The most successful of these have been the low-e coatings. About 84% of the relatively long-wave IR radiation is absorbed when it strikes a window (much of the rest is reflected). In an uncoated single-pane window, much of the absorbed energy is conducted to the other side and reradiated outward. In winter, this means that heat is being lost to the outside through the glass. A low-e coating is (usually) a metal oxide that is applied to the glass surface. If applied to the inner surface of the glass, it increases the reflectance of the glass for IR to 90% or better. This means that absorbance is 10% or less (down from about 84%). This greatly reduces the radiation heat loss through the windows ("low emittance" glass could just as easily have been called "low absorbance" or "high IR reflectance" glass). In areas having large cooling needs in summer, the same approach can reduce long-wave transport into a house from hot surroundings. In this case, a low-e coating is placed on the side of the glass facing outside. This approach can be taken, however, only when using the multiple-pane windows described earlier. The coatings currently used are not resilient enough to stand up to the elements, so the outward-facing layer must face the air- or gas-filled space between the panes. The so called first-generation low-e coatings measurably reduced the amount of visible light allowed through a window. Second-generation coatings (called "spectrally selective") perform as well or better than earlier low-e glass and allow more visible light to make it though.

In the days when window glass had poor thermal performance, there was little motivation to reduce heat transfer through the frames. With the improvements cited here, however, it became increasingly useful to reduce transfer through the nonglass portions as well. Currently, there are frames available made from aluminum, vinyl, fiberglass, and wood, as well as combinations of these materials. In general, aluminum frames are the poorest insulators. Fiberglass frames are relatively new and appear to offer the highest R values. Wood and vinyl are intermediate insulators.

In comparing the performance of windows, the following terms are frequently used:

- *Conductance* (also called U factor), discussed under "Conduction," is the inverse of resistance. A low conductance is the same as a high R value and indicates good insulating properties.

- *Solar heat gain coefficient* (SHGC) is the fraction of incident solar radiation admitted through a window (directly transmitted or absorbed and subsequently reradiated). SHGC has a value between 0 and 1. The lower a window's SHGC, the less solar heat it transmits.

- *Visible transmittance* (VT) indicates the amount of visible light transmitted through a window. VT has a value between 0 and 1. The higher the VT, the more light in the visible range is transmitted.

Table 15-3 compares performances of a variety of window types, with respect to conduction (U factor), prevention of solar gain (SGHC), and transmission of visible light (VT).

Window frames and sashes make up 10 to 30% of the window area, so the thermal characteristics of the frame are important components of overall window performance. There are many frame types manufactured and sold. Each has its strengths and weaknesses, and the various types are attractive for particular applications. Our discussion here is limited to thermal characteristics.

Aluminum frames perform most poorly from a thermal perspective because of their high thermal conductivity (Table 15-4). Thermal performance of aluminum frames can be improved markedly by constructing the inner and outer portions of the frame as separate units and then joining them with an insulating material between (providing a "thermal break"). Wood, wood-clad, vinyl, and "hybrid and composite" (made of combinations of and variations on these materials) frames exhibit similar thermal characteristics and are intermediate in performance. The use of insulated vinyl or fiberglass frames

Table 15-3 Performances of Window Types

These data are for the center of the glass only (do not take into account the frame or spacers) and so should not be used to select a particular window.

Window Type	U Factor	SGHC	VT (No Frame)
Clear glass, single pane	1.11	0.86	0.90
Clear glass, double pane (air-filled space)	0.49	0.76	0.81
Low-e coating facing in only, double pane, argon-filled space	0.30	0.71	0.75
Low-e coating facing in and out, double pane, argon-filled space*	0.25	0.39	0.70
Low-e coating facing in and out, triple pane, argon-filled space*	0.13	0.33	0.56

* Spectrally selective

Source: Efficient Windows Cooperative.

Table 15-4 Whole Window Thermal Performance Using Various Frame Types

Frame Type	Two-Pane (Double-Glazed) Clear Glass Separated by an Air Gap		
	U Factor	SGHC	VT
Aluminum	0.79	0.68	0.67
Aluminum with thermal break	0.64	0.62	0.62
Wood	0.49	0.56	0.58
Wood clad	0.49	0.56	0.58
Vinyl	0.49	0.56	0.58
Hybrid and composite	0.49	0.56	0.58
Insulated vinyl	0.44	0.59	0.62
Fiberglass	0.44	0.59	0.62
Frame Type	Three-Pane (Triple-Glazed) Low-e (Spectrally Selective) Glass Separated by Argon- or Krypton-Filled Gaps		
	U Factor	SGHC	VT
Wood	0.24	0.25	0.40
Wood clad	0.24	0.25	0.40
Vinyl	0.24	0.25	0.40
Hybrid and composite	0.24	0.25	0.40
Insulated vinyl	0.17	0.26	0.43
Fiberglass	0.17	0.26	0.43

Source: Efficient Windows Cooperative.

reduces conductance somewhat. Both fiberglass and insulated vinyl have their hollow cavities filled with insulation.

The thermal performance of windows has clearly come a long way. Top-performing windows now have a resistance to conduction of nearly 6 h °F ft²/Btu (as compared with about 1 h °F ft² / Btu for older units) and have greatly reduced radiant heat gain as well. Although still not comparable to an R18 wall, they have become more manageable energy leaks in the building envelope.

WEATHERIZING

Infiltration, as discussed earlier, is the rate at which exterior air replaces interior air. This replacement contributes to heating or cooling load, because the outdoor air must then be heated or cooled to inside conditions. Ventilation is "planned infiltration." Some daily air exchange is desirable (0.2 to 0.35 ACH). Unplanned infiltration is "leakage." Air leaks in and out of residences in a variety of ways (Figure 15-10). In an average residence, leakage can account for 10% of heating and cooling loads. In homes having high leakage rates, the percentage can be much greater.

Interestingly, infiltration rates at a particular moment depend partly on the pressure difference between outdoor and indoor air. On windy days, short-term pressure increases outside the building envelope (caused by gusts of wind) can markedly increase the rate at which outside air enters a building (see Chapter 21, which discusses the use of landscaping to reduce home energy use). These are the best days for finding air leaks. Locate the leak by moving an incense stick, a lit match (with care), or your hand around potential leak locations to identify places that need attention.

Plugging and Preventing Leaks

There are a variety of ways to minimize leaks in houses.

- *Caulking.* Caulking (Figure 15-11) is often required wherever two different materials or parts of the house meet. This can be around the outside of door frames, windows, chimneys, and foundation sills. On the interior, caulk (or otherwise seal) locations where plumbing enters the building envelope.

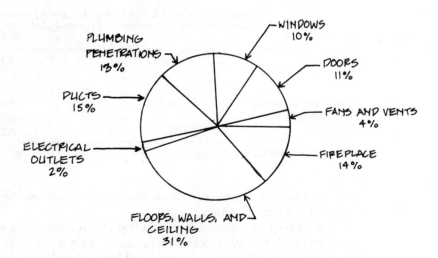

Figure 15-10 Sources of heat leaks in a typical residence. (*Source:* U.S. Department of Energy.)

Figure 15-11 Caulking at the junction of different parts of the house.

- *Sealing around doors.* There are many ways to seal around the edges of doors. These include the use of insulated door stops (purchased as a unit or with insulation added), door sweeps, metal spring or plastic thresholds, and strips of various sorts.

- *Sealing windows.* Older wooden windows don't always seat snugly in the sill. Felt/foam strips can be helpful for sealing these leaks (Figure 15-12). Rubber seals on other types of windows begin to fail as they age. Often, these seals can be replaced.

- *Fireplace.* A fireplace can be a major source of cold air leakage into a house. Make sure that your damper seats properly in the flue. A tightly fitting glass fire screen provides an additional seal.

- *Electrical outlets.* If an electrical outlet is a source of leakage, turn off the power to the outlet, remove the outlet cover, and apply expanding insulating foam to the space around the outlet (available from most hardware stores). Be careful—even "nonexpanding" varieties expand quite a bit. A little goes a long way, and the foam is sticky and hard to clean if misapplied.

- *Ducts.* Exposed ductwork can leak around junctions, wasting both heated and cooled air. Sealants used on ducts age and can fail, and the old stand-by, duct tape, has been shown, in government tests, to be unreliable for this purpose. The same tests showed that foil-backed tape, mastic, injected aerosol sealant, and even clear plastic (package) tape performed quite well to prevent leakage from ducts.

Figure 15-12 Application of self-adhering strip to bottom of window.

Chapter 16

Determining Sun Path

Knowing how to plot the exact location of the sun any day of the year and any time of the day will enable the designer and the engineer to control the heat and light emitted by the sun. Blocking sun heat during the summer can save 30 to 50% on air-conditioning bills. Collecting sun heat can provide 30 to 100% of hot water needs and 20 to 100% of interior space heating needs.

Because the sun provides a significant amount of energy (heat) each day, it is important that we understand how to plot its location so that heat can be absorbed during the heating season and blocked during the cooling season. This chapter discusses how to locate the angle of the sun any time of the day, any day of the year. With that knowledge, you will be able to:

- Site shelters to take maximum advantage of warm winter sunshine
- Site shelters to avoid the summer solar heat buildup
- Design shelter overhangs to allow solar heat gain only during the heating season
- Design shelter overhangs to block sun during the cooling season
- Locate and design outdoor spaces to extend their use during the wintertime
- Locate trees so that they will not interrupt the flow of heat to shelters and outdoor spaces during the heating season
- Locate trees to block the sun on shelter sides and outdoor use areas during the summer

To be able to accomplish these tasks accurately, you will need to compute sun angles for the specific location you are evaluating. To compute sun angles, you must be knowledgeable about latitudes, solar declinations, the solar altitude and azimuth chart, and the analemma chart.

LATITUDES, SUN ANGLES, AND SOLAR HEAT

The earth is divided into latitude lines that enable us to locate areas on the earth and their relationship to the equator (see Figure 16-1). These latitude lines are parallel to the equator line, which is at 0° latitude. The equator is a line or belt around the earth on which the noon sun angle is at 90°, or close to 90°, to the earth. The warm influence of the equator extends north of 0° latitude to the tropic of Cancer at 23 1/2° north latitude, and south of the equator to the tropic of Capricorn at 23 1/2° south latitude. Maximum sun angles north of the tropic of Cancer and south of the tropic of Capricorn will always be less than 90°. The farther away a location is from the equator, the smaller its noon sun angle will be to the earth. This, of course, affects the amount of solar heat, also called solar insolation, delivered to the earth. In Starkville, Mississippi, for example, the noon sun angle is 80° on June 22. This is also when the sun is at its highest point in the sky. On December 22, the noon sun is at an angle of 33°, the lowest point in the sky during the year. The dates of June 22 and December 22 are called the summer and winter solstice. *Solstice* is from the Latin, meaning "sun-stop." It refers to the dates of the extreme positions of the sun each year.

SOLAR DECLINATION

The word *declination* comes from the Latin *declinare,* which means "to fall away." Solar declinations are used to figure the decline of the sun angle north and south of the equator (see Figure 16-2). The declination of the sun is the latitude at which the sun strikes the earth at 90° on a given date. Note that the sun strikes the earth at 90°, at noon, only between the tropical areas on either side of the equator. To be exact, that range of latitudes is between 23°27' north latitude (almost 23 1/2°) and 23°27' south latitude. These latitudes, known as the tropic of Cancer and the tropic of Capricorn, are the imaginary lines that define the extent of the tropics, or the areas of the earth that are always experiencing

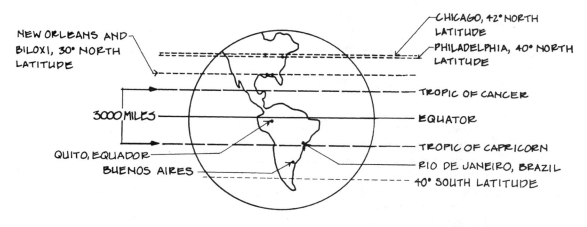

Figure 16-1 Latitude lines and the earth.

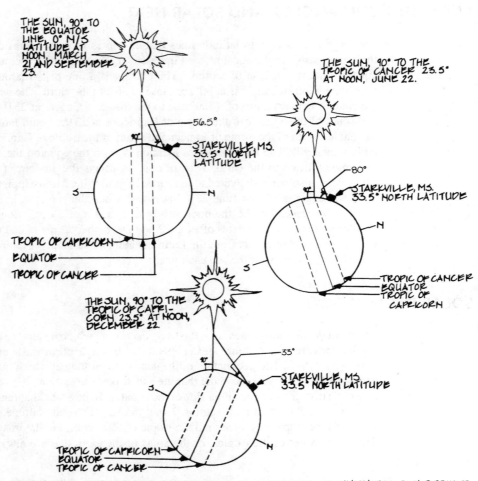

THE SUN, 90° TO THE EQUATOR LINE, 0° N/S LATITUDE AT NOON, MARCH 21 AND SEPTEMBER 23.

56.5°

90°

STARKVILLE, MS. 33.5° NORTH LATITUDE

S   N

TROPIC OF CAPRICORN
EQUATOR
TROPIC OF CANCER

THE SUN, 90° TO THE TROPIC OF CANCER 23.5° AT NOON, JUNE 22.

80°

STARKVILLE, MS. 33.5° NORTH LATITUDE

N

S

TROPIC OF CANCER
EQUATOR
TROPIC OF CAPRICORN

THE SUN, 90° TO THE TROPIC OF CAPRI-CORN 23.5° AT NOON, DECEMBER 22.

33°

90°

STARKVILLE, MS 33.5° NORTH LATITUDE

S

N

TROPIC OF CAPRICORN
EQUATOR
TROPIC OF CANCER

SOLAR DECLINATIONS ARE THE DATES AND LATITUDES AT WHICH THE SUN STRIKES THE EARTH AT A 90° ANGLE. THE LATITUDES ARE USED TO FIGURE NOON SUN ANGLES ANYWHERE ON EARTH.

Figure 16-2   Solar declinations and the earth.

summer. As the earth tilts, seasonal weather occurs because of the change in the amount of light and heat (energy) from the sun. Everyone gets to experience seasons except the people living in the tropics near the equator, where their climate is warm all the time. To explain what is happening when the earth is tilting to create the seasons, consider the motion when you shake your head up and down in agreement. If your head were the earth, the tilting up and down is what is happening when the Northern and Southern Hemispheres tilt toward and away from the sun, creating warm and cold seasons. This is especially true for areas far above and below the equator, like the top of your head and your chin. One complete nod up and down is the equivalent of one year of the earth's tilting and a complete year of seasons.

When North America tilts toward the sun, noon sun angles for the lower states can reach almost 90° and a lot of sun heat (energy) is received. While this is happening, the lower portion of South America is having its version of winter because the noon sun angles are low in the sky and solar heat is not intense. It gets so cold in southern portions of the South American country of Chile that there is even a healthy population of penguins. As winter comes to an end in South America, the earth tilts the opposite way and the noon sun angle in North America becomes low in the sky, and wintertime occurs. The noon sun in southern parts of South America moves higher in the sky, bathing the area with warmth and creating summertime. The latitudes or declinations where the sun strikes the earth at a 90° angle on a given date are listed in Table 16-1.

We will use these declinations to help figure the exact noon sun angles for any location in the world. The process for computing sun angles will be revealed shortly.

SOLAR AZIMUTHS

The solar azimuth is the distance of the sun, in degrees, from true north. Exact north has an azimuth of 0°. Due east has an azimuth of 90°, due south has an azimuth of 180° and due west has an azimuth of 270°. Solar azimuths change throughout the day. Early in the morning the sun may be at a 75° azimuth, at midday it is near a 180° azimuth, and when the sun sets in the summer it is probably at about a 300° azimuth. With true north being 0°, when the sun rises at 5:15 A.M. in Biloxi, Mississippi, on June 22, the solar azimuth is 62°. At 10:00 A.M., the sun is at an azimuth of 96°, and at noon it is at a 180° azimuth. At 3:00 P.M., the sun is at an azimuth of 272°, and it sets at about 6:50 P.M. at an azimuth of 297°. As seen in Figure 16-3, the solar azimuth shown in plan view allows the designer to locate and design shelters and outdoor spaces with maximum consideration of the heat and light from solar energy.

Table 16-1 Solar Declination

(The latitude at which the sun strikes the earth at 90° on a specific date.)

Latitude	Date	
+23° 27′	June 22	Tropic of Cancer
+20°	May 21	
+15°	May 1	
+10°	April 16	
0°	Mar. 21/Sept. 21	Equator
− 5°	Mar. 8	
− 10°	Feb. 23	
− 15°	Feb. 9	
− 20°	Jan. 22	
− 23° 27′	Dec. 22	Tropic of Capricorn

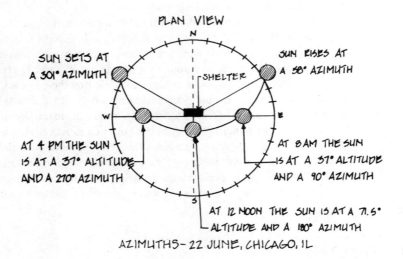

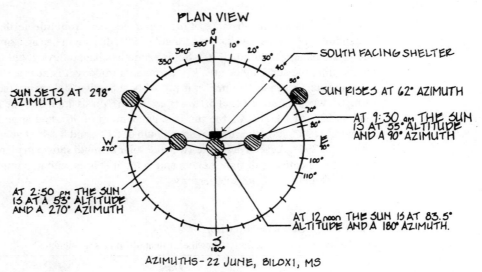

Figure 16-3 Solar azimuths in Biloxi, MS and Chicago, IL.

MOVEMENT OF THE SUN

It is generally true that the sun rises in the east and sets in the west. But did you know that on June 22 the sun rises at about 5:00 A.M. and that you get sun on the north sides of shelters until about 8:30 A.M.? Of course, the exact duration of time depends on your latitude. Examine the movement of the sun for Biloxi in Figure 16-4. The sun on the

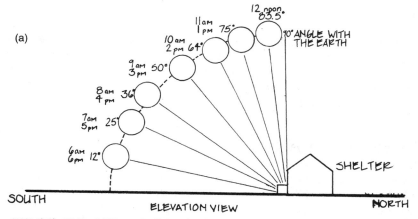

(a)

12 noon
83.5°

11 am
1 pm 75°

10 am
2 pm 64°

90° ANGLE WITH
THE EARTH

9 am
3 pm 50°

8 am
4 pm 36°

7 am
5 pm 25°

6 am
6 pm 12°

SHELTER

SOUTH

ELEVATION VIEW

NORTH

ANALEMA SAYS JUNE 22 DECLINATION FOR BILOXI, MS IS 23.5° NORTH
LATITUDE. TO COMPUTE NOON SUN ANGLE: 23.5° NORTH LATITUDE —
(+ 30° NORTH LATITUDE)= 6.5°+ 90° = 83.5° SUN ANGLE

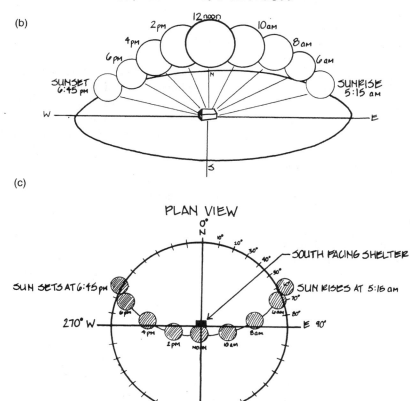

(b)

12 noon

2 pm   10 am

4 pm   8 am

6 pm   6 am

SUNSET
6:45 pm

SUNRISE
5:15 am

W ⸱

N

E

S

(c)

PLAN VIEW

0°
N

10°
20°
30°
40°
50°

SOUTH FACING SHELTER

SUN SETS AT 6:45 pm

SUN RISES AT 5:16 am

6 pm

70°
80°

6 am

270° W

4 pm

2 pm

NOON

10 am

8 am

E 90°

S
180°

SUN PATH & TIMES OF DAY

Figure 16-4 Sun path diagrams for Biloxi, Mississippi—June 22, (a) elevation view throughout day; (b) sun path—3D view; (c) solar azimuths.

longest day of the year in the Northern Hemisphere reaches a high point of 83 1/2° above the horizon at noon in Biloxi, and it sets at about 7:00 P.M. in the northwest. From December 22, the winter extreme, to June 22, the summer extreme, the sun rises in the southeast and sets in the southwest. December 22 is the shortest day of the year, and June 22 is the longest.

COMPUTING NOON SUN ANGLES

Computing sun angles is necessary in order to make sound decisions about the good and bad effects of sun heat gain. The variables needed to determine sun angles include the dates of the beginning and end of the cooling and heating seasons and the sun declinations on those dates. Interestingly, sun angles can also be used to discover whether to site a football field on an east-west axis instead of the usual north-south axis, or to determine where to locate a raised-bed biointensive garden for maximum sun exposure throughout the day.

After selecting dates for which to develop sun angles, begin with establishing the latitude of the site's location. Then refer to the solar azimuth and altitude charts or the analemma chart (see Figure 16-6) that is used to give declinations for each day of the year. After the dates have been selected and declinations have been determined, find the difference between the declination and the latitude of your location. Then take that number and add it to 90° to get the noon sun angle for the project in your latitude. The resulting sun angle can be used to plot and determine overhangs, tree locations, window locations, and outdoor use areas. Table 16-2 is a summary of the steps taken to compute sun angles. In Table 16-3 sun angles are computed using steps 1–5. Sun angles for different dates are computed in Table 16-3.

Let us compute sun angles for Biloxi, Mississippi, which is at 30° north latitude (Table 16-4). We want to know what the sun path will be on June 22, the summer solstice (solstice = sun-stop). Looking at the solar altitude and azimuth chart for 30° north latitude, we see that the sun is at a declination of +23 1/2° (23°27' to be exact) on June 22. We could have looked at the analemma and gotten the same figure. Now we need to relate this declination to Biloxi's latitude. Because the northernmost latitude where the noon sun could be at 90° is at 23 1/2° north latitude, and Biloxi is at 30° north latitude, we must

Table 16-2   Steps for Computing Sun Angles

1. Find the latitude of the area for which you want to determine sun angles.
2. Determine the dates for which you want to evaluate sun angles.
3. Consult the analemma chart or solar azimuth and altitude chart and find the latitude (or declination) where the noon sun will hit the earth at 90° at the selected dates.
4. Find the difference between the solar declination and the latitude of the area you are evaluating.
5. Add that result to 90° to figure noon sun angles .

Table 16-3 Computing Sun Angles for Mississippi State University, 33 1/2° NL

Date	Declination	Mississippi State Latitude		Noon Sun Angle
Jan. 10	−22° south latitude	− (+33 1/2° north latitude)	= −55 1/2° + 90°	= 34 1/2° sun angle
Jan. 28	−18 1/2° south latitude	− (+33 1/2° north latitude)	= −52° + 90°	= 38° sun angle
May 23	+20 1/2° north latitude	− (+33 1/2° north latitude)	= −13° + 90°	= 77° sun angle
Aug. 19	+13° north latitude	− (+33 1/2° north latitude)	= −20 1/2° + 90°	= 69 1/2° sun angle
Nov. 8	−16° south latitude	− (+33 1/2° north latitude)	= −49 1/2° + 90°	= 40 1/2° sun angle

Notes: When solar declinations are south of the equator they are negative, and when north of the equator they are positive.
 • Find the difference between the solar declination (latitude) and Mississippi State's latitude.
 • Latitudes north of the tropic of Cancer and south of the tropic of Capricorn will always have a sun angle less than 90°.
 • Add the difference to 90° to get the noon sun angle.
 • Noon sun angles in North America are low in the sky when the sun is south of the equator and high when the sun is north of the equator.

now compute the difference between the two latitudes so as to determine the less-than-90° noon sun angle that will occur in Biloxi, Mississippi. The difference between 30° north latitude (Biloxi's latitude) and the +23 1/2° declination is −6 1/2°. Latitudes north of the tropic of Cancer and south of the tropic of Capricorn will always be computed as a negative value when finding sun angles because the sun will always be at less than a 90° angle in these areas. Next, we find the sum between the −6 1/2° and the only-in-the-tropics sun angle of 90°, resulting in a noon in Biloxi sun angle of 83 1/2°. We can also look at the solar altitude chart to estimate this noon sun angle.

Looking at the Solar Altitude and Azimuth Chart for 30° North Latitude in Figure 16-5, we find the sun path line for June 22 and note the declination to be +23 1/2°. We see the sun rises at an azimuth of 63° at about 5:00 A.M. At 9:00 A.M., the sun is near an azimuth of 90° and a sun angle of 50° above the horizon. At 12:00 noon the sun is at an azimuth of 180° and a sun angle of 83 1/2°. At about 4:00 in the afternoon the sun is near an azimuth of 280° and at a sun angle of 48° above the horizon. The sun sets on this longest day of the year at about 7:00 P.M. at an azimuth of about 297°. This information can be plotted both in plan view and in elevations or sections to see the effects of the various sun angles throughout the day.

Let us do one more sun angle computation. We will examine the sun path in Biloxi at the opposite extreme of the year on the winter solstice (sun stop) of December 22. We

Table 16-4 Computing Noon Sun Angle

June 22, Biloxi, Mississippi, 30° north latitude
+23 1/2° north latitude (The declination, where the sun will strike the earth at 90° on June 22)
−(+30°) north latitude (We are seeking the difference between the sun's latitude at
  −6 1/2° 90° on June 22 at noon and the latitude of Biloxi.)

 −6 1/2°
 +90° tropic's sun angle at noon
 = 83 1/2° sun angle, noon, in Biloxi on June 22

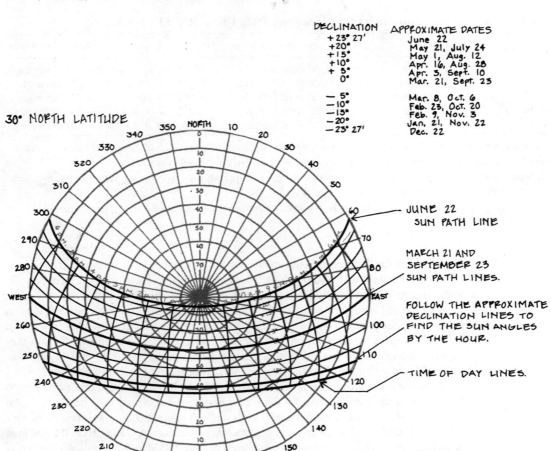

DECLINATION	APPROXIMATE DATES
+23° 27'	June 22
+20°	May 21, July 24
+15°	May 1, Aug. 12
+10°	Apr. 16, Aug. 28
+5°	Apr. 3, Sept. 10
0°	Mar. 21, Sept. 23
−5°	Mar. 8, Oct. 6
−10°	Feb. 23, Oct. 20
−15°	Feb. 9, Nov. 3
−20°	Jan. 21, Nov. 22
−23° 27'	Dec. 22

30° NORTH LATITUDE

JUNE 22 SUN PATH LINE

MARCH 21 AND SEPTEMBER 23 SUN PATH LINES.

FOLLOW THE APPROXIMATE DECLINATION LINES TO FIND THE SUN ANGLES BY THE HOUR.

TIME OF DAY LINES.

Figure 16-5 Solar altitudes and azimuth chart for 30° North latitude.

Table 16-5   Computing Noon Sun Angle

December 22, Biloxi, Mississippi, 30° North Latitude

−23 1/2°
−(+30°) north latitude
─────────
−53 1/2°
−53 1/2°
+90° tropic's sun angle at noon
─────────
= 36 1/2° sun angle, noon, in Biloxi on December 22

can begin either by looking at the analemma (Figure 16-6) and getting the declination for the December 22 date, or we can look at the Solar Altitude and Azimuth Chart and see what the declination and sun path are for that date. If the date of the declination you are seeking is not on the Solar Altitude and Azimuth Chart, then get the declination from

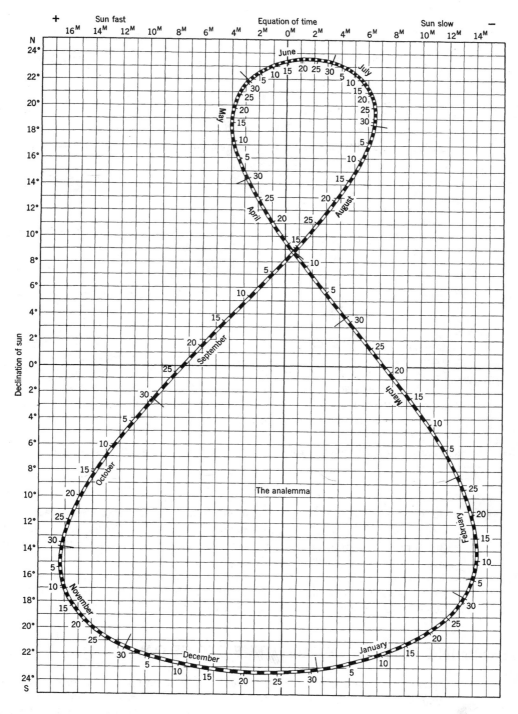

Figure 16-6 Analemma chart showing daily sun declinations. (*Source:* A. N. Strahler, *Physical Geography,* 2d Ed. New York: John Wiley & Sons, Inc.)

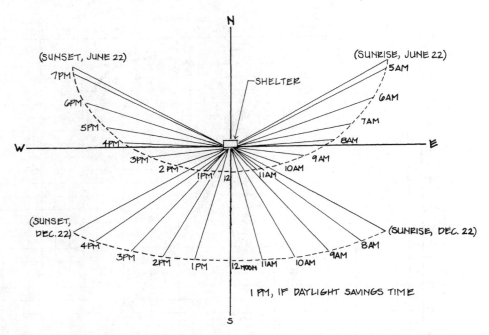

SHELTERS SHOULD BE SITED TO FACE SOUTH IN ORDER TO BE ABLE TO ABSORB THE HEAT FROM THE LOW ANGLE AND REDUCED AZIMUTH RANGE OF THE WINTER SUNSHINE. FACING A BUILDING SOUTH WILL ALSO EXPOSE ONLY ITS NARROW SIDES TO MORNING AND AFTERNOON SUN DURING THE COOLING NEED SEASON, RESULTING IN LESS HEAT GAIN. STUDIES HAVE SHOWN THAT SHELTERS SITED TO FACE SOUTH WILL USE 33% LESS ENERGY FOR HEATING AND COOLING.

Figure 16-7 Sun path diagram—no scale—summer and winter solstice, 33 1/2° North latitude.

the Analemma Chart. Declinations that are below the equator are computed as a negative latitude. For December 22 we have a declination of −23 1/2°. Find the difference with the 30° north latitude of Biloxi. Recall that because sun angles north and south of the tropical zones of the equator will always be less than 90°, these latitudes will be computed as negative or −(+30°) north latitude. Next, find the sum with the 90° sun angle in the tropics to get the noon sun angle, as shown in Table 16-5. Figure 16-7 shows the hourly sun path for the summer and winter solstices in Biloxi, Mississippi, 30° north latitude.

DETERMINING SUN ANGLES ANY TIME OF THE DAY

Now that we know how to figure the sun angle at noon for any day of the year, let us examine how to figure the sun angle for any time of the day. This will be helpful, for example, in determining how much sun will warm the sides of a shelter and come through

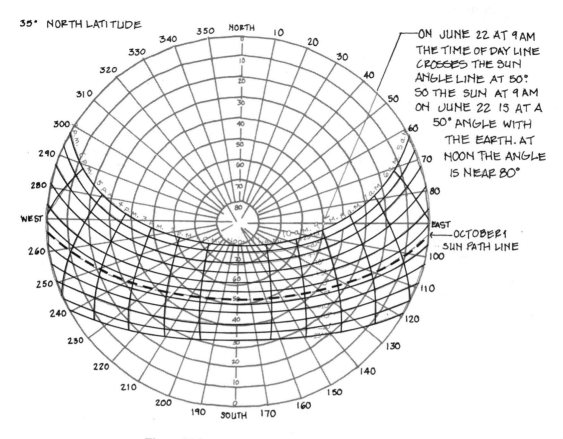

Figure 16-8 Using sun path lines for computing hourly sun angles.

its windows throughout the day. We did studies of this type for our new landscape architecture facility and concluded that we needed 7ft 3in. (2.2 m) overhangs to keep the sun out of the design studios and off the south sides of the shelters during the cooling season (see Figure 16-9). Our calculated overhangs were designed to block the sun when solar heat was most intense from 10:00 A.M. through 2:00 P.M. The overhangs also allowed winter sun to strike the south sides of the buildings and come through the windows to store heat in the thermal mass of the floor.

As the sun rises and moves through the sky toward noon and during the afternoon, it will change azimuths (compass directions) throughout the day, and its angle or altitude with the earth will continously change, reaching a maximum sun angle at noon. To understand the impact of the sun, it is helpful to plot sun angles both in an elevation or section drawing and in plan view, showing the azimuths of the sun throughout the day. Pick the dates for which you want to evaluate the sun's path, and locate their approximate sun path lines on the Solar Altitude and Azimuth Chart. If you are selecting dates not listed on this chart, then use the Analemma Chart to get the specific declination for the date you want. Relate the declination to the declinations on the Solar Altitude and Azimuth Chart and draw a light sun path line on the chart. Remember, you must be using a chart that is made for your latitude. Once you have your sun path line penciled in as shown in Figure 16-8, look at where your sun path line crosses the times

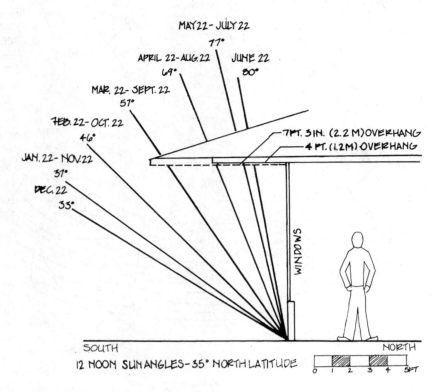

Figure 16-9 Comparing overhangs and monthly sun angles for Mississippi State Campus.

of day lines and approximate the sun angle according to the concentric degree rings on the chart.

In designing the overhangs for our landscape architecture facility, we chose October 1 as the end of the cooling need season and the date for which to plot sun angles throughout the day in order to determine how far to extend a roof overhang to prevent the sun from hitting the sides and windows of the building. In our hot-humid climate, October and November are very pleasant months that usually require no heating or cooling. During this transition season it is a good idea to disallow large amounts of solar heat gain in a building until the heating season, which begins December 1. Our sun control plan was to keep all sun off the building sides until after October 1, and then allow the sun to slowly creep up the sides of the building until December 1, when it would come through the windows to add warmth to the interior spaces. Figure 16-10 illustrates the uncontrolled effect that seasonal solar heat gain has on shelters without overhangs. When creating buildings that do not consider the effect of sun on heating and cooling needs, human comfort is usually achieved through reliance on fossil fuel-driven mechanical cooling systems. A full explanation of sun path diagrams supporting the need for a 7ft 3in. (2.2 m) overhang is found in Chapter 9, "Computing Overhangs for Solar Energy Control." Because a classroom building has substantial internal heat gain caused by machines and the presence of a lot of people, managing heat and creating comfortable interior

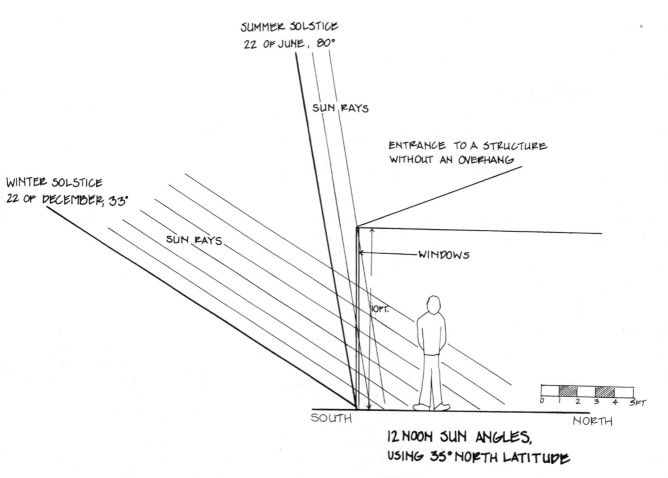

SUMMER SOLSTICE
22 OF JUNE, 80°

SUN RAYS

ENTRANCE TO A STRUCTURE
WITHOUT AN OVERHANG

WINTER SOLSTICE
22 OF DECEMBER, 33°

SUN RAYS

WINDOWS

10 FT.

SOUTH

NORTH

0 1 2 3 4 5 FT

12 NOON SUN ANGLES,
USING 35° NORTH LATITUDE

Figure 16-10 Extremes of sun angles at Mississippi State and sun susceptibility without overhangs.

spaces is of paramount concern. Cooling and dehumidification needs far outweigh heating and humidification requirements in this latitude and hot-humid climate.

Chapter 17

Solar-Powered Hot Water and Space Heating

Using the sun's energy can save 30 to 100% of the fossil fuel energy used for heating water. Solar-heated water can also be used to heat interior spaces, further reducing dependence on fossil fuels and saving 20 to 80% of heating costs.

Solar energy can be used to heat water directly, to heat interior spaces, and to produce electricity when striking a photovoltaic cell. In ancient Egypt the pharaohs used the sun for space heating by capturing solar energy in water contained in black-colored pools during the day and circulating the warm water through pipes under the palace floors at night. Southwestern Native Americans designed and built their masonry cliff dwellings as large thermal masses to absorb and store the heat from the sun for interior space heating on cool desert evenings and during the winter. Throughout the summer thick masonry walls absorbed the daytime solar heat, and when nighttime temperatures began to drop, the stored heat in the walls moved into interior spaces, creating comfortable temperatures. Using the sun to heat water and interior spaces can dramatically reduce dependence on fossil fuels.

SOLAR HOT WATER HEATING

Flat plate solar collectors, the heat-absorbing components of solar water heaters, are generally fabricated of a metal box with glazing on top. Inside the dark-painted metal box are interconnected tubes full of water or a freeze-resistant liquid. Sun heats the liquid-filled tubes, and the heated liquid moves from the collectors to an insulated storage tank, usually located above the collectors. In most cases flat solar collectors are located on rooftops, as shown in Figure 17-1. An auxiliary gas or electric water heater may be connected to the system for maintaining desired water temperatures on cloudy days. Unheated municipal water that is drawn into a water heater is cold, usually 50° to 60°F (10° to 16°C). Energy added to heat the water raises temperatures to 120° to 160°F (49° to 71°C). Generally, a solar water heater can provide about half of the energy needed to heat the water. To make maximum use of the sun, a renewable resource, it is best to

THE FLAT PLATE COLLECTOR IS ORIENTED DUE SOUTH AND TILTED TO BE NEAR A 90°ANGLE WITH THE SUN DURING THE WINTER SEASON.

NOTE: THERE ARE NO OBSTRUCTIONS TO BLOCK SOLAR RADIATION FROM STRIKING THE COLLECTOR.

Figure 17-1 Flat plate collector.

plan to do laundry, dishes, and bathing in the afternoons or early evening when the sun has sufficiently heated the water. Hot water use is usually between 10 and 20 gal (38 and 76 l) per person per day in a home that has a clotheswasher and a dishwasher, in addition to a tub and shower.

Energy Savings

Although the cost of heating water does not seem excessive as compared with space heating and cooling costs, it is the second largest energy user in homes, being approximately 25% of a home's yearly energy bill. The U.S. Department of Energy estimates that a family of four uses as much energy to heat water in a year as it does to drive a car 12,000 mi (19,311 km). Energy used for heating water not only depletes the amount of nonrenewable fossil fuels remaining on earth, but it also produces large amounts of carbon dioxide and other chemicals that are expelled into the atmosphere during combustion, contributing to air pollution and global warming.

Types of Solar Hot Water Heaters

There are two primary methods for heating water with the sun. The first is by directly capturing solar heat with flat plate solar collectors. The second is by producing electricity with photovoltaic collectors and using the electricity to warm water through the use of high-resistance heating elements. High-resistance heating elements are composed of materials that hold tightly to their electrons before releasing them. When electricity flows through the elements, heat is generated and fluids are heated through convection.

Flat Plate Solar Hot Water Heaters

The two types of solar water heaters that collect sunlight and use the solar radiation for heating water are the passive and active systems. The active system uses a pump and a temperature control device, whereas the passive system does not have any moving parts, but relies on the principle of thermosyphon whereby solar-heated water in the flat plate collector expands, becomes lighter, and, because of its lightness, moves up to an insulated storage tank. As water becomes heated, its molecules move farther and farther apart because of the *energy of motion,* thereby becoming less dense. This is how heated water can move vertically in a pipe to storage tanks located above the collector. The word *thermosyphon* comes from two Greek words meaning "heat" and "pipe." Most flat plate solar hot water collectors heat about 1 gal of water a day for each square foot of collector surface. The hot liquid in the pipes expands and rises to a storage tank, usually located at least 18 in. (457 mm) above the collector. The piping of pressurized potable water is arranged so that heated water will be replaced. When hot water is used, fresh unheated water flows into the bottom of the flat plate collector, where it is heated. Heat makes the water less dense, and it moves upward through the pipe into the insulated storage tank. As hot water faucets in the house are turned on, cold water under pressure moves into the collector for heating, and the cycle of water heating begins again. The storage tank can directly provide hot water for use in the household, as in Figure 17-2, or it can serve as a preheating chamber, supplying a conventional electric or gas water heater with preheated water, as shown in Figure 17-3. The conventional water heater can then maintain water at a prescribed temperature setting, such as 120°F (49°C). Water in the solar collector will probably heat up to between 120° and 160°F (49° and 71°C), which is hot enough to burn skin. Users should be aware of how hot water can get when it is piped directly from the solar collector storage tank. The amount of hot water produced depends on how much sun is available for heating water and how much hot water is being used. Of course, when there are periods of reduced sunshine, hot water heating will be reduced because of the reduction of solar radiation.

Freezing Temperatures and the Flat Plate Solar Collector   Water can freeze in flat plate solar collectors, causing broken pipes and leaks. Where freezing is a problem, it is best to use a combination of freeze-resistant liquids in the piping system. When liquids other than water are used, the heated freeze-resistant liquid is circulated to a heat exchanger tank (Figure 17-4). Here it flows through coils located inside the tank, and heat moves by convection from the hot liquid, through the coil walls, and then by convection again to the potable water in the heat exchange tank. This heated water then moves to the conventional hot water tank equipped with electric or gas backup heating for prolonged cloudy days. As the household's hot water faucets are turned on, water under pressure moves through the pipes. A thermostat in the water heater keeps the water within a specific temperature range so that users will not get burned by using water that is too hot.

Locating Solar Collectors   Solar collectors can be installed in any location that will receive uninterrupted sunshine all day and all year long. For that reason, they are usually located on rooftops, facing south in areas north of the equator. Collectors can face up to 20° to 30° on either side of due south and still work, but a due south orientation is best for maximum solar heat gain. The tilt of the collector is best if it is at 90° to the sun at noon. This angle will result in collection of the most solar radiation. See Figure 17-5 for locating a flat plate collector. Noon sun angles can vary more than 40° at seasonal extremes. At 35° north latitude, the noon sun angle on June 22 is 80° and on December 22

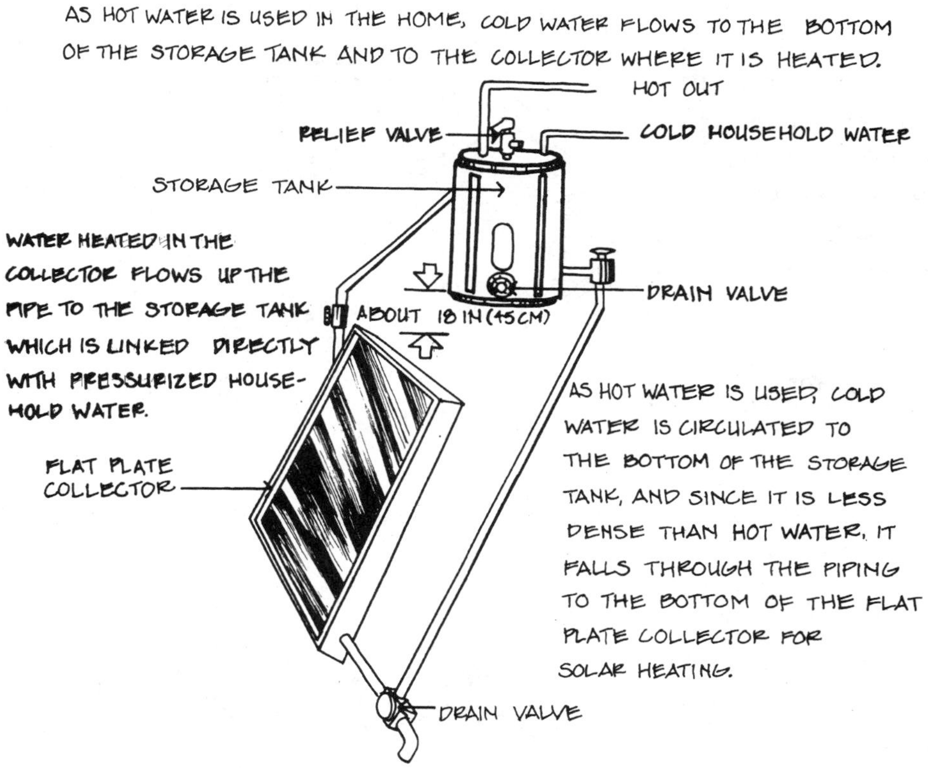

AS HOT WATER IS USED IN THE HOME, COLD WATER FLOWS TO THE BOTTOM OF THE STORAGE TANK AND TO THE COLLECTOR WHERE IT IS HEATED.

HOT OUT

RELIEF VALVE

COLD HOUSEHOLD WATER

STORAGE TANK

WATER HEATED IN THE COLLECTOR FLOWS UP THE PIPE TO THE STORAGE TANK WHICH IS LINKED DIRECTLY WITH PRESSURIZED HOUSE-HOLD WATER.

ABOUT 18 IN (45CM)

DRAIN VALVE

FLAT PLATE COLLECTOR

AS HOT WATER IS USED, COLD WATER IS CIRCULATED TO THE BOTTOM OF THE STORAGE TANK, AND SINCE IT IS LESS DENSE THAN HOT WATER, IT FALLS THROUGH THE PIPING TO THE BOTTOM OF THE FLAT PLATE COLLECTOR FOR SOLAR HEATING.

DRAIN VALVE

Figure 17-2 Thermosyphon solar water heater.

it is 33°. Because it is ideal to tilt the collector to make a 90° angle with the sun, it is best to have an adjustable tilt mechanism that can be tilted for the summer and winter seasons; however, collectors are usually placed flat, and stationary, on a south-facing roof.

Locate collectors as close as possible to the conventional water heater to minimize piping connections. Although thermosyphon and active collectors are usually located on a roof, they can be attached to the side of a house, or even installed on the ground, as long as they will receive uninterrupted sunlight. Remember, your objective is to capture the sun's heat, and that is best done when the collector is at a 90° angle to the noon sun.

Photovoltaic Solar Water Heater

A photovoltaic solar water heater (Figure 17-6) is composed of photovoltaic (PV) modules, a microprocessor controller, and one or two storage tanks with heating elements. The PV modules produce direct current (DC) electricity during the daytime, which goes through the heating elements in the hot water tank. The heating elements have a high resistance to the flow of electrons, so the elements get hot, just like the nichrome elements on an electric stovetop. A lot of heat is given off when electrons travel through materials

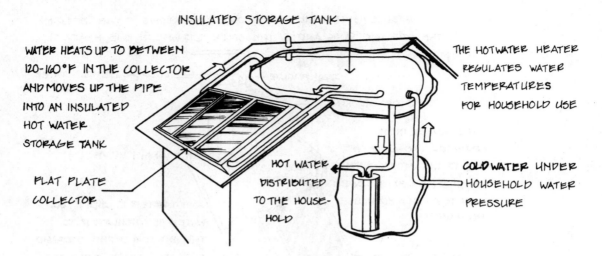

INSULATED STORAGE TANK

WATER HEATS UP TO BETWEEN 120-160°F IN THE COLLECTOR AND MOVES UP THE PIPE INTO AN INSULATED HOT WATER STORAGE TANK

THE HOT WATER HEATER REGULATES WATER TEMPERATURES FOR HOUSEHOLD USE

FLAT PLATE COLLECTOR

HOT WATER DISTRIBUTED TO THE HOUSEHOLD

COLD WATER UNDER HOUSEHOLD WATER PRESSURE

Figure 17-3   Flat plate collector storage tank and water heater.

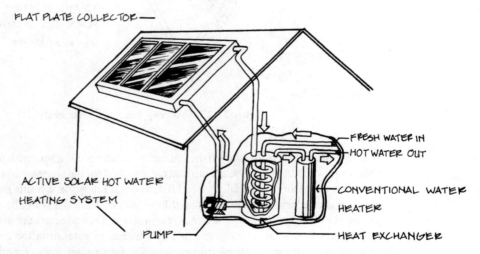

FLAT PLATE COLLECTOR

ACTIVE SOLAR HOT WATER HEATING SYSTEM

FRESH WATER IN
HOT WATER OUT

CONVENTIONAL WATER HEATER

PUMP

HEAT EXCHANGER

IN AREAS OF FREEZING WEATHER, FREEZE-RESISTANT LIQUIDS SHOULD BE USED IN COLLECTOR PIPES. THE ANTIFREEZE LIQUID HEATS UP AND CIRCULATES TO A HEAT EXCHANGER WHERE TAP WATER IS HEATED. WHEN HOUSEHOLD FAUCETS ARE TURNED ON, HOT WATER MOVES UNDER PRESSURE TO THE CONVENTIONAL WATER HEATER, WHERE A THERMOSTAT KEEPS TEMPERATURES CONSTANT. COLD WATER MOVES INTO THE HEAT EXCHANGER FOR PREHEATING.

Figure 17-4   Flat plate collector, pump and heat exchanger.

IN LOWER LATITUDES SUCH AS IN FLORIDA, THE GULF COAST, AND TEXAS, WINTER SUN ANGLES ARE HIGH, THEREBY ALLOWING SOLAR COLLECTORS TO BE PLACED FLAT ON LOW ANGLE ROOFS AND STILL BE CLOSE TO A 90° SUN ANGLE DURING THE WINTER TIME.

Figure 17-5 Flat plate collector.

LOCATE THE P.V. ARRAY SO THAT IT RECEIVES UNINTERRUPTED SUN AND SO THAT IT IS AT 90° TO THE NOON WINTER SUN ANGLE. A SEASONABLY ADJUSTABLE SYSTEM WOULD ENABLE THE ARRAY TO BE AT 90° TO THE SUN DURING THE DIFFERENT SEASONS.

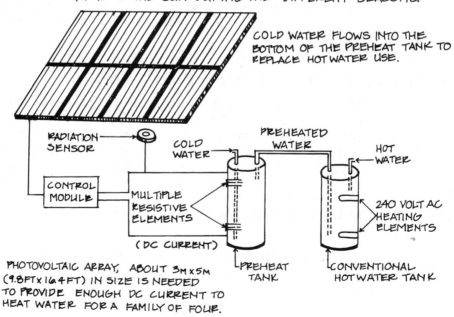

COLD WATER FLOWS INTO THE BOTTOM OF THE PREHEAT TANK TO REPLACE HOT WATER USE.

RADIATION SENSOR

COLD WATER

PREHEATED WATER

HOT WATER

CONTROL MODULE

MULTIPLE RESISTIVE ELEMENTS

(DC CURRENT)

240 VOLT AC HEATING ELEMENTS

PHOTOVOLTAIC ARRAY, ABOUT 3M X 5M (9.8FT X 16.4FT) IN SIZE IS NEEDED TO PROVIDE ENOUGH DC CURRENT TO HEAT WATER FOR A FAMILY OF FOUR.

PREHEAT TANK

CONVENTIONAL HOT WATER TANK

Figure 17-6 Photovoltaic hot water system.

that have high resistance, and very little heat is given off when electrons travel through materials with low resistance. Water in the tank is heated by the high-resistance elements, and because the water heater is connected to the pressurized domestic water system, hot water will flow when the valve in the sink, tub, or shower is turned on, and cold water will move into the bottom of the hot water or heat exchange tank to be heated. When two tanks are used, the first tank (the one wired to the PV array) is called the preheat tank, and this is the one that receives the pressurized unheated water supply. It is heated by DC current from the PV array. The PV array needed to accommodate hot water needs for a family of four is approximately 3 × 5 m (10 × 16 ft) in size. Water from that tank is pushed by the pressurized household water system into the second tank, which is the supply tank for hot water use. Additional heat for hot water in this tank is provided by electricity or gas, and a thermostat is used to keep the water at a certain temperature, ensuring a dependable hot water supply for the residence. See Table 17-1 for the amount of hot water needed for the various residential conditions. The PV solar water system does not require piping that perforates the roof or building wall membrane, and its layout and heating system closely resemble those of an electric water heater.

A photovoltaic hot water system installed for evaluation in the Gaithersburg, Maryland, area provided 56 to 60% of the electricity needed to supply hot water for a family of four. The cost of the system was $8900, with the expense of the PV system being the major cost. The value of a comparable solar flat plate thermal hot water system is about $3000. Because the only moving parts in a PV hot water system are the switching relays, maintenance costs should be low. As photovoltaic cell costs diminish, the energy-efficient PV water heater will become more cost competitive with the flat plate solar hot water heater.

Reasons for Using Solar-Powered Hot Water Heaters

When heating water with the sun, not only will the user save energy costs, but non-renewable fossil fuels will be saved for use by future generations. The production of carbon dioxide and other combustion contaminants like sulfur and nitrous oxides will be reduced or eliminated. These air-polluting contaminants contribute to global warming, acid rain, and smog. By using sun power to heat water, less foreign oil will be used and the need to build additional power plants and high-power transmission lines will be diminished. A typical family of four uses about 70 gal (265 l) of hot water per day at an average electricity cost of $500 per year and a natural gas cost of under $200 per

Table 17-1 Estimating Daily Residential Hot Water Needs

Estimated water use from Solar Direct, Sarasota, Florida.

People	Gallons	Liters	Bedrooms	Gallons	Liters
1	20	76	1	30	114
2	40	151	2	50	189
3	55	208	3	70	265
4	70	265	4	90	341
5	85	322	5	110	416

year. In the hot-humid and hot-arid climate regions, about 80% of water heating costs can be saved by using the flat plate solar water heater. In the temperate climate region of Maryland, a study demonstrated that a flat plate solar water heater saved about 60% of the yearly energy costs incurred by using a conventional hot water heater.

USING HOT WATER FOR SPACE HEATING

Hydronic systems are very effective in heating interior spaces. The word *hydronic*, according to our *Webster's Dictionary,* refers to "a system of heating or cooling that involves the transfer of heat by circulating a fluid in a closed system of pipes." In the hydronic system, heated water or a water-based solution from a solar flat plate collector or a fossil-fueled water heater is used to transport thermal energy to interior spaces for heating. Thermal energy absorbed by the liquid is conveyed by piping and released into spaces by a heat emitter. Heat emitters or heat exchangers can take the form of radiant floors, hot water baseboards, and hot water valances. The heat that is delivered is even and comfortable. No fans or blowers are used to deliver the heat. Interior humidity levels are not dried out as they are with a forced-air convection system. When a flat plate solar collector is used, sunlight enters the panels and heats the liquid to between 130° and 160°F (54° and 71°C). The hot liquid is then pumped through tubes, either within the floor to produce radiant underfloor heating or to the hot water heating system. The floor slab stores and radiates thermal energy. The combination solar collector, hot water heater, and radiant heating system can provide nearly all of a shelter's heating and hot water needs. It works well in sunny climates, but also in cold and overcast climates such as in Vermont and Oregon. As in providing hot water for a household, the flat plate collectors collect solar energy and store it in a fluid medium. The solar energy is released into the shelter by radiation, conduction, and convection.

Structures that are heated hydronically have lower energy bills than those with traditional forced-air convection systems. Because hydronic heating systems do not blow air into spaces, room air pressure levels are not affected. Forced-air systems raise room air pressures and push warm air through the openings of the building envelope to the outside. A study comparing hydronic space heating with forced-air space heating found that the energy used in a forced-air system was 40% greater than that of a hydronic heating system.

Also contributing to heat loss is the difference between how indoor air temperatures are stratified in the forced-air system and in the hydronic system. In a forced-air system, the space is filled with warm air until a thermostat shuts the system down. The warm air rises to the top of the room because it is less dense. Cool air near the ceiling, because it is denser, falls to the floor level. Significant air stratification results, with the warmest air being at the ceiling and the coolest at the floor, as shown in Figure 17-7. Heat is lost by conduction through the ceiling. In the hydronic system, more heat is transferred by radiant energy from warmer objects to cooler objects than it is by convection. The air is not heated as it is with convective heating. When valance radiant systems are used (located above windows, as a valance would be, near the ceiling), the temperature varies about 2° to 4°F (1° to 2°C) between the ceiling and the floor. With radiant floors, the temperature varies about 2° to 4°F (1° to 2°C) from the floor to the ceiling, with the floor

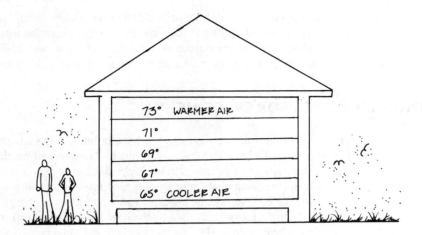

Figure 17-7   Air temperature stratification in a forced air system.

being about 2°F (1°C) warmer than the air. With radiant systems, the air is warmed to the thermostat setting, which is often at 6° to 8°F (3° to 4°C) lower than with conventional systems. Hydronic systems decrease air temperature stratification and reduce heat loss through ceilings.

In sizing a radiant system, the interior temperatures selected are usually 65°F (18°C) in the daytime and 59°F (15°C) at nighttime, versus 70°F (21°C) daytime and 65°F (18°C) nighttime with a conventional system. With the radiant system, space heating analysts figure a reduction in heat needs due to lower building air infiltration, exfiltration, stratification, and heat loss through glass. Building heat requirements can be 25 to 40% lower using radiant heat versus a forced-air convective system.

Hydronic Radiant Floor Heating

In a radiant floor system, heated water or water-based solutions flow through tubing looped throughout a floor, providing radiant heat. Fluid temperatures flowing through polybutylene or polyethylene tubing range from 90° to 105°F (32° to 41°C). This warm, but not hot, temperature range works well with either a ground-source heat pump or an active solar hot water heating system. Hydronic floor heating doesn't directly heat up the air mass by convection; instead, it radiates heat directly to the objects and people within a space. The objects and the floor mass warm the air through radiation, conduction, and convection. One of the reasons people feel comfortable in radiant-heated spaces is that the air temperature is highest at the floor level and decreases toward the ceiling. Because the relative humidity has not been lowered, as it is with the forced-air convection system, the air feels several degrees F warmer than it actually is. Research has shown that with radiant heating systems, people are comfortable in interior spaces that are 6° to 8°F (3° to 4°C) cooler than when heating is provided by a convective forced-air system in which air is the primary heat transfer medium. Operating costs for hydronic floor heating systems can be 20 to 40% lower than with convection systems such as a forced-air gas furnace. Heating a space to lower temperatures will reduce heating costs.

Hydronic systems can be zoned by rooms and controlled with a thermostat. The same type of system can be used to remove ice and snow on walkways and for heating pools and spas. How warm or how cool people feel in spaces is directly related to humidity levels. In a traditional forced-air convection system air is heated, which lowers the relative humidity level. People feel warmer when the humidity is higher in the heating season, and, conversely, cooler during the cooling season when humidity levels are lower. The human body sweats in order to cool and keep the core of the body from overheating. In fact, the human body perspires about 2000 ml each day in hot weather. If the body gets too warm, it will die, so perspiring is an important part of being healthy. The reason the body feels warmer during the heating season when interior humidity levels are high is the reduced rate of evaporation of moisture from the skin. When evaporation occurs, molecules of water heat up to the point where they transform to a gas and rise. This is how heat is removed from the body. It is estimated that 1 kg (2.21 lb) of body perspiration contains about 4 million joules of heat. So, through maintaining high humidity levels during the heating season, the evaporation of perspiration from the skin will be reduced, thereby keeping the body warmer. In a forced-air convection heating system, the relative humidity of interior air is lowered by heating the air. Heated interior air rapidly evaporates moisture from the skin, resulting in a loss of heat and causing the human body to feel cooler—not the effect we are trying to achieve in the wintertime.

When the objective is to make people feel cooler, lowering humidity levels in interior spaces can increase the rate of evaporation and the movement of body heat away from the skin. The use of a fan increases the evaporation of perspiration from the skin and convection of heat from the body. Ceiling fans can make a room feel 8° to 10°F (4° to 6°C) cooler than it actually is.

To construct a hydronic floor heating system, embed polyethylene tubing in a concrete slab placed over a wood subfloor. Wood flooring, tile, or carpet can be placed over the slab. If ceramic tile is placed over the slab, fluid temperatures in the tubing need only be as warm as 90° to 105°F (32° to 39°C). If wood flooring or carpet is used, temperatures will have to be about 130°F (54°C). Figure 17-8 illustrates construction techniques for building a hydronic system on a concrete slab and over a wood subfloor.

As an alternative to the traditional radiant floor heating, hot water or water-based solutions from solar panels can heat a large thermal mass that is a combination of the shelter floor and other storage material like a rock mass located below the floor. One manufacturer calls this storage unit a "massive radiant panel slab." It is composed of a 5 1/2 in. (140 mm) thick concrete floor slab on top of a 24 in. (635 mm) deep thermal mass gravel bed (Figure 17-9). The thermal storage mass is separated from the varying soil temperatures by 2 in. (51 mm) thick polystyrene insulation panels. Heat exchange tubing composed of polyethylene pipe is located both in the concrete slab and in the gravel thermal mass. It transfers the thermal energy in the water (from the sun) into the rock and concrete for storage and radiation. For a 1400 ft² (130 m²) two-story home, about 800 ft (244 m) of 3/4 in. (19 mm) tubing is placed in the slab and 600 ft (183 m) of looped tubing is placed in a 24 in. (610 mm) deep gravel bed. The heated fluid is then pumped from the solar collectors throughout the massive slab, imparting thermal energy for prolonged thermal storage. Thermal energy is conducted through the massive slab and released to the interior spaces passively by radiation, conduction, and convection as the temperatures in the spaces begin to drop. If too much heat is produced, it is

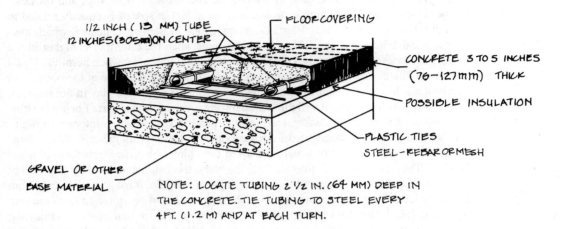

CONCRETE FLOOR RADIANT HEAT

1/2 INCH (13 MM) TUBE
12 INCHES (305mm)ON CENTER

FLOOR COVERING

CONCRETE 3 TO 5 INCHES
(76-127mm) THICK

POSSIBLE INSULATION

PLASTIC TIES
STEEL - REBAR OR MESH

GRAVEL OR OTHER
BASE MATERIAL

NOTE: LOCATE TUBING 2 1/2 IN. (64 MM) DEEP IN
THE CONCRETE. TIE TUBING TO STEEL EVERY
4 FT. (1.2 M) AND AT EACH TURN.

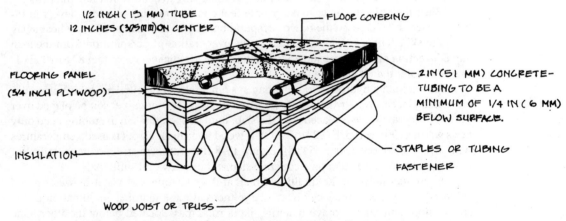

CONCRETE OVER WOOD SUBFLOOR

1/2 INCH (13 MM) TUBE
12 INCHES (305mm)ON CENTER

FLOOR COVERING

2 IN (51 MM) CONCRETE-
TUBING TO BE A
MINIMUM OF 1/4 IN (6 MM)
BELOW SURFACE.

FLOORING PANEL
(3/4 INCH PLYWOOD)

STAPLES OR TUBING
FASTENER

INSULATION

WOOD JOIST OR TRUSS

NOTE: SECURE TUBING EVERY 4 FT (1.2 m) AND AT ALL TURNS

Figure 17-8 Hydronic floor heating system.

diverted to the hot water heater. Testing of a solar massive radiant slab was conducted in a 1400 ft^2 (130 m^2) two-story home in Vermont. Vermont is generally described as having a cold and cloudy climate during the winter. A combination of 210 ft^2 (19.5 m^2) of hydronic flat plate solar collectors and a 720 ft^2 (66.9 m^2) slab and rock bed provided nearly all of the heat the structure needed. Indoor daytime temperatures, from October through April, averaged 65°F (18°C), and nighttime temperatures dropped to 60°F (16°C). Only 1.8 million Btu of auxilliary heating was used during the seven-month heating season.

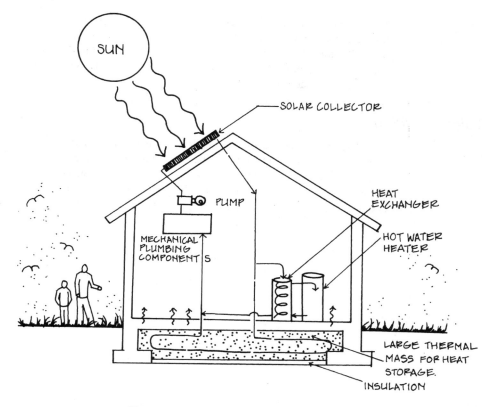

Figure 17-9 Heating with a large thermal mass.

The cost of 1.8 million Btu of natural gas for heating is $15.30. The cost of 1.8 million Btu of electricity for heating is $53.00.

> 1 ft³ of natural gas = 1,000 Btu
> 100 ft³ of natural gas = 100,000 Btu
> 1 therm of natural gas = 100,000 Btu
> 1 therm costs about $.85
> Therefore 1,800,000 Btu divided by 100,000 Btu = 18 therms of natural gas
> 18 therms × $.85 = $15.30
> 1 kWh = 3,412 Btu
> 1,800,000 Btu divided by 3,412 kWh = 528 kWh
> 528 kWh × $.10 per kWh = $53.00

Baseboard Radiation

Baseboard radiant heating heat exchangers are usually composed of a metal pipe with fins to transfer heat to the interior space by convection. A metal cover is placed over these components to protect the user from the hot pipe and fins and to give a more attractive appearance. Units fit against the wall at the floor level and are about 3 in. (76 mm) wide, 8 in. (203 mm) tall, and come in various lengths, from 3 to 8 ft (0.9 to 2.4 m) long. The water temperature for baseboard radiant heating has to be about 130°F (54°C), which is higher than needed for floor heating.

Valance Radiation

When using valance radiant heating, locate the unit close to the ceiling. A valance radiant heater is very similar in form to a baseboard heater, with the heat exchanger composed of a pipe with fins for maximum exposure to the air and convection of heat. The pipe and fins are covered with a valance-like covering for appearance purposes, and, as with floor and baseboard radiant heating, the valance radiant heat emitter is quiet and the units can be controlled with thermostats.

Chapter 18

Using the Earth as a Cooling and Heating Source

Energy Savings: By using the cooling and heating potential of the soil environment 2 m (6.6 ft) belowground, 30 to 100% of the energy used for cooling, dehumidification, and heating can be saved.

Two meters (6.6 ft) belowground the temperature of the soil is nearly the same as an area's yearly average temperature. For example, in much of the South the temperature of the soil is about 58°F (14°C) throughout the year. The soil temperatures for various states at 3 m (10 ft) below grade are shown in Table 18-1.

This belowground energy reservoir and energy sink can be used for cooling and heating shelters. In Mississippi, the seasonal temperature range during the summertime is about 78°F (26°C) in the morning, and in the 90s (°F) (32°C) during the afternoon and early evenings. With a 22°F (12°C) summer temperature spread in an area where the ground temperature is near 58°F (14°C) year-round, it is easy to recognize the earth as a resource that can be used for creating cooler work and home environments. As outside temperatures become cold, the higher temperature belowground becomes a source of energy to extract and use for human comfort. Examine the monthly temperature variations for Nashville, Tennessee, 36° north latitude, in Figure 18-1.

Table 18-1   Average Temperature of the Earth 3 m (10 ft) Deep

New Jersey	54°F	12°C
Illinois	53°F	12°C
Minnesota	49°F	9°C
Michigan	50°F	10°C
California	72°F	22°C
Kansas	55°F	13°C
Kentucky	58°F	14°C
South Dakota	47°F	8°C
Vermont	49°F	9°C

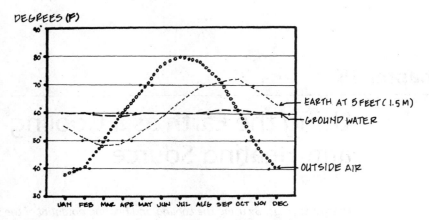

Figure 18-1 Monthly average temperature variations for Nashville, TN. (*Source: Earth-Coupled Heat Pump Manual*, TVA.)

Shelters can transport heat to or from the ground either passively or actively. The constant level of energy underground can be used for cooling and heating. When a shelter is directly in contact with the earth, such as by having soil bermed up on its sides, the shelter interior is passively insulated from outdoor temperatures. Excess heat within the shelter can be moved by conduction through walls to the cooler and lower energy level of the adjacent soil environs. Through the use of heat pumps and pipes filled with water that exchange warm water for cool water, or vice versa, shelters can rely on the constant energy level existing belowground.

GROUND TEMPERATURE

Ground temperatures 2 m (6.6 ft) below grade are often 20° to 40°F (11° to 20°C) cooler than aboveground air temperatures during the summer. There is an opportunity to transport heat from the home to the ground in order to create a more comfortable human habitat. A reservoir of low energy in the soil is waiting to receive higher concentrations of energy, such as interior heat, during the summer. As warm air is moved through tubes or pipes in the soil, the higher energy moves through the tube walls and into the cooler soil, with the potential result of returning air to the shelter 10° to 20°F (6° to 11°C) cooler than the outside air temperature. The soil serves as a heat sink. Warm air circulated belowground will not generally overload the soil with heat (high energy). Instead, the heat being transferred into the soil will move by conduction through the soil and the soil near the tube will remain ready to accept more heat from interior air. Although 2 m (6.6 ft) is ideal for obtaining nearly constant temperatures, at a depth of 30 cm (12 in.) temperatures are cool and the daily temperature is almost constant, with variations of no more than 3.6°F (2°C).

CHANGING THE GROUND TEMPERATURE TO ENHANCE COOLING

The ground's surface temperature can be modified through various means. As the surface temperature is cooled, deeper levels of the soil can be cooled by conduction. Surface temperature also affects the temperature of the air near the surface. Look at the surface temperatures of various materials at ground level in Table 18-2. You will see that the temperature of the ground surface is affected by color, density of the material covering the ground, and whether the ground covering is living, such as with grass, ivy, or vinca. The chart shows that there is a 21°F (12°C) surface temperature difference between asphaltic concrete paving and an area covered with high grass. Note, as well, that during the winter temperature variations are greatly reduced because of the low angle of the sun in North America and the reduced heat gain. Tables 18-3 and 18-4 show the effect of surface treatment on various soil depths.

It is a fact that the temperature of the ground surface can be increased and lowered through various means. When soil is shaded by large shade trees and irrigated, the combination of shade and evaporative cooling will lower the surface temperature. Evap-

Table 18-2 Surface Temperatures of Various Materials in the Washington, D.C., Area

	Asphalt	Bare Soil	Short Grass	Long Grass
Maximum Temperatures	91°F (33°C)	77°F (25°C)	75°F (24°C)	70°F (21°C)
Minimum Temperatures	29°F (−2°C)	28°F (−2°C)	31°F (−1°C)	28°F (−2°C)

Source: Passive and Low Energy Cooling of Buildings, Bernard Givoni, New York: VanNostrand Reinhold, 1994; after "The Effect of Ground Cover on Earth Temperature," T. Kusuda, *Moreland,* 1975, pp. 279–303.

Table 18-3 Temperatures 1.2 Meters Below Various Materials in the Washington, D.C., Area

	Asphalt	Bare Soil	Short Grass	Long Grass
Maximum Temperatures	79°F (26°C)	72°F (22°C)	64°F (18°C)	62°F (17°C)
Minimum Temperatures	58°F (14°C)	53°F (12°C)	52°F (11°C)	50°F (10°C)

Source: Passive and Low Energy Cooling of Buildings, Bernard Givoni, New York: VanNostrand Reinhold, 1994; after "The Effect of Ground Cover on Earth Temperature," T. Kusuda, *Moreland,* 1975, pp. 279–303.

Table 18-4 Temperatures 3.0 Meters Below Various Materials in the Washington, D.C., Area

	Asphalt	Bare Soil	Short Grass	Long Grass
Maximum Temperatures	68°F (20°C)	63°F (17°C)	61°F (16°C)	61°F (16°C)
Minimum Temperatures	48°F (9°C)	43°F (6°C)	47°F (8°C)	46°F (8°C)

Source: Bernard Givoni, Passive and Low Energy Cooling of Buildings, after Kusuda.

orative cooling occurs when molecules of water become heated and the movement of the molecules increases in speed. They become more energetic and less dense because the spaces between them increase to the point that they transform from a liquid to a gas state. When evaporation occurs, heat within the water is carried upward, and this is the point at which the "cooling effect" actually occurs. Over time, the temperature, or amount of thermal energy, in the lower levels of the soil can be reduced.

Another way in which a reduction of surface temperature can be achieved is to cover the soil by at least a 10 cm (4 in.) layer of mulch and irrigate. The mulch intercepts the direct sun heat gain and prevents conduction of heat into the surface soil layer. When selecting mulch types, be aware that an organic mulch layer such as a pine straw or bark mulch has a much lower rate of heat conduction than rock. Shading will provide an environment where the air temperature is about 10°F (6°C) cooler than the air temperature above the same surface exposed to the sun. The difference between the maximum temperature of air in a hot-humid environment during the summer and temperatures 1 m (3.3 ft) below the mulch has been found to be 20°F (11°C). Researchers demonstrated that with a soil-cooling treatment such as mulch and irrigation, a significant cooling opportunity can be provided at a soil depth of 0.5 to 1.0 m (1.6 to 3.3 ft).

HEAT TRANSFER IN THE EARTH

Heat is transferred through soil by conduction and convection. As the soil near the surface heats up, the heat moves toward the cooler soil below. This movement of heat from a region of high thermal energy to one of low energy (from warm to cool) through a solid material is called thermal conduction. Heat flow downward into the earth is by conduction and convection. Irrigation or rainfall occurring during the daytime in the summer cools the soil's surface immediately by conduction and evaporation. As the cool water hits the warm soil surface and the heat in the soil moves into the water, evaporation occurs. During a heavy rain or when large amounts of water are placed on a site through irrigation, the water seeping downward into the soil will carry higher energy from the surface into the ground, thereby increasing temperatures. During the winter the opposite will happen. The cooler water will move through the soil, and the heat in the lower layers of soil will move into the cooler water, resulting in a cooler subsoil environment.

GROUND SOURCE COOLING WITH EARTH TUBES

Air can be cooled as it is circulated in pipes or tubes located 1 to 2 m (3 to 6.5 ft) belowground. When warm indoor air is blown through the tubes into the cool underground environs of the surrounding soil, heat is transferred to the soil. Whether air or water is moved through the soil for cooling, the soil is serving as a heat sink. The heat that gathers around the earth tubes moves through the soil to cooler and lower energy zones away from the tubes. Because of this process, the soil around earth tubes remains cool and able to remove the warm energy contained in the indoor air.

Closed Air Circulation Systems

Air cooled by ground sources can be circulated either from within a shelter or by fresh (ventilation) air from the out-of-doors. In a closed air circulation system the warm air inside the shelter is pulled by a fan through tubes to transfer the energy in the air into the cooler environment of the soil. If high ventilation rates are not required by building codes and adequate ventilation can be obtained by opening windows for fresh air, the closed air system will be more efficient. Pipes can be made of either polyvinyl chloride (PVC) or galvanized steel. Fresh air used for ventilation can be pulled from outside a shelter through the length of the cooling tubes so that its warmth will be deposited in the cooler subgrade. In humid climates, it is necessary to remove water that condenses in tubes when the dewpoint of the air is reached and moisture in the air condenses on tube walls. This can be done by sloping the tubes to a low point where a sump or drain collects and removes water. A sump is a hole filled with gravel or sand for the storage of drainage water.

Soil Temperature Regeneration

Studies have shown that with week-long continuous daytime operation of a fan blowing air through tubes during the summer, the soil next to the earth tubes rose 1° F (0.6°C). During the nighttime, soil would regenerate its ability to cool when outdoor temperatures were lower. A study conducted at a poultry farm in New York demonstrated the cooling potential of earth tubes and the ability of the ground to regenerate its potential to absorb heat. A 45 cm (18 in.) diameter steel tube, 132 m (440 ft) long, was installed 2.4 m (8 ft) deep. During a week of continuous operation in July 1984, the soil temperature near the tubes rose from 52°F to 53°F (11° to 12°C). The outside temperature swing from day to night (also known as the diurnal swing) was 20°F (11°C) and fluctuated from 78° to 98°F (26° to 37°C). The cooled outlet air exiting the tubes was 60° to 63°F (16° to 17°C).

Temperatures Required for Ground Source Cooling

Because deeper soil temperatures are always lower than daytime air temperatures, the potential for cooling ventilation air and indoor air is significant. Where soil temperatures are greater than 72°F (22°C), a partial cooling of ventilation air is still possible, but cooling indoor air in a closed circulation system may not be as feasible, because the ground is not cold enough to provide cool air continuously to indoor spaces. In an experimental house constructed in Georgia in 1981, two air tubes 50 cm (30 in.) in diameter and 30 m (98 ft) long were placed horizontally in the ground 2 m (6.6 ft) deep. The amount of cooling obtained from air pulled by a fan through the system was related to the outside air temperature (aboveground). When the air entering the tubes was 86°F (30°C) and the soil 2 m (6.6 ft) deep was 70°F (21°C), the temperature of the air being drawn into the home was 74°F (23°C). As outside air temperatures rose, so did the temperature of the cooled outlet air. As soil temperatures approach and exceed 72°F, the amount of cooling potential decreases and it would be best to cool only the ventilation air because ventilation air is not provided continuously.

In another study outdoor air was blown by a 1/4 hp (185 W) fan through one 15 cm (6 in.) tube 17 m (56 ft) long. The tube was placed 3 m (10 ft) deep. Air entering the tube was 79.5°F (26°C), and the air at the tube outlet was 69°F (21°C). In addition to the cooling benefit of about 10°F (6°C), this process produced significant dehumidification of the air.

In conclusion, if summertime soil temperatures are 20° to 30°F (11° to 17°C) below daytime air temperatures, there is enough cooling potential to use the earth as a cooling source. If the underground temperatures are below the dew point of the daytime temperatures, water in the air will condense on the sides of the earth tubes, the air will become dehumidified, and people using the cooled space will feel even cooler in a less humid environment.

GEOTHERMAL SYSTEMS

Geothermal refers to using the potential of the heat transfer characteristics of the earth. This discussion centers on geothermal systems that use a continuous loop of buried plastic pipe filled with a freezeproof water solution to provide heating and cooling. During the cooling season water carries unwanted indoor heat to the earth, where the heat moves into the cooler soil. In the heating season the water transfers heat from the earth into the home for distribution into interior spaces.

Types of Geothermal Systems

The three basic types of geothermal systems are the closed loop horizontal, closed loop vertical, and pond or lake loop system. The closed loop systems circulate a water-based solution through small pipes placed underground. The pipes are usually small, up to 1 1/2 in. (38 mm) in size, and made of polyethylene. They are placed either horizontally or vertically (down) into the soil. A heat pump in the shelter connected to the pipes concentrates and distributes heat and cooling through a duct system within the shelter. In the summer cooling season excess heat from inside the shelter is moved from the liquid, through the pipe, and into the cooler soil. In the winter the liquid will collect the heat energy in the soil. Many places in the United States have winter soil temperatures of about 55°F (13°C). Heat from the soil is returned to the shelter heat pump, which will concentrate and deliver that heat throughout the shelter. The pond or lake loop requires no drilling and little trenching to place pipes and is therefore the least expensive to install. Coils of pipe are placed on the bottom in water that is at least 10 ft (3 m) deep. This system takes advantage of the cooler temperatures in deeper water. Figure 18-2 depicts the three types of geothermal energy sources.

Heat Pump Operation

The water source heat pump uses a cooling-refrigeration fluid, such as freon, to absorb inside heat and transfer it in an exchange coil to water that is being circulated underground. The heat in the water then moves into the cooler soil and returns to the shelter, ready to absorb more heat and help make the shelter cool. In winter the heat

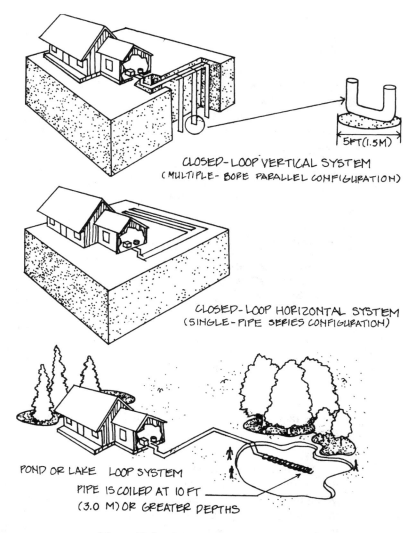

Figure 18-2 Geothermal energy sources.

pump absorbs the heat from the water that has been circulating belowground and releases it inside to provide warmth. The function of the heat pump is based on three key principles:

- Heat flows from areas of high thermal energy (or warm areas) to areas of low thermal energy (cool areas).

- Gases (for example, refrigeration fluids) absorb energy as they expand.

- As gases are compressed, they release the energy they have absorbed.

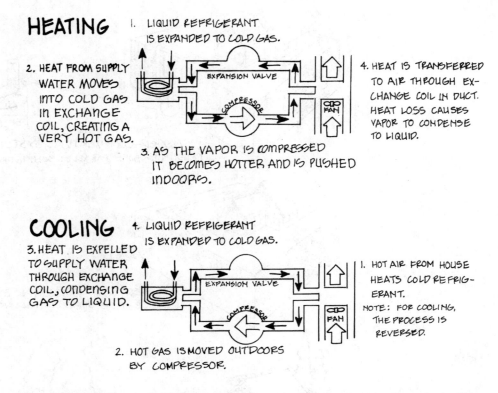

HEATING

1. LIQUID REFRIGERANT IS EXPANDED TO COLD GAS.

2. HEAT FROM SUPPLY WATER MOVES INTO COLD GAS IN EXCHANGE COIL, CREATING A VERY HOT GAS.

3. AS THE VAPOR IS COMPRESSED IT BECOMES HOTTER AND IS PUSHED INDOORS.

4. HEAT IS TRANSFERRED TO AIR THROUGH EXCHANGE COIL IN DUCT. HEAT LOSS CAUSES VAPOR TO CONDENSE TO LIQUID.

COOLING

4. LIQUID REFRIGERANT IS EXPANDED TO COLD GAS.

3. HEAT IS EXPELLED TO SUPPLY WATER THROUGH EXCHANGE COIL, CONDENSING GAS TO LIQUID.

1. HOT AIR FROM HOUSE HEATS COLD REFRIGERANT.

NOTE: FOR COOLING, THE PROCESS IS REVERSED.

2. HOT GAS IS MOVED OUTDOORS BY COMPRESSOR.

Figure 18-3 Heat pump diagram—heating and cooling mode. (*Source: Water Source Heat Pumps*, TVA.)

Figure 18-3 is a diagram of a heat pump in the heating and cooling modes. Note that the flow of refrigerant through the heat pump reverses when in the different modes. When heating, the heat from the warm water circulated from underground moves into the liquid refrigerant, creating a boiling gas vapor. The hot vapor is compressed. It moves through an air exchanger pipe with fins so that interior air around the pipe can become warm and then be blown through the shelters ductwork for space heating.

In the cooling mode, the heat pump moves cold refrigerant in the form of a gas through the air exchanger pipe with fins, where interior heat is transferred into the cold refrigerant and moved to the compressor. Here, an even hotter gas is created and moved to the exchange coil. The captured heat then moves into the water in the pipes and into the soil for transfer of heat from the liquid, so that cool liquid returns to the heat pump. As the heated, compressed gas transfers its heat to the water in the exchange coil, the gas condenses back to a liquid and moves to an expansion valve, which expands the liquid refrigerant into a cold gas, ready to move through the heat exchanger and carry more heat away from interior spaces. The compressor is an important component of the heat pump. It changes the pressure and temperature of the refrigerant and makes the refrigerant move through the heat pump.

Underground Energy Potential

The energy potential belowground is an unlimited and renewable resource. This resource is constantly supplied by the sun, the surrounding soil, the fluctuating groundwater, and the heat supplied by the shelter's cooling system. The reservoir of low temperature or energy contained within earth on a site occupied by a shelter is ten times the thermal energy required during an entire heating season. The reservoir can absorb the heat moved from a shelter by water pipes and contribute to the cooling of interior spaces.

Energy Efficiency

Geothermal systems operate on electricity, they require low maintenance, and they will use up to 45% less energy than a gas or oil furnace for heating. In regard to heating and cooling effectiveness, a geothermal system can save up to 60% of conventional heating and cooling costs. An elementary school with a geothermal system in Cambridge, Massachusetts, consumed 35,900 Btu (37,867,320 J) per square foot for heating and cooling for a year. A similar-sized school nearby with a conventional heating and cooling system used 60,000 Btu (63,288,000 J) per square foot per year. The school with the ground source geothermal system used 40% less energy. In southern Illinois, an area with hot summers and cold winters, a geothermal system was installed in a 2666 ft^2 (248 m^2) unshaded home; the utility costs for both heating and cooling were $280 per year. This geothermal system used a horizontal pipe system in which the pipe was placed about 4 1/2 ft (1.4 m) deep. In the same area, other shelters were being effectively cooled and heated with geothermal systems using the vertical version of pipe layout, in which the small diameter polyethylene pipe is placed in drilled holes 150 ft (46 m) deep.

Other Geothermal System Benefits

A heat pump system is completely contained indoors, rather than having a noisy fan and condensing unit outdoors. The heat pump is both the heating and cooling equipment, which allows owners and building managers to switch to heating and cooling modes quickly. The system provides more comfortable heating and cooling, according to surveys of users. Respondents said that temperatures were more even, especially during the heating season. A conventional system delivers air at about 130°F (54°C) that has been heated and dried out (desiccated) by flames or by resistance heaters. In contrast, the heat pump closed loop system provides heat in the 85° to 95°F (29° to 35°C) range.

Higher First Costs

Geothermal systems cost more initially but are significantly less expensive to operate and maintain than conventional systems. In addition to being used in residences, they are used in schools, offices, hotels, and retirement centers. Real estate brokers say that a geothermal system will boost the resale value of a home or business. A geothermal system is more expensive because the heat exchange pipe has to be buried. But such systems have lower above grade costs because they do not have boilers, chillers, or cooling towers. The mechanical rooms to contain the heat pumps can be up to 75% smaller than rooms containing conventional heating and cooling systems.

PASSIVE GEOTHERMAL SYSTEM

Just as air tubes serve as heat exchangers with the soil, a heat exchanger within a shelter can be of either an active or passive form. An active heat exchanger can take a more mechanical form, with pipes, fins, and a blower, as with the heat pump closed loop geothermal system, to hasten the exchange of energy. A passive form can be a concrete ceiling with interconnected water tubes spaced evenly across the ceiling. These water tubes are connected to the underground tubes located 2 m (6.6 ft) belowground to take advantage of earth cooling. In this situation the concrete serves as a thermal mass, taking the heat from the room and moving it to the cooler water for circulation back to the ground for transfer into the earth.

DIRECT EARTH COUPLING

An earth shelter that has thermal mass walls in direct contact with soil can use the soil as a heat sink, and the wall as a heat exchanger. Insulation should not be used in this case, as it would reduce heat transfer. Only a moisture barrier to prevent ground moisture from getting into the thermal mass wall should be used. Heat that builds up in the shelter, because of the presence of people, machinery, and ventilation, can move into the cooler wall and be conducted into the soil on the earth side of the wall. Through the berming of soil on walls and possibly the roof, the walls and roof will be protected from direct heat gain from the sun. Because wall surfaces may be below the dew point of the outdoor air, moisture in the air may condense on the walls, floors, and ceilings of the earth shelter, making use of a dehumidifier necessary. Moisture in interior air also comes from water vapor produced inside the shelter by cooking, bathing, and the simple act of breathing. Ventilation air can be cooled through the use of a fan and earth tubes in order to prevent condensation of moisture indoors. Another option is to use a heat pump. There are many successful heat pump systems using earth-coupled heating and cooling tubes. Covering a roof with soil can require a significant roof structure to hold the weight of the soil and the moisture in the soil. An alternative is to use a traditional built-up roof with polystyrene insulation to prevent direct solar heat gain.

COOLING ADVANTAGES OF SHELTERS WITH RAISED (CONVENTIONAL) FOUNDATIONS

When a structure is built off the ground, the shaded soil is up to 10°F (6°C) cooler than soil that receives direct heat gain. In measurements we performed, shown in Table 18-5, it was found that the soil surface in crawl spaces under homes with raised foundations was 9° to 16°F (5° to 9°C) cooler. This cooler soil resulted in cooler air above the soil and more comfortable conditions during the summer cooling season. A porch extending beyond the shelter can create shaded soil that will enhance summer air temperatures. If irrigation and subsequent evaporation of moisture occurs, temperatures will be even cooler. Soil and outdoor spaces adjacent to a shelter should be shaded by trees or arbors to ensure a cooler environment. Treatment of the ground with ground covers and irrigation can also result in more evaporation and cooler temperatures. Trees, grasses, ground covers, and shrubs absorb and transpire moisture.

Table 18-5   Comparing Summer Temperatures of Covered and Uncovered Surfaces

Location	Date	Time of Day	Temperature
Under a brick enclosed crawl space	27 July 2001	1:00 P.M.	75°F (24°C)
In the shade	27 July 2001	1:00 P.M.	87°F (31°C)
In the sun	27 July 2001	1:00 P.M.	91°F (33°C)
Under a crawl space with no enclosure	27 July 2001	3:00 P.M.	84°F (29°C)
In the shade	27 July 2001	3:00 P.M.	89°F (32°C)
In the sun	27 July 2001	3:00 P.M.	93°F (34°C)
Under a concrete block enclosed crawl space	29 July 2001	4:00 P.M.	81°F (27°C)
In the shade	29 July 2001	4:00 P.M.	94°F (34°C)
In the sun	29 July 2001	4:00 P.M.	96°F (36°C)
Under a concrete block enclosed crawl space	29 July 2001	7:00 P.M.	80°F (27°C)
In the shade	29 July 2001	7:00 P.M.	86°F (30°C)
In the sun	29 July 2001	7:00 P.M.	89°F (32°C)

Chapter 19

Photovoltaic Energy Production

Photovoltaic energy production is an established technology for creating electricity directly from sunlight. Although it has a high initial cost, it is a reliable method of independently producing electrical power.

Photovoltaic (PV) energy production is the direct conversion of sunlight to electricity. Sunlight that strikes a PV "cell" creates electrical current and voltage.[1] This electricity can be used as it is produced, stored in batteries, or sold to utilities.

Although PV energy production is not part of a regenerative cycle, it has several characteristics that allow us to call it a sustainable practice. First, the source of PV energy is solar radiation, an inexhaustible (at least for the next several million years) resource. Using it now will not impact future generations. Second, use of PV energy produces no waste. Compare this to the 500 million tons of carbon dioxide, as well as other pollutants, produced annually by fossil-fueled power plants in the United States. Third, PV components have relatively low embodied energy and a long usable life (20 years or more for panels, somewhat less for the other components), making them "green" on the production end as well.

HOW PHOTOVOLTAIC ENERGY WORKS

Electricity is the flow of charged particles (electrons, in our household systems). The quantity of charged particles that flow is the current. The ability of the current to overcome resistance (its "electromotive" force) is voltage. Photovoltaic energy production is the conversion of sunlight to electricity. When sunlight strikes a PV cell, electrical current and voltage are created.

---

[1] Electrical current is given in amperes (A). Voltage, as you would expect, is expressed as volts (V). Power (in watts, or W) is current times voltage. Energy, when referring to electrical energy, is commonly denoted using watt-hours (Wh). In PV system design, it is also customary to consider current applied over a particular time period. This is denoted as ampere-hours (Ah). All of these units may be proceeded by kilo, which means 1000 (1 kWh = 1000 Wh).

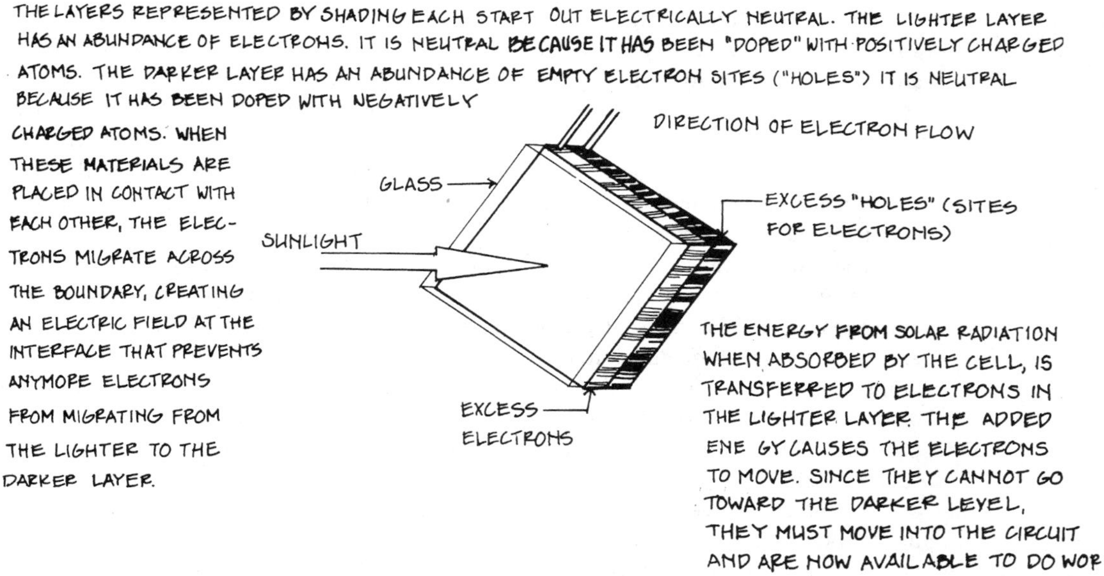

THE LAYERS REPRESENTED BY SHADING EACH START OUT ELECTRICALLY NEUTRAL. THE LIGHTER LAYER HAS AN ABUNDANCE OF ELECTRONS. IT IS NEUTRAL **BECAUSE IT HAS** BEEN "DOPED" WITH POSITIVELY CHARGED ATOMS. THE DARKER LAYER HAS AN ABUNDANCE OF EMPTY ELECTRON SITES ("HOLES") IT IS NEUTRAL BECAUSE IT HAS BEEN DOPED WITH NEGATIVELY

CHARGED ATOMS. WHEN THESE MATERIALS ARE PLACED IN CONTACT WITH EACH OTHER, THE ELECTRONS MIGRATE ACROSS THE BOUNDARY, CREATING AN ELECTRIC FIELD AT THE INTERFACE THAT PREVENTS ANYMORE ELECTRONS FROM MIGRATING FROM THE LIGHTER TO THE DARKER LAYER.

DIRECTION OF ELECTRON FLOW

GLASS

SUNLIGHT

EXCESS "HOLES" (SITES FOR ELECTRONS)

THE ENERGY FROM SOLAR RADIATION WHEN ABSORBED BY THE CELL, IS TRANSFERRED TO ELECTRONS IN THE LIGHTER LAYER. THE ADDED ENERGY CAUSES THE ELECTRONS TO MOVE. SINCE THEY CANNOT GO TOWARD THE DARKER LEVEL, THEY MUST MOVE INTO THE CIRCUIT AND ARE NOW AVAILABLE TO DO WORK

EXCESS ELECTRONS

Figure 19-1   PV Cell.

The PV Cell

A PV cell (Figure 19-1) is a type of diode (a diode is a device that allows electricity to flow in only one direction). When light strikes the cell, it knocks electrons loose from their sites in the cell material. Electrons that have been knocked loose with sufficient energy cross the diode junction, pass through an external circuit, and can do useful work (such as power a lightbulb). Only a small amount of current and voltage come from an individual cell, so some of the cells are usually connected in parallel (to increase current) and others in series (to increase voltage). A solar panel (the framed module that is usually sold) consists of many cells that have been so connected.

PV cells currently have a 10 to 18% efficiency (10 to 18% of the energy of the solar radiation that strikes them is converted to electricity). The least expensive and most commonly sold solar panels use silicon cells. Other materials have the potential to achieve greater efficiencies and may someday displace silicon if their prices can be reduced.

PV Panel Performance

PV panels (or modules) are sealed to protect them from weather. They have a front contact to allow the electrons to enter a circuit and a back contact to allow the electrons to complete the circuit. The panels have "power ratings" (amount of power that they will produce under standard conditions). These ratings depend on their size and material. Common ratings are 16 to 120 W (higher and lower ratings can also be found). Power in a PV system is additive: You can total the power of your panels to determine system power. For example, ten panels of 100 W each make up a 1000 W (1 kW) system.

The power ratings of the panels are the results of lab tests under standard conditions. Although various criteria are included in standard testing conditions, the two most critical are *insolation* (quantity of radiant energy incident on the surface, which is held at 1000 W/m^2 for the tests) and *air mass* (light having the characteristics, including spectral characteristics, of solar radiation when the sun is directly overhead, when the air mass = 1). Acceptance of these testing conditions as the industry standard allows the purchaser to compare the performance of solar panels from various manufacturers. The power output of cells immediately after purchase should closely approximate the rated values.

The rated power of a cell is not the amount of power that the cell always provides. First, even under standard testing conditions, panel performance deteriorates somewhat with age (manufacturers usually guarantee 85 to 90% performance after ten years). Second, in some cases manufacturers appear to overrate (provide slightly overoptimistic ratings for) their products. Third, panel performance varies with the amount of solar radiation available at any particular time. The quantity of current (in amperes) produced by the panel is proportional to the amount of solar energy it absorbs: The greater the incident solar radiation, the greater the current produced. Panel voltage, on the other hand, stays pretty constant across a wide range of insolations. Because only current changes with insolation (voltage remains about constant) and power is current multiplied by voltage, power is proportional to insolation. For example, if the rated panel power is 100 W at standard conditions, then an insolation of 750 W/m^2 (three-quarters of standard insolation) will result in a panel power of a little less than 75 W.

Other Components of a PV System

In addition to the PV panels (often called an *array* when taken in aggregate), the "balance of system" (other) components include the following:

- Wire to connect the panels to other devices (sunlight-resistant USE or UF type cable for exterior use)
- Mounting hardware for the panels (usually corrosion-resistant metal)
- Conduit to enclose cable if damage by rodents or mechanical damage is likely
- System ground wire (#8 copper or larger)
- Watertight junction boxes with strain relief connectors
- Voltage and current meters for monitoring load and performance
- Other hardware components, which depend on the type of PV system used (see the following sections).

Factors That Influence Available Power from a PV System

The amount of photovoltaic power available at a particular location depends on a number of factors:

- *The power rating and number of panels in the system.*
- *The position of the sun relative to the collecting surface of the panels.* The best orientation is for the panel-collecting surface to be at a right angle (perpendicular, 90°) to the path of "direct" solar radiation (direct solar radiation follows a

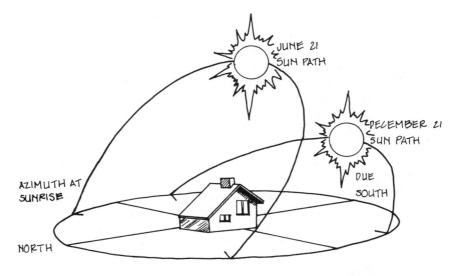

Figure 19-2 Maximum elevation of the sun and day length varies seasonally.

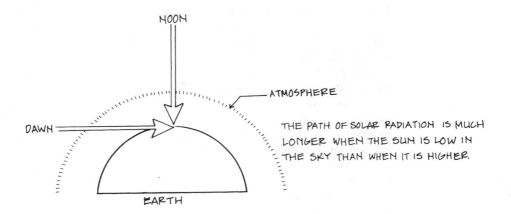

Figure 19-3 Solar radiation and the atmosphere.

straight line from the apparent position of the sun to the panel surface). Any other orientation decreases the effective area of the panel (the area of the panel that is visible from the direction of the sun). For example, if a panel is oriented with its collecting surface 45° from the line of sight to the sun, the collecting area is only about 71% of what it would be at 90°.

- *The time of the year.* In winter, the maximum elevation of the sun is less than during the summer (Figure 19-2). Solar radiation must travel through more of the atmosphere when the sun is lower than when it is higher in the sky (Figure 19-3), and atmosphere reduces the amount of solar radiation that reaches the earth's surface. So, even if your panels are kept at optimum orientation (perpendicular to the path of direct radiation), they will receive less solar energy in winter than in summer. Total energy (kWh) collected during a day also changes seasonally with variations in day length.

- *Tree cover, other characteristics of your site, and cloud cover.* Solar panels receive only diffuse radiation (radiation that has "bounced off" one or more objects) when shaded by any structure or landscape feature. Although diffuse radiation is always present (that's why we can see in the shade), it provides little usable energy. Clouds, like trees, shade solar panels. Depending on the type of cloud and amount of coverage, clouds may effectively eliminate much of the direct radiation (reflected radiation from clouds may occasionally increase insolation, but this is not common).

- *How you use the collected energy.* If you could use all of the PV electricity as it was produced, as direct current (DC), you would get to use a great deal of it. If you decided to store it in batteries or convert it to alternating current (AC), you would get to use less (each time you transform the energy, by storing it or changing its characteristics, some energy is lost).

Of the five factors listed here, some are clearly out of our control: We cannot do much about the season of the year, the time of day, or the weather (cloud cover). Other factors may be only partially amenable to control. Tree cover may preclude or limit PV use unless you are willing to remove trees. Retrofitting an existing residence for DC lights and appliances is difficult. You have no alternative but to use batteries in areas without existing grid service.

We can do something about at least two of these factors. First, we can determine the collecting capacity of the system. As mentioned earlier, total power in a PV system is additive. Under standard conditions (described earlier), we know that ten 100 W PV panels will produce approximately 1 kW of DC electrical power. We also know that when insolation is less than 1000 W/m^2 (and it usually is), we will get a predictable fraction of that power (a bit less than insolation/1000 times the rating). If we know how to calculate power production (in watts) and know how to estimate the amount of insolation a site will receive, we can predict how much energy will be produced per day by PV panels. This is the collecting capacity of the system, and we will see how to estimate power production shortly.

The second factor we can influence is panel orientation. We can mount stationary panels to provide the best possible orientation over an entire year, or part of a year. We can change the panel orientation seasonally. We can even purchase tracking systems that maintain optimal orientation for all seasons and at all hours of the day. In regard to panel orientation, we have to consider some of the terms that describe the various ways panels can be oriented (this will also come in handy when we use software to estimate energy production from a PV system).

Azimuth

Stationary panels can be oriented with their collection surfaces pointed north, south, east, or west (or in any direction between). An azimuth is a convention for describing direction: 90° is east; 180° is south; 270° is west; 0° or 360° is north. Using this approach makes it easy to describe panel direction more exactly (for example, 210° is one-third of the way from due south to due west). In the Northern Hemisphere (particularly north of latitude 23.5°), panels will perform best when facing south (azimuth = 180°). The apparent position of the sun will nearly always, above latitude 23.5°, be south of the system.

The daily apparent motion of the sun confuses this issue slightly. The sun is due south (azimuth exactly 180°) relative to your site for only a short time at midday. At dawn and dusk, the sun is far to the east and west, respectively. So, for much of the day, the stationary panel and direct solar radiation are far from perpendicular. This is not as big a problem as it might seem. When the sun is low in the sky, solar radiation must pass through a great deal of atmosphere to reach your site. The atmosphere scatters, absorbs, and bends (refracts) solar radiation; so the greater the length of the path through the atmosphere, the greater will be the loss of energy delivered to your panels. The amount of solar energy reaching your panels is greatest when the sun is highest in the sky. This is when the length of the path through the atmosphere is relatively short. When the sun is highest, it is also closest to due south (Figure 19-2). Thus, keeping stationary panels pointed south maximizes the amount of radiation you can capture. In fact, pointing stationary panels in any other direction will decrease system performance (we'll see how much, shortly). Solar arrays that track the sun's motion east to west do enhance system performance, but not by as much as you may expect (25 to 40% annually).

Often, panels cannot be conveniently mounted facing due south on a site and an alternate placement must be considered. This will always decrease system performance, but the amount of the decrease is variable. In general, facing the system to the south appears more critical the farther north that you go in the Northern Hemisphere. Table 19-1 predicts the percent loss of performance for three sites along a line from Texas to North Dakota (latitudes 29.5° N to 46.8° N at nearly the same longitude). Predictions are based on a 30-year solar radiation record from the National Renewable Energy Laboratory (NREL) and the array tilt angle set at the site latitude (see the following paragraphs for a discussion of tilt angle). San Antonio, Texas, the southernmost site, shows only about a 4% loss in collected energy between azimuths 135° and 225° (SE to SW). In

Table 19-1 Percent Loss in Energy Collection at Three Locations Due to Mounting Panels Facing Directions Other Than Due South

The "due south" value is 100% in each case. Predictions are based on model PVWATTS at the National Renewable Energy Laboratory Web site.

	45° from South (Average of SE/SW predictions)	90° from South (Average of E/W predictions)	180° from South (Mounted facing N)
San Antonio, TX Latitude 29.53° N	4% loss	15% loss	35% loss
Grand Island, NE Latitude 40.97° N	8% loss	26% loss	60% loss
Bismark, ND Latitude 46.77° N	11% loss	32% loss	68% loss

Grand Island, Nebraska, and Bismark, North Dakota, losses between these limits were predicted to be approximately 8 and 11%, respectively. Loss of performance becomes more pronounced as deviations from due south become larger. Due east and west (azimuths 90° and 270°) showed south-to-north losses of 15, 26, and 32%, respectively. Orienting the panels to the north (azimuth = 0°) decreased panel performance by 35, 60, and 68% along the south-to-north line.

Array Tilt

The array tilt (Figure 19-4) is the angle that the collecting surface of a panel makes relative to a horizontal surface (the ground, if the ground is approximately level). Fully horizontal is 0° and fully vertical is 90°. Just as you can enhance solar collection by choosing the best azimuth, you can also improve collection by choosing the best tilt angle for your site. Remember that in both cases, you want the direction of direct solar radiation and the panel collecting surface to be as close to perpendicular as much of the time as possible (especially when the sun is highest in the sky). This maximizes the size of your "target" (the panel) with respect to the incoming radiation.

For a panel that will remain at the same tilt angle (no adjustments during the year), the tilt angle is commonly set to the latitude of the site (Figure 19-5). At this tilt angle, the collecting surface is perpendicular to direct solar radiation at solar noon (highest elevation of the sun) on two days a year (about March 21 and September 21). In most cases, setting the tilt angle of a stationary panel to the latitude will give the best performance for the entire year. For other azimuths (other than 180°), the optimum tilt angle may be somewhat different.

Certain types of PV mounting hardware allow the tilt angle to be adjusted with relative ease. Some users of nontracking (i.e., stationary) panels adjust the panel tilt during the year (usually two to four times). The position of the sun at solar noon changes during the year by about 47° (Figure 19-2). For most of the Northern and Southern Hemispheres, this represents a progression from a minimum (−23.5° relative to its mean position) in winter to a maximum in summer (+23.5° relative to the mean), with two passes through the mean value (in spring and fall).

It is possible to purchase "solar trackers" that change panel orientation to follow the apparent motion of the sun. Tracking hardware can be single axis (allowing the azimuth

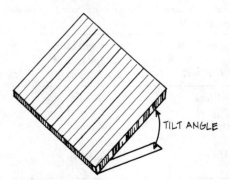

TILT ANGLE

Figure 19-4 Array tilt angle.

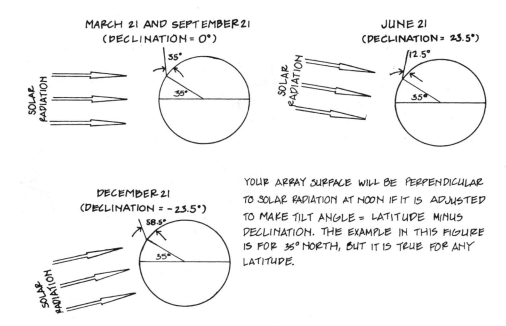

MARCH 21 AND SEPTEMBER 21
(DECLINATION = 0°)

JUNE 21
(DECLINATION = 23.5°)

DECEMBER 21
(DECLINATION = -23.5°)

YOUR ARRAY SURFACE WILL BE PERPENDICULAR TO SOLAR RADIATION AT NOON IF IT IS ADJUSTED TO MAKE TILT ANGLE = LATITUDE MINUS DECLINATION. THE EXAMPLE IN THIS FIGURE IS FOR 35° NORTH, BUT IT IS TRUE FOR ANY LATITUDE.

Figure 19-5 Determining array tilt angle.

to change) or double axis (changing both the panel azimuth and the tilt angle). The use of tracking mounts increases energy collection by roughly 25 to 40% annually. Auto-trackers also increase the complexity and cost of the system.

Estimating Available Power from PV Panels

There are at least three ways to estimate the amount of solar energy that can be collected by a PV array. You can use maps of insolation (solar radiation striking a surface), tables of insolation for specific locations, and interactive computer software. In the United States, all are based on historical data from 239 stations maintained in cooperation with the U.S. Department of Energy (DOE).

Maps and tables are available from many print and Internet sources. One of the best sources of maps is the Renewable Resource Data Center Web site (*http://rredc.nrel.gov/ solar/old_data/nsrdb/redbook/atlas/index.html*). This resource allows you to generate maps of these data for a variety of stationary tilt angles, times of year, and solar trackers. Figure 19-6 is an example of such a map. Maps are helpful if your site is not near one of the 239 collection sites. They can help you refine your estimate of where your site may fall within a particular range.

Tables of the actual (averaged) data are available online (and in print) in the *Solar Radiation Data Manual for Flat-Plate and Concentrating Collectors* (*http://rredc.nrel. gov/solar/pubs/redbook/*). The tables provide a concise summary of measurements for a variety of panel positions and types. Table 19-2 gives an example of these data for

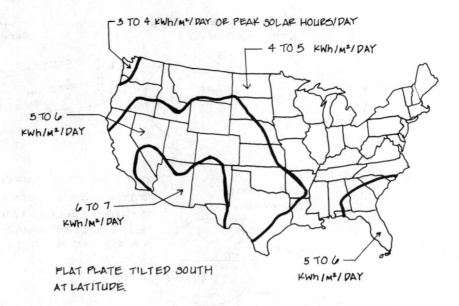

Figure 19-6 Average daily solar insolation for a solar collector facing south and having a tilt angle set to the site latitude. (*Source:* National Renewable Energy Laboratory, U.S. Department of Energy.)

Table 19-2 Daily Insolation Averages at Chattanooga, Tennessee, over a 30-Year Period for a South-Facing Array

(In kWh/m² or peak sun hours; see text.)

	Tilt Angle	Jan.	Feb.	Mar.	Apr.	May	June	July	Aug.	Sept.	Oct.	Nov.	Dec.
Avg.													
Lat − 15		3.1	3.8	4.6	5.6	5.8	6.0	5.8	5.7	5.0	4.6	3.4	2.8	4.7
Lat		3.5	4.1	4.8	5.4	5.4	5.5	5.4	5.5	5.0	4.9	3.8	3.2	4.7
Lat + 15		3.7	4.2	4.6	5.1	4.9	4.8	4.7	5.0	4.8	4.9	4.0	3.4	4.5

Source: U.S. Department of Energy, *Solar Radiation Data Manual for Flat-Plate and Concentrating Collectors (1994).*

three different stationary panel tilt angles in Chattanooga, Tennessee. Tables like these are particularly useful if your site is near one of the 239 collection stations.

In general, maps and tables assume a due south array azimuth (in the Northern Hemisphere) and an unobstructed view of the sun. They are specific for tilt angle, time of the year (annual average, season, or month), and tracker type. The solar data are most commonly presented as either the number of peak sun hours (PSH) available at a site or the total daily energy collected at the site in kWh/m². PSH and kWh/m² are equivalent. Five kWh collected per square meter panel area in an entire day is the same as five hours of collection at a constant intensity of 1 kW/m². Recall that the rated PV panel output (claimed by the manufacturer) is based on standard testing conditions. The standard solar radiation used in the tests is 1000 W/m^2. Use of PSH conveniently emphasizes that the daily panel output can be estimated by multiplying the PSH value by the panel rating. The same multiplication holds true if the map/table has units of kW/m^2, as in Figure 19-6. Make sure that the map or table you use specifies tilt angle, and be aware that actual data can vary significantly from averaged data (the DOE Web sites mentioned earlier also provide minimum and maximum recorded values in addition to average insolation).

EXAMPLE 1. Predict solar energy production during June and December in Chattanooga, Tennessee, using Table 19-2.

We'll use a 1 kW array of panels (1000 W produced under standard testing conditions), facing south and having a tilt angle equal to the latitude of Chattanooga. Table 19-2 tells us that during June and December, average PSH in Chattanooga is 5.5 and 3.2, respectively. Daily predicted performances in June and December are:

June: 5.5 × 1000 = 5500 watt-hours/day (5.5 kWh/day)

December: 3.2 × 1000 = 3200 watt-hours/day (3.2 kWh/day)

For the 30 days of June and the 31 days of December, energy totals are:

June: 5.5 × 30 = 165 kWh

December: 3.2 × 31 = 99 kWh

There is another means of estimating insolation: interactive computer software. PVWATTS is a particularly good example of this to start with, as it requires only access to the Internet (nothing to install) and it is free. PVWATTS was developed by the National Renewable Energy Laboratory and is available online at *http://rredc.nrel.gov/solar/ codes_algs/PVWATTS/index.html*. PVWATTS is based on the same historical data (30 years from 239 sites) as most U.S. maps and tables. It is, however, more flexible than maps or tables. It does require the user to choose the nearest official data collection site (every state has at least two or three; check adjacent states when looking for the closest one), but it allows you to specify system rated size (0.5 to 1000 kW), azimuth (0° to 360°) and tilt angle (0° to 90°) for stationary panels, and single- or double-axis solar tracker. PVWATTS also "derates" panel performance (reduces performance projections) to account for effects of temperature (panel performance decreases with rising temperature), reflection, and soiling of the panel surface. PVWATTS generates monthly PV energy production estimates for an average year. Instructions for its use are quite clear and are available at the Web site.

EXAMPLE 2. Predict solar power generation in June and December using PVWATTS in Chattanooga, Tennessee.

Using PVWATTS, a 1 kW rated system in Chattanooga, having stationary panels (tilt angle = latitude) and facing due south, will produce (based on historical records) 143 kWh in June and 96 kWh in December.

Notice that energy production estimates for December using Table 19-2 and PVWATTS are quite similar (within 3% of each other), whereas the June estimates show a large discrepancy (more than 13%). This is due mainly to the reduction in panel performance caused by warm summer temperatures (which has a larger impact than either soiling or reflection).

EXAMPLE 3. Predict solar power generation in December using PVWATTS in Chattanooga, Tennessee, for a rooftop mount with azimuth not due south.

Let's say our roof is pitched 6 ft vertical for every 12 ft horizontal and our array will be mounted parallel to the roof surface (giving the array the same tilt as the roof). Table 19-3 gives tilt angles for common roof pitches. According to Table 19-3, our roof pitch is 26.6°. Let's also say that the roof orientation is rotated 15° from due south (azimuth = 195°). December PV array performance, according to PVWATTS, will be 90 kWh.

The three approaches described here are similar in that they are based on the same data. Maps may have a slight edge for estimating standard array orientations at sites remote from data collection stations (when estimating PSH may be of great importance). PVWATTS explicitly derates the panels for temperature, reflection, and dirt on the collection surface and facilitates nonstandard orientations (unusual tilt angles and azimuths). When using maps and tables, it is common to derate array performance by 10% to account for all losses (temperature, dirt, reflection, and anything else). Applying the 10% derating in Example 1 slightly overpredicts June performance (148 kWh vs. 143 kWh using PVWATTS) and underpredicts that of December (89 kWh vs. 96 kWh). Given the inherent variability of solar data (which is considerable), this discrepancy is not very important and the use of maps or tables is about as reliable as using software.

It is important to remember when using maps, tables, and software that all of these predictions are based on what has happened in the past. There is no such thing as an "average year," and some years deviate greatly from the average. There is also no guarantee that patterns predominant in the past will persist into the future. Use of historical data is, however, the best approach available on which to base a design.

It is also important to remember that, so far, we have discussed only energy and power produced by the array. The energy delivered to the "load" (the devices that require power) will be diminished further by additional losses in the system. We will look at these losses in the sections that follow.

Table 19-3 Tilt Angles for Pitched Roof Mounted Arrays

Vertical Rise Divided by Horizontal Run	Tilt Angle (°)
0.3	16.7
0.4	21.8
0.5	26.6
0.6	31.0
0.7	35.0
0.8	38.7
0.9	41.2
1.0	45.0

TYPES OF PV SYSTEMS

PV systems are grid-linked, battery storage (off-grid), or hybrid systems.

Grid Linked

A grid-linked (or utility intertied) system, as implied by the name, retains a connection to the conventional power utility grid and has no energy storage capacity. PV-generated electricity is either used as produced or sold to a power company. When power requirements exceed the capacity of the PV system, the difference is drawn from the grid. When PV production exceeds use, the difference is transported to the grid (your meter will actually run backward if permitted by law—more on this later). Because there is no energy storage in this type of system, you remain dependent on the power grid at night or during any daytime period when requirements exceed production. Use of a grid-linked system can allow you to reduce your personal consumption of electricity derived from fossil fuels and can reduce or eliminate your electric bill (excess production during the day can offset use at night).

In addition to the typical components mentioned, a grid-linked system includes:

- An inverter to convert direct current electricity to alternating current. The electricity converted to AC by your inverter and sold back to the utility must match the characteristics of utility power. This places special requirements on your inverter (you should purchase an inverter designated for utility intertie).
- Automatic switching to disconnect the PV system from the utility grid in the event of grid power failure (this protects utility workers from unknowingly working on a line made "hot" by the PV system). Autoswitching is often contained in the inverter.
- Manual switching (lockout) to provide redundant protection for line workers.

Battery Storage

PV-generated electricity can be stored in batteries during the day for use at other times. Battery storage has most frequently been used at locations not currently on or accessible to the utility grid, although some users on the grid have chosen this option as well. A properly designed battery storage system can make you completely independent of the utilities. The design of this type of system requires great care to make sure that the system meets both power and total energy requirements for use (power is the rate at which energy is supplied (W); total energy is the amount of energy (J or kWh) used without reference to its rate of delivery).

In addition to the typical components cited earlier, a battery storage system includes:

- Batteries in series or parallel to meet a specified voltage and current (usually 12, 24, or 48 V)
- A charge controller to protect the batteries during charging and discharge

- An inverter to convert the DC electricity to AC for use by conventional AC devices (not needed for strictly DC systems; does not have the same rigorous criteria as inverters used in utility intertied applications)

Hybrid Systems

More than half of all battery storage systems provide for backup power (when the battery storage system is not operational) and supplemental power (when requirements temporarily exceed supply) from another source. The supplemental source is, most frequently, a gas-powered generator, although other sources (such as wind) have been used. A system that combines two or more different sources of power is a "hybrid."

A gas-powered supplemental power source usually includes:

- A gas (gasoline, propane, or natural gas)-powered generator
- A battery charger
- An inverter (or other device) that has the capacity to incorporate another power source into the household mix

SYSTEM DESIGN

The design of a grid-linked system is simpler than that of a battery storage or hybrid system. This is because less rigor is required in the system sizing (you have the grid to fall back on) and because batteries introduce significant design issues. For this reason, we consider grid-linked systems first.

Design of a Grid-Linked System

Most of the cost of a grid-linked system is on the front end: purchase and installation of the hardware. Although system maintenance is critical, the cost of maintenance is generally quite small (approximately 4% per year) and components are long-lived (panels up to 20 years; balance of system components are variable). The size of the grid-linked system you purchase is more often based on what you are willing to spend than on your actual electrical requirements. Luckily, PV systems are highly modular and can be easily expanded as desired.

Deciding on the Size of Your System

The average U.S. household uses more than 10,000 kWh of electrical energy per year. The cost of a system to provide most or all of the needs of a typical household is in excess of $30,000. Because of the modularity and expandability of PV systems, many grid-linked users start small and work up. The smallest grid-linked systems have a rated capacity of about 500 W. The cost of a small system (hardware plus installation) is approximately $10 per watt capacity. Larger systems (above 4 kW) allow some economy of scale—as low as $8 per watt. Table 19-4 shows predicted energy production from typical small and large systems at two locations.

**Table 19-4   Predicted Energy Production (kWh) for Two Rated System
Capacities at Two Locations**

(Predictions from PVWATTS; azimuth = due south; tilt angle = latitude.)

	System Capacity	
Location	0.5 kW	4.0 kW
Minneapolis, MN (Latitude 45°N)	811 kWh	6486 kWh
Tucson, AR (Latitude 32°N)	1047 kWh	8378 kWh

Most grid-linked systems use the same general types of hardware (Table 19-5). We will consider these components individually and then discuss their assembly into a working system.

PV Panels

PV panels (also called modules) were introduced previously. Panels are connected in series to increase voltage (12 V, 24 V, 36 V, and 48 V are commonly used) or in parallel to increase current. They come in many sizes and rated capacities.

Two types of PV panels make up most current sales. Crystalline panels, as implied by the name, are grown silicon crystals that are later cut and "doped" (supplemental material added) to create PV cells. Thin film panels consist of silicon deposited on backing material. Prices per watt for the two types of cells are about the same. Thin film panels are slightly less efficient than crystalline, and so are slightly larger, but they lose less power under high temperatures (standard testing is performed at 25°C (77°C); all panels lose some power—perhaps as much as 10%—at temperatures above this value). Crystalline panels perform slightly better than thin film panels under low light conditions.

Table 19-6 provides specifications for several commonly used PV panels, which are produced by three different manufacturers. Notice that the "voltage at rated power" figures are nearly identical—about 17 V. As mentioned, panel output voltage decreases as the panel temperature increases. The voltage output from the PV system must typically exceed 12, 24, 36, or 48 V for the inverter to function (and if the inverter does not

Table 19-5   Components Used in a Grid-Linked PV System

- PV Panels (modules)
- Panel rack(s)
- Invertor
- Panel interconnects
- Conduit and conduit box
- Combiner block (for multiple arrays)
- Automatic grid disconnect (may be included in inverter)
- Manual grid disconnect (may be included in inverter)
- Electrical boxes and circuit breakers for DC and AC circuits
- Appropriate cable for indoor and outdoor uses

function, the system does not function). The use of 17 volts is insurance that panel output will always meet minimum system voltage needs, even following a temperature-induced voltage drop or in low light conditions.

The "current at rated power" is the amperage produced under standard test conditions. As temperatures go up at the panel, current drops more quickly than voltage. The "rated power" of the panel is just the rated voltage times the rated current.

"Short circuit current" is the amperage that would occur under test conditions if, for some reason, the current bypassed the load (whatever devices you are operating) and went straight to ground. This is what would occur in the event of a short circuit. It is the maximum current that the panel can produce. The short circuit current is useful in determining the size of the wire and the circuit breakers you should use.

The "open circuit voltage" is the voltage across the panel output terminals under test conditions when there is no load (nothing connected to the terminals). It is the maximum voltage that the panel can produce and is useful for testing panel performance and calculating expected voltages of panels combined in arrays.

Mounting Racks

The dimensions in the panel specifications lead to the next component in system design, the mounting racks. Mounting racks are used to anchor the solar panels securely enough to withstand expected wind and weather conditions. They are usually made of aluminum or steel. Panels can be mounted on the ground, on roofs (flat or pitched), or on poles. You can adjust ground-roof mounts and pole mounts (Figure 19-7) for optimum tilt angles. Panels set at the tilt angle and azimuth of the roof surface are mounted with the use of standoff brackets (Figure 19-8). Such panels appear to be mounted right on the roof surface. In reality, they must be mounted at least 3 in. (7.5 cm) above the surface (hence the use of the brackets). The elevated mount promotes ventilation and prevents the panels from becoming too hot and so losing too much power (dark roofs can heat to 160°F (71°C) during the summer).

Inverter

The next component in a grid-tied system is the inverter. The primary role of an inverter

Table 19-6 Specifications for Commonly Used Panels
(Specifications vary between manufacturers.)

Rated Power	50W	75W	100W	120W
Voltage at rated power	16.6	17.0	17.0	16.9
Current (A) at rated power	3.0	4.4	5.9	7.1
Short circuit current (A)	3.2	4.8	6.5	7.5
Open circuit voltage	21.0	21.7	21.6	21.5
Length (in.)	37.0	47.3	59.0	56.1
Width (in.)	19.7	20.8	23.4	25.7
Depth (in.)	0.9	1.3	1.6	2.0
Weight (lb)	12.5	16.7	24.0	26.2

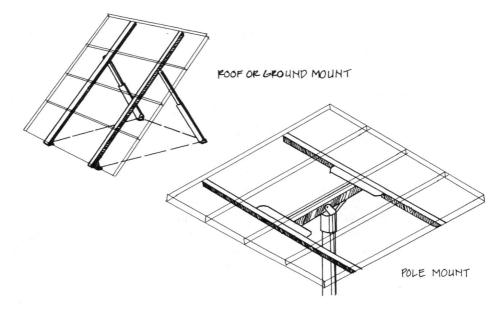

ROOF OR GROUND MOUNT

POLE MOUNT

Figure 19-7 PV array mounting racks.

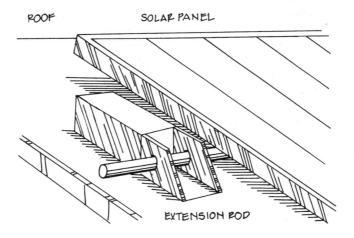

ROOF   SOLAR PANEL

EXTENSION ROD

Figure 19-8 PV panel standoff bracket.

is to convert direct current to alternating current (DC to AC). Inverters require energy to perform this function and have an efficiency of about 90% (somewhat higher at full capacity, somewhat lower at less than full capacity). There are many inverters available for purchase, but only a few are suitable for grid-linked systems. First, the inverter must produce a high-quality true sine wave signal. This leaves out the less expensive modified sine wave inverters. Second, to link your system to the grid, the system must include a number of safety features and must meet standards set by the Underwriters Laboratory (UL) and the National Electrical Code (NEC). An important safety feature has to do with what happens when utility power fails (the power grid "goes down"). Under most circumstances, this will look like a short circuit to the inverter. The inverter will try to supply power to the grid, and the grid requirements will be so much greater than its capability that power flow will trip a *grid short circuit* relay. This internal device disconnects your system from the grid and prevents you from keeping the local lines "hot" (which can endanger utility line workers). It is also possible, however, that the local electrical demand will not be large enough to trip the relay. Under some circumstances, your system may happily continue to supply your home and those of your neighbors. In this case, your system creates an "island" of power that can endanger utility workers. It is possible to detect this condition, called *islanding,* by testing both the frequency and voltage produced by the PV system (both will drift outside utility standards once utility power is lost). When such drift occurs, the connection to the grid is automatically broken.

Your inverter must also be protected from the line. Power surges (due mainly to lightning) can occur on both the AC and DC sides of the inverter. You should install surge (lightning) arresters between the inverter and the panels and between the inverter and the grid.

Maximum Power Point Tracking

Voltage inputs to inverters suitable for grid-tied systems are usually 24, 36, or 48 V. If, for example, your grid-tied inverter requires a 48 V input, you must supply at least 48 V or it will not work correctly. Recall that modules typically have rated voltages of about 17 V (so that actual voltage will always be at least 12 despite temperature and low light effects). This means that you must connect four modules in series to reliably have 48 V (Figure 19-9). This can, under some circumstances, result in a considerable power loss (as when your panel really is producing the rated voltage).

EXAMPLE 4. Calculate power loss at the panel-inverter junction.

For this example, we will use 75 W panels, as described in Table 19-6 (rated 17 V, 4.4 A) and a grid tie inverter having a 48 V input. To ensure adequate voltage under most conditions, we connect four panels in series, giving a rated 68 V. Now, let's

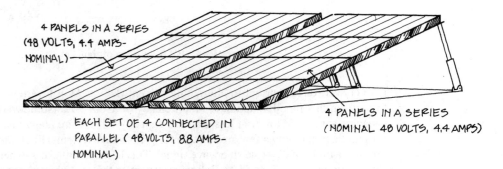

Figure 19-9 PV modules in series and parallel.

say that for much of the time, our panels really do each produce 17 V and 4.4 A. The power produced by the connected panels is:

$$P = 68 \text{ V} \times 4.4 \text{ A} = 300 \text{ W}$$

The usable AC power that makes it into the inverter is:

$$P = 48 \text{ V} \times 4.4 \text{ A} = 211 \text{ W}$$

This represents a loss of 89 W or 30%.

Losses are not usually this bad, but you get the idea. However, there is a solution: It is possible to alter voltage and current in a circuit. We do this all the time in the utility transformers that connect high-voltage utility lines to lower-voltage residences. It's only recently that this approach has been applied to photovoltaics, and it has resulted in *maximum power point tracking* (not to be confused with solar trackers, which physically change panel orientation as the sun moves). Maximum power point tracking (MPPT) has been incorporated into some grid intertie inverters. In the preceding example, the power point tracker would adjust both panel output voltage and current to maximize available power.

EXAMPLE 5.   Apply MPPT to reduce the loss in Example 4.

As in Example 4, panel voltage in series is 68 V. The power point tracker converts this voltage series to approximately 48 V. Because energy is conserved (remains the same), the current becomes:

$$\text{Current} = 300 \text{ W}/48 \text{ V} = 6.25 \text{ A}$$

Now functioning at 48 V and 6.25 A, all the panel power is transferred to the inverter.

Of course, there is no such thing as a completely free lunch. The power point tracker requires energy to make the voltage/current alterations and so reduces inverter efficiency somewhat, but the trade-off is a good one. As mentioned earlier, MPPTs have been built into many of the inverters used in grid-tied PV systems, and they can be added as separate components to others.

Wire and Cable

All outdoor wiring should have sunlight- and abrasion-resistant (XLP/XHHW, TC, or similar) insulation. Wire having other types of insulation should be run in conduit. USE2 2-conductor outdoor wire (also called type TC) is the standard wire for all outdoor applications. It is water and sunlight resistant and UL approved for use without conduit.

Conduit

Conduit is plastic or metal pipe used to contain cables and wires. It should be used whenever wire/cable is not certified for outdoor applications or when abrasion or animals may be a problem. Plastic conduit may be rigid or flexible. Conduit threads onto or otherwise attaches to junction or combiner blocks.

Combiner Block(s)

A combiner block (Figure 19-10) is an electrical box used to wire individual arrays in parallel (the NEC does not approve wiring arrays in parallel in the junction boxes that come connected to a panel). Combiner blocks usually include circuit breakers or fuses for the circuit (to handle the DC side of the system). They may contain surge protection (lightning arresters) to protect the system.

Manual Grid Disconnect and Lockout

Many utilities insist on including a way for line repair workers to manually take the PV system off the grid. This is done to add a level of redundancy (along with the autodisconnects described earlier) for the protection of workers.

Completed System

Figure 19-11 illustrates the organization of components in a complete grid-linked system.

Generally, the system is grounded at two locations: the solar array(s) and the inverter. If the inverter and solar arrays are close enough to the main service entrance, the main utility ground (conducting rod driven 6 to 8 ft into the earth near the main service entrance) may be used for this purpose. If the panels are far from the house, then the

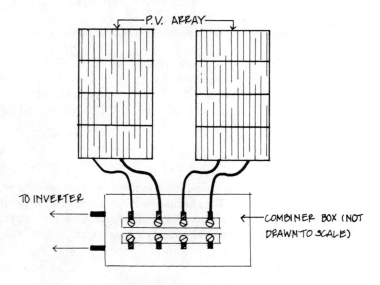

Figure 19-10   Combiner block.

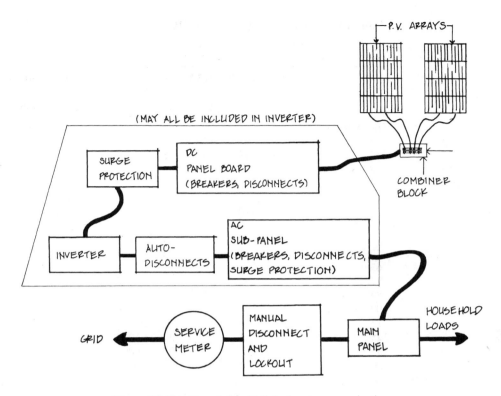

Figure 19-11 Complete grid-linked system organization.

inverter should be mounted outdoors near the panels so as to avoid the voltage drop associated with direct current lines. In this case, a second ground, similar to the utility ground, should be installed. Use #8 or 6 AWG bare copper for wiring to the ground rod.

Solar panels become operational as soon as they are exposed to sunlight. It is good practice to install and/or wire these components last (after all wiring and the rest of the system installation has been completed).

When wiring, be aware that DC circuits require heavier-gauge wire than AC circuits. Table 19-7 gives recommended wire sizes for PV applications.

EXAMPLE 6. Estimate annual energy production for a 3 kW rated capacity grid-linked system in Wood River, Nebraska.

First let's define the system and our management more exactly. The array faces due south. Tilt angle is changed twice per year. October through March, tilt angle is latitude plus 15°. April through September, it is latitude minus 15°. Wood River is quite close to Grand Island (a data collection site), so we can conveniently use the *Solar Radiation Data Manual for Flat-Plate and Concentrating Collectors* or PVWATTS. In either case, we will have to look at two sets of data: one for each tilt angle. Average daily insolation for our site in PSH (which is equivalent to kW/m² per day) is given as follows:

Table 19-7   Wire Sizes (AWG) for DC and AC Circuits of Varying Currents and Lengths

(Wire sizes are consistent with NEC requirements.)

	DC, 12 V Nominal (15 V Rated) Current from PV Array (A)							
				Amperes				
	6	12	18	24	30	36	42	48
One-Way Distance (ft)								
13	13	10	9	7	6	6	5	4
15	13	10	8	7	6	5	4	4
18	12	9	7	6	5	4	4	3
20	11	8	7	5	4	4	3	2
23	11	8	6	5	4	3	3	2
25	10	7	6	4	4	3	2	1
30	10	7	5	4	3	2	1	1
40	8	5	4	2	1	1	0	00
50	7	4	3	1	1	0	00	00
63	7	4	2	1	0	00	000	000
75	6	3	1	0	00	000	000	0000
88	5	2	0	00	000	0000	0000	0000
100	4	1	0	00	000	0000		
113	4	1	00	000	0000			
125	4	1	00	000	0000			
138	3	0	000	0000				
150	3	0	000	0000				

	DC, 48 V Nominal (60 V Rated)							
				Amperes				
	6	12	18	24	30	36	42	48
One-Way Distance (ft)								
13	14	14	12	8	6	6	6	6
15	14	14	12	8	6	6	6	6
18	14	14	12	8	6	6	6	6
20	14	14	12	8	6	6	6	6
23	14	14	12	8	6	6	6	6
25	14	13	12	8	6	6	6	6
30	14	13	11	8	6	6	6	6
40	14	11	10	8	6	6	6	5
50	13	10	9	7	6	6	5	4
63	12	10	8	7	6	5	4	4
75	12	9	7	6	5	4	3	3
88	11	8	6	5	4	3	3	
100	10	7	6	4	4	3		
113	10	7	5	4	3			
125	10	7	5	4	3			
138	9	6	4	3				
150	9	6	4	3				

Tilt Angle	Jan.	Feb.	Mar.	Apr.	May	June	July	Aug.	Sept.	Oct.	Nov.	Dec.
Lat −15	3.6	4.2	5.0	5.8*	6.1*	6.7*	6.8*	6.4*	5.5*	4.7	3.5	3.1
Lat +15	4.4*	4.8*	5.2*	5.3	5.1	5.3	5.5	5.6	5.4	5.2*	4.2*	3.9*

Asterisks are used to denote when each tilt angle will be used. Multiplying daily insolation values by the system capacity and the number of days in the month gives average monthly energy production (in kWh) before derating.

Jan.	Feb.	Mar.	Apr.	May	June	July	Aug.	Sept.	Oct.	Nov.	Dec.	Total
409	403	483	522	567	603	632	595	495	483	378	362	5935

Derating panel performance by 10% to account for temperature, soiling, age, and so on, and accounting for inverter efficiency (reduce by another 10%), the average expected energy production (in kWh) may approach:

Jan.	Feb.	Mar.	Apr.	May	June	July	Aug.	Sept.	Oct.	Nov.	Dec.	Total
327	322	386	417	453	482	505	476	396	386	302	290	4748

Grid Linking Legal Issues

Grid linking appeals to PV users because it eliminates the power storage problem. Excess production is sold to the utility company and offsets the power consumed when solar electricity is not available (night, cloudy days).

There are still problems with this system that have been solved only in certain states. First, the utilities may not have to purchase the electricity at retail rates (the rates they charge you). The Public Utilities Regulatory Policy Act of 1978 (PURPA) required utility companies to purchase output from small power-producing systems at "avoided cost rates." Avoided cost is the cost that the utility would have had to pay to produce the power or purchase the power from another source. Typically, this means 2 to 3 cents per kWh, which is much less than the amount charged by utilities to residential customers (an average 10 cents per kWh in the United States). In places where buyback of power is based on avoided costs, PV producers have had to install a second electric meter that measures the energy exported to the grid. The electric bill is then based on the number of kWh drawn from the grid times the retail rate minus the number of kWh exported times the avoided cost rate.

In 32 states (with five more pending), this problem has been largely corrected through "net metering." Net metering allows the PV producer to use a single bidirectional electric meter (most residential electric meters are bidirectional). The meter turns forward when electricity comes from the grid and backward when it is exported, allowing excess PV production to offset later use at retail value. Most net metering regulations stipulate that excess production at the end of the month (more electricity produced than used) is compensated at the lower avoided cost rate. A small number of states allow net production to be carried over into other months. This allows net production during summer to be used at other seasons (at the retail rate).

In states that allow some form of net metering (Table 19-8), your system must meet a variety of safety and quality criteria, which generally include:

Table 19-8   States That Allow Net Metering

State	Maximum Capacity	State	Maximum Capacity
Arizona	100 kW	Nevada	10 kW
Arkansas	25 kW residential	New Hampshire	25 kW
	100 kW commercial	New Jersey	No limit
California	1 MW	New Mexico	10 kW
Colorado	10 kW	Connecticut	No limit
New York	10 kW	North Dakota	100 kW
Delaware	25 kW	Ohio	No limit
District of Columbia	100 kW	Oklahoma	100 kW & 25,000 kWh/year
		Oregon	25 kW
Georgia	10 kW residential	Pennsylvania	10 kW
	100 kW commercial		
Idaho	100 kW		
Illinois	40 kW		
Indiana	1000 kWh/month	Rhode Island	25 kW
Iowa	No limit	Texas	50 kW
Kansas	10 kW residential	Vermont	15 kW
	100 kW commercial	Virginia	10 kW residential
Maine	100 kW		25 kW non-residential
Maryland	80 kW	Washington	25 kW
Massachusetts	60 kW	Wisconsin	20 kW
Minnesota	40 kW	Wyoming	25 kW
Montana	50 kW		

- *Voltage and frequency regulation.* Certain types of loads (power uses) in the home can temporarily affect system voltage and frequency (electric motors, when they start, can alter both). The utility generally puts limits on the amount of deviation allowed in the PV system.

- *Harmonic distortion in the operating load range.* The AC current and voltage supplied by the grid has a characteristic shape (a sine wave). *Harmonic distortion* refers to the amount of deviation from this wave form that the utility will tolerate in the voltage and current exported by the PV system. Harmonic distortion should be minimal.

- *Power factor.* The power factor is the ratio of the power produced by the system at a particular time to the average power produced by the system. This ratio should be fairly close to 1.0 (usually greater than 0.85).

- *Protection and operation.* These criteria include the automatic grid disconnects for current, frequency, and voltage for protecting line workers, as described earlier.

Because administration of net metering is performed by the various states, there are state-to-state differences in the regulations and requirements. The U.S. Department of Energy Web site (*http://www.eren.doe.gov/greenpower/netmetering/*) is a good source of summary information for your state. In many cases, the rules and agreement forms are available on-line from the individual states (for example, see *http://www.state.vt.us/psd/ee/ee20.htm* for Vermont).

Grid linking in general, and net metering in particular, are still new concepts to many utility employees, so patience is a virtue when making your initial and follow-up contacts. Some utilities have felt threatened by the possibility of individual power producers exporting electricity (there have been a few lawsuits in regard to net metering). Many net metering laws cap the amount of power that can be produced by small "distributed generating" systems. Actually, there are a number of technical advantages for the utility when these systems come on-line. In addition, standards and codes for grid-intertied systems have become available, further allaying institutional fears about the small producers. The standards and codes, in most cases, are established by the Institute of Electrical and Electronics Engineers (IEEE), the American Society for Testing and Materials (ASTM), the NEC, and the International Electrotechnical Commission (IEC). Moreover, individual components are approved by the UL. The individual requirements for your system should be clearly laid out in the state applications, but it is your responsibility to see that your components and system meet these requirements.

Design of a Battery Storage (Off-Grid) PV System and/or Hybrid

A grid-linked PV system offers the luxury of an infinite (more or less) source of backup power. The capacity of a grid-linked system is not critical from an operational standpoint. This is not the case when implementing an off-grid system. The power delivered by your system is all you have. Even when using a source of backup power, such as a gasoline generator in a hybrid system, supplemental energy tends to be costly and inconvenient to use, so system capacity remains a critical factor. However, the composition of an off-grid PV system is quite similar to a grid-linked system.

Differences include:

- Optional use of an inverter—it is possible to have a DC-only home.
- Greater choice of inverters—the user is not required to meet the utilities expectations for signal quality and system performance.
- Use of batteries—batteries are the only viable form of power storage.
- Charge controller—to handle charging from the PV array and protect the batteries.
- Generator (hybrid system)—to provide supplementary power.
- Battery charger (hybrid system)—to charge batteries with supplementary power.
- Electrical bus (connection device)—to combine power sources and prevent back-feed from the batteries to devices that are not in operation.

Figure 19-12 shows a hybrid system that includes battery storage and supplemental power generation.

In this section, we will assume that you have read the sections on grid-linked systems. The contents of these sections are generally applicable to off-grid (battery storage) design as well. This section concentrates on three areas: determining your energy and power requirements, choice and capacity of batteries, and selecting remaining hardware.

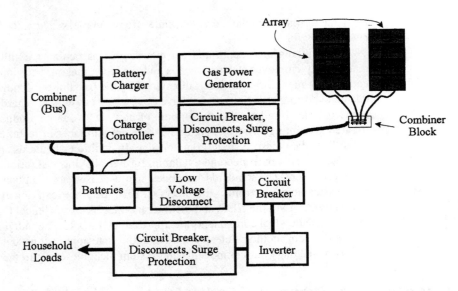

Figure 19-12   Components used in a stand-alone hybrid (back-up generator) PV system.

Determining the Capacity of Your Battery Storage System

There are two aspects to the problem of determining the capacity of your battery storage PV system. The first is determining your energy requirements. Energy is expressed in watts (W) or kilowatts (kW; 1000 W = 1 kW). Your energy requirement per day will be the total of all your energy uses during the day plus the energy lost during the process of storing it in batteries (about 20%) plus the energy lost by converting DC to AC (if AC is used; this is about 10%). The second part of the problem is to determine your power requirements. Power is the rate at which energy is delivered for use.

EXAMPLE 7.   Illustrate the difference between energy and power requirements.

Three devices, A, B, and C, are used once each day. Each device requires 100 W of power and is run for 1 hour each day. Compute total energy use.

$$\text{Energy} = 300 \text{ W} \times 1 \text{ hr} = 300 \text{ Wh} = 0.3 \text{ kWh}$$

- They are operated consecutively. How much power must the system be able to deliver?   P = 100 W, because only one device is used at a time.

- They are operated simultaneously. How much power must the system be able to deliver?   P = 300 W, because each device requires 100 W.

In other words, your system must be able to supply the total quantity of energy you need, and it must be able to supply it at a rate that will allow all required simultaneous operations.

The amount of energy you use and the amount of power required depends on your needs and habits. For an off-grid system, there is no way to avoid considering all of the electrical devices you use in determining what your system must supply. Tables 19-9, 19-10, and 19-11 provide some basic information in this area.

Certain appliances and devices simply require too much electrical power to be used in an off-grid system (unless you have very deep pockets). Electric hot water heating, electric heat, electric stoves, electric clothes dryers, and central air-conditioning fall into this category. Nonelectric alternatives are typically used for heating the home, hot water, cooking, and drying clothes. In low-humidity environments, "swamp (evaporative) coolers" are used. Otherwise, central air is probably not an option.

Other appliances have high energy requirements that may strain your system: window air conditioners, clothes washers, and refrigerators. With respect to clothes washers and refrigerators, extremely efficient models are available. Although their purchase prices are high as compared with conventional alternatives, they more than pay for themselves when compared with the cost of additional capacity in your PV system (they will even pay for themselves in conventional systems). Although they put less strain on your system, the same is true for compact fluorescent lights, which also greatly reduce power/energy requirements for lighting.

As described earlier, the output from your PV system is DC. Use of conventional AC devices require that an inverter be used in your system, which will result in a 5 to 10% reduction in system efficiency. You can avoid this loss by using only DC equipment (Table 19-11). You should be aware, however, that with advances in inverter technology, DC devices are becoming less common (except in developing countries). An exception to this is well pumps, which appear to be good candidates for DC systems.

Determining the Amount of Energy and Power Your System Will Deliver

The size of your system is based on your power/energy requirements plus losses associated with battery storage, and temperature plus losses associated with the use of an inverter.

Table 19-9 Power and Energy Requirements of Small AC Appliances

Item	Average Wattage	Estimated kWh Usage
Automatic blanket	20	0.24/day
Clock	4	0.1/day
Coffeemaker	850	0.85/hr (includes hotplate)
Computer	250	.25/hr
Frying pan	1200	1.2/hr
Hair dryer	1250	1.25/hr
Iron	1100	1.1/hr
Radio	20	0.02/hr
Radio/CD player	40	0.04/hr
Toaster	1100	0.02/min

Table 19-10   Power and Energy Requirements of Large AC Appliances

Item	Average Wattage	Estimated kWh Usage
Air conditioner (room) 6,000 Btu	750	0.75/hr
Air conditioner (central) 2.5 tons	3,500	3.5/hr
Car engine heater	1,000	1 /use
Ceiling fan	60	0.06/h
Clothes dryer	5000	5/load
Clothes washer	600	0.3/load
Clothes washer (high efficiency)	270	0.135/load
Dehumidifier	300	0.3/hr
Dishwasher	1,190	1/day
Freezer, standard (12–15 ft^3)	350	5/day
Freezer, standard (frost free, 12–15 ft^3)	440	6.67/day
Furnace, gas or oil (fans/thermostat)	600	2.5/day
Humidifier	80	0.08/day
Lighting (incandescent)	60	0.06/hr
Lighting (compact fluorescent)	15	0.015/hr
Lighting per room (incandescent)	100	0.1/hr
Lighting per room (fluorescent)	25	0.025/hr
Microwave (large)	1,450	1.45/hr
Microwave (small)	800	0.8/hr
Range	12,000	4/day
Refrigerator, standard (12–16 ft^3)	265	3.5/day
Refrigerator, frost free (16 ft^3)	475	6.5/day
Refrigerator, high efficiency (16 ft^3)	200	0.56/day
Refrigerator, frost free (20 ft^3)	540	8.0/day
Refrigerator, high efficiency (19 ft^3)	200	0.77/day
Television (19 in. color)	250	0.25/hr
Vacuum cleaner	700	0.7/hr
Water bed heater	300	0.3/hr
Water heater (family of 4)	3,800	14/day
Water pump	1,000	1.3/day

EXAMPLE 8. Calculate appliance power and energy requirements in a sample household. In this household, cooking, heating, and water heating are powered by propane. Electrical uses are summarized as follows:

	Energy	Power
Clocks (2)	0.2 kWh	8 W
Coffeemaker (1 hr)	0.85	850
Computer (2 hr)	0.5	250
Iron (1/2 h)*	0.55	1100
Radio/CD player (2 hr)	0.08	40
Toaster (5 min)	0.1	1100
Ceiling fan (3 hr)	0.18	60
Clothes washer (conventional, 1 load)*	0.3	600

Fans/thermostat for heating	2.5	600
Lighting (three rooms, incandescent, 3 hr)	0.3	200
Microwave (small, $1/2$ hr)	0.4	800
Refrigerator (20 ft^3)	8.0	540
Television (19 in., 4 hr)	1.0	250
Vacuum cleaner ($1/2$ hr)*	0.35	700
	15.31 kWh	7098 W

* Not used every day

The appliances in this household would (if all electrical devices were used in a given day) require over 15 kWh of electrical energy and (if all were in use at once), have to be able to deliver more than 7 kW of power.

The numbers in the preceding example are starting points. Most PV users attempt to minimize costs by keeping their systems as small as possible. This can include setting up rules for how electrical devices are used.

EXAMPLE 9. Set rules for using electrical devices to minimize power and energy use.

Rule 1. Do only one of the following in a day: iron, vacuum, wash clothes. This will decrease appliance daily energy requirements by 0.65 kWh (by the two smallest components), bringing it to 14.66 kWh / day.

Rule 2. Use only one of the following at a time: coffeemaker, iron, toaster, clothes washer, microwave, or vacuum cleaner (they can be used on the same day, but not simultaneously). This brings the maximum power use down to about 3050 W.

EXAMPLE 10. Replace the refrigerator and clothes washer with high-efficiency models.

A high-efficiency refrigerator has energy and power requirements of 0.77 kWh and 200 W, respectively (down from 8 kWh and 540 W). A high-efficiency clothes washer has requirements of 0.135 kWh and 270 W (down from 0.3 kWh and 600 W). Energy and power savings are the differences between the old and new values:

Table 19-11   Power and Energy Requirements of Selected DC Appliances

Item	Average Wattage	Estimated kWh Usage
Refrigerator (12 ft^3)	93	0.81
Well pump	200	0.5/day
Blender	96	0.016/day
Ceiling fan (6 hrs / day)	25	0.15
Coffeemaker	120	0.12/day
Refrigerator (16 ft^3)	200	0.54/day
Television (19 in. color, 3 hr/day)	90	0.27/day
Swamp cooler (8 hr/day)	50	0.4/day
Radio/tape player (2 hr/day)	35	0.07/day
Fan (8 in.) (2 hr/day)	15	0.03/day
Lighting per room (6 hr/day)	25	0.15/day

$$\text{Refrigerator: } 8 - 0.77 = 7.23 \text{ kWh} \qquad \text{Clothes washer: } 0.3 - 0.135 = 0.165 \text{ kWh}$$
$$540 - 200 = 340 \text{ W} \qquad\qquad\qquad 600 - 270 = 330 \text{ W}$$

Savings for the clothes washer will occur only on days when it is used, so we will leave it out of the totals. The refrigerator represents a daily and substantial savings, bringing daily appliance energy and power requirements down to about 7.5 kWh and 2710 W, respectively.

As shown in the preceding examples, a high efficiency refrigerator decreased energy use by almost 50%. Being careful about when devices are used (not on the same day or at the same time for certain devices) also decreased energy use and had a large impact on peak power demand.

Notice that this system did not include air-conditioning or other electric devices that we often have in our homes. It is possible to include these devices (you can see from Example 8 how to determine energy and power requirements). In general, though, off-grid system users get used to living without some of the luxuries that others take for granted.

Battery Storage for an Off-Grid System

Batteries in an off-grid PV system store electrical energy for use at night or on cloudy days. Those used in most PV systems are deep-cycle batteries, designed to provide steady power over extended periods. They can discharge up to 80% of their energy without being damaged and can be discharged and recharged over and over again. Automobile batteries are not deep-cycle batteries. They are designed to provide short, intense bursts of power and fail if they repeatedly discharge more than 20% of their capacity. There are many different types of batteries (lead-acid; nickel-cadmium, etc.) that can be used. The most common variety is lead-acid. We will confine our discussion to this type.

The size of the battery "bank" you need depends on a number of factors:

- Your desired storage capacity (for how many consecutive cloudy days you wish your system to function)

- Battery efficiency (the ratio of energy discharged from a battery to the energy used to charge it—usually assumed to be 80%)

- Inverter efficiency (usually assumed to be 90%)

- The maximum discharge rate of your batteries (the rate at which power can be delivered and still provide all of the stored power)

- Their maximum charge rate (batteries should be brought back to full charge after each cycle)

- The battery storage temperature (batteries perform more poorly when cold than when warm)

Storage Capacity

Storage capacity in a battery is expressed in ampere hours (Ah). A battery storing 100 Ah can (in theory) deliver any combination of current multiplied by time that equals 100. Ten A for 10 hours and 1 A for 100 hours are mathematically the same. Ah and kWh are a bit alike in this respect. There are, however, two differences. First, not all of the stored energy is actually available. Even in deep-cycle batteries, only about 80% of the energy can be extracted before you begin to damage the battery. Most battery manufacturers recommend 50% discharge (depth of discharge, DOD) as a regular practice to extend battery life. Second, you must take the maximum discharge rate into account.

Maximum Discharge Rate

The actual storage capacity of a battery depends on the rate at which energy is withdrawn (its discharge rate). The ratings you see on a battery are usually based on 20 hr of discharge. A 100 Ah capacity based on 20 hr would give you 5 A per hour for 20 hr, at which time it would be completely drained (sometimes you will see 100 hr used instead, but 20 hr is more the norm). For a battery rated at more than 20 hr, allowing it to drain over a longer time period will actually increase the amount of energy you can extract. Draining it more quickly will decrease the amount of energy you can extract (sometimes considerably). So the rate of draining actually affects the amount of energy that you can recover.

Maximum Charge Rate

The rate at which the battery is charged by the panels is also a factor. If a battery is charged too quickly, it will heat up, which can damage the battery. A slow charge, with a current not more than $1/10$ of its Ah capacity, will not harm the battery.

Temperature

The process of storing and extracting energy actually involves a chemical reaction. Like many chemical reactions, it is affected by temperature. Rated battery capacities are at 80°F (27°C). At temperatures of less than 80°F (27°C), the amount of stored energy will be less (Table 19-12).

Table 19-12   Battery Performance Loss Due to Temperature (For Worst-Case Sizing)

Temperature	Loss (%)	Temperature	Loss (%)
80°F (27°C)	0	40°F (4°C)	30
70°F (21°C)	4	30°F (−1°C)	40
60°F (16°C)	11	20°F (−7°C)	59
50°F (10°C)	19		

Determining the Size of Your Battery Bank

The size of your battery bank refers to the number of batteries you must use to meet your power and energy needs. The number of batteries depends on the following:

- The types of batteries you will use
- The amount of daily energy you require (including system losses)
- Your power requirements
- The number of days of storage your batteries will provide (usually three to seven)
- The minimum temperature at which the batteries will be held

EXAMPLE 11. Determine the battery bank size required for the home in the previous example (energy = 7.5 kWh/day; maximum power = 2710 W) .
We will select:

- Battery efficiency: 80%.
- Energy loss due to inverter: 10%.
- Number of days of storage: 3 (for three days of bad weather).
- Maximum design discharge: 50% (to protect the batteries).
- Battery characteristics (this battery frequently appears in off-grid systems): 6 V, 225 Ah (each cell in a battery is 2 V; therefore, a 6 V battery has three cells—this will matter when we get to charging voltage).
- Voltage at the inverter: 24 V (this means that four 6 V batteries must be connected in series).
- Battery storage temperature: 60°F.

Start with the daily energy requirement. The daily requirement must account for appliance needs, the efficiency of the batteries (80%), and the efficiency of the inverter (90%).
Total energy requirement = 7.5 kWh/day × 1/0.8 × 1/0.9 = 10.5 kWh/day
Multiply this by the number of days of storage.

$$\text{Stored energy} = 10.5 \text{ kWh/day} \times 3 \text{ days} = 31.5 \text{ kWh}$$

This is the amount of deliverable energy you want your system to store. Next, multiply this value by 2 to account for the fact that you want battery discharge limited to 50%.

$$\text{Battery storage for 50\% discharge} = 31.5 \text{ kWh} \times 2 = 63 \text{ kWh}$$

Now account for storage temperature losses (winter storage at 60°F (16°C)).

$$\text{Battery storage at 60°F} = 63 \text{ kWh}/0.89 = 70.8 \text{ kWh} = 70,800 \text{ Wh}$$

We have converted kWh to watt hours (Wh) for the next step: determining the total Ah delivered by the storage system. (Recall that power, in watts, is equal to current times voltage; we can convert watts to amps by dividing by 24 V.)

$$\text{Storage Ah} = 70{,}800 \text{ Wh}/24 \text{ V} = 2950 \text{ Ah}$$

The number of 24 V series we need to connect in parallel is then:

Number of 4-battery series connected in parallel = 2950 Ah/225 Ah per battery = 13.1 = 14 series

There are four batteries in each 24 V series, so the total number of batteries required is $14 \times 4 = 56$ batteries.

Because we rounded up the number of 4-battery series (from 13.1 to 14), actual storage capacity is about 3.5 days at 50% DOD or (when needed) 5.5 days at 80% DOD.

Note: this system would probably use higher-voltage batteries to decrease battery-to-battery connections (the number of battery connections for similar 12 V batteries would be half that needed for 6 V batteries).

EXAMPLE 12. Determine whether this system will meet peak power demand.

Peak power demand for this system is 2710 W. Each four-battery series can deliver the rated current over a 20 hr period (225 Ah/20 hr = 11.25 A). The power available is the available current times the number of 4-battery series times the system voltage (24 V):

Available power from batteries = 11.25 A per series $\times$ 14 series $\times$ 24 V = 3780 W

This power can be delivered to the inverter. The amount of power converted to AC for use in the house is 90% of 3780 W (10% lost to inverter).

Available AC power = 3780 W $\times$ 0.90 = 3402 W

This exceeds peak demand.

Battery Operation and Maintenance

Batteries require regular and careful attention. Battery terminals and electrical connections should be periodically cleaned (use water and clean cloths, no detergents) to avoid energy losses. In lead-acid batteries, cells must be routinely checked (every four weeks or so) to make sure that the lead plates are covered with liquid (a solution of water and acid). Distilled water should be added to capacity when checking (cells are "topped" with water). Battery holding temperature should not be much above 80°F (27°C), as this decreases battery life. Temperatures lower than this increase battery life but decrease capacity (Table 19-12).

Proper battery charging is essential to get the maximum performance and life from your batteries.

- The rate at which lead-acid batteries are charged (in A) should be between "capacity/10" and "capacity/20" (referred to as C/10 and C/20). For a 225 Ah battery, such as used in our sample system, C/10 is 225/10 = 22.5 A. C/20 = 225/20 = 11.25 A. Charging more quickly than at C/10 causes a battery to heat and may damage the plates of deep-cycle lead-acid batteries.

- The leading cause of battery failure is incomplete charging following periods of discharge. Battery recharging is accomplished by either the PV array or an alternate power source (such as a gas-powered generator). In relying on the array, recharging current may vary, battery recharging may compete with household use for available power, and sunlight may be lost prior to completion of recharging. All of these factors conspire to prevent complete recharging between cycles. It is possible to complete the charge using a gas-powered generator, but this requires considerable run-time at low generator load. There are at least two possible solutions to this problem:

  1. Increase your array-to-load ratio (energy production of solar array divided by the expected load). A minimum array-load ratio is usually 1, to avoid excess use of the generator. Some designers suggest using an array-load ratio of 1.3 (30% more array capacity than load demand) to ensure adequate battery charging.

  2. Perform high energy tasks (doing laundry, vacuuming, etc.) during times that the gas-powered generator is in use for charging.

- Another important cause of battery failure is water loss due to overvoltage. Overvoltage (using a high charging voltage late in the charging process) causes excessive heating and bubbling, both of which contribute to water loss and can expose battery plates.

- Batteries should be periodically "equalized." Not all battery cells are created equal. Some take longer to charge than others. After a battery has been fully charged (brought back to about 2.12 V/cell), it is then overcharged (maximum voltage = 16.5 V, current = C/10 to C/20) for two to three hours to make sure that all cells are brought back to full charge. Not doing this will cause the batteries to age more quickly. Equalizing usually requires the use of a generator.

Battery Safety

Batteries are potentially dangerous and should be kept apart from living spaces. When working on batteries, always have someone within shouting distance. There are also other things to keep in mind:

- Batteries store your system's energy and power. Your system's discharge through you could be deadly. Be careful when working with metal tools. Handles should be insulated. Battery terminals should be taped or otherwise covered. Remove jewelry (including rings and watches) when working with batteries.

- Lead-acid batteries contain acids that can spill. Avoid contact with spilled liquids. Wash with soap and water if contact occurs. Keep baking soda near batteries to neutralize spills. Use protective eyeware. Do not touch your eyes when working with batteries. Have water nearby for flushing and rinsing in the event of spills or contact.

- When near full charge, batteries can outgas hydrogen, which is flammable. Battery storage areas should be well ventilated. Do not smoke or have an open flame in the vicinity of the batteries.

Choosing an Inverter for an Off-Grid System

Grid-linked inverters must generate true sine wave AC signals and must incorporate safety features specific to the grid intertie. This is not the case in an off-grid system and, as a result, inverter costs can be reduced.

The absolutely cheapest inverter is the square wave inverter. This type of inverter is so inefficient that it should not be used to power AC devices.

The next step up from the square wave is the modified sine wave (MSW) inverter that generates a sine wave that has up to 40% harmonic distortion. This type of inverter can power most AC devices except photocopiers, laser printers, and some types of cordless battery rechargers (all may be damaged by the MSW). The distortion from the MSW inverter may also introduce an annoying hum into audio devices. Otherwise, MSW inverters are completely adequate for most home systems. The most expensive type of inverter is the true sine wave inverter. Prices for such inverters have come down in recent years, so the difference between a true sine wave and a MSW inverter may not be great. The absence of grid-linking autodisconnects makes inverters for stand-alone systems somewhat less expensive than those linked to a grid.

Determining Inverter Size

Inverters are rated for continuous wattage and surge wattage. Continuous wattage is the amount of power the inverter can handle indefinitely. Your inverter should exceed the maximum power demand of your system (2710 W, in the previous example). Surge wattage (surge capacity) refers to the additional power required to start induction motor devices (compressor refrigerators, clothes washers, etc.). Surge requirements for individual devices can be two to three times their continuous operating power. If your system is to include such devices (our example system does), then you should ensure that your inverter provides ample capacity. Many MSW and true sine wave inverters provide surge capacity that is two to three times their rated power (this specification will be listed with the inverter).

Inverters for Hybrid Systems

More than half of all battery storage PV systems are actually hybrid systems. There will be times when your PV system fails to meet your power and energy needs due, perhaps, to a malfunction, an extended period of bad weather, or unusually high power demands. Many owners prepare for this eventuality by wiring their system to accommodate a gas-driven power generator. The generator can be used to meet excess demand or to recharge the battery bank. Inverters are available to accommodate two or more power sources (sometimes wind is combined with PV). The use of such inverters simplifies the process of combining these sources.

Sizing the Photovoltaic Array for a Battery Storage System

The number and size of the photovoltaic panels you will use depends on the amount of power required by your system, your geographical location, and your overall collection and power management strategy. The last category (power management strategy) suggests that there are further decisions for you to make in the design of your system. This is very much the case.

Designing for the Annual Average

Let's say that you want to base your PV array size on the average annual PSH for your site. In this case, your PV system would supply all of your electrical energy needs for a portion of the year and require a generator to supplement power for part of the year. Let's continue with the system used in the preceding example. We now have to pick a location for our site, because the amount of solar radiation available depends on where the system is. We will place our stand-alone system in Grand Junction, Colorado.

EXAMPLE 13. Use the example system in Grand Junction, Colorado, to determine how many solar panels are needed.

Our array will face due south and have a tilt angle equal to the latitude at Grand Junction (this is the best choice if you don't plan to adjust tilt angle during the year). The *Solar Radiation Data Manual* tells us that annual average PSH in Grand Junction is about 5.8. On average days, our array capacity should be designed to equal or exceed the daily electrical load (including battery losses). For this example, we will design with an array-load ratio of 1. This daily load was 10.5 kWh/day (Example 11). Recall that the daily load included the appliances in the house as well as the extra energy required to account for battery losses (20%) and the efficiency of the inverter (90%).

Let's use 100 W panels from Table 19-6 (17 V and 5.9 A at standard test conditions). We'll derate the panels by 10% to account for aging, dirt, and reflection. We'll also assume that we have maximum power point tracking.

The number of solar panels required to meet the daily load is equal to the daily load divided by the number of PSH divided by the derated power of each solar panel:

$$10.5 \text{ kWh/day} \times 1/5.8 \text{ PSH} \times 1/0.090 \text{ kW per panel} = 20 \text{ panels}$$

This makes the actual number of panels 20 and the rated capacity of the array 2 kW (2000 W). How will this system do over a number of years? We can project performance using other months of the year and including average, minimum, and maximum PSH averages from the *Solar Radiation Data Manual* (Table 19-13).

Table 19-14 shows the percentage of daily load the design system will meet based on historical data.

Table 19-13 Average, Maximum, and Minimum PSH for Grand Junction, Colorado

(South-facing stationary array having tilt angle set to the latitude of the site, 39.12°.)

	Jan.	Feb.	Mar.	Apr.	May	June	July	Aug.	Sept.	Oct.	Nov.	Dec.
Average	4.4	5.2	5.7	6.4	6.6	6.8	6.7	6.7	6.6	5.9	4.6	4.1
Maximum	5.7	6.6	6.6	7.1	7.1	7.6	7.0	7.2	7.3	6.8	5.8	4.1
Minimum	3.2	4.2	4.3	5.6	6.0	5.7	6.4	5.7	5.2	4.2	3.3	2.3

Source: National Renewable Energy Laboratory (USDOE).

Based on the projections of Table 19-14, the system in Example 13 would meet daily energy requirements for 8 of 12 months in an average year, 11 of 12 months in a very good (high insolation) year, and 5 of 12 months in a very poor year. For the months having inadequate insolation, a power generator would have to be used to make up the difference.

There are two things you should notice about the system in Example 13. First, it looks as if the array is somewhat overdesigned for conditions during the warm months. Recall, however, that the warmer months see a decrease in panel performance because of high temperatures, so part of the surplus would likely not occur during summers (we did not account for temperature in our derating; PVWATTS, which does account for high summer temperature, shows substantially less surplus).

Second, a surplus (when it does occur) will help the array to adequately charge the batteries even when household power needs are being met (surplus capacity was one of the solutions to battery charging presented in an earlier section).

The criteria used to size the PV array in Example 13 were not the only ones that you could use. You could size the array to more closely meet needs in December (the month having the poorest insolation). You could alter the array-load ratio to maximize battery charging by the array (the suggested array-load ratio for battery charging is about 1.3). You could plan on two tilt angles during the year (latitude + 15 degrees, latitude − 15 degrees for a half year each) to increase collected energy. The method presented here will allow you to estimate production for whatever criteria you choose to investigate.

Here's another point to keep in mind. Whatever criteria you accept, and no matter how big your system, you will probably need to run a generator at least part of the time. The first law of thermodynamics tells us that "energy is conserved." A kWh of energy

Table 19-14 Projected Percentage of Daily Load Met by the 2 kW Array in Example 13

(Values were calculated as PSH × 2 kW/10.5 kWh.)

	Jan.	Feb.	Mar.	Apr.	May	June	July	Aug.	Sep.	Oct.	Nov.	Dec.
Average	84	99	109	122	126	130	128	128	126	112	88	78
Maximum	109	126	126	135	135	145	133	137	139	130	110	97
Minimum	61	80	82	107	114	109	122	109	99	80	63	44

can be used directly to run a refrigerator, or it can be stored for later use. It cannot do both. Let's say that we have had two days of no insolation because of bad weather, so our storage is down to one day. The next day, we have insolation that exactly matches our needs for that day. At the end of that time, we still have only one day of storage left. The only sure way to bring your system back to full storage (other than curtailing your power use and hoping for good weather) is to use a gas-powered generator to recharge your batteries. Because extended periods of bad weather will undoubtedly occur, your system will require recharging periodically. This is one reason that most off-grid PV users have gas-powered (gasoline, liquid propane, etc.) generators connected to their systems (other reasons are to provide for times when you have overnight guests, which increases your energy consumption, and to periodically "equalize" your batteries, as discussed earlier).

Connecting the Panels in an Array

The panels used in our sample configuration were 100 W, rated at 17 V (12 V nominal), and 5.9 A. They can be connected in more than one way. It would be logical, given that we are using batteries connected in 24 V series, to connect two panels in series and use ten 2-panel series (nominal 24 V, 59 A) to make up a 20-panel array. Alternately (if our charge controller has maximum power point tracking; see the following paragraphs), we could use five parallel strings of four panels each to do the same thing (nominal 48 V, 30 A). This configuration would reduce line loss between the array and the charge controller (as a result of reduced current).

Adding a Charge Controller

There are only three more major components to be added to our battery-storage PV system (Figure 19-12): the charge controller, the battery charger, and the gas power generator.

A charge controller manages the power from the array. It fulfills a number of useful purposes:

- It prevents overcharging of the batteries (attempting to charge beyond their capacity). Overcharging can cause damage to batteries and battery heating (which can degrade performance), and it is a safety hazard (due to bubbling out of flammable hydrogen gas).
- As a battery is charged, its cell voltage increases. Older charge controllers worked in an on-off mode: They were either charging at maximum capacity or not charging. Newer controllers (having pulse-width modulation, or PWM) decrease the charging current in two or three stages by monitoring battery voltage. The voltage set points correspond to changes in charging strategy.

  Stage 1—below set point 1: Charge at maximum safe rate (bulk charge).

  Stage 2—between set points 1 and 2: Gradually decrease charging current.

  Stage 3—above set point 2: Charge at a very low rate to compensate for self-discharge by batteries (float charge).

- Some charge controllers monitor battery temperature. Charging requirements (and voltages) vary with the temperature of the battery. Temperature-compensated controllers vary the set points to correspond to these altered voltages.
- Charge controllers prevent reverse current from the batteries to the solar array at night.
- For DC loads (not included in our example system), some charge controllers will guard against overdischarge (below 80% of capacity), which can damage deep-cycle batteries (nearly all inverters guard against overdischarge, so this feature is not needed for strictly AC loads).
- Some charge controllers include MPPT. As in Example 5, MPPT will ensure that batteries receive the maximum current possible when bulk charging at a specified voltage. In addition, MPPT allows additional flexibility when configuring your PV array, because (as described in the previous section) a larger array voltage can be shifted to service batteries connected in series at a lower voltage (for example, a 48 V array can potentially service 24 V batteries via a charge controller having MPPT).

Sizing the Charge Controller

The maximum charging rate for deep-cycle batteries is usually considered to be C/10, where the C refers to the batteries' capacity. The 56 batteries in our example system have a combined capacity of 3150 Ah (14 four-battery series × 225 Ah per series). The maximum charging rate is therefore 315 amps (3150/10). Recall, though, that our array-load ratio was about 1, which means that we sized our array to deliver 10.5 kWh on an average day. This translated (in Example 13) to a 2 kW array. When working at maximum capacity, the solar array will provide only about 83 A (2000 W/24 V), so we are in no danger of exceeding C/10 with our array. In general, if a system has multiple-day storage capacity and the load-array ratio is about 1, the upper limit for charging will not be a factor in controller selection.

The aspect of sizing that we do have to be concerned about is selecting a charge controller capable of handling the current produced by the array. For a charge controller not having MPPT, the maximum panel current is the short circuit current. For our panel (Table 19-6), this is 6.5 A. For a charge controller equipped with MPPT, the maximum current is the power of the array divided by the voltage of the batteries (in our example system, 2000 W/24 V = 83 A). The UL and the NEC want the controller to be able to handle 156% of the design current. For our example system (which has MPPT), this would be 83 A × 1.56 = 130 A. Although charge controllers of this size are available, you may find it more convenient to use multiple controllers having a total capacity adequate for the current. If you choose to do this, each controller should have its own array (sized appropriately for the controller). The parallel controllers can then service the batteries through a common DC bus (the DC bus is described in the following section).

Adding a Battery Charger and a Gas-Powered Generator

The primary purpose of a battery charger/gas-powered generator in a stand-alone PV system is to recharge batteries following periods of poor weather or especially heavy use of the system. The majority of systems that use supplemental gas power (and about half of all stand-alone PV systems do) use an AC power generator. This is by far the most common type of commercially available power generator, and it has an advantage in that it can directly power AC devices in addition to being used for battery recharging. Use of an AC power generator, however, requires that an AC-to-DC battery charger be used as well.

The maximum charge rate that can be used in PV deep-cycle batteries is C/10 (where C designates total battery storage capacity). For the example system (capacity = 3150 Ah), the maximum charge current is 315 A. Commonly used charge rates are between C/10 and C/20. C/20 is considered by some to be the optimum rate for equalizing batteries and a good choice for general recharging.

In our example system, C/20 corresponds to a charge current of ~158 A (3150 A/20). For a 24 V system, this current represents about 3.8 kW of power (158 A × 24 V). Because of the nature of the load that a battery charger places on a power generator, it is likely that a power generator would have to be of about twice this power to actually perform at this level, requiring a generator capacity of about 7.5 kW. Because of the nature of the charging process (current tapering after bulk charge, as described in the section "Adding a Charge Controller"), it is likely that the time required to completely charge a battery bank will be longer than expected as well (by about 30 to 50%). In the example system, charging the storage batteries from a depth of discharge of 50% to full charge would be expected to require 13 to 15 hours.

It is a good idea to use the power generator while it is operating to perform tasks that require a great deal of energy. First, using the generator directly to perform these tasks hastens the speed of recharging, inasmuch as the power for such tasks would otherwise come through the batteries. Second, although the generator is working as hard as it can on the *resistive* load of the battery charger, there is excess capacity for *inductive* loads (motor-driven devices, such as a clothes washer and vacuum cleaner). Third, by adding an inductive load to balance the capacitative load, you actually improve the overall efficiency of the generator, so that it performs both tasks better.

There is another option for charging deep-cycle PV batteries: using a DC power generator. DC generators are not as commercially common as their AC counterparts. Although DC generators cannot provide backup power for AC devices, a properly sized DC generator will obviate the need for a battery charger. The journal *Homepower* published a description and instructions for constructing your own DC generator from a small motor and an automobile alternator (see *http://www.homepower.com/gengo.htm*). This appears to be an inexpensive solution to an important issue in developing a stand-alone PV system.

DC Electrical Common Bus

When different power sources are connected in a hybrid system, the power sources are typically combined with the use of a common bus. The bus includes components to prevent reverse current (from batteries to power source) when the source is not producing power. Note that some inverters provide the common bus as a part of their internal circuitry.

Monitoring Tools

Keeping track of a battery's state of charge is necessary for proper management of your system. It is also helpful to have an idea of how the rest of your system is doing. There are a variety of tools and components that can help you do this.

Portable Voltmeter

A good portable voltmeter is a necessary tool in a battery storage PV system. It provides a good indication of the battery's state of charge (where your batteries are relative to your depth of discharge). A fully charged lead-acid battery will have a voltage of ~2.12 to 2.15 V per cell. At 50% discharge, it will be ~2.03 V. Fully discharged voltage is 1.75 or less.

Hydrometer

A hydrometer measures the specific gravity of a liquid (its density relative to pure water). A liquid with a specific gravity greater than 1 is denser than distilled water. A hydrometer is an excellent indicator of a battery's state of charge, provided that you can make reliable readings. Some knowledgeable people assert that there are so many opportunities to make mistakes that most of us shouldn't even try, but this opinion is not universally held. The specific gravity of a fully charged lead-acid cell is ~1.265. A discharged cell has a specific gravity of 1.13 or less.

Battery System Monitor

A battery system monitor is another means of keeping an eye on battery voltage. Some system monitors track a variety of functions, including power or Ah into and out of the batteries, battery percent full, days since fully charged, and days since equalized. The latter two items are helpful for extending battery life through proper maintenance. Although not strictly necessary, battery system monitors are convenient sources of useful information and can help to protect the investment in your PV system. This capability varies somewhat with different batteries.

CONCLUSION

This chapter has presented a great deal of information. Its purpose was to acquaint you with the many considerations of grid-linked and off-grid photovoltaic design and provide a basic understanding of how these considerations are addressed. Its purpose was not to provide "do it yourself" instructions. The financial investment in a significant home PV system is large, and the electrical currents produced are potentially hazardous. For this reason, it is important that your actual system be designed and installed by qualified professionals.

Chapter 20

Using Biomass to Heat Your Home

With the use of biomass, you can meet all of your home heating needs. You can do this without using a nonrenewable resource and without adding carbon dioxide to the atmosphere.

Biomass, in its most general sense, is material that has been synthesized within living creatures. When used to describe an energy source, biomass refers to solar energy that has recently been trapped in living organisms by photosynthesis. This energy is stored in chemical bonds that can be broken later to release it in a usable form. When you burn wood for heat or digest a meal, you are releasing the solar energy that was trapped in these high-energy bonds.

Current interest in biomass-derived energy is based on two characteristics. First, biomass is renewable. We can always grow more biomass. Second, ongoing biomass energy production contributes no "new" carbon dioxide (CO_2) to the atmosphere. The CO_2 that we release today, through the use of biomass, to meet our energy needs was withdrawn from the atmosphere just a short time ago. The CO_2 that we will release in the future is being assimilated right now. The CO_2 is cycling, not accumulating. In contrast, when we burn fossil fuel, our energy practices only add CO_2 but never remove it from the atmosphere. To the extent that our energy can come from sustainable biomass sources, our use of energy is a sustainable practice.

Biomass energy production has always been with us. When we eat, we release energy from biomass to meet our metabolic needs. We have burned wood and other biomass materials for thousands of years for heat and to cook our food. Biomass provides 50% of the energy for heating and cooking in Asia and 70% in Africa.

In places where biomass use results in the destruction of forests and damage of ecosystems, it is not a sustainable practice. To the extent that biomass can be grown specifically for energy and is based on stable and sustainable cultural practices, it shows much promise as an energy source. In addition to providing heat through direct combustion, biomass can be used to generate electricity, provide transportation, and power industrial engines. Many industries and some municipalities currently meet part or all of their electricity needs by burning biomass for power generation.

Biomass can be used to produce fuels having properties similar to natural gas and petroleum. In these forms, the energy from biomass can be conveniently stored and transported.

Wood, wood wastes, agricultural residues (e.g., corn husks, rice hulls, peanut shells, sugarcane stalks, grass clippings, and leaves) and "energy crops" grown especially for this purpose are used most frequently for biomass energy. It is also possible to use municipal wastes and manure in this way.

In the United States, biomass for electricity production has grown to 7,800 megawatts (MW); 1 MW = 1,000,000 W of power. Power plants with a capacity as large as 80 MW are fueled with biomass in the United States. Many industries are now burning their wastes to produce in-house power. The United States has the potential to produce up to 20% of its electricity needs using biomass if a concerted effort is made in that direction.

EXTRACTING THE ENERGY OF BIOMASS

Home use of energy from biomass can take two forms. We can convert the biomass to energy in the home itself, or we can use a gas or liquid conversion product that was created from biomass at some other location.

In the United States and most other places, extracting the energy from biomass in the home means burning it in a stove or fireplace and using the released energy primarily for heat. Wood is overwhelmingly the fuel of choice, although other biomass materials are sometimes used.

The second method of using biomass energy for residential purposes is to combust a biomass-derived material that was created at a central location and then transported to the point of use (home, business, or vehicle). There are many ways to implement this approach, but most are still relatively small-scale methods or under development. Approaching the theoretical maximum of 20% of total U.S. energy use requires that some or all of these methods be implemented on a larger scale. The following is a short survey of the various methods currently in use or under development.

Pelletized Fuel

Various forms of organic waste can be shredded, dried, and compressed into pellets that can be burned to produce heat. The pellets can be made from wood, cardboard, mixed papers, and vegetative agricultural wastes. Residential heating units typically produce 7,000 to 50,000 Btu/hr (2 to 15 kW) and can be up to 80% efficient. The energy content of various pellet fuels (assuming no more than 10% moisture content) typically falls between 7,200 and 8,500 Btu/lb (17 to 23 million J/kg).

Electricity Generation

Energy from biomass can be delivered to the point of use in various forms. One of these is electricity.

Biomass has been incorporated into electrical energy production in a number of ways. Various industries have used organic wastes to fire in-house power plants. Towns have burned municipal wastes and converted the energy to power to defray part of the disposal costs. Utilities have used biomass-only plants and have also developed "recipes" and equipment for combining biomass with fossil fuels (mainly coal). The coal-biomass mixtures allow the utilities to use biomass when available and coal at other times.

Biomass-driven power plants tend to be relatively small. The range in capacity is 2 to 100 MW, with the average about 20 MW. The use of smaller plants reflects the tendency in industry toward in-house-only plants but is also consistent with trends in the utilities, which are emphasizing smaller "distributed power generation" systems.

Wood wastes, agricultural wastes, and municipal wastes make up the bulk of the biomass fuels used for this purpose. The efficiencies of biomass-driven power plants have been 15 to 30 percent. Some applications, called cogeneration systems, use the heat that the plants produce to meet the heating needs of industrial processes or adjacent buildings. When this occurs, the overall efficiency of these systems can climb to 60%, which is much higher than that of conventional utility power production.

Alcohol Fermentation

Yeast can ferment (digest) organic material to produce ethanol. Ethanol has a high energy content and is particularly well suited to replace some or all of the gasoline in internal combustion engines. This approach has been used on a small scale in the United States and on a larger scale in some other countries. Ethanol derived from biological sources can supply all of the energy needed by cars, provided that the engines are modified to account for the differing properties of alcohol and gasoline.

Biodiesel Fuel

Diesel engines were originally developed to run on vegetable oils. High-energy oil-producing plants (rapeseed oil, sunflower seed oil, and others) can be processed to produce a fuel for slightly modified diesel engines. These oils can also be added as a supplement to conventional diesel fuel without modifying the engine. Currently, there is interest in using waste products for this purpose, including waste oils from restaurants and other sources.

Anaerobic Digestion

When organic materials are degraded in the absence of oxygen, specialized bacteria will convert a portion of the waste to methane, a burnable biogas. Methane can be used for cooking, heating, and powering engines for transportation, industry, and generating electricity. A variety of materials have been used for this purpose, including manure from animals and humans, other organic wastes, and many types of plant material. Individual residence-scale systems have been used in developing countries (most easily in areas having warm climates). Larger-scale pilot operations have been attempted, and are still under development, in many countries.

Because the anaerobic digestion process is based on the activity of living creatures, management of conditions in reactors must promote the activity and reproduction of microorganisms. Temperature, pH, prevention of air leakage (which will kill the bacteria), contaminants in the waste, and other factors must be carefully regulated. Sulfur compounds in the methane gas can also produce acids in the gas, which makes storage of the gas more difficult.

Pyrolysis

Pyrolysis is the application of heat in the absence of oxygen to convert complex organic molecules to simpler combustible molecules. If oxygen were present, the material would simply "burn" (be converted to carbon dioxide and water with the release of a great deal of energy). By heating biomass to temperatures between 800° and 1400°F (425° to 760°C) without oxygen, the material is converted to energy-rich compounds that can be stored and used for fuel.

Products of pyrolysis include charcoal, gas, and liquid fuel. Altering the rate of the process largely determines which component dominates. Low temperature results in a longer process that mainly produces charcoal. Very rapid heating to about 900° F (500°C), followed by rapid "quenching," will maximize the production of liquid fuel. Higher temperatures and longer duration results mainly in gas production.

Gasification

Gasification, like pyrolysis, can be used to convert organic materials to burnable fuel. The gasification process is typically carried out at about 1400°F (750°C). It differs from pyrolysis in that a small amount of oxygen is allowed to react with the organic material. The resulting gas tends to have a somewhat lower energy content than gas derived from pyrolysis.

MATERIALS ESPECIALLY SUITED FOR BIOMASS USE

Any naturally occurring material that is organic has been developed by trapping solar energy. This energy can always be released or transformed to a recognized fuel via combustion, gasification, or digestion. Table 20-1 shows the energy content of a variety of

Table 20-1   Energy Content of a Variety of Biomass Materials

Green wood—8 MJ/kg
Oven-dried plant matter—20 MJ/kg
Methane—55 MJ/kg
Coal—23–30 MJ/kg
Canola (rapeseed) oil—40.4 MJ/kg
Sunflower oil—39.7 MJ/kg
Safflower oil—39.7 MJ/kg
Diesel fuel (conventional, for comparison)—38.5 MJ/kg

materials. Certain materials are particularly suited to biomass use, either because they have an especially high energy content per unit of mass or because they have a low intrinsic value for other purposes. Such materials include:

- *Agricultural crops.* Crops having a high starch, cellulose, or oil content are especially useful for biomass production. These include sugarcane (especially a specialized version called "energy cane"), corn, wheat, sorghum, sunflower seed, rapeseed (canola), and soybeans. Most of these crops are processed to create liquid fuels, such as ethanol, biodiesel fuel, and heating oil.

- *Agricultural wastes.* These agricultural materials remain after the removal or extraction of components that have intrinsic value (usually as a human food source).

- *Animal wastes.* Animal wastes are by-products of commercial animal production. The solid waste produced by pigs, cows, chickens, and other animals has an energy content that can be extracted or converted to a useful fuel.

- *Industrial wastes.* By-products of industrial processes that use organic materials can frequently be used for energy production.

BIOMASS USE IN THE HOME

In the United States, most of the energy extracted from biomass used in residences comes from direct combustion of wood and wood by-products. Interestingly, the most common device for direct combustion is also the least useful. The various devices currently in use for this purpose are discussed in the following sections.

Conventional Fireplaces

Conventional fireplaces are not considered viable heat-producing units for homes. The amount of heat actually added, as compared with the pollution produced (particulates and other pollutants), makes them marginally useful for this purpose.

Conventional fireplaces burn wood in a firebox using air that is mainly drawn from the inside of the house. In most fireplaces, heat production is 20% radiant heat and 80% directly heated air/gas. Virtually all of the household air used in combustion is lost up the chimney. To this is added "tramp air," up to ten times the combustion air volume, which is also drawn out of the house by the powerful convection produced by the fire. Most of the heating value of the fireplace is in the radiant 20%. Glass fireplace doors, if well sealed, can reduce the amount of tramp air lost from within the house. The tempered glass is, however, a very poor radiator of heat, so much of the heating value of the fireplace is lost as well. Conventional fireplaces do not typically combust all of the wood fuel. Heated burnable gases and particulates often escape. They either accrue on the sides of the flu and chimney or escape into the atmosphere.

Table 20-2 provides estimates of the efficiencies of fireplaces and other direct combustion devices. Open fireplaces (without glass screens) may have a negative efficiency, depending on the amount of household tramp air drawn up the chimney (a roaring fire may cause more than one household air change per hour). Fireplace doors made from

Table 20-2   Estimated Efficiencies of Biomass Heating Units

Conventional fireplace	−10–10%
Advanced combustion fireplace	50–70%
Conventional woodstove	55–70%
High-technology woodstove	70–80%
Masonry heater	60%

tempered glass may cut radiant heating by half, resulting in roughly 10% efficiency. Supplemental heat-scavaging techniques (air circulators, radiation enhancers) can improve efficiency by about 10%, but the percentage is usually lower.

It is difficult to create optimal conditions for combustion in conventional fireplaces. Incompletely burned material routinely escapes up the flu, contributing to air pollution. Conventional fireplace particulate emission rates are about 40 g/hr, which is so high that fireplaces have been banned in some areas.

Advanced Combustion Fireplaces and Woodstoves

Advanced combustion fireplaces (Figure 20-1) reflect an attempt to incorporate the features of advanced technology woodstoves into fireplaces (see the later section "Free-standing Woodstoves"). The advanced combustion units use ducts to bring in air from outside the house and are tightly sealed around the glass doors, effectively eliminating

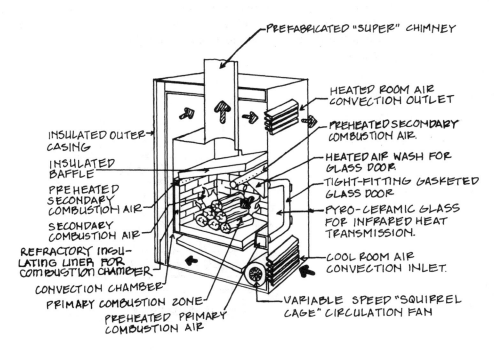

Figure 20-1   Advanced combustion fireplace.

tramp air loss. They create conditions in which all of the burnable fuel is ignited, improving efficiency and reducing pollution. The doors are made of a ceramic glass that radiates well. They also do a better job conducting the heat from the fire to the house than conventional fireplaces. The pollution from an advanced combustion unit is approximately 10% of that produced by a conventional fireplace.

Pellet Fireplaces and Stoves

Pellet fireplaces and stoves have many of the features of the advanced combustion fireplace. They use fuel pellets made from wood or wood/biomass waste material. Automated pellet feeding systems are available for these units, simplifying daily use. The pellets are also easier to carry and handle than split wood. Efficiency and pollution reduction in pelleted fireplaces and stoves tend to be slightly better than in the best split-wood systems because of the high surface-area-to-volume ratio of the fuel.

Masonry Heaters

Masonry heaters consist of a high thermal mass outer shell. Very hot fires are used for a relatively short time to heat the thermal mass. The heat and hot gas are routed through the masonry in a way that results in the capture of much of the heat. The system is designed so that the surface of the heater gets warm but not too hot to touch (~100°F [38°C]). The captured heat is then slowly released via radiation and convection. A properly designed masonry heater can provide heat for eight or more hours and can achieve efficiencies comparable to those of advanced combustion fireplaces. Pollution production is similar to that of advanced combustion fireplaces.

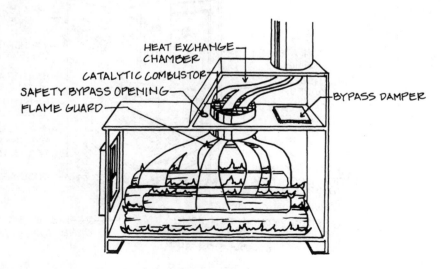

Figure 20-2 Catalytic wood stove.

Freestanding Woodstoves

Older woodstoves burn less efficiently and release more pollution than newer stoves. The newer stoves can be divided into two groups: catalytic (Figure 20-2) and noncatalytic stoves. Both types of stoves promote secondary combustion, or "light off" to ignite volatile gases that were not burned in the fire. Most of the enhanced efficiency and lowered pollution are due to the secondary combustion. Catalytic stoves use a ceramic screen coated with a noble metal (usually palladium) to ignite the combustible gases at a lower temperature than would otherwise be possible (~500°F [260°C]). Noncatalytic stoves rely on a higher burn temperature (~1000°F [540°C]), often in combination with a secondary air feed, to accomplish the same task. In both cases, light off occurs in a secondary combustion chamber that also helps to capture and use the heat.

CONCLUSION

Most biomass technologies are still developmental in the United States. Direct combustion devices, on the other hand, are an established technology able to assume a significant role in American heat production.

Chapter 21

Use of Trees for Sun and Wind Control

Energy Savings: *Studies have shown that trees planted next to buildings to block the warming effect of sunlight can reduce cooling costs from 15% to more than 75%. When the sun is allowed to strike the south sides of shelters during the heating season, 30 to 100% of interior space heating needs can be met. Shading an air-conditioning unit can save up to 10% on cooling costs. Outdoor temperatures under trees can be 8° to 12°F (4° to 7°C) cooler than in the sunlight. Where there are few trees and a concentration of hardscape materials absorbing heat from the sun, built-up urban and suburban areas can be 8° to 15°F (4° to 8°C) warmer than less developed and moderately forested areas. By using trees to deflect the cold winter wind and create still air spaces around a shelter, 20 to 40% in winter energy savings can be achieved.*

Shelters need the warming benefit of the sun during the heating season in all of the U.S. climate zones (see Figure 11-1). Because most locations in the United States are at a significant distance from the equator, the wintertime noonday sun will always be at a low angle in the sky and will strike primarily the south sides of shelters. Figure 21-1

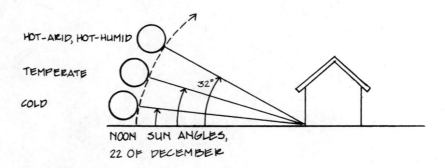

Figure 21-1   Noon sun angles on December 22nd for climate regions in the United States.

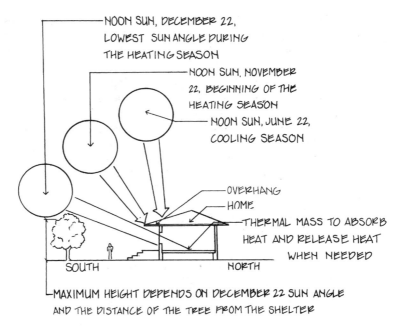

NOON SUN, DECEMBER 22, LOWEST SUN ANGLE DURING THE HEATING SEASON

NOON SUN, NOVEMBER 22, BEGINNING OF THE HEATING SEASON

NOON SUN, JUNE 22, COOLING SEASON

OVERHANG

HOME

THERMAL MASS TO ABSORB HEAT AND RELEASE HEAT WHEN NEEDED

SOUTH   NORTH

MAXIMUM HEIGHT DEPENDS ON DECEMBER 22 SUN ANGLE AND THE DISTANCE OF THE TREE FROM THE SHELTER

Figure 21-2   Overhangs and sun control.

shows the lowest noon sun angles for the four climate zones in the United States at the time of the winter solstice (December 22). What is the designer to do about preventing the summer sun from striking the south sides of shelters and allowing winter sun? Ideally, it is best to block all of the summer sun from the sides of a shelter and passive outdoor use areas when trying to keep interior spaces cool and outdoor spaces comfortable for human use. In the wintertime, sunlight can be allowed to enter windows and bathe the south sides of buildings with solar radiation, as shown in Figure 21-2, so that heat can be absorbed and stored in thermal masses for release when temperatures drop below human comfort levels.

DEFINING HEATING AND COOLING SEASONS

To control heat from the sun, heating and cooling seasons have to be determined in order to set the dates when sun is needed and when it should be blocked. This is best accomplished by studying yearly energy use data for a facility whose use is similar to that of the facility with which you are working. Plot energy use by month, and create illustrative charts that will help you to see how and when energy is being used. The charts will indicate when energy is being used for cooling or heating and the transition seasons when there are no heating or cooling expenses. Through examining energy use charts, the beginning and end of the heating and cooling seasons can be determined. Next, to be more exact, you can consult monthly historical temperature charts. Refer to Figure 9-2 for a chart showing yearly electric and gas energy use for a residence. Table 21-1 shows account histories for a residence's yearly use of electricity and natural gas. Note that the natural gas account shows gas use in ccf, which is 100 cubic feet, or 1 therm of gas. For the electric account, the meter usage amounts are given in kilowatt hours (kWh). In this residential example, natural gas was being used for space heating, two hot water heaters, and a stove. All other appliances and the air-conditioning system used electricity. See Tables 9-1 and 9-2 in Chapter 9, "Computing Overhangs for Solar Energy Control," for more information on selecting heating and cooling season dates. The ccf of natural gas and the kWh of electricity can be plotted directly, or they can be converted to joules (J) of energy for comparison purposes. Various energy units and their conversion rates are listed in Table 21-2. The joule is the internationally accepted unit for the measurement of energy.

Energy use planners also need to know exactly how to plot the daily sun path movement so that building and site amenities such as overhangs, setbacks, awnings, trees,

Table 21-1   Electric and Natural Gas Account Histories

Electric Account

Month	Days Billed	Usage	Cost
Jan. 1997	32	940kWh	$58.80
Feb. 1997	30	605	39.84
Mar. 1997	28	598	39.45
Apr. 1997	33	508	34.36
May 1997	29	466	31.98
June 1997	33	600	39.56
July 1997	29	1760	105.18
Aug. 1997	30	2281	134.66
Sept. 1997	33	2013	119.50
Oct. 1997	28	1184	76.70
Nov. 1997	31	704	47.89
Dec. 1997	32	673	46.02

Natural Gas Account

Month	Days Billed	Usage	Cost
Jan. 1997	31	141ccf	$90.13
Feb. 1997	29	202	107.93
Mar. 1997	31	125	61.50
Apr. 1997	29	64	38.15
May 1997	29	64	39.15
June 1997	30	37	22.85
July 1997	32	36	21.61
Aug. 1997	31	35	21.24
Sept. 1997	33	40	25.29
Oct. 1997	29	34	24.63
Nov. 1997	29	52	35.35
Dec. 1997	32	146	78.23

Table 21-2   Energy Conversion Factors

1 kWh = 3412 Btu
1 kWh = 3,601,707 J
1 ft³ of natural gas = 1000 Btu
100 ft³ (ccf) of natural gas = 100,000 Btu
100 ft³ (ccf) of natural gas = 105,560,000 J
1 therm = 100,000 Btu
1 Btu = 1055.6 J

thermal mass, and indoor and outdoor use areas can be located and designed. Once the heating and cooling season and sun path information are known, the correct placement of trees around a shelter for sun control can be determined. Today, trees are most often planted for purely aesthetic reasons—for enframement, seasonal color, and their use as sculpture. An energy-conscious alternative to planting for aesthetic reasons is to plant for energy savings functions first, and then consider enframement, seasonal color, and the sculptural value of trees.

THE VALUE OF TREES IN REDUCING SUN HEAT GAIN

Planting to block the sun was a matter of necessity before heating and cooling systems were driven by fossil fuels. Our ancestors knew the value of well-placed trees to shade walls, windows, and roofs, and the comfort the shade would bring to the indoors in the summertime. By blocking the sun's heat from walls and roofs, trees prevent structures from heating up to temperatures above the ambient or the general air temperature in a specific area. In addition, shade from trees prevents the area around structures from gaining solar heat. When the sun hits the ground and paving near a shelter, the ground acts as a heat sink or heat storage area, converting the solar radiation into thermal energy and releasing it in the afternoon and evening when midday temperatures begin to drop below the temperature of the stored energy. Figure 21-3 illustrates an ideal energy-efficient planting design.

A tree placed between a shelter and the sun will cool the shelter 5° to 12°F (3° to 7°C). When properly located, both evergreen and deciduous trees can prevent 70 to 100% of sunlight from hitting a shelter or outdoor space. A study done in Miami, Florida, showed that trees and shrubs planted around a mobile home reduced cooling costs by 40%. A study in Pennsylvania showed that trees shading a mobile home reduced cooling costs by 75%. Considering that about 50% of the total energy used in a residence is for interior space heating and cooling, significant savings can result from shading with trees.

Cooling through Evapotranspiration

In addition to preventing absorption of heat, trees cool an area through the process of transpiration. Evapotranspiration (ET) is the process of evaporation of water from the soil and transpiration of water from plant leaves. As part of their living and breathing process, plants are always secreting water from small pores in their leaves and stems. A

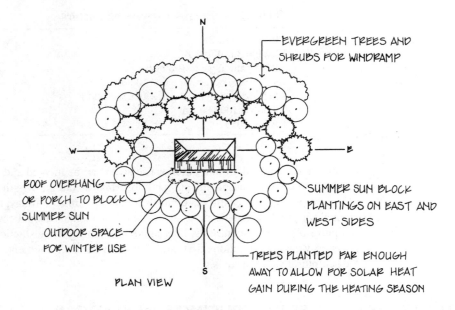

Figure 21-3 Ideal planting design for the reduction of energy use.

large tree can transpire more than 200 gal (757 l) of water per day. Some trees remove more than their weight of water from the soil each day and transpire it into the air. Solar energy evaporates water from plant leaves, resulting in a cooling effect. An abundance of trees planted in an urban area can reduce ambient air temperatures by 5°F (3°C) through evapotranspiration alone.

The collective cooling effect of a large number of trees and shrubs in a neighborhood or city can have a significant influence on reducing energy use. In a notable tree planting program in the 1940s the city of Nanjing, China, planted 34 million trees in an effort to reduce energy use and make the city more comfortable for habitation. That massive tree planting endeavor resulted in a 5°F (3°C) drop in summer temperatures. For energy conservation and a host of other benefits, the city of Tucson, Arizona, is planting 500,000 desert-adapted trees. In addition to energy conservation, the benefits include abatement of dust and storm water runoff. Many communities have street tree planting programs that provide multiple advantages. The benefits include providing edges to the roadway space, which helps to slow drivers and make them more cautious, shading the roadways and preventing heat absorption, and contributing to the collective cooling effects of evapotranspiration. Street tree plantings are a smart way to begin to reduce the unnaturally warm temperatures in our built landscapes.

Additional Benefits of Trees Planted in the City

In addition to providing cooler environments in which to live, trees can also filter particles out of the air, reduce noise through absorption, and reduce soil erosion through their soil-holding root systems. Moreover, through the creation of a ground plane mulch of leaves and twigs dropped by trees, rainfall is soaked up and water is stored for future use by plants. Forest floor mulch provides nutrients to trees, ensures habitat for beneficial insects and animals, and filters runoff water, thereby passing on clean and clear water to the next user in the ecosystem (Figure 21-4). Trees sequester carbon from the atmosphere by absorbing carbon dioxide for photosynthesis and storing some of it in their trunks and branches. Trees provide oxygen for use by oxygen-breathing organisms, and they help to create greater biodiversity by providing habitat for animals, insects, and microbes. Finally, trees are desirable and attractive to people, providing feelings of comfort and protection.

Sequestered Carbon

Because trees are the major means of recycling carbon from the atmosphere, let us discuss the amount of carbon they are able to take from the atmosphere, and examples of how trees are being used to reduce the huge buildup of carbon already overloading the atmosphere throughout the world. First of all, it is important to know who is producing the large amounts of carbon that are beginning to affect the world's climate. Table 21-3 lists the major producers of CO_2. It is apparent that the industrialized countries are burning the largest amounts of the ancient reserves of carbon that have been stored in the ground for millions of years. In fact, the United States produces nearly twice the CO_2 per person than the next major producer, the United Kingdom. With 5% of the world's population, we in the United States produce 21% of the world's greenhouse gas emissions, which include methane, nitrous oxide, and carbon dioxide, among other minor greenhouse gases. Oil, coal, and natural gas, when burned, produce large amounts of carbon dioxide. When only wood biomass is burned, the trees on the earth can remove from the atmosphere the amount of CO_2 produced and keep the amount of CO_2 in the at-

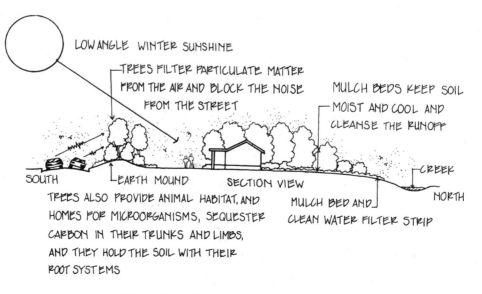

Figure 21-4 Environmental benefits of trees.

mosphere balanced. When the ancient reserves of carbon from the ground are burned and the CO_2 produced is added to that being produced by the combustion of wood, there is no way that the plants on earth can remove the carbon from the atmosphere fast enough.

To compute the amount of CO_2 for which you are responsible, use the conversion factors in Table 21-4. On average, in the United States, a household produces about 45,000 lb (20.385 kg) of CO_2 per year. This would require planting about 1730 trees to sequester the family's yearly production of CO_2 from the atmosphere. The carbon becomes tree leaves, twigs, branches, roots, and trunks. A tree planting effort at any scale will help to clean our air and protect the atmosphere.

There are organizations that are planting trees to remove the amount of CO_2 their employees produce. This is a start, of course. There are also power-producing companies that are buying existing tracts of large rain forests to offset the carbon produced when they create electricity from ancient fossil fuel reserves. These efforts guarantee that an equal amount of the gas is absorbed from the atmosphere by growing trees in forests or is stored as carbon in mature forests. This is an effective way to preserve the vast forested areas in Central and South America that are so important to the removal of CO_2 from the atmosphere. At the University of Texas-Houston Health Science Center, Sustainability Officer George Bandy has created an environment-friendly campus by requiring that the

Table 21-3   Major Producers of Carbon Dioxide

(Approximate production of CO_2 per person per year.)

United States	43,000 lb
United Kingdom	22,000 lb
Denmark	20,000 lb
Japan	19,000 lb
South Africa	18,000 lb
France	14,000 lb
Mexico	8,000 lb
China	5,000 lb
Brazil	3,000 lb
India	2,000 lb

Source: Oak Ridge National Laboratory.

Table 21-4   Determining Carbon Dioxide Production

1 kWh of electricity produces 1.3 lb (0.6 kg) of CO_2.
An average family of four uses 13,000 kWh per year.
1 ccf of natural gas produces 12 lb (5.4 kg) of CO_2 per year.
An average family of four uses about 1000 ccf (1,000,000 Btu) of natural gas per year.
1 gal (4.4 l) of gasoline produces 22 lb (10 kg) of CO_2 per year.
An average person drives about 10,000 mi (16,093 km) per year.
Cars average about 20 mi (32 km) per gal.
Jet airplanes release 0.68 lb (308 g) of CO_2 per mi.

An average growing tree removes 26 lb (11.3 kg) of CO_2 per year.
An average forest is composed of approximately 400 trees per ac (0.2 ha).

Source: Consumer Report (September 1996).

amounts of CO_2 being produced are computed and trees planted on campus for removal of the carbon from the air. Limits on CO_2 production in the near future are predicted by many environmentalists and scientists.

DECIDUOUS TREE BRANCHES AND SOLAR INSOLATION

Solar insolation is solar radiation that is received by an object or place on the earth. Ideally, south sides of shelters should be protected with roof overhangs that block sunlight or solar insolation during the cooling season and allow sun heat gain during the heating season. If the south side of a building is planted with trees, it is best that they be located so that limbs and trunks do not block the low-angle winter sunlight and interfere with solar heat gain by the shelter in the heating season. Winter sun angles should be plotted so that trees will not interfere with the lowest angle of the sun during the heating season, which occurs on December 22. That date, December 22, is significant in that it is the time of the year when the Northern Hemisphere is tilted the farthest away from the sun. This is the time of the winter solstice in the Northern Hemisphere, and it is the shortest day of the year. In the southern hemisphere the winter solstice occurs on June 22. *Solstice* comes from Latin and French words that basically mean "sun standstill" or "sun stop."

When a deciduous tree loses its leaves in the wintertime, it may appear that most of the winter sunlight will still come through the tree branches. However, this is not true. Be aware that the leafless branching structure of a tree will block winter sunlight, allowing only 50 to 80% of the sun's heat to pass through the tree's branches and warm the shelter. This is a significant amount of heat loss. Be cautious about using deciduous trees on the south side of a building when an objective is also to capture sun for winter heating (Figure 21-5). Locate trees far enough from a structure so that they will not interfere with the sun angles during the heating season, and close enough to the structure that they can provide shade on the ground plane next to the shelter in the summer, thereby preventing solar heat gain and warmer outdoor air temperatures. See Table 21-5 for the percentages of sun energy that pass through different types of deciduous trees.

CLIMATE REGIONS AND TREE LOCATION STRATEGIES

Tree placement should consider the climate region in which a project is located. In the United States, the four climate regions are the cold, temperate, hot-arid, and hot-humid regions. Figure 21-1 illustrates the lowest noon sun angle of the year in each of the four climate zones. Each region has its own shelter and planting relationships that must be considered in order to create environments that are as comfortable as possible for people living there.

Tree Placement in the Cold Climate

In the cold climate region, where there are long, cold winters and short, mild summers, trees should be located so they don't block the potential for heat gain in the wintertime. Because shelters in the cold region receive winter sunlight only along their south faces,

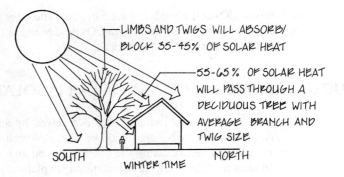

Figure 21-5a Deciduous trees and solar heat gain.

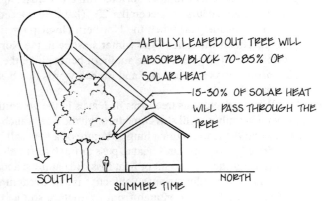

Figure 21-5b Deciduous trees and solar heat control.

tree placement should not interfere with the low sun angle in the fall, winter, and spring. Wintertime sunlight is needed by shelters for supplemental heating. Overhangs on shelters provide the best solution for control of undesirable heat gain in the summertime. If trees are used to control summer heat gain, they should be planted on the western side of a shelter to block afternoon sun. Trees planted on the west side can be either deciduous or evergreen. When the heating season begins, the sun's path will be such that sunlight will primarily strike the south side of the shelter. If trees are planted on the south side of the structure, they should be located either far enough away that they don't block winter sun, or close to the shelter so the branches can be pruned to allow sun heat during the heating season. See Figure 21-6 for winter sun angles and tree locations on the south side.

Tree Placement in the Temperate Climate

The temperate climate zone has moderately cold winters and mild to hot summers. *Temperate* means moderate, mild, and not excessively hot or cold. In regard to heating and cooling a shelter, it is more difficult to cool than to heat. Therefore, when planting for

Table 21-5 Transmissivity of Solar Radiation through Trees

| Common Name | Scientific Name | Transmissivity | | Ultimate Height |
		Summer	Winter	
Red maple	Acer rubrum	8–22%	63–82%	65–115 ft (20–35 m)
Sugar maple	Acer saccharum	16–27%	60–80%	98–130 ft (30–40 m)
White birch	Betula pendula	14–24%	48–88%	50–98 ft (15–30 m)
Shagbark hickory	Carya ovata	15–28%	66%	98–130 ft (30–40 m)
Green ash	Fraxinus pennsylvanica	10–29%	70–71%	60–115 ft (18–35 m)
Red oak	Quercus rubra	12–23%	70–81%	75–100 ft (23–30 m)
Colorado spruce	Picea pungens	13–28%	13–28%	90–135 ft (27–41 m)

Source: R. D. Brown and T. J. Gillespie, *Microclimatic Landscape Design* (New York: John Wiley & Sons, Inc.).

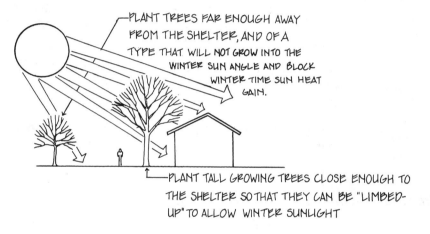

Figure 21-6 Tree locations for sun control and heat gain.

sun control in this climate, it is best to keep the heat out of the structure and the sun off its east, west, and south sides during the cooling season. Because of the latitude range of the temperate zone, not much sun will hit the north side of the shelter in the summer. In a south-facing shelter with overhangs along the south side, little to no solar radiation will get into the structure. Plant trees on the west and east sides of the structure to block the low angle of the morning and afternoon sun. Trees planted on the north side should be selected and located to deflect the winter winds. Shrubs can be planted along with the trees to create a wind ramp to better deflect the winter winds that can cause cooling of the shelter by convection, as well as infiltration of cold air and exfiltration of heated air. Trees planted on the south side of the building should be selected to be short enough, and located far enough away from the south side of the building, to shade only outdoor spaces near the building and not interfere with the warming benefit of sun

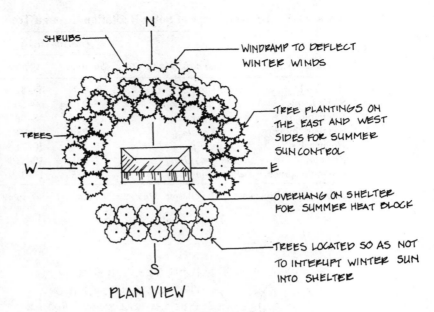

SHRUBS

N

WINDRAMP TO DEFLECT
WINTER WINDS

TREE PLANTINGS ON
THE EAST AND WEST
SIDES FOR SUMMER
SUN CONTROL

TREES

W

E

OVERHANG ON SHELTER
FOR SUMMER HEAT BLOCK

TREES LOCATED SO AS NOT
TO INTERRUPT WINTER SUN
INTO SHELTER

S

PLAN VIEW

Figure 21-7 Temperate climate planting layout for ideal sun control and heat gain.

heat gain during the heating season. See Figure 21-7 for tree locations in the temperate region.

Tree Placement in the Hot-Arid Climate

Planting and shelter design objectives in the hot-arid climate should include blocking sun heat gain during the cooling season and allowing winter sunlight on the south side of a structure during the heating season. Because a shelter is more difficult to cool than to heat, keep the heat out of the structure by keeping the sun off its east, west, and south sides during the cooling season. Conduction of heat gain in this climate is the major contributing factor in causing interior spaces to heat up. This zone has short but mild winters and long, hot summers, making shade highly desirable. Trees should be planted on the east, west, and north sides of a shelter to prevent sun heat gain during the cooling season. If trees will not grow in an arid area, then the shelter itself should be designed to prevent heat gain on these sides. Thick masonry walls themselves can protect against the heat; such construction can prevent conduction of daytime heat through the walls until the heat is needed in the interior during the cool desert evenings. The south, east, and west sides of shelters should be protected by roof overhangs, awnings, or arbors that prevent the sun from hitting the buildings in the cooling season and allow heat gain during the heating season. See Figure 21-8 for tree, arbor, and porch locations for sun control.

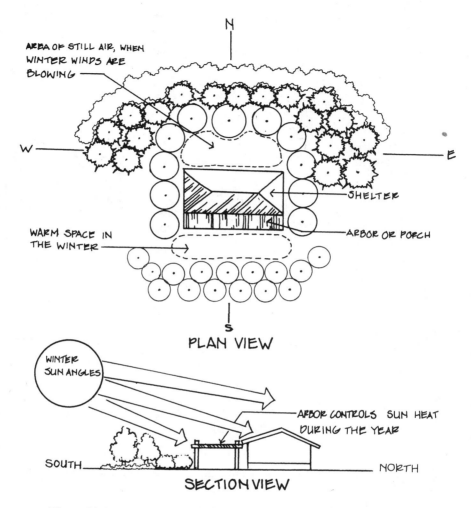

Figure 21-8 Hot-arid climate planting layout for sun control and heat gain.

Tree Placement in the Hot-Humid Climate

In the hot-humid climate, planting and shelter design objectives should be to block sun heat gain during the cooling season and allow winter sunlight on the south sides of a structure during the heating season. As in the hot-arid climate zone, conduction of heat gain in this climate is the major factor in causing interior spaces to heat up. If the heat is not allowed to enter the interior spaces, the structure will probably not heat up beyond the ambient air temperature. This zone has short but mild winters and long, hot summers. It is basically a zone with a hot climate, and one where energy bills for cooling may be two-thirds of the yearly combined heating and cooling costs. Shade is highly desirable in

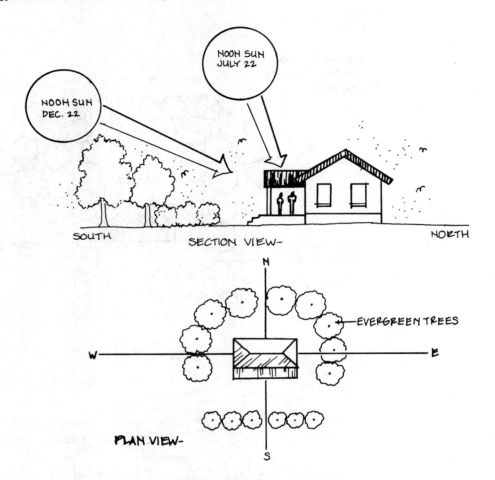

Figure 21-9 Hot-humid climate planting layout for sun control and heat gain.

this climate zone. Trees should be planted on the east, west, and north sides of shelters to prevent heat gain by the sun during the cooling season. South sides of shelters should be protected by roof overhangs or awnings that prevent the sun from hitting the buildings in the cooling season and allow heat gain during the heating season. Because sun heat gets into a structure primarily by transmission through windows, conduction into a thermal mass, and convection and radiation as interior air and objects are heated, if the sun does not hit the building, there will be no significant transmission and conduction of heat into the interior. The south side should be planted so that tree limbs and trunks do not block the low-angle winter sunlight. Deciduous tree branching structures can block 50 to 80% of the warming benefit of the sunlight in the wintertime. Planting on the east and west sides can be of either deciduous or evergreen trees. See Figure 21-9 for locations of trees and roof overhangs. Chapter 9, "Computing Overhangs for Solar Energy Control" explains how far overhangs need to be extended according to winter sun angles.

WINDBREAKS AND WIND RAMPS

Trees can be used as windbreaks or in wind ramps to deflect predictable winter winds from hitting a shelter's sides and roofs. A study in South Dakota evaluating linear windbreaks demonstrated that wind deflection plantings saved 25% of the residential winter heating energy cost. When windbreaks were extended from one side of a shelter to three sides, winter fuel savings jumped to 40%. Actual electrical energy use was an average of 422 kWh per month to keep indoor temperatures at 60°F (16°C) when homes had no wind protection, and 270 kWh per month with wind deflection plantings. Using $0.10 per kWh, the monthly electric heating bill in the homes with no windbreaks was $422, but only $270 for the homes with windbreaks. The effectiveness of planting to deflect wind is significant for shelters in the cold and temperate climate regions. Wind deflection plantings in the hot-humid and hot-arid climate regions will also reduce heat loss in shelters and will extend the use of outdoor spaces in the wintertime.

PART V

Waste Processing in the Sustainable Landscape

Chapter 22

Treating Sewage Using Constructed Wetland Ecosystems

By treating large amounts of sewage with settling lagoons and constructed wetlands, 75 to 95% of energy costs can be saved, as compared with using traditional concrete, steel, and energy-intensive sewage treatment plants. Installation costs of a constructed wetland sewage treatment system are usually 20 to 30% less than those of traditional sewage treatment facilities, and management needs will be 50 to 75% less.

BIOLOGICAL SEWAGE TREATMENT

An alternative to operating the traditional energy-intensive concrete and steel sewage treatment plant is to use natural ecosystems to treat sewage. Most of the processes involved in treating sewage with either method are biological and physical and include the microbial degradation of organic matter and settling of solids in water. Treatment in conventional plants is more intense and requires more energy. The benefits of natural systems like a pond or wetland include the fact that they are powered by the sun, the wind, the flowing of water, and the nutrients within the water.

The natural marsh or wetland (Figure 22-1) is the model on which constructed ecosystem sewage treatment systems are based. Both natural and constructed wetlands provide water quality enhancement, including filtration, sediment removal, oxygen production, nutrient recycling, and chemical absorption. They also serve as habitat for the production of fish, shellfish, waterfowl, other birds, and fur-bearing animals. Wetlands have both social and economic importance, absorbing water from floods, protecting from wave damage, controlling erosion, recharging groundwater, serving as a habitat for production of timber, and providing for recreational benefits, including hunting, trapping, fishing, wildlife observation, and aesthetic experiences. The biological processes employed by wetlands using sunlight, plants, and microbes will treat sewage and cleanse runoff pollution, break down toxins, and assimilate heavy metals. Simply stated, plants need nutrients and water, and human sewage is composed of nutrients and water.

Figure 22-1 Natural wetland—the model for the constructed wetland ecosystem.

In contrast, traditional, industrial style sewage treatment plants are more expensive to build, require large amounts of energy to run aerators and pumps, and they require two to three times the manpower for operation and management. Because the industrial system is energy intensive, it can treat sewage in 30 hours, versus 75 days for the constructed ecosystem method, and it requires much less land area for treatment. The lagoon-constructed wetlands method is land intensive.

TRADITIONAL SEWAGE TREATMENT

To understand the value of treating sewage with constructed ecosystems, it is important first to understand how it is usually treated in industrial systems. The comparison between the two systems will probably persuade you to consider using constructed ecosystems, which are less energy, chemical, and manpower intensive than the traditional treatment systems commonplace in the United States. An industrial system is composed of structures and equipment made from concrete and steel, clustered together to intensely treat large volumes of sewage. See Figure 22-2 for a well-constructed and managed industrial style sewage treatment plant. This plant, which treats 4 million gal (15,140,000 l) of sewage a day in Starkville, Mississippi, cost $8,000,000 to build. The facility serves a combined university and town community of about 30,000 people. Electrical energy costs are $10,000 per month, or $120,000 per year. The plant needs four full-time personnel, who conduct water sampling, check pump stations throughout the city, do grounds

Figure 22-2   Industrial style sewage treatment plant.

maintenance, and wash down facilities being serviced for regular cleaning. Table 22-1 shows, step-by-step, the treatment process for a successful plant that removes solids and cleans nutrients and pathogens from the water. Appendix A illustrates a traditional septic tank and fixed absorption system useful for smaller sewage treatment conditions.

ECOSYSTEM SEWAGE TREATMENT

Wetlands

In nature, wetlands clean water and release it to be stored in the ground or to flow into creeks, rivers, or larger water bodies. The combination of plants and the microbes attracted to those plants helps to cleanse water of substances before it is returned to the ground. Beneficial microbes are primarily bacteria, fungi, and single-celled organisms like protozoans and dinoflagellates. The microbes will consume nutrients, as well as pathogens, including viruses and bacteria. Pathogens are organisms that can make people and animals sick. The word *pathogen* comes from the Greek *pathos,* which means "suffering." Warm temperatures enhance microbial activity. When temperatures climb from 10° to 20°C (50° to 68°F), microbial activity will increase, on average, by 100%. Blackened trees from the great fire at Yellowstone National Park are still in place more than 20 years after the fire because it is cold in that area nearly year-round and microbial activity is reduced. Microbes attracted to plant leaves, stalks, and roots help plants to fend off disease and insects and help to convert organic matter into a form that plant roots can absorb. Elements in wastewater, including carbon, hydrogen, oxygen, nitrogen, phosphorus, micronutrients, and metals, are assimilated by wetland plants. As the water gets deeper in a wetland, the species of plants that are best adapted to the various water depths change. There is often a visual zone or band of plants along a pond or wetland

Table 22-1 Traditional Industrial Sewage Treatment Plant Process

(For an oxidation ditch system in Starkville, Mississippi, where sewage is pumped into aeration ponds for treatment. Total treatment time = 30 hours.)

Step 1 Incoming sewage goes through an aerated grit chamber where organic and inorganic materials are separated. A 1/4 in. (6 mm) screen removes larger inorganic objects like bobby pins and plastics. The grit, plastics, and steel are augured out to a dumpster for placement in a landfill.

Step 2 The organic solids and liquid sewage are pumped to an oxidation ditch or aeration unit, as shown in Figure 22-3, where the wastewater is aerated and mixed for 24 hr. Aerators inject oxygen into the muddy brown mixture in order to culture bacteria. Aerobic bacteria consume the solids, dissolved nutrients, and pathogens, creating nearly clear water, which flows to clarifiers.

Step 3 The clarifiers, as shown in Figure 22-4, are quiet pools where water is detained for 3 hr, allowing further settling of any remaining solids. Persisting solids settle to the bottom of the clarifiers and are pumped back either to the aeration unit for further treatment or to a 20 ac (8 ha) sludge pond for long-term storage and further decomposition by bacteria. Clear water from the clarifier flows to a chlorine contact chamber.

Step 4 The chlorine contact chamber disinfects the water and kills any remaining pathogens. See Figure 22-5 for a picture of the chlorine chamber.

Step 5 Chlorinated water is then treated with sulphur dioxide to convert the chlorine to chloride. Chloride is a salt and in low concentrations will not cause damage to aquatic systems. Chlorine is a strong oxidant that can chemically damage an organism, such as the roots and surfaces of plants.

Step 6 Oxygen is added back into the water in a reaeration unit after it has been treated in the chlorine unit. Treated wastewater is then released into a nearby creek.

that are a result of increasing water depth. Figure 22-6 shows a typical pond edge with the types of plants that will grow at the different water depths.

Wetlands also take sediment out of water. Sediment consists of inorganic particles, like silt and clay, that are dislodged from ground surfaces by flowing water. When flowing water gets to a flat, wetland area, sediments drop out because the velocity of water slows. Pollutants often attach themselves to sediments, especially clay particles, and thus will drop out along with the heavier sediments. Sediment and pollution are thereby detained by the wetland and kept from flowing into a creek, a river, or the sea.

Wetlands are the most productive of all ecosystems, producing more biomass than any other type of landscape. See Table 22-2 for a comparison of biomass produced by different types of ecosystems. Biomass is important because it is primarily carbon, the essential building block for the growth of all organisms. In summary, wetlands remove and recycle nutrients, they settle out sediment, and they allow suspended organic and toxic compounds to be digested by microbes. Wetland plants take up and store heavy metals in their roots, stems, and leaves, and they provide an environment for the destruction of pathogens. Wetlands are the earth's kidneys, cleaning water and recycling nutrients, thereby preventing adverse environmental impacts.

Figure 22-3 Oxidation or aeration unit for treatment of organic solids.

Figure 22-4 Suspended solids settle in the clarifier pools.

Oxidation Pond

An oxidation pond can be used for treating sewage when drainage through soils is not good or when large amounts of sewage needs to be treated in a large body of water. An oxidation pond treats sewage using sunlight, bacteria, algae, and air. It can be used at

Figure 22-5 Chlorine contact chamber for final water disinfection.

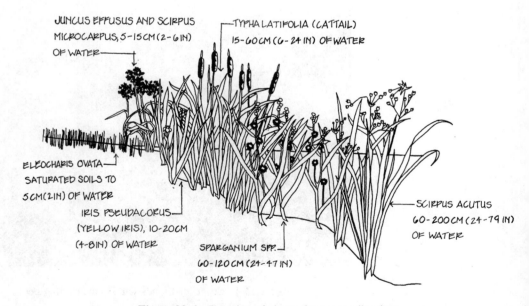

Figure 22-6 Zonation of plants along a pond's edge.

a residential scale where soil conditions preclude the use of a septic absorption field, and it can also be used at a city scale, such as in Lima, Peru, where large oxidation ponds treat both the solid and liquid components of sewage for about 100,000 people. In the oxidation ponds for Arcata, California (population of 15,000), solids are removed

Table 22-2   Biomass Production of Various Plant Communities

Ecosystem	Dry Weight in Metric Tons per Year per Hectare
Freshwater temperate submerged plants	6
Freshwater tropical submerged plants	17
Marine temperate submerged plants	29
Marine tropical submerged plants	35
Marine emergent plants salt marsh	30
Freshwater temperate emergent plants	38
Freshwater tropical emergent plants	75
Marine and lake phytoplankton	2
Desert, arid plants	1
Deciduous temperate forest	12
Coniferous temperate forest	28
Rainforest	50

conventionally in large settling tanks. The daily load of 2.3 million gal (8.9 million l) of liquid sewage per day is treated in 94 ac (38 ha) of oxidation ponds.

In the natural treatment process, algae assimilate the carbon dioxide resulting from the action of aerobic bacteria consuming organic matter. Through photosynthesis the algae produce the oxygen needed to sustain the bacteria. Pathogens in the water are killed either by the presence of predator bacteria or by the wide pH swing between day and night. This wide swing in the ponds at Lima, Peru, ranges from a pH of 10 during the day to a pH of 6 at night. During the daytime, algae pull the CO_2 expelled by aerobic bacteria out of water and use the carbon for building biomass. As the algae respire at night, they expel CO_2 just as we do. When CO_2 is expelled in water, it causes most water bodies to become more acidic. If the water body is well buffered, it will not change much from day to night. When water bodies are buffered, they are resistant to pH change because they contain components such as carbonates and bicarbonates. Buffering components will use up the acids that might normally make the water more acidic. During the detention period, the objectionable components of sewage largely disappear. See Figure 22-7 for a plan and section view of an oxidation pond for a residence. Primary treatment can be provided with a septic tank, which will remove solids and pass on the liquid sewage to the pond, where secondary treatment to remove nutrients and pathogens will occur. Oxidation ponds should be fenced to keep out people and animals. A pond should be located at least 50 ft (15 m) from dwellings, and at least 100 ft (30 m) from any well supplying drinking water. For best performance, the oxidation pond should receive six to eight hours of sunlight per day.

Constructed Wetlands

The two types of constructed wetlands are the surface flow system and the subsurface flow system. In the constructed wetland, landscape architects and engineers are seeking to recreate a natural ecological system for treatment of sewage or storm water. Besides performing water cleansing tasks, the wetland can be a recreational asset and a

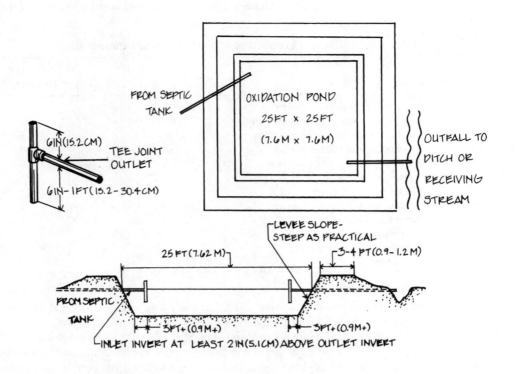

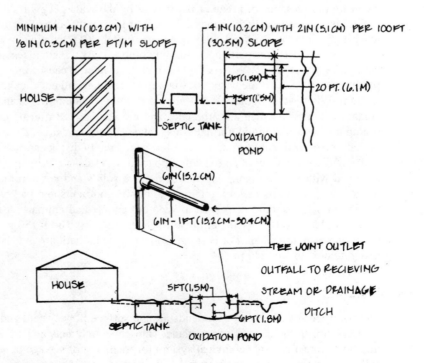

Figure 22-7 Plan and section views of an oxidation pond.

wildlife attractant, providing habitat and food. A constructed wetland is generally self-maintaining but requires some maintenance efforts, such as mowing levees, clearing obstructions in the wetland, and harvesting or burning dead biomass during the wintertime. A constructed wetland is very much like a natural wetland in that it is powered by the sun and by nutrients in the wastewater. Constructed wetlands are simple to construct and operate. They can be composed of emergent plants, floating plants, open water, and either a soil or gravel substrate placed over a thick liner to prevent contaminated water from polluting groundwater. The impermeable liner can be either a layer of clay or a thick plastic sheet. Sewage water must be exposed to natural cleansing processes for 12 to 14 days for thorough cleaning. This detention time may have to be increased during colder times of the year.

Kevin Elliott, operations manager at the award-winning West Jackson County, Mississippi, Regional Land Treatment Facility, operates both conventional and constructed wetland treatment plants. He compared for us the size requirements, and the cost of construction, management, and power consumption, of traditional industrial style sewage treatment plants and constructed wetlands.

For a traditional plant treating 3 million gal per day (mgd, 11.6 mld), Elliott said that a minimum of 2 ac (0.8 ha) is required for the physical plant. In contrast, his 3 mgd (11.6 mld) lagoon and constructed wetlands facility is built on 185 ac (75 ha). Construction costs for the conventional system were $1.2 to 1.3 million per million gal (3.85 million l) of sewage treatment, and for a lagoon and wetland system $1 million per million gal (3.85 million l), or 20 to 30% less. Regarding manpower, the conventional system needs three to four persons working eight hours a day to do testing, check equipment, wash down facilities, and maintain the grounds. The lagoon and constructed wetland plant can operate with one person working four hours a day doing water sampling, observing systems, mowing levees, and clearing biomass from the wetlands in the late fall. This natural system generally uses about 75% less manpower for operation and management. Electrical power costs for the conventional system are $5,000 to $7,000 per month, or $60,000 to $84,000 per year, and this is for running all of the pumps and aerators. The lagoon and wetland system uses $1,000 worth of power a month, or $12,000 a year, and this is for pumps and infrequent use of aerators. The amount of power used by the conventional industrial treatment system is five to seven times greater (or 500 to 700% more power used) than that used by the lagoon and wetland system.

The mechanical industrial system, despite the land area savings, is clearly much more energy intensive than the natural system. Once sewage is fully treated in the conventional system, the remaining biosolids must be land applied somewhere, incinerated, or heated and dried to kill all pathogens and prepared for reuse as commercially available fertilizer. In the ecosystem process it takes 60 days for treatment in the settling lagoons and 12 to 14 days in the constructed wetlands. This substantially longer detention period, which allows biological methods to work without extensive use of electricity, is the reason for the larger land area requirement. The wetlands ecosystem treats sewage as well as the energy-intensive industrial system does.

How does the lagoon-constructed wetland ecosystem work? First, large settling ponds or lagoons receive raw sewage. Contaminants like bobby pins, grit, plastics, and snail shells are screened out and taken to a landfill. Organic materials remaining in the water are allowed to settle and be consumed by both aerobic and anaerobic bacteria.

After a 60-day settling period, the liquid effluent flows to the constructed wetland. Solids that remain in the liquid sewage (effluent) from the settling ponds (lagoons) settle out as they slowly flow through the first one-third of the wetland. Waste in the water is digested by microorganisms, primarily bacteria that colonize on the soil, rocks, and plants and in the leaf litter on the bottom. Very little of the waste is taken up by the plants. It is estimated that plants assimilate less than 10% of the waste. Plants can, however, assimilate heavy metals into their biomass (Table 22-3). When metal concentration is a problem, biomass should be harvested and either the metals removed or the biomass stored as a hazardous waste. Heavy metals include cadmium, chromium, mercury, lead, arsenic, and antimony, among others. They are called *heavy metals* because of their higher atomic weights relative to some of the other metals. When heavy metals are assimilated into animals, they can be poisonous and cause illness and death.

Constructed wetlands are built so that storm water runoff cannot drain into the wetland and flush out wastewater being held for the 12- to 14-day treatment period. Excessive rains can reduce sewage detention time in a constructed wetland, but this can happen in a conventional sewage treatment plant as well. The result of rainwater flushing either type of system is that some wastewater will flow untreated into local creeks, rivers, or bayous.

Emergent plants can survive in the wetland even if there is little oxygen in the sediment because they take air from above the water level and send it to the root system. This process also allows aerobic bacteria around the roots to survive in water with low dissolved oxygen (DO). Plant leaves create shade and thereby reduce the amount of algae or phytoplankton in the water. Algae need plenty of sunshine, so blocking solar radiation will reduce phytoplankton. The problem with algae in the wetland is when they die, their biomass contributes to the amount of organic material to be treated. Emergent plants also reduce the amount of wind that can cause mixing, which decreases the uniformity of flow in the system. Wetlands remove solid and soluble organic compounds and reduce biological oxygen demand (BOD) and total suspended solids (TSS). Wetlands also lower levels of nitrogen, phosphorus, metals, and hydrocarbons. Wetlands are ideal habitats for predator bacteria that feast on harmful bacteria, viruses, and other pathogens. The longer sewage effluent is detained, the higher the treatment level will be. The use of natural systems to treat human wastes is an evolving low-technology process, and many

Table 22-3 Wetland Plants Noted for Their Ability to Assimilate Heavy Metals

Scientific Name	Common Name
Typha latifolia	Common cattail
Sparganium spp. (americanum)	Bur reed
Eichhornia crassipes	Water hyacinths
Alternanthera philoxeroides	Alligator weed
Scirpus californicus	Giant bulrush

Sources: B.C. Wolverton, *Growing Clean Water* (Picayune, MI: WES, Inc., 2001); Craig Campbell, M. Ogden, *Constructed Wetlands in the Sustainable Landscape* (New York: John Wiley & Sons, Inc., 1999).

experts have changed their original opinions on detention times. There now seems to be a consensus that 12 to 14 days is necessary for best treatment of sewage effluent. Because constructed wetlands are living ecosystems constructed for the benefit of people, they need regular observation and evaluation in order to be managed properly. Any problems must be determined as early as possible, as constructed wetlands are not like machines that can be fixed with a new part. It can take several weeks to correct a problem in a natural ecosystem.

Surface Flow Wetlands

Surface flow wetlands can be built either within an area that is excavated or on top of the ground and contained with berms. They are generally used where larger wastewater quantities have to be treated. During the treatment process, solids are first settled in quiet lagoons or septic tanks, where decomposition by anaerobic bacteria begins. If the lagoons are aerated, aerobic bacteria also participate in decomposition of the solids. After the solids have settled in lagoons for about 60 days, liquid effluent flows into the surface flow wetlands, and any remaining solids suspended in the water settle to the bottom and are consumed by bacteria and fungi on plant stems, leaves, roots, and the bottom substrate. This usually happens in the first one-third of the wetland. Because the wastewater surface is exposed to the air in a surface flow marsh, the facility must be fenced to control access so as to limit the potential for human contact with the effluent water because of the possibility of contracting disease.

A surface flow wetland hosts a very vigorous ecosystem composed of microbes, insects, plants, fish, amphibians, mammals, and birds. The wetland ecosystem is, in fact, the most productive biomass producer of all ecosystems. Animal and insect life teems around wetlands because of all of the carbon and other nutrients produced by wetland plants. Surface flow constructed wetlands are about one-half as expensive to build as subsurface flow systems. A 1 ac (0.4 ha) surface flow wetland can cost about $45,000 to $50,000 to build.

Subsurface Flow Wetlands

Subsurface flow treatment systems are also called rock-reed or plant-reed systems (Figure 22-8). They are composed of gravel and pipes that evenly distribute effluent water and keep water levels below the top of the gravel beds. Often, there are plants growing in the gravel beds. Their purpose is to pump oxygen down to the bacteria on the rocks and roots below the water level in order to maintain healthy populations of aerobic bacteria. If plants are not used, aerobic bacteria can be sustained by a system of pipes that deliver air to the gravel bed. A septic tank or settling lagoon first removes the solids from the sewage. If the septic tank or lagoon is big enough, anaerobic bacteria will consume organic solids so they will never have to be removed from the lagoon or pumped out of the septic tank. The 75 ac (30 ha) solids settling lagoons at the Ocean Springs, Mississippi, sewage treatment plant settle out the solids from a mostly residential flow of 3 mgd (11.6 mld) of sewage. According to wetland manager Linwood Tanner, after ten years of treatment there was only 1 in. (25 mm) of solids on the bottom of the lagoons,

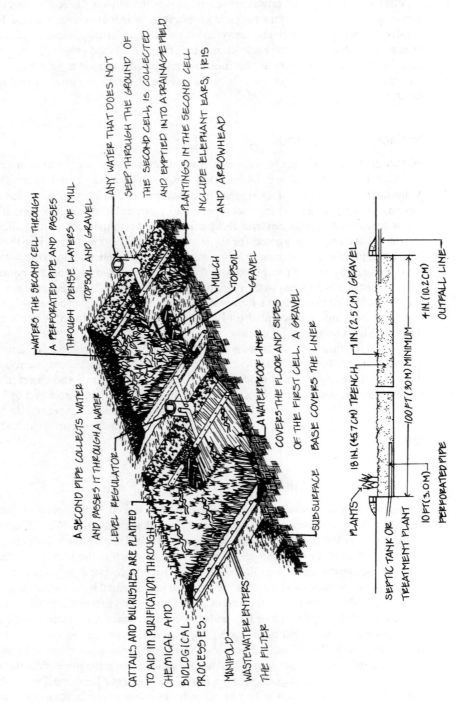

WATERS THE SECOND CELL THROUGH
A PERFORATED PIPE AND PASSES
THROUGH DENSE LAYERS OF MUL

ANY WATER THAT DOES NOT
SEEP THROUGH THE GROUND OF
THE SECOND CELL, IS COLLECTED
AND EMPTIED INTO A DRAINAGE FIELD

PLANTINGS IN THE SECOND CELL
INCLUDE ELEPHANT EARS, IRIS
AND ARROWHEAD

A SECOND PIPE COLLECTS WATER
AND PASSES IT THROUGH A WATER
LEVEL REGULATOR

TOPSOIL AND GRAVEL

MULCH

TOPSOIL

GRAVEL

A WATERPROOF LINER
COVERS THE FLOOR AND SIDES
OF THE FIRST CELL. A GRAVEL
BASE COVERS THE LINER

CATTAILS AND BULRUSHES ARE PLANTED
TO AID IN PURIFICATION THROUGH
CHEMICAL AND
BIOLOGICAL
PROCESSES.

SUBSURFACE

MANIFOLD
WASTEWATER ENTERS
THE FILTER

PLANTS

18 IN. (45.7 CM) TRENCH

1 IN. (2.5 CM) GRAVEL

100 FT (30 M) MINIMUM

4 IN. (10.2CM)
OUTFALL LINE

SEPTIC TANK OR
TREATMENT PLANT

10 FT (3.0M)

PERFORATED PIPE

Figure 22-8 Rock reed subsurface flow wetland.

composed of grit, sand, and plastic materials. The organic solids had been consumed by the microbes, which were composed primarily of anaerobic bacteria.

Once the solids have settled out in either a septic tank or a settling lagoon, liquid effluent flows into the subsurface flow filter. The purpose of the gravel in the beds is to provide large surface areas for the culture of microbes. Most microbes are simple heterotrophs that digest organic materials. As the liquid effluent flows through the rocks from one end of the system to the other, it will receive treatment by aerobic bacteria. It is best to use large gravel that is 1½ to 3 in. (37 to 75 mm) in diameter. Also called railroad ballast, its primary use has been as a bedding for railroad tracks. The pore spaces of gravel of this size are large and therefore not easily clogged, and the rock provides enough surface for colonization of a large population of aerobic bacteria. Some larger-scaled subsurface flow treatment systems do not have plants growing in the gravel. Instead, they use pipes and pumps to aerate the gravel for the culture of aerobic bacteria. Plant biomass often clogged the gravel voids in many of the early systems, where small-sized gravel was used.

Let us restate that the main purpose of the plants growing in the beds is to supply oxygen to the bacteria that are colonizing on the rocks. This will ensure healthy populations of aerobic bacteria, which are more effective consumers of organic matter than anaerobic bacteria. Anaerobic bacteria do not need oxygen to flourish. Plant leaves transport oxygen from aboveground to submerged roots anchored in the gravel. Plants suitable for growing in these gravel beds, besides cattails, include yellow iris, bulrushes, common reeds, canna lilies, banana trees, elephant ears, ginger lilies, and arrowroot. But plants other than those that enjoy wet feet will also grow in rock-reeds.

There is a unique plant-reed treatment system at a community college in northern Mississippi designed by biological sewage treatment pioneer B. C. Wolverton. This indoor tropical plant system (Figure 22-9) treats sewage from rest rooms on the third floor of the math and science building. Sewage first goes to interior raised planters, where both the solids and liquids are treated. The planters are designed so that solids can be pumped out if necessary. However, bacteria in the planters have been consuming all available solids produced for the past ten years. See Table 22-4 for a list of bacteria that

Figure 22-9   Indoor sewage treatment system with tropical plants and rock filled planters.

have been identified in the interior plant-reed system. The solids are separated and decomposed by anaerobic and aerobic bacteria, and the liquid flows through tropical plant beds to an exterior plant-reed bed planted with ornamental shrubs and trees. The trees and shrubs enjoy the small amount of nutrient-filled water that flows from the tropical planters. Interestingly, the outdoor plantings in the plant-reed system on the east side of the building, are outgrowing the same plants on the other side of the building which are planted in soil and which do not receive the nutrient-filled water from the indoor treatment planters.

On a larger scale, a subsurface flow constructed wetland system will cost about $100,000 to $105,000 per acre (0.4 ha) to construct, with gravel making up 45% of the total cost. This is nearly double the per acre (0.4 ha) cost of the surface flow wetland.

We conclude this review of subsurface flow wetlands with a quote from an Environmental Protection Agency (EPA) report authored by professional engineer Sherwood Reed. Reed and selected reviewers drew the following conclusions regarding the state of the art of subsurface flow wetlands:

> Subsurface flow wetlands can be a reliable and cost-effective treatment method for a variety of waste waters. These have included domestic, municipal, and industrial waste waters as well as landfill leachates. Applications range from single family dwellings, parks, schools, and other public facilities to municipalities and industries. It can be a low-

Table 22-4 Bacteria Colonized in the Math and Science Building Rock-Reed

Bacillus pumilis
Bacillus sphaericus
Bacillus mycoldes
Bacillus megaterium
Bacillus thuringlensis
Bacillus cereus
Pseudomonas putida
Pseudomonas fluorescens
Pseudomonas nitroreducens
Rhodabacter
Flavobacterium
Acinetobacter
Enterobacter
Aureobacterium
Ochrobactrum
Agrobacterium
Xanthomonas
Micrococcus
Listeria
Methylobacterium

Source: M. Wardlow, S. O'Bannon, and A. Mikell, "Characterization of a Tertiary Wastewater Treatment System Utilizing Plant-Microbe Interactions" (University of Mississippi, 1994).

cost, low-energy process requiring minimal operational attention. As such, the concept is particularly well suited for small to moderate sized facilities where suitable land may be available at a reasonable cost. Significant advantages include lack of odors, lack of mosquitoes and other insect vectors, and minimal risk of public exposure and contact with the water in the system.

COMPONENTS OF SEWAGE

Wastewater Elements

Typical sewage components found in residential wastewater include nitrogen, phosphorus, potassium, calcium, carbon, sulfur, sodium, and very small amounts of other micronutrients. The sewage also contains bacteria, viruses, and protozoans. We automatically think that water with all of these components is bad for the environment and harmful to people. Consider, however, that many of these constituents are essential to communities of organisms that naturally live in water. Plants and bacteria that form much of the bottom of the food chain in aquatic systems depend on the nutrients in the water. Bacteria, for example, require organic molecules for their energy and growth. Without these substances that constitute the bottom of the food chain, organisms that feed farther up the food chain, including many commercially important species, would starve. See Table 22-5 for a list of both macro and micro nutrients on which the plant kingdom depends.

Eutrophication

Problems occur when the good components of water become so abundant that they damage or alter the biological communities that use them. Recall from Chapter 4, "Water Quality," that eutrophication happens when a body of water becomes overenriched with dissolved nutrients and organic compounds and an oxygen deficiency occurs. A water body over rich in nutrients is eutrophic. The word *eutrophic* comes from the Greek *eutrophos,* which means "well nourished." Organic materials that enter water via the collection of household sewage often exceed the capacity of the water to process them. Microorganisms, especially aerobic bacteria, multiply to consume the large quantity of

Table 22-5   Nutrients Essential for Plant Growth

Macronutrients in the Soil		Micronutrients in the Soil		Nutrients in Air and Water	
Nitrogen	N	Iron	Fe	Carbon	C
Phosphorus	P	Copper	Cu	Hydrogen	H
Potassium	K	Manganese	Mn	Oxygen	O
Calcium	Ca	Zinc	Zn	Nitrogen	N
Magnesium	Mg	Molybdenum	Mo		
Sulfur	S	Boron	B		
		Chlorine	Cl		

Source: Edward C. Martin Jr. and Pete Melby, *Home Landscapes, Planting Design and Management* (Portland, OR: Timber Press, 1994).

organic matter, and in doing so, they deplete all of the dissolved oxygen in the water, thereby killing themselves and rendering the aquatic environment uninhabitable to all living creatures that are oxygen breathing. This condition can lead to fish kills, the production of noxious odors, and the culture of pathogenic organisms. Aeration of the water can help to prevent anoxic (low oxygen) conditions. It should be noted, however, that not all eutrophic conditions become anoxic.

Dissolved Oxygen

Adding too much organic material to a body of water may result in the decline of the dissolved oxygen (DO) concentration. Even a moderate DO drop in aquatic communities can cause stress. When all of the oxygen becomes depleted, there occurs a DO crash that can wipe out all of the oxygen-breathing species that cannot escape. The challenge then is being able to measure the organic carbon in water so that a DO crash can be predicted and prevented. Organic carbon is carbon that has been incorporated into compounds in living tissue as a result of photosynthesis. People have it in their bodies as a result of eating foods that originated from photosynthesis. Organic carbon is the primary constituent in all of our food and is the source of all our metabolic energy. Metabolism is the process by which living organisms break down food for energy and produce waste matter. Most carbon in the world, though, is inorganic, like the CO_2 we exhale and like that contained in limestone and chalk deposits.

Biochemical Oxygen Demand

Although it is possible to measure organic carbon in water bodies, the most commonly used method is to measure the oxygen consumed over a specific period of time. This test for biochemical oxygen demand (BOD) indicates the rapidity with which microorganisms consume oxygen in a water sample. It is a measure of the amount of oxygen required to oxidize and stabilize the organic materials in sewage. When food is oxidized, it is combined with oxygen and the chemical structure of the food is changed so that its components can be used by organisms. BOD is a measure of the concentration of the organic material suspended in water that is readily biodegradable. The higher the BOD level, the greater the amount of oxygen required to achieve oxidation of suspended organic matter. Organic matter attracts aerobic bacteria, which will multiply to consume it as long as there is oxygen in the water. Therefore, BOD is also a measure of the pollution load in a river, stream, lake, or wetland. BOD levels for discharge into large rivers are often set by state regulators at 30 mg/l. In a smaller body of water, such as a stream, where the impact of suspended organic matter would be greater, acceptable BOD levels can be as low as 10 mg/l. BOD units are measured in milligrams per liter (mg/l) or parts per million (ppm). Because there are about 1 million milligrams in a liter of water, the two terms can be used interchangeably. If water has high BOD, the microorganisms will use up a lot of oxygen while chewing up the organic matter. If water has low BOD, not much oxygen will be used by the microorganisms in the water and aquatic life will not be harmed by depleted oxygen levels. In treating sewage in a traditional industrial style plant, lower BOD levels are achieved by using energy to aerate water. This creates environmental conditions that will accommodate large numbers of aerobic bacteria. The greater amounts of bacteria, in turn, consume more organic matter. In constructed wetlands, BOD levels are lowered through detention of sewage solids in settling lagoons for long periods of time and treatment primarily by anaerobic bacteria.

Turbidity and Total Suspended Solids

Turbidity is a term used by scientists involved with water quality issues. The turbidity, or "cloudiness," of a body of water, affects the ability of light to pass through the water. It refers to dissolved constituents in water that are not filterable. If they are filterable, then we are discussing total suspended solids. Turbidity is important, because dissolved matter can block solar radiation through the water column, decreasing the growth of phytoplankton and submerged vegetation.

The term *total suspended solids* (TSS) refers to the amount of solid organic particles in water, such as clay and phytoplankton. Solids in water can be a significant consideration—for example, when a large quantity of sediment settles and covers the stony bottom of a creek, thus altering the habitat type. In sufficient amounts, solids can choke existing organisms, causing the loss of species or a change in species composition. By reducing suspended matter, water clarity will improve. Although sewage water is held for about 12 days for treatment in a wetland, in treating storm runoff from yards and roadways, both BOD and TSS treatment standards are usually achieved by detaining water for 2 days, according to Bill Wolverton.

Nitrogen

Ammonia (NH_3, NH_4^+), exists abundantly in wastewater. It starts in human waste as urea. Once in water, ammonifying bacteria convert the urea to ammonia. Aerobic bacteria (nitrifiers are aerobic) that depend exclusively on ammonia for energy will then convert the ammonia to nitrite and, in a second step, to nitrate (NO_3). This two-step process is called nitrification. Anaerobic bacteria called "denitrifiers" then convert the nitrate to a nitrogen gas, such as N_2, which will diffuse into the air. Ammonia, the form of nitrogen that is usually regulated, must be treated to achieve a level of less than 2 mg/l for most conditions. To meet this level, some form of nitrogen removal within the sewage treatment process is needed. Nitrate (NO_3) is not usually toxic except when present in large quantities, when it can cause health problems in both people and animals. Nitrite (NO_2) and ammonia are toxic in smaller quantities and can affect the oxygen-carrying capacity of the blood in aquatic life, including fish. Nitrate affects the oxygen-carrying capacity of the blood in animals.

Constructed wetlands, especially surface flow wetlands, promote the nitrification and denitrification performed by the various types of bacteria.

Transformation of Nitrogen in Sewage

urea	ammonia	nitrite	nitrate	nitrogen gas
$CO(NH_2)_2$	NH_3, NH_4^+	NO_2	NO_3	N_2

Ammonia within wastewater at the Starkville, Mississippi, city sewage treatment plant comes into the plant at 14 mg/l. It is treated with the use of oxidation ditches (aeration ponds), and when wastewater is released from the plant, the ammonia level is at 2 mg/l. The vigorous thrashing by aerators in the oxidation ditch helps to transform the nitrogen by creating a habitat for bacteria that will convert it to a gaseous form to be released harmlessly into the air. The composition of air is roughly 78% nitrogen, 21% oxygen, and less than 1% carbon dioxide. This treatment process is partly pH dependent. At high pH (> 8), most of the ammonia is in the NH_3 form. At a lower pH, most is in the NH_{4+} form, which is not a gas and does not diffuse out of the system. Nitrogen, especially ammonia NH_3, can be toxic to fish and invertebrates (e.g., snails and crawfish) and insects in water. Nitrogen can also cause rapid growth or "blooms" of algae. When algae go through their life cycle, nutrients that were absorbed and compose their biomass are released back into the water, where they are consumed by aerobic bacteria, depleting oxygen levels. Once the oxygen in the water is depleted by the aerobic bacteria consuming the nutrients, anaerobic bacteria proliferate. They digest matter incompletely, causing noxious gases to be released and generating a stink.

Human Waste Components

Human manure is the waste produced by the digestion process. It takes form as it moves along the large intestine by involuntary muscular contractions called peristalsis. The normal daily output of manure from human adults is about 250 g (9 oz). Besides food products, up to 20% of this weight is intestinal bacteria. Other constituents are digestive secretions, enzymes, fats, cell debris, electrolytes, water, and small amounts of protein.

The characteristic odor of feces is caused by certain organic chemicals, primarily skatole. Fecal odor results from gases produced by bacterial metabolism, including skatole, mercaptans, and hydrogen sulfide. Normal feces are roughly 75% water and 25% solids. The bulk of fecal solids are undigested organic matter, fiber, and bacteria. The characteristic brown color of feces is due to stercobilin and urobinin, both of which are produced by bacterial degradation of bilirubin. Bilirubin is basically a by-product from the use of blood in the body.

Nitrogen is contained primarily in urine in the form of urea $CO(NH_2)_2$, but is also contained in human manure. Nitrogen concentration is lower in plants than in people because plants do not have a need for large quantities as people and animals do. People need it for muscle development. Nitrogen is converted into protein, which builds muscle mass. The average composition of human manure is noted in Table 22-6. Table 22-7 lists the nutrient composition of human urine. Table 22-8 lists both the components and the characteristics of residential sewage, according to EPA accounts.

Table 22-6   Components of 50 to 60 Liters (13 to 16 Gallons) of Human Manure

0.1 kg (0.22 lb) nitrogen
0.2 kg (0.44 lb) phosphate
0.2 kg (0.44 lb) potassium
(Other nutrients are contained within manure, but content depends on diet.)

Table 22-7 Components of 400 to 500 Liters (106 to 132 Gallons) of Human Urine

5	kg nitrogen
0.4	kg phosphate
0.9	kg potassium
Sodium	130–260 mEq
Chloride	110–250 mEq
Potassium	25–100 mEq
Calcium	100–250 mg
Magnesium	15–300 mg
Inorganic phosphorus	9–1.3 g

Note: mEq = milli-equivalents.

Table 22-8 Residential Sewage Components and Characteristics

Element	Strength (milligrams per liter)
Total solids	680–1000 mg/l
Volatile solids	380–500
Suspended solids	200–290
Volatile suspended solids	150–240
Biological oxygen demand	200–290
Chemical oxygen demand	680–730
Total nitrogen	35–100
Ammonia	6–18
Nitrites and nitrates	<1
Total phosphorus	18–29
Phosphate	6–24
Total coliforms	10_{10}–10_{12}
Fecal coliforms	10_8–10_{10}

Source: Onsite Wastewater Treatment and Disposal Systems (EPA, 1993).

Sewage Water pH

Acid or alkaline wastewater conditions will affect the health of microorganisms. Most bacteria cannot live in acid or low pH conditions. Bacteria demand a slightly acid to alkaline range, from pH 6 to pH 8.5. Consider the effect of pH on microbial life in oxidation ponds. Oxidation ponds use the presence of algae and sunlight to purify sewage. During the daytime, algae pull CO_2 out of the water and use the carbon for building biomass. At night, the algae expel CO_2 as we do. The CO_2 makes the water more acidic and lowers the pH. If water is naturally buffered, it will not change much from day to night. Consider the following examples of sewage treatment and how daily pH changes are used to help cleanse municipal sewage.

Oxidation Ponds, Lima, Peru

Sewage treatment ponds in Lima, Peru, treat the sewage waste for 100,000 people. Wastewater is first detained in large settling lagoons. Raw sewage flows into these ponds, where solids settle to the bottom and are consumed by anaerobic bacteria. Inorganic objects that cannot be biologically treated are screened and removed. Liquid effluent then flows to the oxidation ponds, where it is treated by algae, sunlight, and bacteria for 20 days in order to create safe water conditions. To help purify sewage, the natural fluctuation of pH from day to night, when algae are present, is used to kill pathogens in the water. Because of the abundant sunlight and algae in the treatment ponds, the pH will be 10 during the day and 6 during the night. While the algae assimilate the dissolved nutrients in the water, it is the wide range of pH that kills the pathogens in the water. After the 20 days, water flows into a third set of ponds, which are used for growing and harvesting tilapia, a fast growing tropical fish known for good eating. The tilapia are herbivores, and they consume the algae flowing into their pools from the oxidation ponds. Waste is used as a resource in Lima, Peru.

Co-Composting at the Earth Complex, Memphis, Tennessee

At the Earth Complex, a sewage treatment center in Memphis, Tennessee, plant manager Peter Alfonso uses sewage biosolids along with residential yard waste to create a marvelous compost (Figure 22-10) that is used on municipal gardens and golf courses. To kill bacteria and to ensure that there are no pathogens in the compost, lime is added and thoroughly mixed into the compost. A fluctuation of pH 6.5 to pH 14 kills all microorganisms in the compost pile. After the compost has been in the open air for a few days, its pH reverts back to its normal level and bacteria again proliferate in the pile

Figure 22-10 Co-composting sewage biosolids with community yard waste.

and continue degradation of the organic matter. In general, compost left to sit or mixed with soil will be completely consumed by microorganisms in three years. Again, waste is used as a resource, but this time in Memphis, Tennessee.

Constructed Wetlands Sewage Treatment Facility, Ocean Springs, Mississippi

At the Ocean Springs constructed wetlands sewage treatment facility (Figure 22-11), waste being treated by constructed ecosystems arrives at the 3 million gal (11,355,000 l) per day facility and goes directly to a series of settling lagoons (Figure 22-12). Here it spends 60 days, during which organic solids are settled and consumed by aerobic and anaerobic bacteria. At this first stop, grit and solids settle out in a 20 ac (8 ha) lagoon cell. Sometimes the effluent is also aerated in this cell for BOD reduction. In testing for solids accumulation in the lagoons, after 10 years of plant operation there was only 1 in. (25 mm) on the bottom and this was composed primarily of grit, sand, and plastics. From the first cell, water flows to cell 2, which is 50 ac (20 ha) in size. Here suspended and dissolved organic materials are reduced by further settling and consumption by bacteria. The water next flows to cell 3, a 5 ac (2 ha) storage pool, where it is detained for further treatment either in constructed wetlands or for land application.

Wastewater then moves from the storage pool by gravity flow to one of three constructed wetlands below (Figure 22-13) or is pumped to a 120 ac (48 ha) hay field for spray application. Each surface flow wetland is 39 ac (15.6 ha) in size and treats the gravity-fed effluent with naturally occurring bacteria and fungi attached to vegetation and located in the wetland sediment. Relatively clear sewage effluent spends 12 to 14 days in the wetlands, where microbes break down the remaining organic compounds and assimilate nutrients in the water. During this breaking down process, most of the organic molecules are oxidized and converted aerobically to CO_2 and water. Refractory, or hard-to-digest, materials such as lignin remain, but they are quite stable and don't cause problems. The digestion of organic compounds containing nitrogen and phosphorus results in inorganic or mineralized phosphorus (also called ortho-phospate) and ammonia. The ammonia then undergoes nitrification followed by denitrification. Treated effluent then flows to an aeration basin (Figure 22-14) to increase oxygen levels, and to an ultraviolet light system for final disinfection, prior to flowing to a local bayou running through the property. Ultraviolet light disinfects because it is a high-energy form of radiation. Ultraviolet light from the sun can damage human skin cells. In general, the treated water flowing from the constructed wetlands is cleaner than the water from Bayou Costapia to which it flows.

When water is needed for the hay fields (Figure 22-15), it is pumped under pressure from the storage lagoon and applied by rain guns (large sprinkler heads). Here naturally occurring bacteria and fungi on the hay and in the soil cleanse the primary treated sewage. The large hay field is also fertilized with dried biosolids from a nearby conventional sewage treatment plant. The biosolids, which originated as human manure, are dried microbial biomass from the decomposition of organic sewage solids. The decaying shells of the microbes that decomposed the sewage solids, as shown in Figure 22-16, are important sources of slow-release fertilizer. Human manure is spread over the 120 ac (48 ha) hay fields with conventional manure spreaders. Lime and potash are the

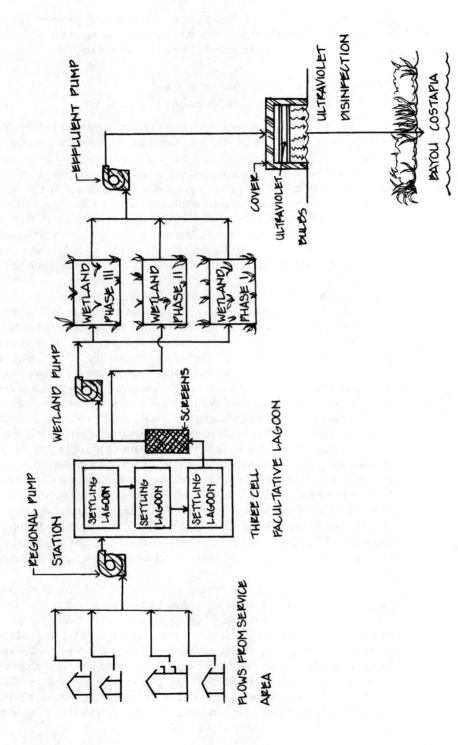

Figure 22-11 Ocean Springs constructed wetlands sewage treatment facility.

Figure 22-12 Settling lagoons—Ocean Springs, Mississippi, ecosystem sewage treatment facility.

Figure 22-13 Constructed wetlands—Ocean Springs, Mississippi, ecosystem sewage treatment facility.

Figure 22-14 Ultraviolet Light Disinfection Unit—Ocean Springs, Mississippi, ecosystem sewage treatment facility.

only supplemental nutrients added to the hay fields. The fields are cut five to nine times a year and produce 45,000 to 60,000 square bales of hay. The hay is rich in nutrients, especially nitrogen, and area farmers line up to buy all that is produced for cattle and horse feed.

Indicators of Sewage Contamination

There is a need to ensure that adequate safeguards are in place to prevent the spread of disease when treating and reusing human wastes—urine and feces. Although urine is rarely a source of human pathogens, many human illnesses can be transmitted via feces. Fecal coliform bacteria that occur in the intestines of all warm-blooded animals (including humans) are mostly nonpathogenic, but some strains can be virulent, and when entering the body orally or through a cut, they can cause health problems such as diarrhea and even more serious illnesses. Their presence in water is used as an indicator of possible sewage contamination. Two tests are routinely performed to determine the presence of coliform bacteria. The "total coliform" test is simple to perform but indicates only the presence or absence of the bacteria that are from mammal guts or types that are

Figure 22-15 Sewage effluent application on hay fields—Ocean Springs, Mississippi, ecosystem sewage treatment facility.

Figure 22-16 Microbial biomass from conventional treatment facility—Ocean Springs, Mississippi, ecosystem sewage treatment facility.

not from animal guts. The fecal coliform test is more complex and is used to measure the number of coliform bacteria per 100 ml sample. Often, the total coliform test is used to screen samples, and the fecal coliform test is then used to provide quantitative results on samples that tested positive. Water that tests positive for coliform bacteria may also be tested for pathogenic bacteria and specific internal parasites and viruses, depending on need. Water having any coliform bacteria per 100 ml of water is not suitable for drinking. Water having counts in excess of 200 per 100 ml is unsafe for swimming. Water with counts greater than 1000 per 100 ml is unsafe for any contact.

Treating Sewage for Release Back into the Landscape

To prepare contaminated water for release into the landscape, BOD, TSS, and nitrogen level are usually considered for reduction. It is the goal of many sewage treatment facilities to lower BOD, remove as many suspended solids as possible, and reuse nitrogen for plant growth. At the Starkville sewage treatment plant, 95% of the BOD is removed, which beats the state regulation level requiring 85% removal before discharging into a water body. The suspended solids level coming into the sewage treatment plant is 60 to 100 mg/l, and going out after treatment is 6 to 10 mg/l. The state requires that no more than 30 mg/l of suspended solids be discharged. If treated effluent is going into a creek or river, nitrogen will have to be reduced to low levels so as not to stimulate algae blooms in the water. The state's Department of Environmental Quality regulations require Starkville's treated wastewater to be prepared so that its constituents meet the following limitations, as shown in Table 22-9.

Production of Sewage

The EPA estimates that an individual in the United States will produce 47 to 52 gal (178 to 200 l) of wastewater per day. This figure includes the water from flushing a toilet, bathing, cooking, washing dishes, and doing laundry. In conducting a weeklong assessment of personal water use, students at our university estimated that they used 40 to 90 gal (154 to 345 l) of water per day. It takes 25 to 50 gals (96 to 192 l) of water to do a load of wash, and 5 to 15 gal (20 to 50 l) of water to shower. Each flush of a commode takes 3.5 to 7 gal (13 to 26 l) for the older commodes and 1.5 gal (6 l) for the newer low-flow toilets. Cooking water needs are estimated at 3 gal (11.5 l) per person per day. In contrast, in the poorest areas of Peru around Lima, the total amount of water each user gets for all uses is about 0.5 gal (2 l) per day. The actual amounts of urine and fecal matter produced are approximately 2.5 gal (10 l) of urine and 3.85 lb (1.75 kg) of fecal matter per week.

John Beeby, in his book *Future Fertility* (Willits, CA: Ecology Action, 1995) says the yearly amount of some nutrients contained within a person's manure is about 2.8 lbs (1.2 kg) of nitrogen, 1.9 lbs (.86 kg) of phosphorus, 0.8 lbs (0.4 kg) of potassium, and 2.0 lbs (0.9 kg) of calcium. Because of its fertilizer value and that it also contains many micronutrients, it is processed by some municipal areas for use as a fertilizer. An example is Milorganite, which is made from dried and pasteurized biosolids from Milwaukee area sewage. It is a desirable, slow release fertilizer valued by the turfgrass

Table 22-9 Requirements for Treating Wastewater

(Discharge limitations—monthly average, Starkville, Mississippi.)

Biochemical oxygen demand (5 day)	10 mg/l
Suspended solids	30 mg/l
Ammonia nitrogen	2 mg/l
Fecal coliform	200 colonies per 100 ml
Chlorine	0.011 mg/l
Pentachlorophenol	0.0021 mg/l
Silver	0.00105 mg/l (maximum weekly average)

industry. Beeby also states that a year's worth of human urine is generally composed of 7.5 lbs (3.4 kg) of nitrogen, 1.6 lbs (0.72 kg) of phosphorus, 1.6 lb (0.72 kg) of potassium, and 2.3 lbs (1.0 kg) of calcium. John Jeavons, Executive Director of Ecology Action states that the nutrients from one person's human waste for one year may contain enough nutrients to grow all the food for one person for all year on a small-scale basis (personal correspondence with the author 21 November, 2001).

Diseases That Can Be Contracted from Sewage

Diseases are caused by pathogens. As mentioned earlier, *pathogen* comes from the Greek *pathos* "suffering." A pathogen can indeed make you suffer. Pathogens found in water include viruses, bacteria, helminths, and protozoans. Typhoid, polio, and cholera are all pathogens that can cause disease in humans through consumption of contaminated water. Groundwater polluted by human waste can infect people with hepatitis A, a viral infection. Although it seems logical that one would have to be infected with a disease for a particular system's sewage to be contaminated, according to the official United States Geological Survey Web site discussing water supplies, diseases affecting water can be spread by air and precipitation:

> Unfortunately, some pathogenic bacteria, viruses and protozoans may have special survival mechanisms, such as cyst formation in Cryptosporidium, or attachment of viruses to particles, so that waters free of fecal indicator bacteria may still harbor these microorganisms. [Cyst formation with cryptosporidium occurs when the protozoan becomes encapsulated and goes dormant as a means of protecting itself from low pH water or the acid conditions in the stomach.] In this encapsulated form it can be transferable in air or moving water. The possibility exists that the pathogen could wash or blow into a sewage treatment system that does not have pathogens in the system. This is even true of water which has undergone treatment for drinking water purposes.

Table 22-10 presents a list of pathogens potentially found in sewage, and possible human sufferings that can occur by coming in contact with the pathogens.

In the 30 hours that sewage was detained at the Starkville oxidation plant and the 75 days it was treated at the Ocean Springs constructed wetlands plant, solids were removed from the liquified sewage mix, most of the nitrogen and other nutrients were assimilated by microbes, and pathogens in the water were destroyed, resulting in clean water.

Some Final Thoughts

In conclusion, consider these thoughts conveyed to us by Bill Wolverton and Asahi Takasano, two early pioneers of treating sewage with natural systems and reusing the nutrients within sewage. Wolverton says that sewage is like a potent liquid fertilizer. Being full of nutrients, it acts like a slow-release organic fertilizer, providing a broad range of both macro- and micronutrients. Because sewage is a resource for plants and animals, it is easily treated by plants and waterborne microbes. Wolverton does caution people to treat sewage with care because of the potential for acquiring pathogens.

Takasani has said that sewage water has great potential for use as a fertilizer for food and fiber plants. When using sewage components such as biosolids or liquid effluent

Table 22-10   Pathogens Potentially Present in Household Sewage Wastewater

Pathogen	Affliction
Protozoans	
Entamoeba histolytica	Amoebiasis dysentery
Giardia lamblia	Giardiasis
Balantidiumce	Coli balantidiasis dysentery
Helminths (flatworms)	
Lascaris lumbricoides	Ascariasis—roundworm
Ancylostoma duodenale	Ancylostomiasis—hookworm
Necator americanus	Necatoriasis
Ancylostoma	Cutaneous larva migrans—hookworm
Strongyloides stercoralis	Strongyloidiasis—threadworm
Trichuris trichiura	Trichuriasis—whipworm
Taenia	Taeniasis—tapeworm
Enterobius vermicularis	Enterobasis—pinworm
Bacteria	
Shigella	Shigellosis—dysentery
Salmonella typhi	Typhoid fever
Salmonella	Salmonellosis
Vibrio cholerae	Cholera
Escherichia coli	Gastroenteritis
Yersinia enterocolitica	Yersiniosis
Leptospira	Leptospirosis
Viruses	
Enteroviruses (71 types) (polio, echo, Coxsackie)	Gastroenteritis, heart anomalies, meningitis, others
Hepatitis A virus	Infectious hepatitis
Adenovirus (31 types)	Respiratory disease
Rotavirus	Gastroenteritis
Parvovirus (two types)	Gastroenteritis

for food crops, it is essential that the sewage not come in contact with the fruit of the crops. He says that the EPA has considerable restrictions on the use of sewage for food crop fertilizer because there is a remote possibility that pathogens can be transferred to people. But with care, sewage can be used safely and effectively for food and fiber crop production.

DESIGNING AND MANAGING CONSTRUCTED WETLANDS

A surface flow constructed wetland is designed so that wastewater can flow slowly from one end of the wetland to the other and receive maximum exposure to the bacteria colonized on plant leaves, stems, and the bottom surface. The treatment objectives are the same for a subsurface flow wetland, except that the bacteria are colonized primarily on large gravel or rock surfaces. Sewage effluent that has had most of the solids removed by settling ponds or septic tanks will probably still contain some organic compounds. Suspended and dissolved materials may include nutrients, such as nitrogen and phosphorus, and pollutants such as heavy metals. In addition, the water will probably contain sediment and organisms like protozoa, bacteria, and viruses. As the wastewater moves through the wetland, pollutants and organisms are exposed to a large variety of microbes in the water, on plant leaves and litter, on stems and roots, on the surfaces of gravel, and in the mud. These microbes are primarily responsible for cleaning the sewage, but water is also cleaned by the assimilation of nutrients into plants and by sedimentation, a physical process whereby particles settle out. Plants assimilate no more than 10% of the nutrients in a system.

Maximizing Exposure of Wastewater to Microbes

It is the responsibility of the wetland designer to make sure that polluted water gets maximum exposure to as many microbes as possible. The two major factors that affect exposure of wastewater to microbial treatment are an evenly distributed flow of water through the wetland and detention of the dirty water for a specific amount of time. For effective treatment, sewage effluent should be detained 12 to 14 days. A molecule of dirty water should take the required amount of detention time to get from its entrance into the wetland, through the wetland, to the outfall point. Water should flow evenly apportioned among the plants in order to maximize exposure of dirty water to microbes. If water starts to channel, as shown in Figure 22-17, microbes in certain areas of the wetland will

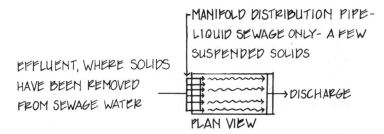

EFFLUENT, WHERE SOLIDS HAVE BEEN REMOVED FROM SEWAGE WATER

MANIFOLD DISTRIBUTION PIPE- LIQUID SEWAGE ONLY- A FEW SUSPENDED SOLIDS

→ DISCHARGE

PLAN VIEW

EVEN FLOW DISTRIBUTION ACROSS WETLAND - DIRTY WATER IS EVENLY DISTRIBUTED TO MICROBES FOR TREATMENT

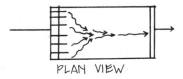

PLAN VIEW

FLOW THROUGH THE CONSTRUCTED WETLAND- DIRTY WATER IS CONCENTRATED, THUS OVERLOADING THE MICROBES ALONG THE FLOW ROUTE

Figure 22-17 Channeling of flow in the constructed wetland.

become overexposed to pollution and the water will not be fully cleaned. The opposite of channeled flow is plug or uniform flow, and that's what the designer and manager are trying to achieve in the wetland. The longer dirty water is detained and exposed to microbes, the cleaner it will become. A conventional concrete and steel sewage treatment plant can usually treat wastewater in 30 hours, but the treatment technology relies heavily on energy to aerate the water for enhancement of aerobic microbial activity, and on chemicals like chlorine to kill any remaining pathogens in the water. Undigested solids that result from traditional sewage plants have to be stored in a lagoon, incinerated, or land-applied to hay, fiber crops, or tree plantations.

Sizing the Constructed Wetland

There are three basic steps to consider when sizing a constructed wetland. The quantity of wastewater that will flow through the wetland must be determined, and the amount of time the wastewater will be detained has to be decided. These first two considerations will constitute the information needed to complete the third step, which is to determine the volume and dimensions of the wetland.

The volume of the wetland needed can be determined by multiplying the daily volume of wastewater to be treated by the wetland detention time for treating the wastewater. This will yield the total volume of constructed wetland needed. Design depths of constructed wetlands vary from 12 to 30 in. (30 to 75 cm). A constructed wetland that is 12 in. (30 cm) deep will require a treatment area twice the size of one that is 24 in. (60 cm) deep. When figuring the total volume for treating a given capacity in a subsurface flow wetland, consider the void or pore spaces in the gravel that will contain the water. A subsurface flow marsh treating the same amount of wastewater as a surface flow marsh will be larger than the surface flow wetland because of the space taken up by the gravel. The amount of space or volume taken up by gravel will have to be considered in determining the final volume needed in the marsh. If gravel has 33% void space, then the total volume of marsh space will have to be three times larger than the surface flow marsh in order to include the space taken up by the gravel. In computing the required space for a surface flow marsh, the amount of space taken up by the plants will have to be considered in determining the final volume needed. From observations of surface flow marshes it appears that plants can take up 10 to 25% of the total water volume. Many surface flow treatment system designers do not increase the volume of the wetland to account for the space taken up by plants; they say it is unnecessary and that the water treatment works fine with the slightly reduced volume.

Generally, the flow of water through a wetland works better when the shape of the wetland is two to three times longer than it is wide. This aspect ratio of 2 to 3:1 has been determined by trial and error over the years of constructing and evaluating wetlands. A square-shaped wetland will work only when the size is very small, such as 10 × 10 ft (3 × 3 m).

Wetland Sizing Problem 1

Let us size a surface flow wetland to treat the sewage effluent from five single-family residences. The residences have three to four bedrooms each, and each residence has five occupants. There is a septic tank at each residence to remove solids. From the tanks, liquid effluent will flow to a single constructed wetland, where it will enter a distribution pipe or manifold for an evenly distributed entrance into the wetland. In this example the effluent will be held 12 days for treatment, and then the water will flow out of the wetland and be stored for irrigation use.

Sizing a Surface Flow Wetland for Five Houses
Assume 50 gal of wastewater produced each day by each user:

> 5 houses × 5 users each house × 50 gal wastewater per user per day
> = 1250 gal of wastewater produced per day
> 1250 gal/7.48 gal per ft^3 = 167 ft^3 of wastewater per day produced
> by the five houses

With a retention time of 12 days in the wetland:

> 12 days × 167 ft^3 of wastewater = 2004 ft^3 volume of wetland needed
> to treat 1250 gal of wastewater per day, with a 12 day retention time.

Assume an aspect ratio of approximately 3:1 and a design depth of 1.5 ft (0.45 m). The system surface area = 2004 ft^3/1.5 ft = 1336 ft^3. For an aspect ratio of 3:1, the area is: length × width = 3 times width times width = 3 times width^2.

> Width^2 = 1336/3 = 446 ft^2. Width = the square root of 446
> = slightly less than 22 ft

When excavating, standard practice is to use whole feet, so we'll call width 22 ft. The length is then 1336/22 = approximately 61 ft.

A wetland that has 2004 ft^3 of volume could have a configuration of 22 × 61 × 1.5 ft = 2013 ft^3.

Therefore, a wetland that is 22 × 61 ft by 1½ ft deep will be able to treat 167 ft^3 or 1250 gal of wastewater each day. After 12 days of detention time, the 167 ft^3 of daily wastewater flow will be released from the wetland into a vegetated swale to slowly drain into the soil, or to a tank or pool where it is stored for irrigation use.

Metric Version:
Figuring 189 l of wastewater produced by each user:

> 5 houses × 5 users each house × 189 l wastewater per user per day
> = 4731 l of wastewater produced per day
> 4731 l/1000 l (there are 1000 l in 1 m^3) = 4.33 m^3 of wastewater per day
> produced by the five houses

With a retention time of 12 days in the wetland:

12 days × 4.33 m^3 of wastewater = 52 m^3 volume of wetland needed to treat

4731 l of wastewater per day, with a 12 day retention time

Assume an aspect ratio of approximately 3:1 and a design depth of (0.45 m). The system surface area = 57 m^3/0.45 m = 124 m^2. For an aspect ratio of 3:1, the area is:

length × width = 3 times width times width = 3 times width^2.

Width^2 = 124 m^3 = 41.3. Width = the square root of 41.3

= slightly less than 6.7 m

When excavating, standard practice is to use whole feet, so we'll call width 7 m. The length is then 124 m/7 m = approximately 18 m.

A wetland that has 57 m^3 of volume could have a configuration of 18 × 7 × 0.45 m = 57 m^3.

Therefore, a wetland that is 18 × 7 × 0.45 m deep will be able to treat 4.33 m^3 of wastewater each day. After 12 days of detention time, the 4.33 m^3 of daily wastewater flow will be released from the wetland into a vegetated swale to slowly drain into the soil, or to a tank or pool where it is stored for irrigation use.

Treatment Capacity of Wetlands

The ability of a wetland to treat a certain amount of polluted water in a specified time is called its hydraulic capacity. The Ocean Springs wetland treatment facility has a hydraulic capacity of treating 5 million gal (18,925,000 l) of sewage per day, with a retention time of 60 days in the solids settling ponds and 12 days in the wetlands. The hydraulic retention time is the amount of time it takes for an average molecule of wastewater to travel through the lagoon or wetland to the outfall point. Once it makes it through the wetland, the water should be cleansed to an acceptable level.

Form of the Constructed Wetland

Whether a wetland should be laid out in a square, rectangular, or freeform style relates to how best the wastewater will receive the maximum amount of treatment as it flows through the given form. In the sewage treatment process, solids are first settled out in a settling pool or septic tank, and the liquid part of the sewage, also known as the effluent, flows into the wetland. Effluent is the liquid outflow from a septic tank. The word *effluent* comes from the Latin word *effluere,* which means to flow out. When effluent flows from a settling pond into a wetland, it must be evenly distributed along one side via a perforated pipe or other device for distributing that flow equally to all parts of the wetland. Figure 22-18 is a photograph of a manifold delivering effluent from the solids settlement lagoons at Ocean Springs, Mississippi. Distributing wastewater uniformly at the entrance end can help to ensure that the water will be dispersed equally over the entire wetland and get maximum exposure to microbes for treatment. Regular observation is

Figure 22-18   Manifold delivering sewage effluent from settling lagoons—Ocean Springs, Mississippi, ecosystem sewage treatment facility.

needed to ensure that the flow of sewage effluent is not being blocked in certain areas, which will cause channeling.

In regard to the form of the constructed wetland, let us consider the advantages and disadvantages of a rectangular and a square configuration. As stated earlier, the conventional wisdom about aspect ratio has been that the length of a wetland should be at least two to three times its width. The reason for this is the tendency of wetlands to become patchy over time and to evolve into sections of open water surrounded by dense stands of emergent plants. The banks and the plants help to make the flow uniform by dissipating flow energy (velocity is lost due to friction when the flowing water comes in contact with plant stems or the bank). If a constructed wetland has a large open area providing little frictional resistance, this area will become a relatively high-velocity "channel" through the wetland. In a short, wide cell, an open area may cover much of the cell length. If this happens, the cell has been "short circuited" and flow is not uniform. As pointed out, uniform flow is essential for effective treatment.

Yet this argument does not always hold true. Recall that a manifold is used in constructed wetlands to distribute incoming water uniformly across the width of the wetland cell. Channeling, even in the presence of some patchiness does not occur immediately. The channel will begin to become a factor some distance from the upper end of the cell. If the length of the cell is less than the distance required to establish channeling, then channeling will not become very noticeable in the system. If the short cell has a vigorous growth of emergent plants, channeling will be even more inhibited.

When can the conventional wisdom about aspect ratio be disregarded? The answer is, when the wetland can be kept small. If we assume that from the perspective of land use, the most efficient shape is square, then a constructed wetland consisting of small square cells would be a viable option. Although determining distance required to establish channeling is a complicated problem, examples drawn from the literature suggest that cells approximately 10 ft × 10 ft (3 m × 3 m) will perform reliably.

The rectangular form of the subsurface flow constructed wetland can be prone to clogging of solids in the gravel. This can happen as wastewater flows from the settling ponds through the wetland and drops remaining solids in the effluent. If the gravel voids are small, they can fill up and liquid can no longer flow through. When this occurs, the sewage begins to flow along the top of the gravel, with the result that it receives minimal exposure to microbes and, thus, minimal treatment. Untreated wastewater can flow out of the treatment system. This occurrence is called *surfacing* (Figure 22-19), a sign that there is a significant problem in the subsurface flow system.

In a rectangle-shaped surface flow system, solids are prone to dropping out in the first one-third of the system, causing an overload of solids for the aerobic bacteria to treat. This can result in depletion of oxygen in the water and a surge in the population of anaerobic bacteria. Anaerobic bacteria incompletely digest organic solids, resulting in foul-smelling gases and a wetland that becomes inefficient and unappreciated because of its offensive smell.

Wetland Sizing Problem 2

Let us calculate the flow expected for a classroom building and size a subsurface flow wetland. An average residence in the United States has 3.2 occupants and generates 50 gal (189 l) of sewage per person per day. In contrast, wastewater created at an office or school is estimated at 15 gal (57 l) per day per person (Table 22-11), inasmuch as using water for bathing, cooking, and cleaning is not normally a part of the office or

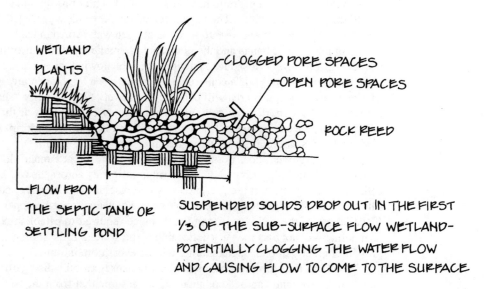

Figure 22-19 Surfacing of untreated wastewater in the constructed wetland.

Table 22-11   Estimated Wastewater from Facility Types

Type of Facility	Estimated Flow in Gallons per Day (Liters per Day)
Food service	
Restaurant	35 gpd (133 lpd) per seat
Restaurant (24-hour)	50 gpd (189 lpd) per seat
Short order	35 gpd (133 lpd) per car or parking space
Bar	20 gpd (76 lpd) per seat
Motel	40 gpd (152 lpd) per bed
Motel with kitchen	50 gpd (189 lpd) per bed
Personal Care Home	190 gpd (719 lpd) per bed
Resort, camp, cottage	125 gpd (473 lpd) per unit
Offices, factories	15 gpd (57 lpd) per employee
Offices, factories with showers	25 gpd (95 lpd) per employee
Day school with cafeteria	16–20 gpd (61–76 lpd) per student
Day school without cafeteria	10–15 gpd (38–57 lpd) per student
Swimming pools	10 gpd (38 lpd) per maximum swimmer occupancy
Airport (small)	10 gpd (38 lpd) per employee
Laundry	580 gpd (2200 lpd) per machine
Shopping center	1 gpd (4 lpd) per parking space, 10 gpd (38 lpd) per employee
RV park with sewer hookups	100 gpd (379 lpd) per space
Churches with kitchens	6 gpd (23 lpd) per seat

Source: Mississippi State Department of Health, 1991.

classroom experience. Now let us project the wastewater flow produced by a proposed classroom facility on a university campus. The department will have 250 students and staff members. Sewage will be treated on-site with a subsurface flow constructed wetland. Solids will be separated from the liquids by septic tanks located in series—that is, one behind the other. Liquid wastewater will flow from the septic tanks (where solids have settled) into the subsurface wetland for treatment. Treated water flowing out of the wetlands will flow to a rock-reed planting for use by plants and distribution into the soil. When sizing a subsurface flow wetland, be sure that the volume of the excavated space considers the pore spaces the water will fill in the gravel. If pore spaces are only 33% of the gravel volume, the total volume of the wetland will need to be three times the computed wastewater volume to be treated.

Sizing a Subsurface Flow Wetland for a Classroom Facility

250 people × 15 gal per day production = 3750 gal of sewage produced per day

3750 gal/7.48 gal per ft^3 = 501 ft^3 of water to treat per day

Detaining water for 12 days, the hydraulic capacity of the wetland will be 501 ft^3/day × 12 days = 6012 ft^3.

Gravel that has a pore space of 33% will triple the volume of the 6012 ft^3 wetland to accommodate the sewage and gravel.

$$6012 \text{ ft}^3 \times 3 = 18{,}036 \text{ ft}^3$$

501 ft³/day × 12 days detention time × 3 (gravel with a pore space of 33%)
$$= 18{,}036 \text{ ft}^3$$

Divide the ft³ of wetland by a 1½ ft depth to get the required ft².

$$18{,}036 \text{ ft}^3/1.5 \text{ ft} = 12{,}024 \text{ ft}^2$$

Therefore, a subsurface flow wetland 75 ft × 160 ft × 1.5 ft deep has an area of 12,000 ft² and a volume of 18,000 ft³. This will be sufficient to detain the 501 ft³ of daily wastewater flow for 12 days, resulting in fully cleaned wastewater in the subsurface flow wetland.

Another way of determining the space that gravel will need is to figure the void loss of the gravel. If the gravel that is being used takes up 40% of the void area of the wetland volume, then we would have to take 40% of the projected volume needed and add that to the volume projection to provide room for the gravel.

Metric Version

250 people × 57 l each per day production = 14,194 l of sewage produced per day
14,194 l/1000 l = 14.1 m³ of water to treat per day

Detaining water for 12 days, the hydraulic capacity of the wetland will be 14.1 m³/day × 12 days = 169.2 m³

Gravel that has a pore space of 33% will triple the volume of the 169.2 m³ wetland to accommodate the sewage and gravel.

$$169.2 \text{ m}^3 \times 3 = 507.6 \text{ m}^3$$

14.1 m³/day × 12 days detention time × 3 (gravel with a pore space of 33%)
$$= 507.6 \text{ m}^3$$

Therefore, a subsurface flow wetland 23 m × 49 m × 0.45 m deep has a volume of 507 m³, and this will be sufficient to detain the 14 m³ of daily wastewater flow for 12 days, resulting in fully cleaned wastewater in the subsurface flow wetland.

Physical Components and Costs

The physical components of a constructed wetland impoundment include the excavation, levees, plastic or clay liner, soil, gravel, plantings, and structures for water control. Gravel is used only in a subsurface flow wetland, and it is the most expensive material and installation part of that wetland, being nearly half the total cost. A plastic or impermeable clay liner, which is used in both a surface flow and a subsurface flow wetland, can be up to 25% of the total cost. The costs of the excavation and compaction of soils, the plants and planting, and the water control structures constitute the remaining expenditures.

LEMNA MINOR
"DUCKWEED"

NELUMBO LUTEO
"AMERICAN LOTUS"

LIMNOBIUM SPONGIA
"FROG'S BIT"

Figure 22-20 Hydrophytic plants used in the constructed wetland.

Plants in a Wetland Sewage Treatment System

Hydrophytic plants are those that enjoy a constant water source. Floating plants useful for treating water include the water hyacinth (*Eichhornia crassipes*), a plant native to areas along the equator, and duckweed (*Lemna minor*), a plant native to North America. Both of these plants are very effective in removing nutrients and other pollutants from water. Submergent plants that grow beneath the surface and do not have to be rooted in a substrate include *Hydrilla, Elodea,* and *Egeria.* See Figure 22-20 for illustrations of typical hydrophytic plants. In addition to hosting bacteria, these plants are also able to absorb nutrients on the surfaces of their leaves and stems, to and provide oxygen to water.

Emergent plants useful in constructed wetlands include cattails (*Typha latifolia*), yellow iris (*Iris pseudacorus*), bulrushes (*Scirpus*), and common reeds (*Phragmites australis*). Cattails, among others, can grow to a height of about 5 to 6 ft (1.5 to 1.8 m) and will grow into thick matts of rhizomes, with roots extending into the soil to a depth of about 1 ft (0.3 m). Yellow iris are vigorous spring flowering plants that enjoy wet feet. They will grow to about 5 ft (1.5 m) tall, and although they will tolerate dry, upland conditions, they are more vigorous in wet soils. Their root system will extend about 8 in. (20 cm) below the substrate. Bulrushes, although not as vigorous as cattails and yellow iris, will grow to a height of 5 to 7 ft (1.5 to 2.1 m), and roots will extend 3 ft (0.9 m) deep. Bulrushes are effective in removing nitrogen and providing oxygen deep into the gravel substrate of subsurface flow treatment systems. Common reeds are actually grasses that enjoy wet feet. They will grow to a height of about 6 to 12 ft (1.8 to 3.6 m), and their root structure will extend to a depth of about 1½ ft (0.46 m). Table 22-12 lists hydrophytic plants suitable for growing in plant-reed systems.

Wetland Plants and Oxygenation

Most emergent plants are very effective in transferring oxygen from their leaves above the water level to the submerged root zone. This is an important feature, especially in

Table 22-12   Plants Suitable for Use in Plant-Reed Filter Systems

Common Name	Scientific Name	Height	Rooting Depth
Arrow arum, tuckahoe	*Peltrandra virginica*	3.3 ft (1m)	8–15 in. (203–381 mm)
Arrowhead, duck corn	*Sagittaria sagittifolia*	2 ft (0.6 m)	—
Arrowhead, duck potato	*Sagittaria latifolia*	2–4 ft (0.6–0.8 m)	10–12 in. (254–305 mm)
Water iris, blue	*Iris versicolor*	3 ft (0.9 m)	8 in. (203 mm)
Water iris, yellow	*Iris pseudacorus*	0.8–3.3 ft (0.2–1.0 m)	8 in. (203 mm)
Bog arum, wild call	*Calla palustris*	0.5–0.75 ft (0.2–0.3 m)	9–10 in. (229–254 mm)
Bulrush	*Scripus americanus*	10 ft (3 m)	12–18 in. (305–457 mm)
Calla lily	*Zantedeschia aethiopica*	2–3 ft (0.6–0.9 m)	8–12 in. (203–305 mm)
Canna lily	*Canna flaccida*	1.3–5.9 ft (0.4–1.8 m)	10–12 in. (254–305 mm)
Cardinal flower	*Lobelia cardinalis*	2.6 ft (0.8 m)	6–8 in. (152–203 mm)
Cattail, broadleaf	*Typha latifolia*	3–6 ft (0.9–1.8 m)	6–12 in. (152–305 mm)
Cattail, narrowleaf	*Typha angustifolia*	3–6 ft (0.9–1.8 m)	6–12 in. (152–305 mm)
Cyperus sedge	*Carex pseudocyperus*	2.6 ft (0.8 m)	—
Elephant ear	*Calocasia esculentia*	3 ft (0.9 m)	12–18 in. (305–457 mm)
Flowering rush	*Butomus umbellatus*	2–3 ft (0.6–0.9 m)	12–24 in. (305–610 mm)
Giant reed	*Phragmites australis*	—	18 in. (610 mm)
Great blue lobelia	*Lobelia siphilitica*		
Horsetail	*Equisetum hyemale*	1–3.3 ft (0.3–1 m)	6–8 in. (152–203 mm)
Japanese water iris	*Iris laevigata*	2.6 ft (0.8 m)	—
Marsh marigold	*Caltha palustria*	1 ft (0.3 m)	6 in. (152 mm)
Pickerel weed	*Pontederia cordata*	0.8–4.9 ft (0.2–1.5 m)	15 in. (381 mm)
Plantain lily	*Hosta* species	0.5–2 ft (0.2–0.6 m)	8–10 in. (203–254 mm)
Rushes	*Juncus* species	0.5–6 ft (0.2–1.8 m)	12–18 in. (305–457 mm)
Rushes	*Scirpus* species	3–4 ft (0.9–1.2 m)	—
Sedges	*Carex* species	—	—
Sweet flag-calamus	*Acorus calamus*	2–2.5 ft (0.6–0.8 m)	—
Umbrella sedges	*Cyperus* species	2–6 ft (0.6–1.8 m)	12–18 in. (305–457 mm)

subsurface flow systems where treatment is dependent on aerobic bacteria covering the surface of submerged gravel. The oxygen ensures that there will be aerobic bacteria on the rocks for water treatment, instead of anaerobic bacteria. Aerobic bacteria grow in the presence of oxygen, and anaerobic bacteria grow without oxygen. The aerobic bacteria are vigorous consumers of organic matter and will completely digest material, whereas the anaerobic bacteria are incomplete digestors of matter and the remaining, undigested matter will give off gases that we sense as offensive odors. For maximum treatment, it is important to cultivate aerobic bacteria in the substrate of subsurface flow treatment systems. Bulrushes and common reeds are noted for their ability to transport oxygen to gravel substrates in order to meet the needs of aerobic bacteria. Sometimes subsurface flow wetlands are grown without plants and oxygen is supplied to submerged gravel surfaces by aerators. See Figure 22-21 for pictures of oxygenation plants in both surface flow and subsurface flow wetlands.

Design of a Rock-Reed or Plant-Reed Filter for Small-Scaled Facilities

A rock-reed filter is a subsurface flow wetland that can be used where soils are not suitable for absorption fields. The plant and rock filter consists of a lined cell that receives

Figure 22-21 Oxygenating plants in surface flow and subsurface flow sewage treatment filters.

effluent from a septic tank, and an unlined cell where treatment is still occurring and some of the effluent is allowed to percolate into the soil. The following design criteria must be used in designing rock-reeds at a residential scale.

1. Primary treatment must be provided by a septic tank, in which all human urine and manure are collected. Solids are allowed to settle to the bottom of the tank, where they will be treated by anaerobic bacteria. If the tank is large enough, the bacteria will consume all of the organic solids and there will never be a need to pump out the tank. The recommended septic tank sizes in many states are based on the number of bedrooms in a house. See Table 22-13 for recommended tank sizes for residential use.

2. Secondary treatment of sewage effluent is provided in the subsurface filter or plant bed, where one cell must be lined to hold the sewage effluent that flows from the septic tank. The liner can be two thin layers of polyethylene sheeting or a single sheet of 20 mil polyethylene. In the cells, microbes and plants assimilate nutrients and destroy pathogens, rendering the effluent water clean after a 12- to 14-day detention time.

Table 22-13 Septic Tank Sizes for Residential Use

Number of Bedrooms	Liquid Capacity of Tanks
2	750 gal (2839 l)
3	900 gal (3407 l)
4	1000 gal (3785 l)
5	1250 gal (4731 l)
Add 250 gal (946 l) for additional bedrooms.	

3. The standard depth of the plant-rock filter is 18 in. (457 mm), with a static water level of 12 in. (305 mm). A shallower system can be built that is 12 in. (305 mm) total depth with 6 in. (152 mm) of liquid depth.

4. Include a manifold of perforated 4 in. (101 mm) pipe for the inlet from the septic tank.

5. Plant-rock filters should be sized as follows:

Number of Bedrooms	18 in. (457 mm) deep bed	12 in. (305 mm) deep bed
3 or fewer	300 ft^2 (28 m^2) bed	600 ft^2 (56 m^2) bed
4 or more	400 ft^2 (37 m^2) bed	800 ft^2 (74 m^2) bed

6. The outfall line should be at least 4 in. (102 mm) below the outlet of the septic tank. On level ground, it may be necessary to lower the rock bed so that the top of the rocks are as far below the natural ground surface as necessary.

7. Effluent from the bed can be disposed of by overland flow or subsurface absorption, depending on site evaluation by regulating authorities.

Management of Constructed Wetland Treatment Systems

In many parts of the world there is a dormant season for the plant kingdom. As constructed wetland plantings die back during the winter, the nitrogen, phosphorus, and other nutrients taken up by the plants from the wastewater is released back into the wetland in the spring as the biomass undergoes decomposition. This increases the waste load. To prevent the decaying plant matter from making water quality worse, harvest dead biomass from plants whose tops have died as a result of freezing. Plants like pickerel weed will freeze, and their tops will fall back into the water. It is best to harvest these plants after killing frosts. Bulrushes die in the winter, but their foliage does not fall back into the water until spring, allowing a site manager to delay the harvesting of plant biomass until later. After plants die back, like the cattails illustrated in Figure 22-22, harvesting and composting biomass can recycle these nutrients to locations where they will be beneficial.

Management Costs

The cost of managing a constructed wetland can be 50 to 75% less than the cost of managing a conventional treatment facility. Management of the Ocean Springs, Mississippi,

Figure 22-22 Cattails that have died back during the winter.

constructed wetlands plant, serving a population of about 30,000 people, requires one person four hours a day, five days a week. This costs about $20,000 per year. At the Starkville, Mississippi, traditional sewage treatment plant serving a population of about 30,000 people, management requires three to four people a day, eight hours a day, five days a week. This costs about $100,000 or more per year.

There are not as many tasks that need attention in wetland management as there are in a conventional sewage treatment plant. Operational tasks that need regular attention in a wetland landscape include adjusting water levels, general observation, and testing water to ensure that treatment levels are being met. Regular inspection is needed in sub-surface flow wetlands to make sure that surfacing is not occurring and that there is water flowing through the system. Surfacing occurs when the gravel clogs and sewage seeps to the top of the gravel and flows across the surface. In all public sewage treatment systems both influent and effluent must be tested in order to meet state regulations. Maintenance tasks for wetlands can include mowing levees, weed control, harvesting dead biomass in the late fall, and ensuring that there is adequate flow distribution. When plant matter is harvested, nitrogen in the plants is being taken out of the wetland instead of decomposing in the wetland and being released the next spring. Removing biomass also results in more vigorous growth during the spring. Constructed wetlands use simple or low technology and have low operation and installation costs.

Effect of Cold Climates on Constructed Wetland Performance

Constructed wetlands in cold climates in the United States and Canada will continue to treat sewage effluent at an acceptable rate even during the coldest parts of the year. However, treatment rates will be lower than during the warmer growing season, which is more suitable to more bacteria. A study in Ontario, Canada, showed that during the coldest parts of the winter when there was a 4 in. (102 mm) thick layer of ice on treatment marshes and cattails were completely dormant, effluent continued to flow beneath the surface and treatment levels were acceptable. The study showed that an effluent retention time of seven days proved to be ideal for obtaining the best sewage treatment. Biological wastewater pioneer Wolverton says that a different set of bacteria take over treatment of effluent during cold weather.

The lagoon and constructed wetland plant at Ouray, Colorado, also has a successful wintertime operation, despite cold weather and ice on the lagoons and the wetlands. Normally, the city has about three months of cold weather with temperatures that drop to the single digits during the evening, and in the 30s and 40s (°F) (-1 to 4°C) during the daytime. Ice accumulates to about 6 to 8 in. (15 to 20 cm) thick over the lagoons and the dormant cattail-dominated wetlands. The plant operates aerators both in the lagoons and in the wetlands during the winter to ensure full treatment and to make certain that the wetlands contain plenty of oxygen and do not go anaerobic. The winter of 2001 was especially cold, with nighttime temperatures around 0°F (-18°C) and below and daytime temperatures in the 30s (°F) (-10°C). Ice accumulated to a thickness of 2 ft (0.6 m) both in the lagoons and in the wetlands. Water Quality Coordinator Ed Witherspoon said that through aeration, treatment was still significantly below state limits, despite the 2 ft thick ice cover. He also said that although a constructed wetland is a very effective, environment-friendly way of treating sewage effluent, it does need constant observation and evaluation. If a problem arises, it can take weeks to alter, so diligent observation is important.

At the Ocean Springs, Mississippi, constructed wetlands plant, cold winter weather causes the cattails and bulrushes to die back to the water level. Wetland manager Linwood Tanner says that when the warm weather plants die back, then other plants like dollargrass and pennywort appear, providing living structure for bacteria to attach, and the water continues to be cleansed. Although the plants assist in treating the water in winter, aerobic bacteria will still cleanse effluent water even if all of the green plants are in a dormant condition, as long as oxygen is available.

Chapter 23

Recycling

Recycling saves energy, reduces pollution, and decreases the use of virgin natural resources.

Recycling is the collection and separation of materials from waste and their subsequent processing to produce marketable products. Recycling is inherently a cyclical process, in which the same material is used multiple times. By reusing a material, virgin (particularly nonrenewable) resources are conserved. The remanufacturing process typically uses much less energy than manufacturing from virgin material, reducing the consumption of fossil fuel energy. Reduced fossil fuel energy consumption reduces pollutants, including carbon dioxide, released as a result of manufacturing. Reuse of certain materials (such as lead batteries, motor oil, antifreeze) reduces pollution resulting from disposal of the material itself.

The definition of *recycling* given here is specific to the subject of this chapter, the removal of material from the waste stream followed by its reuse to create the products we need. In a more general sense, recycling is a central tenet of living sustainably. Sustainable practices, as pointed out in the introduction to this book, help us to live without damaging the regenerative cycles on which we depend for life. Chapter 6, on gray water, and Chapter 25, on composting, are both about recycling. By using our water more than once, we fill part of our need for water with "used" water. In this way, we reduce pressure on our drinking water supplies, reduce the energy required to treat and pump water, and reduce the amount of water that must be treated by expensive treatment plants. Through composting, we reuse organic material and reduce the resources, energy, and pollution involved in processing that material as a part of the municipal waste stream.

Recycling, as used in the rest of this chapter, refers to returning used materials in order to manufacture new commodities. Most often, the materials we think of recycling are glass, paper, plastics, and metals. There are, however, many other materials or objects that either are, or can be, recycled: batteries, industrial solvents and other chemicals, appliances, computers, automobile tires, motor oil.

The recycling of metal, paper, and plastic has been with us for so long that it is possible to become a bit complacent about it. Curbside recycling is established in many areas, but there are large segments of our population that do not have this service. Even in the areas that do have curbside pickup, a decision on whether to continue the practice still comes up periodically in many town government meetings. The markets for recycled materials continue to be extremely volatile, causing some recycling services to refuse acceptance of certain materials for variable periods of time. Plastic, the food container material experiencing the fastest growth, has become a continuous headache for recycling center managers. Even glass, a material that can be recycled forever, is no longer accepted in some locations.

Questions have also been raised in the recent past about whether recycling really does any good. There is a significant segment of our population that would like to see most recycling disappear altogether (the section at the end of this chapter, "Responses to Common Criticisms of Recycling," addresses some of these questions). Recycling is not yet a sustainable success story. It is no longer in its infancy, but has not yet made it through its turbulent adolescence.

The astute reader will notice that we do not address the reuse of existing commodities in this chapter. This is a broad topic by itself, and beyond the scope of this book. Indeed, reuse is the method of choice for some types of items. Personal computers and packaging "peanuts" (Styrofoam packing material), for example, appear at present to be better suited for reuse than recycling. We also do not address the broad topic of recycling building materials.

Americans generate about 4 lb (1.8 kg) of solid (municipal) waste each day. In theory, we should be able to recycle (via composting, remanufacturing, or some other method) or reuse all of this waste. There are organizations whose goal is the elimination of all wastes—an admirable but distant goal. We certainly can, however, make an impact on the amount of waste we produce by maintaining a firm commitment to recycling.

RECYCLABLE MATERIALS

Many products can be recycled. The listing that follows is extensive but by no means complete. These are merely the materials that we have traditionally recycled, along with some that we really should recycle.

Paper

Paper and paperboard make up the largest component of solid waste by weight. In the United States, more than 40% of municipal solid waste is paper (more than 70 million tons each year). Paper includes office paper, junk mail, paper bags, books and magazines, cardboard, and other forms of packaging. Most types of paper can be recycled. Americans use over 700 lb (320 kg) of paper each year per person.

Every ton of paper recycled saves (as compared with manufacturing from virgin materials):

- $\sim$ 7000 gal (2700 l) of water
- $\sim$ 450 gal (1700 l) of petroleum
- $\sim$ 3 yd^3 (2.3 m^3) of landfill space
- $\sim$ 4100 kWh of energy

Newspaper

The fact that there is a great deal of "newsprint" in circulation each day, and that it has uniform characteristics, makes it easily recyclable. Newspaper inserts can generally be recycled with the paper itself, provided that they are not plastic or sealed in plastic. Brown paper grocery bags are often used to hold old newspapers and usually may be recycled with the newsprint (or with corrugated paper).

Corrugated Paper

Corrugated cardboard, along with newsprint, is the most commonly recycled paper product. Annual recovery of corrugated boxes is approaching 70%. Manufactured boxes almost always contain some material that has been recovered, and frequently it is labeled with its postconsumer content. Like newspapers, corrugated paper is universally accepted for recycling. Corrugated can be distinguished from "cardboardlike" materials by the ruffled layer between its two smooth sheets. Remanufacture of cardboard does not produce the huge energy savings of other materials, but it does reduce energy use by about one-quarter and reduces emissions of some air pollutants as well.

Office Paper

Office paper is a general paper category that can include white paper (copier, computer, letterhead, nonthermal fax, and writing paper, and nonglossy brochures and advertising), light pastel-colored paper, white or light/pastel-colored envelopes (plastic windows are OK), and manila or light/pastel-colored file folders. Recycled office paper should not include paper clips, tapes, self-adhesive envelopes, bright colors, cardboard tablet backing, paper ream wrappers, newspaper, magazines, telephone books, food wrappings, paper towels, trash, or other recyclable materials. Well-sorted recycled office paper is a high-value and salable material.

Phone Books

Some phone books are assembled with the use of water-soluble glue that makes them easy to recycle; others are not. Information about materials and glue can often be found in a phone book. Not all recycling centers will take phone books. Some phone books contain information about where they can be recycled.

Mixed Papers

Mixed papers sometimes include desirable items such as office (junk) mail and newsprint circulars. They often consist of boxboard or chipboard (such as cereal, tissue, and shoe boxes), beverage boxes (such as 12-pack and case can containers), and magazines. Mixed paper can be used to manufacture low-value chipboard products. If you wish to give your local recycler a break, chipboard and the like can also be composted and end its life in your garden.

Paper That Cannot Be Recycled

Contaminated paper and paper that has been coated or combined with other materials usually cannot be recycled. Examples include the following:

- Paper contaminated with food or oil
- Used tissues of any sort and any sanitary products
- Waxed milk and juice containers
- Waxed paper
- Carbon paper
- Thermal fax paper
- Stickers
- Plastic-laminated paper (fast-food wrappers and pet food bags)

Overall, the United States is recycling about 40% of its paper products (this includes recovery of unused material in the manufacturing process). The recovery rates for the "easy" types of paper, corrugated and newsprint, are at about 70% (if you include recovery of industrial "scraps"). Further expansion depends on several factors:

- Willingness of consumers (individual and institutional) to rigorously separate recyclable paper. Mixed paper has a lower intrinsic value than grade-separated paper. Office paper and printer paper, for example, have good value but tend to be mixed with other grades. A purer recyclable paper stream would allow more paper to be used for higher-grade purposes.
- Advances in technology for processing paper. Inks and glues can make recycling more expensive and make it difficult to generate a high-quality product. These and other contaminants must be removed in order to reuse the paper. This can be expensive and may make some paper impractical to use for recycling. Improved technologies would allow more paper to be used and higher-quality end products to be generated.
- Consumer acceptance of simpler packaging. Much of the packaging used for hard-to-recycle items could be replaced with recycling-friendly packaging. The impetus for this must, however, come from the consumer.

Unlike metal and glass, paper cannot be recycled indefinitely. Paper is made of wood fibers, and each round of recycling weakens and shortens the fibers. Eventually, the fibers have to be disposed of via landfills, incineration, or composting/mulching.

Plastics

Plastics come in a variety of types, each with its own chemical composition. Mixing plastics types can damage the equipment used to reprocess recycled plastics. The code stamped on (most) plastic containers corresponds to the type of plastic (Table 23-1).

Table 23-1 Plastic Codes and Their Meanings

Code	Composition	Used For
1	Polyethylene terephthalate (PETE/PET)	Soda and water containers, some waterproof packaging
2	High-density polyethylene (HDPE)	Milk, detergent, and oil bottles; toys and plastic bags
3	Vinyl/polyvinyl chloride (PVC)	Food wrap, vegetable oil bottles, blister packages
4	Low-density polyethylene (LDPE)	Many plastic bags; shrink wrap, garment bags
5	Polypropylene (PP)	Refrigerated containers, some bags, most bottle tops, some carpets, some food wrap
6	Polystyrene (PS)	Throw-away utensils, meat packing, protective packing
7	Other	Usually layered or mixed plastic; cannot be recycled

In many locations, only containers made from codes 1 and 2 plastics (PET and HDPE) are recycled. Plastic bags are generally code 2 or 4. Plastic bag recycling is often available in retail stores. Bags with these codes can often be mixed, but not always.

Like paper fiber, plastics cannot be recycled indefinitely. With each cycle, the plastic molecules (polymers) become weaker. Estimates place plastic life at a maximum of about five cycles.

At the present time, about two-thirds of the U.S. population can recycle PET (#1) and HDPE (#2) containers. The percentage of containers recycled in the United States has leveled off or may be dropping, although the total weight of recycled bottles has continued to increase. This is because the number of containers (especially bottles) being produced has grown faster than the recycling rate. Much of this expansion has been fueled by the production of small bottles that often are not recycled by consumers. Expanding access to PET and HDPE recycling and consumer willingness to recycle are key factors in increasing the rate of recycling of these materials. There is also concern that the falling rate of PET and HDPE recycling may be due to a lack of interest among food container manufacturers in using these materials to make new food containers. Government certification for this purpose is rigorous and, unlike aluminum cans, these materials do deteriorate with repeated use. These issues may explain the apparent lack of interest among food and beverage producers in promoting recycling of food containers. Whatever the reason, the near absence of a "same commodity" use for recycled PET and HDPE appears to be hurting the recycling of these materials.

The other types of plastics, although heavily used, are not often recycled. Packaging often contains mixed plastic types, making separation very difficult. There are exceptions, however. Expanded polystyrene blocks (usually molded to fit around and protect electronic equipment) have been regarded as difficult to recycle. The Alliance of Foam Packaging Recyclers (*http://www.epspackaging.org/info.html*) now provides drop-off locations in all states for this material. We tried the site by calling a nearby contact number and received a courteous reply and directions to the drop-off point.

Glass

Glass is made of sand, sodium carbonate (soda), and lime (limestone). When glass is produced from virgin materials, it must be heated to a very high temperature (more than 2000°F, 1200°C) in order to melt the materials together. Recycled glass, on the other hand, melts at a much lower temperature and requires about a third less energy to manufacture the equivalent amount of glass.

The glass we recycle is from bottles and jars. These cannot be mixed with other types of glass (windows, light bulbs, mirrors, drinking glasses, Pyrex or auto glass). The other grades of glass have different chemical compositions and melting temperatures than bottle and jar glass. Using them can cause defects in new containers.

Clear glass is the most valuable. Mixed colored glass is nearly worthless, and broken glass is hard to sort (hand sorting is still the norm). Glass containers, if unbroken and properly sorted, can be recycled indefinitely.

Metals

Metals include ferrous metals such as steel and iron and nonferrous metals such as aluminum and copper. These are all recyclable and are nearly universally accepted.

Recycling aluminum saves about 95% of the energy used to make aluminum from bauxite (the virgin ore). It has traditionally been one of the higher-value recycled commodities, often creating revenue that offsets the costs of recycling of other materials. The turnaround time for aluminum cans is remarkably short. The average life span of an aluminum can is six weeks. That is the time it takes for a beverage can to be manufactured, filled, sold, recycled, and remanufactured.

Batteries

Batteries use a variety of chemicals. Lead-acid, nickel-cadmium, and mercury-containing batteries have to be recycled in such a way to avoid contaminating landfills with heavy metals and acid (automobile batteries contain about 18 lb (8 kg) of lead and about 1 lb (0.45 kg) of sulfuric acid).

Lead-acid batteries are normally accepted for recycling at retail outlets (in most states, such establishments are obligated to take up to five batteries from anyone, even noncustomers). For other kinds of batteries, you can find drop-off locations by calling 1–800-8BATTERY (that's not a typo: There is one extra digit).

Automobile Tires

Auto tires are still more a waste disposal problem than a recycling opportunity. Although many different approaches have been attempted, there is still no proven or universally accepted method to successfully recycle tires. Later in the chapter, we discuss some of the methods that are under development and appear to show promise.

Motor Oil

It is important to recycle motor oil for the same reason that it is important to recycle many types of batteries: Any other method of disposal will release harmful chemicals into the environment. A gallon (3.85 l) of oil can pollute a million gallons of water (1 ppm of oil in water renders the water seriously polluted). By recycling motor oil, you are actually adding to our store of petroleum. The dirty oil from your engine can be cleaned and reused in a variety of ways that will preserve our finite oil resources. For example, 2 gal (7.7 l) of oil, less than two oil changes in your car, can supply all the electricity needs for a typical house for an entire day. Recycling oil is a win-win proposition.

About 75% of motor oil is currently being recycled in some way. As compared with other materials, this is a fairly high rate. Given its toxicity, the fact that 325 million gal (1.2 million m³) of motor oil (25% of the total) are still getting into landfills or are illegally dumped each year is disturbing.

USE OF RECYCLED MATERIALS

Recycled materials can follow two general paths: remanufacture of a commodity similar to that from which the recycled material came or manufacture of a different material (usually a lower-value material), based on the limits of the material or the process used in recycling. In the following sections, we will look at the various materials that we now recycle to see where they end up.

Paper

Recycled paper can be used for many purposes. Much recycled paper is remanufactured as its original grade. Office paper, newsprint, corrugated paper (cardboard), and kraft paper (paper bags) can all be made using recycled stock of the same grade. Mixed paper (any of the aforementioned papers, mixed with other grades of paper) can be used to make newsprint, food packaging (for example, cereal and cracker boxes), and paper towels. With the exception of newsprint, the mixed paper products are usually "last use" products and are subsequently landfilled or composted.

Of the recycled paper, about 94% is used to make new paper products (in the United States or abroad). The remaining 6% is used to make a variety of products, such as insulation, mulch, kitty litter, and molded packaging.

Plastic

There are different views about the ways in which plastics are being used and reused, and the overall success of plastics recycling. A number of sources, including the plastics manufacturing associations, tout the large and growing list of products that include recycled plastics (more than 1300 products, at last count). A listing of many of these can be found at the United States and Canadian Recycled Plastics Product Directory (*http://sourcebook.plasticsresource.com/*).

A second view is that the plastic bottling and container industry could be doing more to incorporate recycled material into food containers. According to this view, maintained by a number of environmental groups, a relatively small percentage of recycled PET and HDPE actually makes it back into food containers (less than 2%, by some accounts). Some large manufacturers have reneged on promises to use recycled plastics. Most of what is being used is for lower-value end-use applications such as carpeting and jacket linings. Among recycling center managers, plastics are judged to be among the lowest-valued recycled materials.

Expanded polystyrene blocks have been among the plastic waste materials deemed difficult to recycle. Although not convenient for everyone, there are more than 200 drop-off points for this material in the United States (see the information on locating these sites given earlier in this chapter). The blocks are used to make new foam packaging, as well as cameras and videocassette casings. This material is highly resilient for a plastic and can be recycled many times.

Packaging peanuts, used to protect shipped items, is hard to recycle. Reuse is often a better option for the peanuts. Some look like plastic but are, in fact, made from vegetable starch. Test the peanuts by placing one in water (it will dissolve within minutes if it is starch). Starch peanuts can be composted.

Glass

Glass "cullet" (pieces of ground glass) is most often used to make new glass containers. It can also be used in fiberglass, and a small amount ends up in roadways as "glassphalt" (a glass-asphalt mix).

Metals

Metals, in general, suffer no loss of usefulness or strength following recycling. Metals can be recycled almost indefinitely and are used to manufacture new metal products.

Ferrous Metals (Iron and Steel)

Recycled metal is the most economical raw material available to steelmakers and, as such, has become indispensable. It accounts for about 45% of all steel produced world-wide. Iron and steel foundries depend on a steady intake of highly competitive secondary material to provide the major proportion of their furnace feed. Using recycled metal in place of iron ore to make steel has many advantages. Recycled material is nearly 100% metal and is readily available or can be purchased in bulk. In contrast, iron ore has to be mined, freed from impurities, and smelted in a blast furnace before it can be converted into steel. This entire process is obviated by using recycled steel and iron, with dramatic reductions in the energy and water used and the air pollution created. Using weight as a criterion, more iron and steel are recycled than any other material. Iron and steel, following processing, are used to manufacture new items of the same materials. This process can continue almost indefinitely.

Nonferrous Metals (Aluminum and Copper)

Aluminum has one of the highest values of all recycled materials. Recycled aluminum is used to manufacture new aluminum products. About half the aluminum in beverage containers is recycled. Copper has an even higher residual value than aluminum and is used to manufacture new copper products.

Batteries

Batteries are broken open to extract heavy metals and treat toxic chemicals. The heavy metals (lead, cadmium, mercury) are sent to manufacturers for reuse in many areas (all of these heavy metals have multiple commercial uses).

Automobile Tires

Probably the most promising method to "reuse" tires is to burn them. Tire-derived fuel (TDF) appears to have potential as an energy source. Likely users of this fuel are electric power plants, cement kilns, and paper mills. There are operations in California and the southeastern United States that process millions of tires into fuel. Each tire contains 2 to 3 gal (8 to 11 l) of petroleum, giving it a high energy value. Proponents claim that TDF can be burned more cleanly than coal if it is processed correctly. Each year the United States produces about 3.6 million tons of used tires, which could be used to produce about 2.5 million tons of fuel. Current operations use only about 5% of this total, so the market would have to expand to about 20 times its current size to use the entire resource.

Other uses of scrap tires, either under development or in operation, include mixing "crumb rubber" (ground tires after metal is removed) with plastic to make a material having greater resiliency than plastic, rubberized asphalt (for use in paving), and stream bank armor for erosion control.

Motor Oil

The largest part (about 75%) of recovered motor oil is reprocessed (cleaned and filtered) to be used as fuel. In order of end use (high to low), the fuel is sold to asphalt plants, factories, electric utilities, steel mills, cement/lime kilns; used as marine fuel; sold to paper mills; and used as fuel for building heat.

About 15% of used oil goes through a re-refining process. This oil can replace oil from virgin sources in cars and trucks.

About 10% of recovered motor oil is used unprocessed to heat service stations and garages; the space heaters used are especially designed for this purpose. This practice is not recommended for homes.

PROCESSING RECYCLED MATERIALS

Sorting and separating usually occur many times during the recycling process. Items are sorted at a recycling center to keep like materials together. Sorting may then occur at the manufacturing facility to remove contaminants and further refine or complete the likes-with-likes process. Finally, it may occur just prior to the remanufacturing step in order to get the right combination of materials for the "recipe" being used.

Paper

Following the final sorting process, recycled paper is mixed with water to form a slurry, washed and screened to remove contaminants, and spread over screens for draining and to form a mat. The matted material is dried and can then be rolled up for transport and ultimately cut for use in the remanufacturing process.

Plastics

Most plastics are recycled with the use of a mechanical process. With this method, recycled plastics are converted to plastic pellets.

The process begins at the recycling center. In most instances, plastic containers start out in combination with metal and glass items. At a *materials recovery facility,* the mixed materials are separated manually or automatically. The types of plastics are then separated by type (usually PET and HDPE), and the separated plastics are then baled and shipped to a *reclaimer.* Reclaimers usually deal with specific plastic types (HDPE or PET). The bales are broken and the plastic moves across a shaker screen, where small loose contaminants are separated from the desirable plastic. The plastic is then automatically cut, ground, and washed. The cutting and grinding process removes or loosens labels and attached debris. The ground materials are washed, often with a detergent, to remove dirt and much of the labeling. Ground plastics, labels, and dirt are then rinsed in a flotation tank. HDPE is less dense than water and is separated by skimming it from the surface. PET is denser than water, and it collects on the bottom of the tank. The rinse water is usually filtered and reused. The ground-up plastic is dried and then goes through a blower designed to separate the plastic particles from labels and debris. The plaster flakes are melted in an *extruder,* the liquid plastic passes through a screen that separates the remaining contaminants, and is then forced through the *die* that extrudes the plastic as spaghetti-like strands. The strands are chopped into pellets, ready for use in manufacturing.

Glass

Although glass must arrive at the recycling center unbroken (broken glass is hard to sort), it is deliberately broken once sorting is complete in order to reduce volume and make it easier to ship. The broken glass (called *cullet*) is shipped to intermediate preprocessors for cleaning or directly to the manufacturer.

Metals

Metals must be separated from nonmetals, and ferrous metals must be separated from nonferrous metals. In most instances, this is an automated and highly efficient process.

Ferrous Metals (Iron and Steel)

Recycled items with ferrous metals include everything from steel cans and appliances to dismantled bridges, old cars, and even entire ships. All of the large items must be cut or sheared to get them down to a manageable size. Lighter materials, such as cans, are compacted into blocks. Shredders cut large items into fist-sized chunks that can be fed directly into furnaces (big shredders can do an entire car in about a minute). Ferrous materials that are mixed with other materials are removed in rotating magnetic drums.

Nonferrous Metals (Copper and Aluminum)

Copper and aluminum are removed from mixed metals by forced air or "sink-float" processes that separate them from other materials based on density differences. There is also a process, the "eddy-current method," that allows nonferrous metals to be separated on the basis of their differing electrical conductivities when placed in a magnetic field.

Aluminum Cans

Following collection, aluminum cans are shipped to smelting plants. The cans are tested for quality and moisture content, shredded, and then passed through a "delacquering" oven to remove the paint, residual moisture, and volatile impurities. The hot shredded aluminum is passed over a screen to remove dirt and other contaminants and then melted at 1400°F (760°C). The melting process allows the aluminum parts to blend together to a uniform grade and removes the last of the impurities, which can be skimmed from the liquid material. The melted aluminum is poured into rectangular molds and allowed to cool. These aluminum ingots then pass through a series of steel rollers to make sheet aluminum with the desired thickness and hardness. The sheet aluminum is rolled up and shipped to product manufacturers. Aluminum ingots and rolls can be very large; for instance, the rolled material may be 2 mi (3 km) long and made from more than 1 million cans.

Batteries

Most batteries contain either strong acids or bases. Recycling such batteries entails neutralizing or collecting these chemicals. The process for recovering heavy metals varies with the battery type. Once recovered, the heavy metals are sold for a variety of purposes.

Nickel-Cadmium

In recycling lead-cadmium batteries, the batteries are shredded or broken open with the use of a hammer mill. The cadmium is recovered by pyrometallurgical processes (the metals are melted and then separated based on density or other differences).

Lead-Acid

Lead-acid batteries are broken with a hammer mill. The lead is chemically extracted with the use of controlled-temperature processes. These processes can include low-temperature melting of the lead and chemical treatment with a variety of salt solutions or acid to extract and purify the lead.

Mercuric-Oxide and Silver-Oxide

Silver oxide also contains mercury. These batteries are shredded, and the mercury is extracted with controlled-temperature processes.

Other Types of Batteries

The remaining battery types are shredded. Metallic components are extracted and sold for use in commercial operations.

Motor Oil

Used motor oil can be filtered and cleaned to remove gross contaminants if it is to be burned as fuel.

The re-refining process to reuse it as lubricating oil in your car is more elaborate. A vacuum distillation process removes dirt, water, fuel, and old oil additives. The oil then undergoes hydrotreatment (a process that maximizes the contact between the oil and the contaminant-removal medium) to clean it further. Finally, the re-refined recycled oil is combined with fresh additives and the oil can be reused in a car or truck.

Oil that is burned in specially designed space heaters in service areas undergoes no preliminary treatment.

BUYING RECYCLED PRODUCTS

Recycling means making the effort to send recyclable items to appropriate processors. Learning about what can and cannot be recycled is an important part of this process. There is, however, another facet to recycling: the use and purchase of recycled products. We often do this without thinking about it. A number of products already contain recycled material. Table 23-2 contains a partial listing of these.

There are opportunities to push this process along, however, and to make recycling work requires that we actively engage in rewarding manufacturers that provide quality products using recycled materials.

There are extensive databases on the Internet indicating commercially available products that contain recycled materials:

- California's Integrated Waste Management Board's Recycled Products Database (*http://www.ciwmb.ca.gov/RCP/*)
- American Plastics Council's Recycled Products Database (*http://www2.plasticsresources.com*)

Table 23-2　Products That Frequently Contain Recycled Materials

Aluminum cans	Newspapers
Cereal boxes	Paper towels
Egg cartons	Carpeting
Motor oil	Car bumpers
Nails	Anything made from steel
Trash bags	Glass containers
Comic books	Laundry detergent bottles

When buying products made from recycled materials, you will probably encounter terminology like the following:

- *Post-consumer content.* If an item contains recycled material that was actually purchased, used, and returned for recycling, it has "post-consumer content."

- *Recycled or recovered content.* Products so labeled are made from materials that would otherwise have been discarded. These can include items with post-consumer content or leftovers from manufacturing. The term also can indicate that the product was rebuilt or remanufactured. Printer cartridges frequently fall into this category.

- *Recyclable.* A product that is labeled "recyclable" or "100% recyclable" means that it can be recycled. It does not necessarily contain any recycled material at all.

RESPONSES TO COMMON CRITICISMS OF RECYCLING

Critics of recycling have made a number of arguments pertaining to the overall usefulness of recycling. The National Recycling Coalition (*http://www.nrc-recycle.org/*) has presented the following responses to some of these criticisms. See also *Advantage Recycle: Assessing the Full Costs and Benefits of Curbside Recycling*, which is available at the Web site of this book (http://www.wiley.com/go/melby) and provides an in-depth look at these arguments.

1. Recycling costs too much.
   - Well-run recycling programs cost less than landfills and incinerators.
   - The more people recycle, the cheaper recycling gets.
   - Recycling helps families save money, especially in communities with "pay-as-you-throw" programs; for example, trash pickup that charges based on quantity of trash.
   - Recycling generates revenue to help pay for itself, but incineration and landfilling do not.

2. Recycling should pay for itself.
   - Landfills and incinerators don't pay for themselves; in fact, they cost more than recycling programs.
   - Recycling creates more than 1 million U.S. jobs in recycled product manufacturing alone.[1]
   - Hundreds of companies, including Hewlett Packard, Bank of America, and the U.S. Postal Service, have saved millions of dollars through their recycling programs.
   - Through recycling, the United States is saving enough energy to provide electricity for 9 million homes per year.[2]

3. Recycling causes pollution.
   - Recycling results in a net reduction in ten major categories of air pollutants and eight major categories of water pollutants.[3]

- Manufacturing with recycled materials, with very few exceptions, saves energy and water and produces less air and water pollution than manufacturing with virgin materials.
- Recycling trucks often generate less pollution than garbage trucks because they do not idle as long at the curb. If you add recycling trucks, you should be able to subtract garbage trucks.[4]
- By 2005, recycling will reduce greenhouse gas emissions by 48 million tons, the equivalent of the amount emitted by 36 million cars.[1]

4. Recycling doesn't save trees or other natural resources.
   - 94% of the natural resources America uses are nonrenewable (up from 59% in 1900 and 88% in 1945). Recycling saves these nonrenewable resources.[1]
   - With recycling, 20% more wood will have to be harvested by 2010 to keep up with demand. Without recycling, 80% more wood would have to be harvested.[4]
   - 95% of our nation's virgin forests have been cut down, and less than 20% of paper manufactured in the United States comes from tree farms.[4]
   - It takes 95% less energy to recycle aluminum than it does to make it from raw materials.[5] Making recycled steel saves 60%, recycled newspaper 40%, recycled plastics 70%, and recycled glass 40%. Landfilling never saves energy.[4]
   - Recycling saves 3.6 times the amount of energy generated by incineration and 11 times the amount generated by methane recovery at a landfill.[2]
   - Using scrap steel instead of virgin ore to make new steel takes 40% less water and creates 97% less mining waste.[3]
   - Tree farms and reclaimed mines are not ecologically equivalent to natural forests and ecosystems. Recycling prevents habitat destruction, loss of biodiversity, and soil erosion associated with logging and mining.

5. There is no landfill crisis.
   - Recycling's true value comes from preventing pollution and saving natural resources and energy, not landfill space.
   - Recycling is largely responsible for averting the landfill crisis.
   - Most states have less than 20 years of landfill capacity—who wants to live next to a new landfill?[6]
   - The number of landfills is decreasing, but the cost to send waste to them is on the rise.[6]

6. Landfills and incinerators are safe.
   - Landfills and incinerators can be major sources of pollution. For example, leachate from solid waste landfills is similar in composition to that of hazardous waste landfills.[2]
   - About one-quarter of the sites on the Superfund list (the nation's most hazardous sites) are solid waste landfills.[3]
   - Landfills are responsible for 36% of all methane emissions in the United States, one of the most potent causes of global warming.[2]
   - About two-thirds of operating landfills do not have liners to protect groundwater and drinking water sources.[4]
   - Landfill owners are required to check for groundwater contamination for only 30 years. What happens afterward?

7. If recycling makes sense, the free market will make it happen.
   - Government supports lots of services that the free market wouldn't provide, such as the delivery of running water, electricity, and mail to our homes.
   - Unlike most public services, recycling does function within the market economy, and quite successfully.
   - If the market were truly free, long-standing subsidies that favor virgin materials and landfills would not exist, and recycling could compete on a level playing field.

8. There are no markets for recyclables.
   - Prices may fluctuate as they do for any commodity, but domestic and international markets exist for all materials collected in curbside recycling programs.
   - Demand for recycled materials has never been greater. American manufacturers rely on recyclables to produce many of the products on your store's shelves.
   - By the year 2005, the value of materials collected for recycling will surpass $5 billion per year.[1]
   - All new steel products contain recycled steel.[7]
   - More than 1400 products and 310 manufacturers use post-consumer plastics.[8]
   - In 1999, recycled paper provided more than 37% of the raw material fiber needed by U.S. paper mills.[9]

9. We are already recycling as much as we can.
   - The national recycling rate is 28%. The U.S. EPA has set a goal of 35%, and many communities are recycling 50% or more.[3]
   - Many easily recycled materials are still thrown away. For example, 73% of glass containers, 77% of magazines, 66% of plastic soda and milk bottles, and 45% of newspapers are not recycled.[3]
   - We are nowhere near our potential, especially if manufacturers make products easier to recycle.

10. Recycling is a burden on families.
   - Recycling is so popular because the American public wants to do it.
   - More people recycle than vote.[10]
   - More than 20,000 curbside programs and drop-off centers for recycling are active today because Americans use and support them.[3]

Statistical sources: (1) Office of the Federal Environmental Executive, (2) Environmental Defense, (3) U.S. Environmental Protection Agency, (4) Natural Resources Defense Council, (5) Aluminum Association, (6) *Biocycle* magazine, (7) *Steel Recycling Institute,* (8) *American Plastics Council,* (9) *American Forest and Paper Association,* (10) *Resource Recycling* magazine.

PART VI

Landscape Management in the Sustainable Landscape

Chapter 24

Managing Human Landscapes

Through understanding the biophysical processes that occur in the natural landscape and basing the management of human landscapes on this model, the costs of landscape management can be reduced by 38 to 80%. A sustainable landscape management plan will assess the possibility of rescheduling management tasks and reducing the need for labor, energy, and materials.

A discouraging aspect of gardens and landscapes is the overwhelming amount of time required to make them perform in just an average manner. Let us discuss how to manage a garden or landscape to be in harmony with nature, utilizing the least amount of resources, and keeping the time required for maintenance and improvements within practical limits. A landscape that is balanced works with the forces of nature, including seasonal temperatures, moisture levels, exposure to the sun and wind, existing plant and animal inhabitants, and characteristics of the soil. Understanding the ecology of an area and designing and managing to blend with the processing characteristics of the natural ecological system will ensure the harmonious accommodation of the human landscape to natural systems. A balanced landscape results in the healthiest landscape possible, without the need for excessive fertilizer, chemicals, or water, and without the need for excessive infusions of energy for maintenance.

THE NATURAL LANDSCAPE

An area that is undisturbed by human influence and activities is usually in a healthy, natural condition. When a disturbed landscape altered by human disruption is let alone, it will usually evolve into a vigorous natural system that is self-sustaining. By *self-sustaining* we mean that it will be able to provide for all of its own nutritional needs and remain in a healthy condition. The landscape will support a population of plants and animals adapted to the existing natural conditions. Being made up of living creatures and non-living materials that are interacting with one another, the self-sustaining natural area is dependent on renewable resources such as sun, rain, and plant and animal matter for sustenance and energy. The landscape itself provides sustenance, habitat, protection of habitats, recycling of plant and animal wastes, and cleansing of pollutants from air and water. Planners working with human landscapes must recognize the working processes within the natural landscape and seek to become partners in these processes. Five basic ecosystem processes that contribute to the regeneration of natural systems are the following:

- Conversion
- Distribution
- Filtration
- Assimilation
- Storage

A great example of conversion is what happens through photosynthesis with the light from the sun. The sun's rays are collected by plants and *converted* into food and energy for the plants, and for whatever eats those plants. Once the sun's energy is converted to plants and the plants are eaten, the plants are then converted into the biomass of animals. Milk and meat are produced, through conversion, to feed people.

Nature provides many ways for energy and materials to get to all the users in the ecosystem. Wind, water, and traveling animals *distribute* materials naturally to the users.

Nature's air and water purification system is composed of plants, microbes, humus, soil, and rock. As air moves over and through the landscape, organic and inorganic matter is removed through *filtration* by plant leaves and through consumption by bacteria located on plant leaves and stems and within decaying plant matter. Water is filtered to remove organic and inorganic matter by plant detritus or organic matter on the forest floor, in our planting beds, and in freshwater wetlands and saltwater marshes.

To be assimilated means to be absorbed and incorporated. When animals consume plant biomass, the plants are *assimilated* into the living tissue of animals. As plants shed their leaves and die, plant matter is consumed by microorganisms or decomposers that assimilate the matter and transform it into soil minerals for eventual use by living plants. Decomposers include insects, worms, bacteria, and fungi. When animals create waste or die, they undergo the same decomposition by microbes as did the plants, and their waste or dead bodies are transformed into soil minerals.

In the natural system materials are usually *stored* for a period of time before they are reused. The humus on the forest floor is stored plant food, awaiting further decomposition before being made available as mineralized plant food. Aquifers store water, and even fossil fuels are created and stored underground, sometimes for millions of years.

These five basic processes of regeneration that occur within ecosystems are the keys to creating sustainable environments. The term *ecological system* is defined by ecologist Eugene Odum in his book *Fundamentals of Ecology* as "any area of nature that includes living organisms and nonliving substances interacting to produce an exchange of materials between the living and nonliving parts." Examples of ecosystems are a pond, a lake, a forest, an aquarium, a desert, the tundra, and a prairie grassland. Ecological systems can also be of any size, from the whole earth, to a pond or forest, or the shaded area under a porch.

When a site is being evaluated for restoration to its native, natural state, examine the soils for drainage, pH, and water-holding capacity. Note the aspect or slope of the

Figure 24-1 Fire managed landscape on a grassland savannah.

site as related to the sun. Scout the local area for existing native plants and habitats, and note what seems to do well and what combinations of plants are vigorous and healthy looking. When recreating the natural site ecosystem, don't forget the detrital layer on the ground plane that is an integral part of all healthy, naturally occurring areas. Long-term management of the site is important. Look at natural sites and inquire as to how they are being managed. Many natural landscapes are managed by periodic fires ignited by lighting strikes, and those fires result in an assortment of fire-resistant species that can survive burnings. Fire management is what gives many natural landscapes their intrinsic character. Figure 24-1 shows a fire managed pine savannah at the Sandhill Crane National Wildlife Refuge. Fires are set every three to four years to keep dense undergrowth from becoming established and to attract a broad variety of native grasses.

A BALANCED LANDSCAPE

A balanced landscape is one that requires the absolute least amount of attention in order to perform well and to look attractive. It is created when attention is given to the following factors:

- Soil conditions
- Geographic conditions such as sun, shade, slopes, land forms, and prevailing winds
- Selection of plants that matches soils and geographic conditions
- Selection of plants that considers their mature sizes and their relationship to the sizes of the spaces in which they will be located

- Planning and regular management tasks for reduced landscape maintenance
- Relating design form and landscape management tasks that reflect form and processes in local, natural ecosystems

An undisturbed natural landscape is the model for the balanced landscape. In nature, the forces of sunlight, wind, rain, fire, and biological life maintain the natural landscape. In human developments, it is usual for the forces of the local landscape management crews to maintain the landscapes. Energy, materials, and manpower can be reduced when landscape designs and management plans are based on the forces of nature. Ignorance will increase costs and contribute to upsetting the balance of energy and materials and, ultimately, the health and longevity of a landscape.

Many people first experience trying to create a balanced environment with an aquarium, striving to get that perfect balance of aquarium components. Once the right amounts of catfish, snails, aquatic plants, and other fish are determined, the water quality remains sparkling, the bottom clean, and algae are continuously removed from the glass sides of the tank. A balanced fish tank requires very little upkeep to be healthy and look its best. In contrast, an unbalanced aquarium keeps one busy cleaning the tank and medicating the fish. The same principle of balance versus unbalance applies to management of a landscape.

LANDSCAPE MANAGEMENT PLAN

A landscape management plan is a year-long determination of tasks that have to be accomplished in order for an area to look its best and to be healthy and productive without the need for excessive infusions of energy and materials. Its purpose is to provide an organized direction for management of the landscape over an entire year. A sample landscape management plan is shown in Appendix B. The usefulness of a landscape management plan is in knowing what and when something should happen and what equipment, supplies, and labor will be needed to effectively accomplish the job. By matching maintenance chores with seasons and dates, more efficient management of labor and equipment will be possible and the use of machines and materials, such as compost, mulch, and fertilizers, will be affected. Organized landscape management results in a healthy and attractive landscape with lower overall maintenance costs.

When developing a landscape management plan, a time and task study of the landscape will help in determining the tasks that require the greatest time, energy, and material expenditure during certain seasons of the year. See Table 24-1 for a time and task expenditure analysis for an unbalanced, $1/2$ ac (0.2 ha) residential landscape located in the hot-humid climate zone. The hours required to accomplish the tasks reflect the hours spent managing this landscape. Table 24-2 provides monthly and seasonal breakdowns. Incorporating techniques that will bring design and management of the residential landscape closer to the form and processes of a natural system will result in reduced expenditures as shown for the newly balanced landscape in Table 24-3. In comparing the requirements of a balanced landscape with those of an unbalanced landscape, there is a 38% savings in hours needed for landscape maintenance in the balanced landscape. Table 24-4 is the accompanying task and time chart by months and seasons. This table illustrates how, in a balanced landscape, some of the time spent managing a garden or

Table 24-1   Task and Time Expenditure
(0.5 ac (0.2 ha) unbalanced landscape)

Task	Frequency	Time in Hours	Total Hours per Year
Mow, summer	20 times a year	2.0	40.0
Edge	10 times a year	1.5	15.0
Weed	April–May	20.0	
	June–July	9.0	
	September	3.0	32.0
Prune	February	8.0	
	June	3.0	11.0
Plant			
trees, shrubs	December	2.0	2.0
annuals, perennials	March–May	10.0	10.0
Fertilize			
lawn	Spring, fall	3.0	6.0
flowers, shrubs, trees	March–July	5.0	5.0
Watering, by hand and movable sprinkler	June–September	12.0	12.0
Rake leaves	October–November	5.0	10.0
Cleanup	December–January	1.0	2.0
	Total		145.0

Source: Pete Melby, Ed Martin, *Home Landscapes, Planting Design and Management* (Timber Press, 1994).

Table 24-2   Annual Time Expenditure
(0.5 ac (0.2 ha) unbalanced landscape)

Task	Jan.	Feb.	Mar.	Apr.	May	June	July	Aug.	Sept.	Oct.	Nov.	Dec.	Hours
Mow	—	—	—	6.0	8.0	8.0	8.0	6.0	4.0	—	—	—	40.0
Edge	—	—	—	1.5	4.5	4.5	1.5	1.5	1.5	—	—	—	15.0
Weed	—	—	—	12.0	8.0	6.0	3.0	—	3.0	—	—	—	32.0
Prune	—	8.0	—	—	—	3.0	—	—	—	—	—	—	11.0
Plant	—	—	6.0	2.0	2.0	—	—	—	—	—	—	2.0	12.0
Fertilize (lawn)	—	—	—	3.0	—	—	—	—	3.0	—	—	—	6.0
Fertilize (other)	—	—	1.0	1.0	1.0	1.0	1.0	—	—	—	—	—	5.0
Watering	—	—	—	—	1.5	4.5	4.5	1.5	—	—	—	—	12.0
Raking	—	—	—	—	—	—	—	—	—	5.0	5.0	—	10.0
Cleanup	1.0	—	—	—	—	—	—	—	—	—	—	1.0	2.0
Total hours:	1.0	8.0	7.0	25.5	25.0	27.0	18.0	9.0	11.5	5.0	5.0	3.0	145.0

	Spring	Summer	Fall	Winter
Percent effort by season:	40%	37%	15%	8%
Total hours by season:	57.5	54.0	21.5	12

Source: Pete Melby, Ed Martin, *Home Landscapes, Planting Design and Management* (Timber Press, 1994).

landscape in the summer can be distributed to the fall and winter months, thereby freezing summer time that can be used for recreation or other pursuits. This result of distributing tasks more evenly throughout the seasons can enhance the management of employees

Table 24-3 Task and Time Expenditure
(0.5 ac (0.2 ha) balanced landscape)

Task	Frequency	Time in Hours	Total Hours per Year
Mow			
summer	20 times	1.0	20.0
winter	5 times	0.5	2.5
Edge	6 times a year	1.0	6.0
Weed	April–May	6.0	
	June–July	2.0	
	September	2.0	10.0
Prune	February	4.0	
	June	2.0	6.0
Plant			
trees, shrubs	December	2.0	2.0
annuals, perennials	March–May	7.0	
	October	1.0	8.0
Fertilize			
lawn	March	2.0	2.0
flowers, shrubs, trees, with compost	February, June, September	2.0	6.0
Watering, automatic drip and sprinkler irrigation	June–September	0.25	1.0
Irrigation system maintenance	March, July, November	1.0	3.0
Rake leaves	October–November	4.0	
		3.0	7.0
Compost, turn weekly	April–September	1.0	
	October–November	2.0	10.0
Test soil			
nutrients	October	0.5	0.5
pH	January	0.5	0.5
Mulch	March	1.0	
	November	2.0	3.0
Winter overseed	October	1.0	1.0
Cleanup	January, December	1.0	2.0
		Total	90.5

Source: Pete Melby, Ed Martin, *Home Landscapes, Planting Design and Management* (Timber Press, 1994).

by spreading management efforts throughout the year instead of concentrating them in one or two seasons. As shown in Table 24-2, 57 1/2 hr will be spent maintaining the unbalanced landscape during the spring. In the balanced landscape, for which expenditures of labor, energy, and materials are reduced, only 29 hr, or 50% of the time spent in the unbalanced landscape, will be spent maintaining the balanced landscape in the spring. Maintaining a landscape can be a complex endeavor. Creating a landscape management plan as a guide for directing the use of labor, energy, and materials throughout the year will allow more logical maintenance of the garden or landscape, which will also result in more enjoyment. Table 24-5 is a summary of landscape management for a balanced landscape.

Table 24-4   Time Expenditure
(0.5 ac (0.2 ha) balanced landscape)

Task	Jan.	Feb.	Mar.	Apr.	May	June	July	Aug.	Sept.	Oct.	Nov.	Dec.	Hours
Mow													
summer	—	—	1.00	3.00	4.00	4.00	4.00	3.00	1.00	—	—	—	20.00
winter	0.50	0.50	—	—	—	—	—	—	—	—	0.50	1.00	2.50
Edge	—	—	—	1.00	1.00	2.00	1.00	1.00	—	—	—	—	6.00
Weed	—	—	—	3.00	3.00	1.00	1.00	—	2.00	—	—	—	10.00
Prune	—	4.00	—	—	—	2.00	—	—	—	—	—	—	6.00
Plant													
trees, shrubs	—	—	—	—	—	—	—	—	—	—	—	2.00	2.00
annuals, perennials	—	—	2.00	3.00	2.00	—	—	—	—	1.00	—	—	8.00
Fertilize													
lawn	—	—	2.00	—	—	—	—	—	—	—	—	—	2.00
flowers, shrubs, trees, with compost	—	2.00	—	—	—	2.00	—	—	2.00	—	—	—	6.00
Watering	—	—	—	—	—	0.25	0.25	0.25	0.25	—	—	—	1.00
Irrigation system maintenance	—	—	1.00	—	—	—	1.00	—	—	—	1.00	—	3.00
Rake leaves	—	—	—	—	—	—	—	—	—	4.00	3.00	—	7.00
Compost	—	—	—	1.00	1.00	1.00	1.00	1.00	1.00	2.00	2.00	—	10.0
Test soil													
nutrients	—	—	—	—	—	—	—	—	—	0.50	—	—	0.50
pH	0.50	—	—	—	—	—	—	—	—	—	—	—	0.50
Mulch	—	—	1.00	—	—	—	—	—	—	—	2.00	—	3.00
Winter overseed	—	—	—	—	—	—	—	—	—	1.0	—	—	1.00
Cleanup	1.00	—	—	—	—	—	—	—	—	—	—	1.00	2.00
Total hours:	2.00	6.50	7.00	11.00	11.00	12.25	8.25	5.25	6.25	8.50	8.50	4.00	90.50
		Spring			*Summer*			*Fall*			*Winter*		
Percent effort by season:		32%			28%			26%			14%		
Total hours by season:		29.00			25.75			23.25			12.50		

Source: Pete Melby, Ed Martin, *Home Landscapes, Planting Design and Management* (Timber Press, 1994).

Table 24-5 Landscape Management Plan for the Pete Melby Family, Starkville, Mississippi: Yearly Summary

Activity	Jan.	Feb.	Mar.	Apr.	May
Mow lawn as needed.	—	—	Mow once. 1 hour	Mow three times. 3 hours	Mow four times. 4 hours
Mow rye grass planted in front landscape.	Mow once. 1/2 hour	Mow once. 1/2 hour	—	—	—
Edge and trim grass from walks and along plant beds. Remove from around trees.	—	—	—	Trim grass from edges. 1 hour	Trim grass from edges. 1 hour
Weed garden, shrubs, and ground cover beds by hand or hoe.	—	—	—	Remove weeds. 3 hours	Remove weeds. 3 hours
Prune trees, shrubs, and ground covers.	—	Prune trees, shrubs, and ground covers. 4 hours	—	—	—
Plant trees and shrubs.	—	—	—	—	—
Plant annuals, perennials.	—	—	Divide perennials and replant. 2 hours	Add bedding plants. 3 hours	Add bedding plants. 2 hours
Fertilize lawn	—	—	Spread fertilizer if needed at beginning of month. 2 hours	—	—
Fertilize flowers, shrubs, and trees in plant beds with compost.	—	Apply 2 in. (5 cm) of compost. 2 hours	—	—	—
Water—use drip irrigation, water manually as needed. Set lawn sprinklers for automatic control.	—	—	—	—	—
Check irrigation—sprinkler coverage, pressure, clogging.	—	—	Check system for operation and coverage. Run manually through each circuit. Flag inoperable heads. 1 hour	—	—
Rake leaves from turf areas, compost leaves.	—	—	—	—	—
Attend to compost. Add organic matter, turn as needed, check moisture.	—	—	—	Attend compost. 1 hour	Attend compost. 1 hour
Test soil nutrient levels in lawn, flower, and vegetable garden areas.	—	—	—	—	—

June	July	Aug.	Sept.	Oct.	Nov.	Dec.
Mow four times. 4 hours	Mow four times. 4 hours	Mow three times. 3 hours	Mow once. 1 hour	—	—	—
—	—	—	—	—	Mow once. 1/2 hour	Mow once. 1/2 hour
Trim grass from edges. 2 hours	Trim grass from edges. 1 hour	Trim grass from edges. 1 hour	—	—	—	—
Remove weeds. 1 hour	Remove weeds. 1 hour	—	Remove weeds. 2 hours	—	—	—
Prune trees and shrubs for form if needed. 2 hours	—	—	—	—	—	—
—	—	—	—	—	—	Plant trees and shrubs. 2 hours
—	—	—	Plant spring-blooming bulbs. 1 hour	—	—	—
—	—	—	—	—	—	—
Apply 2 in. (5 cm) of compost. 2 hours	—	—	Apply 2 in. (5 cm) of compost. 2 hours	—	—	—
Check for soil moisture. turn on drip when needed. 15 min.	Check for soil moisture. Turn on drip when needed. 15 min.	Check for soil moisture. Turn on drip when needed. 15 min.	Check for soil moisture. Turn on drip when needed. 15 min.	—	—	—
—	Check system for operation and coverage. 1 hour	—	—	—	Winterize— sprinkler system. 1 hour	—
—	—	—	—	Rake leaves. 4 hours	Rake leaves. 3 hours	—
Attend compost. 1 hour	Attend compost. 1 hour	Attend compost. 1 hour	Attend compost. 1 hour	Attend compost. 1 hour	Begin new pile. 2 hours	Attend compost. 2 hours
—	—	—	—	Test soil sample or deliver to testing lab. 1/2 hour	—	—

(Continued)

Table 24-5 Continued

Activity	Jan.	Feb.	Mar.	Apr.	May
Test soil pH of lawn, garden beds, and shrubs (azaleas).	—	Use test kit to check soil pH. 1/2 hour	—	—	—
Adjust soil pH if needed.	—	Spread material on lawn; use cultivator, work into garden soil. 2 hours	—	—	—
Apply mulch of shredded bark, leaves, pine straw, or other organic material.	—	—	Apply mulch. 1 hour	—	—
Winter overseeding—plant rye grass over dormant warm-season grass.	—	—	—	—	—
Cleanup	Cut back spent stalks of annuals and perennials. Pick up fallen limbs, trash. 1 hour	—	—	—	—
Check for pest and disease damage.			Throughout year as needed.		

Historical climatic data: Starkville, Mississippi

	Jan.	Feb.	Mar.	Apr.	May
Rainfall (inches)	5.55	5.52	5.93	4.47	3.76
Evapotranspiration[1]	0.79	1.03	2.15	3.78	5.85
Net	4.65	4.49	3.78	0.69	−2.09
Temperature (degrees F)					
Normal high	58	67	72	81	87
Maximum	81	84	89	93	99
Normal low	29	31	37	46	54
Minimum	−6	−1	14	28	38

Frost expectancy: last frost March 27, first frost October 29.

[1]Evapotranspiration (EVT) is the amount of water evaporating from the soil and transpiring from leaves and twigs. Note that EVT rates are lowest in January and highest in July for this section of Mississippi. Local EVT rates are available from irrigation equipment suppliers and many experiment stations at land grant universities.

Source: Pete Melby, Ed Martin, *Home Landscapes, Planting Design and Management* (Timber Press, 1994).

June	July	Aug.	Sept.	Oct.	Nov.	Dec.
—	—	—	—	—	—	—
—	—	—	—	—	—	—
—	—	—	—	—	Apply mulch. 2 hours	—
—	—	—	—	Overseed with rye grass. 1 hour	—	—
—	—	—	—	—	—	Cut back stalks of annuals and perennials. Pick up fallen limbs, trash. 1 hour

Throughout year as needed.

June	July	Aug.	Sept.	Oct.	Nov.	Dec.	Total
3.48	5.27	3.20	3.16	2.54	3.93	4.48	51.48
7.43	8.04	7.49	5.50	3.33	1.52	0.89	47.80
−3.95	−2.77	−4.29	−2.40	−0.79	2.41	3.95	
92	94	93	92	83	72	63	
105	111	108	103	96	88	82	
62	67	66	56	43	32	30	
41	53	52	40	28	10	−8	

SOILS

The most critical ingredient in the recipe for a healthy, flourishing landscape is well-conditioned soil. Through understanding that there are various soil types, differing in structure, drainage, and fertility, a significant beginning can be made toward creating a sustainable landscape. Soil is composed of weathered minerals, organic matter, air, and water. The ideal soil can be described as having 50% pore space for air and water movement, 5% organic matter, and 45% mineral content. Weathered minerals are potential plant nutrients that contribute to plant health and growth. Ideal soils will also be teeming with microflora and microfauna—the fungi, bacteria, and tiny animals that break down organic matter into forms beneficial and usable to plants. Table 24-6 illustrates different soil types and their characteristics.

Organic matter helps to provide the mineral nutrient needs of plants. As plant and animal matter decays, humus is formed. Humus is that dark, moist, decayed matter found on the forest and prairie floor (Figure 24-2). It is similar to finished compost. Leaves and twigs become humus when they rot beyond recognition. Microorganisms, the microscopic bacteria and fungi, decay plant and animal matter and transform it into a pool of nutrients to be used by plant roots for growth and production. A rich soil is alive with these microorganisms. Because microbes are constantly breaking down organic matter into fertilizer, a soil with a good humus content may not need supplemental fertilizer. Humus, or composted organic matter, supplies plant nutrients in a manner similar to that of a slow-release fertilizer. Soils with a high humus content are very fertile and are wonderful growing mediums for plant roots. Interestingly, roots don't grow in soil; instead, they grow in the voids within soil. Organic matter at rates up to 30% of soil volume will enhance the presence of these voids and the accommodation of roots. When microbes break down organic matter, they release minerals, such as nitrogen, phosphorus, and potassium contained within the decaying plant and animal matter. In addition, microbes in the humus help to reduce plant disease by attacking the diseases or pathogenic (disease-causing) organisms. Plants grown in soil containing composted matter have fewer disease and insect problems.

Air is a must in soils, as plant roots need it to take up nutrients, and many microorganisms would die without it. Air is usually abundant in the top 8 to 12 in. (20 to 30 cm)

Table 24-6 Soil Characteristics

Soil type	Permeability	Erodability	Reservoir of Available Water	Drainage (porosity)	Nutrient Holding Capacity
Sand					
Sandy loam					
Loam					
Silt loam					
Clay loam					
Clay					
	low	low	high	low	high

Source: Pete Melby, Ed Martin, *Home Landscapes, Planting Design and Management* (Timber Press, 1994).

Figure 24-2   Humus, the decayed leaf and twig matter on the forest floor.

of healthy soils. In forests, almost all of a tree's feeder roots are in this upper soil area. The humus layer on top of the soil acts like a sponge to hold water and slowly release it as needed by plants. Humus can hold up to 200 times its weight in water. To recreate this condition when rejuvenating a landscape, place composted materials or plant detritus like pine straw and/or shredded plant leaves on top of the ground three times a year to a maximum depth of 6 in. (152 mm) according to the following schedule:

- First application, three to four weeks before the growing season
- Second application, in the summer during active plant growth
- Third application, in the fall, to prepare planting beds for winter

When applying composted organic matter, make sure the compost is cured and that the carbon-to-nitrogen ratio is 10:1. If the compost has not thoroughly cured, or uncomposted pine straw and leaves are used, the ratio of carbon to nitrogen will be greater than 10:1 and microorganisms working to decay the organic matter will take available nitrogen for their own energy and growth, thus creating a short-term nitrogen deficiency for nearby plants. As organic matter becomes depleted, the soil environment can no longer meet the food, air, or even pH demands of the fauna that help in aerating soil and producing nutrients.

To retain good soil structure and reduce unwanted compaction, covering soil with an organic mulch will cushion pressure from human feet and pounding rain. A protective mulch cover will break the impact of raindrops and protect soil from the eroding effects of flowing water and wind. Adding composted or organic material will keep soils, in both human and natural landscapes, ideal.

Figure 24-3   Meadow landscape thriving without fertilizer and irrigation.

FERTILIZER

Why is there a need to fertilize landscapes when forests, prairies, and meadows thrive effortlessly (Figure 24-3)? If planting beds were managed as Mother Nature manages her fields and forests, supplemental nutrients would not have to be added to the soil. In nature, organic matter is constantly returned to the soil through the dropping of plant and animal matter. Decomposed organic matter, or humus, is the soil's storehouse of nutrients. Decomposed organic matter along with other natural sources can provide nearly all of the essential nutrients for plants. For example, the average amount of nitrogen released yearly when the top 6 in. (15 cm) of soil contains 19% organic matter is 15 to 20 lb (7 to 9 kg) per ac (0.4 ha). Nitrogen comes from other sources as well. Approximately 10 lb (4.5 kg) of nitrogen per ac (0.4 ha) is provided by microorganisms that can extract nitrogen from the air and bring it down into the soil. Rain and snow bring about 10 lb (4.5 kg) of nitrogen per ac (0.4 ha) from the atmosphere. Heat from lightning in the atmosphere causes the nitrogen in the air we breathe to mix with oxygen to form nitrogen oxide. Air is composed of 79% nitrogen.

Through nurturing soil with composted organic matter, or regular mulching with pine straw or shredded leaves, most plant nutrient needs can be met. Sustainable landscapes rely on naturally available resources and processes for sustenance and health. Table 24-7 lists nutrients essential for plant growth.

Water

Water is an essential part of all landscapes. Although in many parts of the country it appears as though water supplies are inexhaustible, we are approaching or exceeding

Table 24-7   Nutrients Essential for Plant Growth

Macronutrients in Soil		Micronutrients in Soil		Nutrients in Air and Water	
Nitrogen	N	Iron	Fe	Carbon	C
Phosphorus	P	Copper	Cu	Hydrogen	H
Potassium	K	Manganese	Mn	Oxygen	O
Calcium	Ca	Zinc	Zn	Nitrogen	N
Magnesium	Mg	Molybdenum	Mo		
Sulfur	S	Boron	B		
		Chlorine	Cl		

Source: Martin and Melby, *Home Landscapes, Planting Design and Management* (Timber Press, 1994).

water supply limits in many areas. To reduce the use of water, creating and maintaining low-water-need landscapes should be considered. Low-water-need landscapes are popularly called *xeriscapes.* The word comes from the Greek word *xeros,* which means "dry." When applying xeriscape techniques, it is best to select native plants from the local area. These plants can probably take the extremes of local climatic conditions. Through using native plants, the use of irrigation water can be reduced. Because research has shown that automatic irrigation systems often use 75% more water than a manual hose and sprinkler system, doing with less irrigation water is probably beneficial to the environment. When using native plants, be aware that they will have to be irrigated for as long as two years to get them established. Some plants that provide important site functions, such as sun or wind control, will benefit from longer-term irrigation in order to enhance growth. Spray or drip irrigation techniques are appropriate to accomplish this requirement for plant establishment. In creating xeriscapes, the following can be helpful in reducing the need for water:

1. Consider whether screening a view can be best accomplished with a row of plants, a fence, or a wall.

2. Evaluate the various areas as to whether they should be paved, covered with a mulch, or planted with grass.

3. Incorporate shade into the planting design. Shaded landscapes are up to 15°F (8°C) cooler than areas in the sun. Water loss by evaporation is greater in sunny areas. Shade can be provided by trees but can also be the result of using arbors and tall fences.

4. Create water need zones in a landscape. Public areas of high visibility may need the most water, whereas service areas may need the least amount. A landscape can be divided into three water use zones: high use, requiring regular watering; moderate use, with occasional watering; and low use, where natural rainfall is relied upon. Recall, though, that newly planted material will require regular irrigation until established. In the Starkville, Mississippi, Street Tree Planting Program, trees were watered with 5 gal (19 l) of water per week during the summer for two years. After that time period, they were sufficiently established to sustain themselves with natural rainfall.

5. Concentrate plantings with high water needs together, such as water-loving annual flowers, as opposed to scattering them throughout a landscape.

6. Fit plants to the size of the space in which they will be located instead of choosing plants that will need constant pruning to maintain a certain size. Cutting plants back during the growing season stimulates growth and increases water demand.

7. Feed the soil with composted organic matter that will become a slow-release fertilizer. This will reduce growth spurts caused by large infusions of fertilizer and thus reduce the need for water.

8. Mulch around plants with an organic material like shredded leaves and pine straw to slow evaporation of water from the soil and to reduce heat stress to plants. This will reduce water consumption.

9. Where grassed areas are desired, mow turf so that no more than one-third of the leaf is removed. This reduces growth surges, which demand water. Raise mower blades during drought periods and at the end of the growing season to encourage deeper rooting. When grassed areas are used as visual void spaces in a design, convert the lawn to a meadow that needs mowing seasonally. For a different appearance, grasses can be cut occasionally to a height of 6 to 9 in. (152 to 229 mm), which will reduce the need for mowing and the use of water.

10. Irrigate just before plants become stressed. When they are becoming stressed, grasses will dull in color and will not spring back when stepped on, tree leaves will begin to droop and shed, and shrubs will dull in color and begin to wilt. Keep plants healthy, but don't encourage optimum growth all of the time.

Chapter 25

Composting Kitchen and Yard Wastes

Like most sustainable practices, the composting of kitchen scraps and yard wastes will provide multiple benefits. It will reduce the quantity of waste sent to a landfill (kitchen plus yard wastes can make up as much as 30% of household wastes). It will also provide a rich soil amendment that will greatly improve garden and lawn soil.

Composting is the controlled decomposition of organic materials. When materials such as vegetable peels, fruit skins, food scraps, paper towels, grass clippings, and tree leaves are allowed to degrade in the presence of sufficient oxygen and moisture, they quickly and inoffensively convert to a rich humuslike material that is useful in the home and garden.

Organic residues from kitchens and yards have, in the past, been regarded as wastes and sent to a waste "sink," usually a landfill. Treating them in this fashion requires paid labor, fuel, trucks, and a landfill. Existing landfills in the United States are filling up, and new regulations have increased the effort, materials, and energy needed to build new landfills.

The organic materials deposited in landfills are not really valueless. They have an inherent value based on their nutrient content and their potential for improving soil. The energy and materials required to transport and process these "wastes" can be saved and their inherent value realized if they are processed on-site (on the homeowner's property). Composting is a simple and efficient way to process wastes on site and create a useful product. Hence, composting is a sustainable practice.

COMPOSTING—THE MODEL IN NATURAL SYSTEMS

In the natural world, most dead animals and plants are ultimately decomposed by microorganisms and a variety of invertebrate organisms. When adequate moisture and oxygen are available, the process advances rapidly and few offensive odors are produced (most offensive odors develop when oxygen is used up in the vicinity of the degradation process; at that time anaerobic bacteria become active and typical rotting smells are produced).

Decomposing microorganisms mineralize phosphorus, nitrogen, and other nutrients, making them available to plants. Bacteria and fungi convert the easily digested carbon compounds to carbon dioxide and water, as seen in the following reaction of carbohydrate:

$$CH_2O + O_2 \longrightarrow CO_2 + H_2O$$

(carbohydrate + oxygen yields carbon dioxide + water)

The structural molecules that are resistant to microbial decay (lignin, complex polysaccharides, structural proteins) end up becoming incorporated into soil. They will ultimately be degraded over a period of years (by earthworms and bacteria). In the meantime, though, they improve soil characteristics such as water retention (in sandy soil) and drainage (in packed and heavy clay soils). The slowly degrading organic material also helps to maintain the complex population of soil microorganisms that directly or indirectly benefit plants.

ADAPTING THE NATURAL MODEL TO HUMAN NEEDS

We humans create a steady stream of organic kitchen and yard wastes. Kitchen wastes are so readily degradable that if we put them in a garbage can, they will quickly develop anaerobic "micro-environments" that produce bad odors and attract flies. If we wish to adapt the natural model to process these wastes without sending them to a landfill, we must find a way to provide an adequate supply of oxygen to the waste or, failing that, provide a covering material that filters out the bad-smelling anaerobic by-products that occur when oxygen runs out.

A Not-So-High-Technology Solution

The solution to the odor problem is a properly constructed compost pile. Yard waste (leaves, grass clippings, and perhaps some topsoil) can be used to provide the bulk of the compost pile. Leaves break down very slowly. They are, however, excellent surfaces for microorganisms to colonize. In a pile, they create air pockets that allow oxygen diffusion into the pile. When segments of the pile become anaerobic (which they will, from time to time, after new kitchen waste is added), the user will never know it, provided that a layer of leaves is at the surface. A leaf covering and its colonizing microorganisms effectively filter odors escaping from the pile. The rate of air movement through the pile is slow enough that the pile retains moisture and heat. The retention of heat speeds the process by allowing heat-loving (thermophillic) microorganisms to become established.

Some people have been following this practice for years. The leaves that fall in autumn constitute the bulking material of the pile for the rest of the year. Rather than send the leaves to a landfill in plastic bags, they pile them in an unobtrusive corner of the backyard. Then, until the next fall, they add their kitchen waste to the pile. The large pile of leaves becomes a small pile of leaves by the following fall, as the leaves and other wastes break down together. Between that autumn and the following spring, all of the previous year's pile is added to the garden or spread on the lawn (landscapers call this a "soil dressing"). In the meantime, the recently arrived newly fallen leaves are gathered to provide the bulk for the next year's pile. As mentioned earlier, this cycling has been going on for years, to the benefit of many vegetable and flower gardens, with no kitchen waste or leaves transported from the homeowner's property.

A Slightly-Higher-Technology Solution

Many properties produce a bountiful leaf harvest each year. Perhaps you do not have access to leaves or you don't want to devote a part of the yard to a "pile" of anything. Kitchen scraps, mixed with yard waste, can be composted in small volumes, and more quickly, in compost bins. A variety of prefabricated bins are commercially available. Some of these can be rotated or rolled to mix the composting material, thereby avoiding anaerobic degradation, speeding the process, and providing a finished product of more uniform quality. The commercially available bins are fairly attractive while still providing all the benefits of composting. It is also possible to construct your own enclosed bin.

Composting, no matter what the scale or approach, is easy and practical for all but the most urbanized.

THE COMPOSTING PROCESS

As we step through the basics of the composting process, we may refer occasionally to the "best" conditions for composting. In most cases, providing optimum conditions for composting microorganisms is not critical in residential systems. In composting at the industrial or municipal level, it is important to speed compost production as much as possible to use up the waste and, perhaps, to get the best-quality product possible to sell. At the residential level, rushing the process is not usually important. If the pile dries out for a few days, the process will slow. But when it eventually gets wet again, it will speed up. Having the right balance of nutrients will push the process along. But if the balance is a bit off, the process does not grind to a halt. It just goes a bit more slowly (remember, no one is managing the composting that occurs in the natural world). The details of the composting process are interesting, but not critical for the residential composter. Home composters are more interested in keeping dogs out and avoiding bad odors (which is actually pretty easy).

Oxygen

Adequate oxygen keeps the composting process aerobic. This means that decomposition will proceed with few of those smelly anaerobically produced intermediate products. Our atmosphere is about 21% oxygen. Concentrations well below this level, however, are adequate for keeping the microbes happy in the pile. Constructing the pile with adequate bulking material (such as leaves) or periodically turning the pile will ensure that adequate oxygen is available.

Water

All living creatures require water to survive, and this includes microbial organisms. In general, a water content between 40 and 65% (by weight) is adequate to support microbial activity. Recall that the aerobic composting process actually results in the production of water (see the reaction given earlier). The important issue is how quickly the compost dries because of air circulation in the pile. The outer surface of the compost usually dries first. Many composters wet the pile with a garden hose following extended periods without rain.

Too much water can be a problem for the composting process. At a content of more than about 70%, the water will actually block the diffusion of oxygen to the surface of the material. This is why some materials (such as animal waste from stockyards) must be "dewatered" before they can be composted.

Nutrients

Any component in food that is necessary to sustain life is a nutrient. In this sense, both water and organic carbon molecules (which we digest to capture the energy stored in their chemical bonds) are nutrients. Usually, though, when we speak of nutrients, we mean nitrogen, phosphorus, potassium, and many other elements and compounds that we require in small quantities. The critical nutrient (the one most referred to) in composting is nitrogen. Other nutrients are usually available in adequate concentrations. A ratio of carbon to nitrogen (C:N)—atoms of organic carbon to atoms of nitrogen—of 20:1 to 30:1 is usually considered optimum. In fact, it's the ratio of *available* carbon to *available* nitrogen that matters. Atoms of carbon or nitrogen locked away in hard-to-digest compounds are really not available (at least for a couple of years) and so don't enter into the C:N ratio.

A C:N ratio greater than about 30:1 indicates that there is too little nitrogen for an optimum composting rate; composting will continue, but at a slower rate than would otherwise occur. A ratio less than about 20:1 indicates that there is too much nitrogen in the composting material. Generally, this occurs only when there is a great deal of animal tissue in the composting material (which does not usually occur in household waste).

Particle Size

In general, the smaller the particles in composting material, the greater will be the rate of degradation. Smaller particles have a greater ratio of surface to volume (amount of surface area to per unit volume). Because microbes attack (digest) from the outside of a particle, the greater the amount of exposed surface, the greater the speed with which it will be eaten.

Very small particle size, however, can mean that the composting material will become compacted, preventing the diffusion of oxygen to the surfaces colonized by microorganisms. If this occurs, then the rate at which the material composts will decrease. Under extreme conditions, it can even result in large anaerobic pockets (which degrade very slowly and smell very bad). One backyard composter used to simply pile the leaves into a mound. Because there were a number of large oak trees on the property, they produced a huge pile of leaves. Now this person has begun to use a power vacuum system that shreds the leaves. This creates an initial pile that is perhaps one-quarter the size of the unshredded leaves, making the pile a bit easier to manage. There is no indication that shredding the leaves impairs oxygen diffusion in the pile during the year.

Bacteria and Fungi

The organisms that do the work of composting are important parts of the process. Both bacteria and fungi readily take up residence in a compost pile, beginning the process of degradation almost as soon as the pile is established.

Like all living organisms, bacteria and fungi give off heat as they digest organic molecules. The inside of a compost pile is generally well insulated, so the heat that microbes produce tends to accumulate in the pile. A large population of microbes, starting at outdoor air temperature with adequate organic material to digest, will produce enough heat that they will first stress and then kill themselves (this can happen in as little as one to three days). As the temperature of the pile reaches 105°F (40°C) or so, heat-loving, or thermophillic, bacteria and fungi will begin to dominate the microbial population. The best temperature for these heat-loving organisms is actually about 130°F (55°C). At about 150°F (65°C), accumulated metabolic heat will actually slow growth, so temperatures in active piles tend to level off in the 140° to 150°F (60° to 65°C) range. At this point, the temperature of the pile has exceeded the temperature tolerance of most human pathogens, so the piles (if temperature is uniform) will "disinfect" themselves.

There is no need to inoculate piles with bacteria and fungi. Even thermophillic microorganisms become readily established on their own. A typical residential compost pile will not reach and maintain the consistently high temperatures of industrial or municipal operations. As a rule, most people simply do not add enough readily degradable material to their home piles (which is good, because these piles are harder to manage). You will find, however, that parts of such a pile will support thermophilic organisms from time to time. This is an indication that composting is proceeding at a furious rate.

CONTAINERS FOR COMPOSTING

A compost pile can be just that, a pile with nothing surrounding it. If you have an out-of-the-way corner that is sheltered from the wind and free of pesky animals, a pile may be just the thing for you. This was the strategy of the aforementioned composter for a number of years. The wind didn't blow the leaves around, and animals mainly left the pile alone (provided that the kitchen waste was buried a good foot or so in the pile). Then Jack arrived in the neighborhood—a big friendly dog with long legs, who loved to dig, and had the run of the neighborhood. So much for the uncontained pile.

The solution was chicken wire, wood slats, and a staple gun (an idea from a site on the Web; see Figure 25-1a). It took about an hour to build the bin, and it has worked flawlessly.

There are many other solutions to the bin selection problem. Some people like the multiple bin solution (Figure 25-1b). This allows the composter to transfer ("turn") the

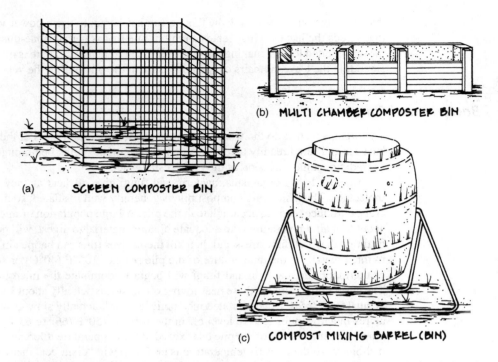

(a) SCREEN COMPOSTER BIN

(b) MULTI CHAMBER COMPOSTER BIN

(c) COMPOST MIXING BARREL (BIN)

Figure 25-1 There are a variety of types of composting bins that can be built or purchased. Simple designs (a) can consist of little more than wood slats and nails or staples. Multiple-bin systems (b) allow convenient mixing and sequencing of compost batches. Purchased systems (c) enclose the compost and facilitate mixing.

pile from one bin to the other. Turning the pile mixes the compost, which both speeds the process and results in a more homogeneous final product.

Other users like the "top in, bottom out" approach. Material to be composted is added at the top of the bin. The finished product is removed from an opening at the bottom.

There are also bins that allow you to roll or turn the bin itself in order to mix the contents (Figure 25-1c).

Thus, a bin can be nonexistent or an extremely cheap and simple one. It can be more sophisticated; it can even be somewhat attractive. There are many do-it-yourself designs on the Internet and many types of bins that you can purchase. Many people avoid the use of treated lumber in their bins because of the possibility of harmful constituents leaching into the compost.

MANAGING A COMPOST PILE

Managing a compost pile can be as simple or elaborate as you wish. The pile will compost if you let it alone (just add kitchen scraps). It will compost a bit faster and more homogeneously if you turn it occasionally. It will move along quite briskly if you mix it regularly and keep it moist. It will race forward if you monitor pH and add lime if needed, add fertilizer, and turn it regularly. Depending on your approach, the compost will be ready for use in several weeks to a year. It just depends on your schedule and level of interest.

CONTENTS OF A COMPOST PILE

Practically any organic waste generated in the house or yard (with the exception of sewage) can go into a backyard compost pile. Common items include the following:

- Vegetable peels
- Corn husks and cobs
- Fruit skins and cores
- Seeds and pits
- Eggshells
- Plate scrapings
- Moldy leftovers
- Shrimp, crayfish, lobster, and crab shells
- Ancient boxed or bagged foods (cereal, flour, etc.)
- Cereal boxes
- Paper towels
- Leaves
- Grass clippings
- Twigs
- Plants (dead or pulled from the garden, but not diseased plants)

One of the fascinating aspects of composting is that waste goes in looking like waste and then quickly disappears, never to be seen again. A sealable plastic container can be used to hold the kitchen scraps until enough have accumulated to take out (perhaps about every day or two). Cereal boxes should be ripped into a few pieces prior to composting. Both boxes and paper towels should be wetted prior to composting (a dry paper towel that makes it to the surface of the pile can hang around for months; a wet towel in the interior disappears in a few days). Even junk mail (not the ceramic coated slicks, but everything else) can be composted. Junk mail disappears in the pile as well, with the exception of the little plastic envelope windows, which will surface after a while.

Note that meat scraps and oils are not included in the preceding list. The conventional wisdom is that meat scraps attract pests and oils do not degrade well. Also, pile temperature may not always be hot enough to kill pathogenic microorganisms in meat and dairy wastes. This is probably true in many instances. Both can be added to a pile, in moderation, without apparent problems (bones do persist for a while).

THE FINISHED COMPOST

Determining when compost is "finished" is up to you. The ultimate end products of aerobic degradation of organic materials are water and carbon dioxide, but that takes years. Commercial and municipal operations allow the pile to return naturally to the temperature of the surroundings and then usually give it some time to "cure" (continue degrading) at a low rate. The time of the curing process appears quite variable.

For the backyard composter, the batch is really finished when the pile appears to be a homogeneous mass that looks like humus (obviously organic but of undetermined origin). A slightly more liberal definition of "finished compost" allows some of the leaves to still look like leaves, with everything else pretty much indistinguishable. The "gardener in a hurry" definition is that the compost is finished when nothing looks like kitchen scraps and you need it. All of these definitions work.

APPLICATION OF THE FINISHED COMPOST

Compost can be spaded or tilled into a garden. A 50:50 mix of compost and soil is about the maximum that should be used. Because organic material in soil is usually completely degraded over two to three years, a garden can be a continuous repository for finished compost.

Compost can be laid on the surface of the garden like mulch. Earthworms will plow it into the soil in time.

Finished compost can also be raked over grass as a soil dressing, provided there are few large fragments or uncomposted leaves. Ideally, the compost will fall between the blades of grass and form an organic layer that contributes to the development of turf.

Compost can be used for house plants and outdoor container plants during the re-potting process.

Some composters choose to not use their finished product for much of anything, regarding composting mainly as a process for disposal of wastes. This is actually a viable approach, as the material continues to "disappear" until it is gone (it may have to be spread about from time to time). The soil in the vicinity of the compost pile becomes remarkably rich and healthy, teeming with earthworms (great for fishing bait).

THE VALUE OF COMPOST TO SOIL AND PLANTS

The addition of compost nearly always improves soils and plant growth in a number of ways:

- Compost provides "time release" nutrients. Much of the nutrient content of compost is incorporated into bacteria biomass. As the bacteria die, these nutrients gradually become available to plants and soil microorganisms.

- When spaded or tilled into sandy soil, compost improves the soil's water retention properties. The organic material absorbs water like a sponge, keeping it at the root zone of the plants.

- When spaded or tilled into densely packed clay soils, compost improves both drainage and the structure of the soil.
- Compost supports a rich population of soil microorganisms and invertebrates. Healthy soil is characterized by a diverse population of bacteria, fungi, and other organisms that play a role in the complex chemical transformations of nutrients in the soil. Many studies have shown that plants grow better in compost amended soils even after accounting for the water-holding, drainage, and nutrient effects.
- When used as a mulch, compost helps to retain moisture in the soil and inhibit weed growth.

COMPOST PESTS

The list of composting pests is remarkably small. We have already mentioned dogs. Dogs can be excluded by a barrier around the sides of the pile. In areas where rats may be a problem, a fully enclosed compost bin (commercial or homemade) should prevent entry.

Relatively few insects or invertebrates can be called pests. Your compost pile contains a rich population of insects and worms, but most of these belong there and contribute in some way to the decomposing process. Anaerobic degradation or scraps left on the surface can attract flies. By burying kitchen scraps 6 in. (15 cm) or so in the pile, this is generally not a problem. In the southern United States, fire ants may occasionally take up residence in a pile. These pose a potential problem because they both swarm and sting. A solution to fire ants is a pot of boiling water, which quickly incorporates the ants into the composting process. Biodegradable sprays are also available for those who do not wish to handle hot water.

A COMPOSTING VARIATION: VERMICULTURE

Vermiculture is the use of worms to convert waste to a stable end product. Bacteria and fungi still play a role (they are part of the worms' diet). Vermiculture bins can be kept indoors or in the garage. They are mainly used to process kitchen scraps.

Vermiculture uses worms that are adapted to eating and living in organic material. The most common variety used are the "red worms" available in many bait shops. The worms are grown in bedding made from shredded leaves, shredded newspaper, or some other shredded organic material. The bedding is kept damp, and kitchen scraps are buried in it to feed the population of worms.

The worms will ingest practically all small particles, including the aforementioned bacteria and fungi as well as nematodes, protozoans, and whatever else is small enough for ingestion. It is all ultimately converted to worm castings (feces), and this material is then applied as compost to the garden. A liquid also accumulates, which makes a fine fertilizer when it is drained off.

Vermiculture is particularly suited to people who wish to compost but have limited space in which to do it. You do not have to have a big pile of leaves and other bulking materials. People have treated their kitchen scraps in their apartments using vermiculture.

The size of the bin you use depends on the amount of kitchen waste you generate. It is common to use 1 ft^2 (0.09 m^2) of surface area for each 1 lb (0.37 kg) of waste generated in a week. The bin(s) should be 8 to 12 in. (20 to 30 cm) deep, with holes in the bottom to allow accumulated liquid to drain out (the bin should be slightly elevated on small boards or bricks). The bin should be covered to prevent drying.

About 2000 worms are needed to process 1 lb (0.37 kg) of waste in a day. Typically, you will start with a smaller number of worms and then increase the amount of waste added as the population increases.

The wastes that you can process are somewhat more restricted with vermiculture than with conventional composting. In addition to meat and oil, grains and dairy products should be avoided because of the possibility of attracting flies (there is less opportunity to "hide" these materials in a vermiculture bin than in a compost pile).

Bedding should be changed every two months or so (when everything in the bin looks like compost). Do this by pushing the bin contents to one side of the bin, adding new bedding and waste, and then removing the compost when the worms have migrated to the improved quarters (about two to three days later). The compost can then be removed and used.

CONCLUSION

Composting is a sustainable practice that is very easy to incorporate into most lifestyles. As landfills become more restrictive in what they will accept (especially in regard to yard wastes), composting is a logical way to close the natural cycle with respect to the nonsewage wastes that we generate.

Chapter 26

Managing Runoff Water

Runoff from human landscapes, including urban and suburban areas, roadways, and agricultural regions, is generally polluted and contains sediments, organic matter, hazardous chemicals, and metals. The volume of water runoff from human landscapes has reached enormous proportions and is having an adverse effect on the quality of waterways and offshore water bodies, causing erosion and affecting aquatic life habitats.

Water that is not soaked up and stored on a site flows off the land and is called runoff. Runoff can adversely affect the quality of water bodies by introducing sediments and pollutants such as organic matter, chemicals, and metals. Runoff can also be destructive when flowing in large volumes and at high velocities, causing impairment and destruction of aquatic habitats, making ditch and stream banks cave in, and inducing roadways and bridges to fail.

THE NATURAL MODEL

When precipitation falls on natural and undisturbed landscapes, the descent of water to the ground surface is slowed by leaves and branches or stems of plants. This cushioned fall to the earth prevents the hammering of the ground surface and compaction of the layer of organic matter covering the soil. Once at ground level, water soaks into a 6 to 9 in. (152 to 229 mm) layer of plant and animal matter. This soft organic layer beneath the forest canopy and covering the prairie floor acts like a sponge, soaking up and holding most of the precipitation for use by plant roots, animals, insects, and microorganisms. The small amount of water that runs off the land is filtered by the layer of organic matter so that only clean, clear water flows from the site. We estimate the amount of water that, in the past, ran off naturally occurring sites with thick layers of organic matter to be only 10% of current runoff amounts.

In addition to protecting the soil surface from rain impact and soaking up water, the thick layer of organic matter is a storehouse of nutrients. Carbon and other elements from plant leaves and animal droppings are continuously degrading or composting, building nutrients for plant growth. Nutrients are made available by decomposers like insects and microbes, whose job it is to break down organic matter so that a nutrient pool can be developed and the cycle of life can continue. In comparing the ground coverings of human landscapes with the natural model of the forest and prairie floor, we find a great difference in the ability of the two surfaces to perform environmental housekeeping tasks. For those in charge of the design and management of human landscapes, there are great leaps of progress to be made in reflecting the processes contained in the natural model of the forest and prairie floor.

WATER MANAGEMENT IN HUMAN DEVELOPMENTS

Even though water quality has become a major environmental and economic development issue, efforts to protect water from the harmful effects of runoff have been limited. For a developer to get a building permit, public policies, in general, require runoff levels to be no higher than predevelopment levels. Although this may sound reasonable, when comparing the water runoff levels of a proposed parking lot and shopping mall to be built on a cattle pasture, the "predevelopment runoff level" of the grassed pasture is significantly higher than it was when that pasture was a forest or prairie with a thick layer of detritus. Land development policies should require runoff volume and quality to be the same as when a site was in a natural state.

The amount of water that runs off a home landscape, for example, is enormous as compared with runoff in the natural model. Let us consider just the amount of water that runs off the roof of a 2000 ft^2 (186 m^2) home. If we assume that the roof is also about 2000 ft^2 (186 m^2) and the home is located in a climate zone where it will get 58 in. (1473 mm) of precipitation per year, about 70,000 gallons (264,950 l) of water will run off the roof to the ground and most of that will run off to ditches, creeks, rivers, and, ultimately, the ocean. The Gulf of Mexico is currently suffering from polluted runoff and has numerous hypoxic zones (areas depleted of all oxygen) including one very large, 7000 mi^2 (18,130 km^2), area off the coast of Louisiana.

EXAMPLE 1. Compute roof runoff.
Rainfall is 58 in. (1473 mm) per year. Converting it to feet (meters), we divide the 58 in. (1473 mm) by 12 in. (305 mm) to get 4.83 ft (1.47 m). That is, a year's worth of rainfall collected on the roof would be 4.83 ft (1.47 m) deep.

Now, take the roof area of 2000 ft^2 (186 m^2) × 4.83 ft (1.47 m) of rainfall per year to get the quantity of water, which is 9666.66 ft^3 (273 m^3).

Thus, 9666.66 ft^3 × 7.48 gal = 72,306.66 gal (273,000 l) of water that will run off the roof each year. Of that amount, probably only 10%, or 7230 gal (27,300 l), of water per year ran off the 2000 ft^2 (186 m^2) area covered by the roof when it was a natural area with a thick humus layer covering the ground plane.

A landscape architect with the Maine Department of Transportation who spoke to a group of university students applied the model of runoff from the natural forest or prairie floor to a soccer field. He said that by tilling 12 in (305 mm) of composted organic matter a foot deep into the soil of a sports field, the field will hold all of the water from a 2 in.

(51 mm) rainstorm. No water would run off the field because of the spongy condition of the forest floor created within the playing field.

WATER QUALITY AND THE BUILT ENVIRONMENT

Nearly all runoff from human developments is polluted with some or all of the following: sediments, organic matter, bacteria and viruses, chemicals, and metals. The impact of built developments on water quality and on the balance of water distribution in the landscape is great and demands regular consideration. The most polluted part of runoff is the first flush of water. The first flush is the first 1/2 in. (13 mm) of water that runs off a site, and it is usually the dirtiest water that will run off in a rainstorm. It may be carrying hydrocarbons, heavy metals, nitrogen, phosphorous, bacteria, viruses, and toxic chemicals from roadways, lawn care, and home landscape management. Water runoff beyond the first flush will be cleaner. First-flush runoff from roadways in the Denver, Colorado, area was found to include constituents as noted in Table 26-1. The pollutants found in these roadway samples should compel designers and engineers to include technologies for considering water quality on projects with which they are involved.

BEST MANAGEMENT PRACTICES

Best management practices (BMPs) in the management of runoff water are construction techniques and maintenance procedures for reducing water quantity and for cleaning water that flows from built landscapes. BMPs have been created for storm water management, erosion control, water runoff quality, and protection of natural waterways. Water runoff management can be divided into the categories of construction site impact

Table 26-1   Roadway Stormwater Runoff Constituents

Constituents	Primary Sources
Nitrogen, phosphorus	Atmosphere, roadside fertilizer application
Lead	Auto exhaust, tire wear
Zinc	Tire wear, motor oil, grease
Iron	Auto body rust, steel highway structures
Copper	Metal plating, bearing wear, engines, brakes, insecticides
Cadmium	Tire wear, insecticide application
Chromium	Metal plating, engines, brake lining wear
Nickel	Diesel fuel, gasoline exhaust, oil, metal plating, asphalt
Manganese	Moving engine parts
Cyanide	Anti-cake compounds
Sodium, calcium, chloride	Deicing salts
Sulphate	Roadway beds, fuel, deicing salts
Petroleum	Spills, leaks, antifreeze

Source: Urban runoff monitoring in Denver and Aurora, Colorado, by the Colorado Department of Environmental Quality.

reduction, source reduction, erosion control, water volume management, water quality treatment, and constituent entrapment. Let us review a few BMPs in two categories of water management.

Water Volume Management

The emphasis in water volume management is on controlling the rate of storm water flow to receiving streams. For example, a *dry detention basin* (Figure 26-1) is an impoundment or excavated basin used for the short-term detention of storm water runoff, followed by controlled release from the downstream side of the basin. Release of water can be set at predevelopment rates, or at rates at which the designer thinks will have the least impact and be nearest the runoff in the natural model. The main reasons for using dry detention basins are to reduce peak storm water discharges, control floods, and prevent downstream channel scouring. This low-cost alternative for controlling large runoff volumes will also remove a limited amount of pollutants, as shown in Table 26-2.

Figure 26-1   Dry detention basin—a best management practice.

Table 26-2   Typical Dry Basin Pollutant Removal Efficiencies

Pollutant	Total Phosphorus	Total Nitrogen	Total Suspended Solids	Lead	Zinc	Oil and Grease	Bacteria	BOD
Estimated Removal Efficiency	Low	Low	High	Moderate to high	Moderate	Low	High	Moderate

Source: Center for Sustainable Design, Mississippi State University, Starkville, MS, 1999. *Water Related Best Management Practices in the Landscape.* (Watershed Science Institute, USDA).

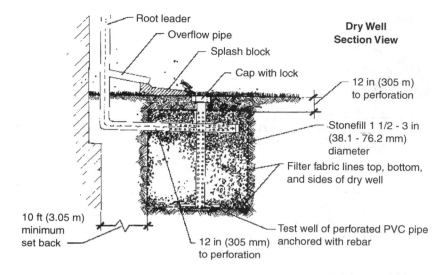

Figure 26-2 Dry well—a best management practice.

A *dry well* is an underground trench located to reduce the runoff from impervious surfaces like roofs. It is usually connected to roof drains and will help remove particulate pollutants in water and reduce erosion in downstream environments. A dry well, as shown in Figure 26-2, depends on soils that are permeable for percolation of rainwater into the soil.

Another device that is useful for reducing storm water volume from parking lots is the *parking lot perimeter infiltration trench,* as shown in Figure 26-3. In addition to holding the first flush of runoff, a trench can be an effective means of removing particulate and soluble pollutants. Trenches are installed on underutilized perimeters of a site. Besides helping to maintain low flows and control stream bank erosion, this BMP technique also recharges groundwater.

Water Quality Treatment

There are a host of BMPs used for trapping solids and treating water to remove pollutants. The *basic biofiltration swale,* as shown in Figure 26-4, is used to treat storm water runoff from small sites such as driveways, parking lots, and roadways. The swale is an open and gently sloping vegetated channel, designed for treating runoff water from sites of less than 5 ac (2 ha). Treatment swales can be designed to have a pleasing aesthetic quality in the landscape. Because biofiltration swales rely on grasses to impede and filter the flow of water, they are not suitable for continuously wet or shady conditions (less than six hours of sun per day) because grasses would become stressed and die under such circumstances. Swales must be allowed to dry between storms. When they dry, air moves back into the soil and root zone for the benefit of both the grasses and the microbes within the soil.

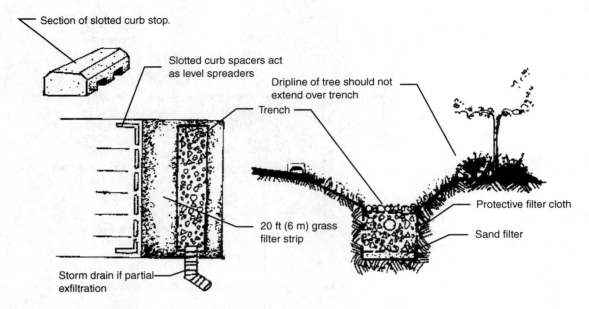

Figure 26-3 Parking lot perimeter infiltration trench—a best management practice.

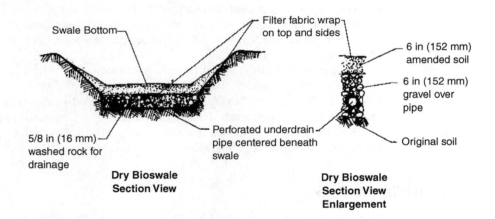

Figure 26-4 Basic biofiltration swale—a best management practice.

The *wet biofiltration swale* (Figure 26-5) is a variation of the basic biofiltration swale but is developed for wet soil conditions. This swale is used for treatment of storm water runoff on small sites where slopes are not excessive, water tables are high, and soils are often saturated. Plants that will perform well in a wet biofiltration swale are listed in Table 26-3.

An *infiltration/detention basin* is used to provide removal of soluble and fine particulate pollutants in urban runoff for large drainage areas. This BMP technique also helps

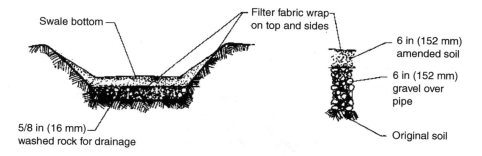

Figure 26-5 Wet biofiltration swale—a best management practice.

Table 26-3 **Recommended Plants for Wet Biofiltration Swales in King County, Washington**

Common Name	Scientific Name	Spacing on Center
Short foxtail	*Alopecurus aequalis*	Seed
Water foxtail	*Alopecurus geniculatus*	Seed
Spike rush	*Elocharis* spp.	4 in. (200 mm)
Slough sedge	*Carex obnupta*	6 in. (152 mm)
Sawbreak sedge	*Carex stipata*	6 in. (152 mm)
Sedge	*Carex* spp.	6 in. (152 mm)
Western mannagrass	*Glyceria occidentalis*	Seed
Velvet grass	*Holcus mollis*	Seed
Slender rush	*Juncus tenuis*	6 in. (152 mm)
Water parsley	*Oenanthe sarmentosa*	6 in. (152 mm)
Harstem bulrush	*Scirpus acutus*	6 in. (152 mm)
Small-fruited bulrush	*Scirpus microcarpus*	12 in. (305 mm)

Source: Surface Water Design Manual, King County, Washington: Department of Natural Resources, 1998.

Note: Cattail (*Typha latifolia*) is not appropriate for most bioswales because of its very dense and clumping growth habit, which prevents water from filtering through the swale.

to control peak discharges from large storms and is used for groundwater recharge. The small, temporary pool (Figure 26-6) uses a riprap settling basin to trap coarse sediment from runoff entering the pool. As the runoff filters through the riprap apron, it spreads over the basin floor, where suspended particles settle. An orifice located several feet above the pool bottom ensures detention of storm water and allows for infiltration of the water into the ground. This BMP technique is a very cost-efficient treatment system that can be designed to maintain the natural water balance of a site as large as 50 ac (20 ha).

A *constructed wetland* (Figure 26-7) is a human-made wetland designed to remove contaminants from storm water. Like other natural biological treatment technologies, this system is useful where runoff is contaminated with oils, pesticides, nutrients, fertilizers, and animal wastes. The natural wetland process allows microbes on plant roots and stems, and on the bottom, to consume contaminants, rendering the water clean and

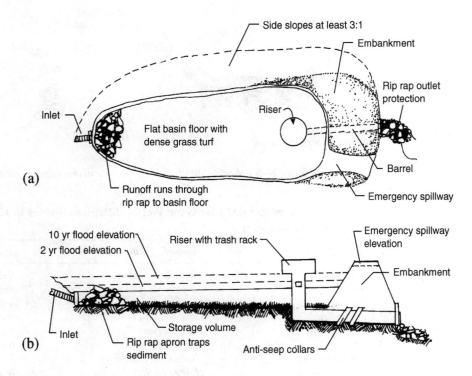

Figure 26-6 Infiltration/detention basin—a best management practice; (a) plan view, (b) section view.

ready for reuse. Wetlands also provide valuable habitat for wildlife and enhancement of the environment.

CONSTRUCTED WETLANDS AND DETENTION POOLS

Let us compute the size of a constructed wetland needed to treat polluted storm water runoff from an urban area. A 1 in. (25 mm) rainstorm covering one square mile of an urban area can produce about 17 million gal (64,345,000 l) of runoff. The challenge is to find out how big a constructed wetland will be necessary to treat the first flush of polluted runoff from the built-up area. The first flush is usually the first 1/2 in. (13 mm) of water that runs off a site, and it is the dirtiest water that will run off during a rainstorm. To begin, we compute the first flush and determine the size of a constructed wetland to contain and detain the first flush for treatment.

EXAMPLE 2.   Size the flow from an urban area.
   1 mi^2 of an urban area = 5280 ft × 5280 ft = 27,878,400 ft^2.
   1 in. converted to ft = 1 in./12 in. = .083 ft (to check, take .083 ft × 12 = 1 in.)
   27,878,400 ft^3 × .083 ft = 2,313,907 ft^3.

Figure 26-7 Constructed wetland—a best management practice.

2,313,907 ft^3 × 7.48 gal of water per ft^3 = 17,308,025 gal, which is the amount of flow from 1 in. of rain running off 1 mi^2 of urban area.

In reality only 10 to 50% of water will run off, with the remaining water puddling and soaking into permeable materials, including soil. Water running off a slate roof will be reduced by 10%, and off a flat roof by about 50%. We will reduce our runoff figure by 10%, which leaves us with approximately 15,577,223 gal of runoff. Because this is the runoff from a 1 in. storm, and we are going to detain the first flush of ¹/₂ in. for treatment, we will take half of the 1 in. total, and that figure will be 7,788,611 gal of water to be detained for treatment.

Metric Version

1609 m × 1609 m = 2,588,881 m^2, or 1 mi^2 of an urban area
2,588,881 m^2 × .0254 m (.0254 m is the equivalent of 1 in., or 25.4 mm)
= 65,757 m^3

This is equivalent to 65,756,999 l, which is the amount of flow from 25.4 mm of rain running off 1 mi^2 of urban area. Because this is the runoff from a 25.4 mm storm, and we are going to detain the first flush of ¹/₂ inch (13 mm) for treatment, we will take half of the 25.4 mm total, and that figure will be 32,878,500 l of water to be detained for treatment.

Experience suggests that by detaining the first flush for a two-day period, the biological oxygen demand (BOD) and total suspended solids (TSS) will reach acceptable permit levels. The area of wetland needed is computed as in the following example.

EXAMPLE 3. Size a constructed wetland.

Water to be detained is 7,788,611 gal/7.48 gal per ft^3 = 1,041,258 ft^3

Let us set the depth of the constructed wetland at $1\frac{1}{2}$ ft—1,041,258 ft^3/1.5 ft = 694,172 ft^2. Therefore 694,172 ft^2 of constructed wetland, $1\frac{1}{2}$ ft deep, are required. The form of the wetland may be 700 ft × 1000 ft, which is about a 16 ac pool.

Metric Version:

32,878,500 l = 65,756 m^3/0.46 m = 142,948 m^2

Therefore, a wetland that is 142,948 m^2, 0.46 m deep, is required. This can have a shape that is 290 m × 500 m.

Design depths of constructed wetlands vary from 12 to 30 in. (305 to 762 mm). Having a constructed wetland that is 12 in. (305 mm) deep will require a treatment space twice the size of one that is 24 in. (607 mm) deep.

Let us now design a surface-flow storm water detention pool for a 120 ft × 180 ft (37 m × 55 m) parking lot that accommodates 72 vehicles. The collected storm water will be detained for treatment and discharged over a two-day period. The first $\frac{1}{2}$ in. (13 mm) of runoff from the parking lot is 6732 gal (25,480 l). This is the first flush of water, and the dirtiest water, that will run off during a rainstorm. Refer to Table 26-2 for a list of typical roadway storm water constituents. Water runoff beyond the first flush will be cleaner and will bypass the detention facility. This detention period provides time for treatment of pollutants and allows for a more natural release of water instead of a torrential release all at once, which damages structures, erodes soil, and exposes the plant roots attempting to hold the soil together. The area of wetland needed for the 72 car parking lot is computed in the following example.

EXAMPLE 4. Size a parking lot detention wetland pool.

Figure the first $\frac{1}{2}$ in. (25 mm) of runoff from the parking lot. This is the first flush and the dirtiest water. It is also the runoff water that will be detained 2 days for treatment to remove pollutants.

The parking lot is 120 ft × 180 ft, or 21,600 ft^2, nearly $\frac{1}{2}$ ac (0.2 ha) in size.

Convert the first $\frac{1}{2}$ in. of water to ft: $\frac{1}{2}$ in. or 0.5 in./12 in. = 0.0417 ft.

21,600 ft^2 of parking surface × 0.0417 ft (first $\frac{1}{2}$ in. of runoff) = 900 ft^3 of runoff water to be detained for treatment. One ft^3 = 7.48 gal.

900 ft^3 of dirty water × 7.48 gal/ft^3 = 6732 gal of water, the amount of the first flush.

Wetland volume = 6732 gal (the first $\frac{1}{2}$ in. flush). This is the amount of volume the wetland will have to hold in order for the $\frac{1}{2}$ in. to be detained for treatment. Thus, 6732 gal/7.48 gal per ft^3 = 900 ft^3 of wetland volume needed to hold the first flush of dirty parking lot water. We will create a wetland that is $1\frac{1}{2}$ ft deep (900 ft^3/1.5 ft = 600 ft^2, $1\frac{1}{2}$ ft deep).

A wetland that is $1\frac{1}{2}$ ft deep, and 20 × 30 ft, will be able to detain and treat 900 ft^3 of storm water over a two-day period.

Metric Version:

The parking lot is 37 m × 55 m or 2035 m^2, or 0.2 ha in size.

Converting the first flush of 13 mm of water to meters = .013 m.

The volume of water to be treated is 37 m $\times$ 55 m $\times$ .013 m $=$ 26.5 m^3. This is the water to be detained for treatment, the amount of the first flush.

26.5 m^3 $\times$ 1000 l $=$ 26,500 l

Wetland volume $=$ 26,500 l; this is the volume of water the wetland will have to hold in order for the first 13 mm to be detained for treatment.

Therefore, a wetland that is 0.46 m deep, and 6 $\times$ 9 m, will be able to treat 26.5 m^3 of storm water over a two-day period.

It is important to note that when treating water in constructed wetlands, there must be enough water in the wetland to maintain hydric (saturated) soils and emergent plants. Additional volume within the wetland may be needed if the frequency of runoff will not create continuously moist soil conditions to provide habitat in which emergent plants can flourish.

Appendix A

Septic Tank and Field Absorption Systems

The traditional sewage treatment system, using a septic tank and field absorption, relies on natural processes and can be used for small sites, such as residences, and for larger, remote facilities such as park rest rooms and beach bathhouses. The treatment process is similar to that of large municipal systems in which organic solids are settled and the nutrients and germs in the water are removed. First, the septic tank, as shown in Figure A-1, collects all human waste and allows solids to settle and become digested by anaerobic bacteria. If the tank is large enough, the bacteria will consume all of the biosolids and there will never be a buildup in the tank. See Table A-1 for septic tank sizes. Many states have regulations suggesting that septic tanks be pumped out every three to five years to ensure that solids do not flow into the soil absorption field and clog soil pores. If that should happen, sewage water will flow to the ground surface instead of percolating down into the ground for treatment by soil bacteria. Next, clear water flows from the septic tank to the absorption field. A combination of pipes and gravel beds, as shown in Figure A-2, distributes sewage effluent to undisturbed soil, where microbes treat the liquified sewage, solids in the water are filtered, and cleaned water finally flows to natural groundwater reservoirs. The following health department specifications direct the design and construction of septic field absorption systems.

Primary Treatment—Septic Tank

For residential uses, the septic tank shall, as a minimum, comply with the following:

1. Schedule 40 PVC pipe, 4 in. (102 mm) in diameter shall be used to connect to the septic tank and to flow from the tank to the field.
2. The inlet invert shall enter the tank at a minimum of 2 in. (51 mm) above the liquid level and be equipped with a tee or baffle that extends at least 6 in. (152 mm) below the liquid level of the tank.
3. The effluent discharge line from the tank shall be 4 in. (102 mm) schedule 40 PVC. Septic tanks shall have a tee or baffle that extends at least 18 in. (457 mm) below the liquid level of the tank.

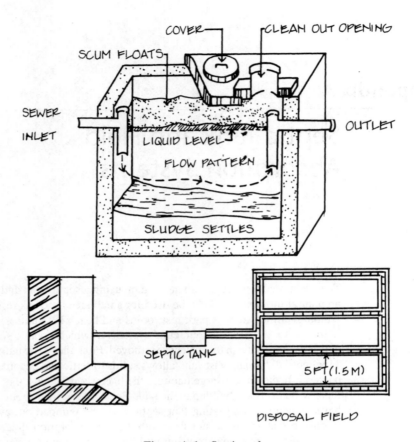

SEWER
INLET

OUTLET

Figure A-1 Septic tank.

Table A-1   Septic Tank Sizes for Residential Uses

Number of Bedrooms	Liquid Capacity of Tanks
2	750 gal (2838 l)
3	900 gal (3406 l)
4	1000 gal (3785 l)
5	1250 gal (4731 l)
Add 250 gal (946 l) for each additional bedroom.	

4. The effluent discharge line shall extend to a length sufficient to allow a minimum of 3 ft (1 m) of undisturbed soil between the excavation for the treatment plant or septic tank and the beginning of the absorption trench, bed, or effluent line.

5. Treatment plants and septic tanks shall be installed level.

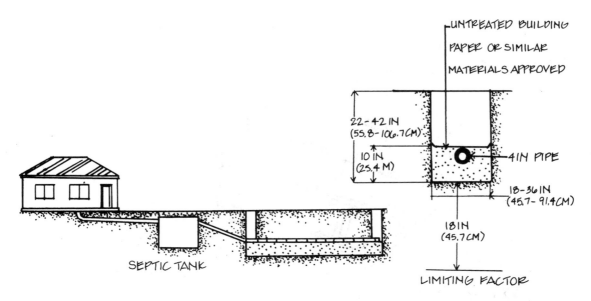

Figure A-2 Soil absorption field.

Secondary Treatment—Soil Absorption Field

1. The overall size of the subsurface disposal system shall be determined by soil texture and the ability of the soil to absorb sewage effluent and treat it effectively with aerobic and anaerobic bacteria in the soil.

2. Subsurface disposal systems shall be no deeper than 36 in. (914 mm) below the surface.

3. The minimum distance between absorption trench sidewalls shall be 6 ft (1.8 m).

4. Trenches shall be a minimum of 24 in. (610 mm) deep and a maximum of 36 in. (914 mm) wide.

5. The bottom of the septic tank outlet must be 1 in. (25 mm) above the gravel for gravel absorption systems.

6. The bottom of the trenches and the effluent lines shall have a grade from level to no greater than 2 in. (51 mm) fall per 100 ft (30 m). This is a slope of almost 0.2%.

7. When a change in elevation of the disposal trench is required, such as in a serial distribution system, a connecting lateral or crossover shall be used (see Figure A-3). At the point where a crossover line leaves a lateral, the trench for the crossover line shall be dug no deeper than the top of the gravel for the gravel absorption line (Figure A-4).

8. Absorption beds/trenches should be located a minimum of 10 ft (3 m) from a tree.

NOTE: SLOPE 6IN(15.2 CM) OR MORE FROM SEPTIC TANK TO DISPOSAL AREA

4 IN(10.2CM) NONPERFORATED
EFFLUENT LINE FROM SEPTIC TANK.

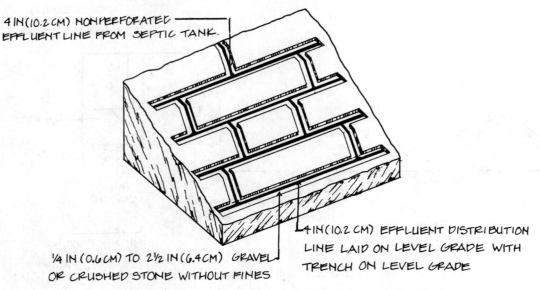

¼ IN (0.6 CM) TO 2½ IN (6.4CM) GRAVEL
OR CRUSHED STONE WITHOUT FINES

4 IN(10.2 CM) EFFLUENT DISTRIBUTION
LINE LAID ON LEVEL GRADE WITH
TRENCH ON LEVEL GRADE

NOTE: LINES LESS THAN 40 FT(12.2M) LONG IN THE DISPOSAL
SYSTEM WILL REQUIRE ONLY ONE CROSSOVER
TO AND FROM FIELD LINES.

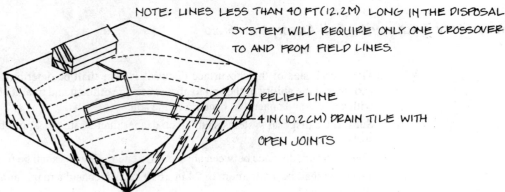

RELIEF LINE
4 IN (10.2CM) DRAIN TILE WITH
OPEN JOINTS

Figure A-3 Serial distribution system including cross over.

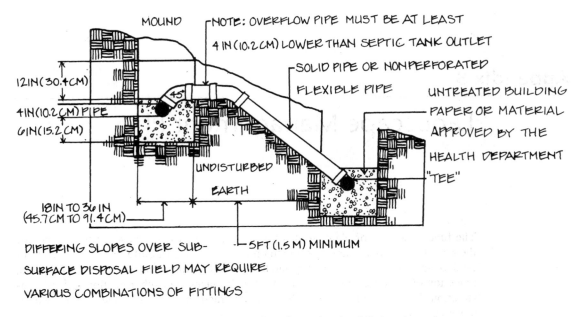

Figure A-4 Subsurface disposal under differing slopes.

Construction Specifications and Installation

1. Trenches should not be excavated when soil is wet enough to smear and compact easily. This could damage the ability of the undisturbed soil adjacent to trenches to absorb and treat sewage effluent.
2. Gravel for the disposal field shall extend from at least 2 in. (51 mm) above the top of the perforated pipe to at least 6 in. (152 mm) below the bottom of the pipe.
3. Crushed rock or gravel shall vary in size from 1/2 to 2 1/2 in. (13 to 64 mm).
4. Disposal field trenches shall be covered with a medium that will protect the trench from absorbing water when it is raining, and will keep fine soil particles from moving down into the trenches and clogging the gravel pores.

Landscape Management Plan

The functional uses of plants in this turn-of-the-century courthouse landscape include the reduction of solar energy heat gain on the west and east building sides, creation of outdoor spaces, direction of pedestrian flow, accent of major entries, control of erosion, reduction of the need to mow grass in difficult places, and subordination of hard construction elements. Mulch is used throughout to retain soil moisture and reduce the need to weed.

This landscape management plan directs maintenance so as to ensure a quality landscape for the public to enjoy. The plan was developed in order to solicit bids from landscape contracting and landscape management companies. Figure B-1 depicts the planting design on which the landscape management plan is based.

Attala County Courthouse Landscape

Kosciusko, Mississippi

for the Attala County Board of Supervisors

Pete Melby, ASLA, Landscape Architect

Landscape Management Plan

LANDSCAPE MANAGEMENT REPORT

Submit a faxed or e-mailed weekly landscape management report on Mondays to the landscape architect, describing work accomplished, materials used, and condition of the landscape.

LAWN

Mow weekly or as needed to remove one-third of the grass blade. The landscape architect shall take a pH test in May of each year from the four lawn quadrants around

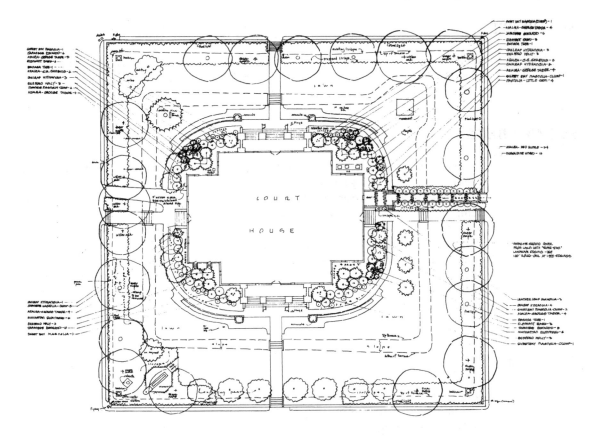

Figure B-1 Plan view of the Attala County Courthouse Landscape, Kosciusko, Mississippi.

the courthouse. From the pH reading, soil modification plans, if needed, shall be developed by the contractor and presented to the landscape architect. Work shall be funded on an addendum basis. Lawns will be fertilized, if needed, in March as directed by the landscape architect, and efforts shall be funded on an addendum basis. Contractor will observe lawn areas for pest and disease damage and shall contact the landscape architect when problems are noted.

LITTER

Remove all litter and fallen limbs on grounds by Friday noon each week.

EDGING

With a push style steel-blade mechanical edger, cut grass back from all edges every third mowing. Edges shall include all concrete walkways and along all planting beds.

SHRUB BEDS

Remove all weeds in shrub beds by 31 May and by 31 July. Add additional pine straw to beds by 31 October to create a total mulch depth of 6 in. (15.2 cm).

FLOWER BEDS

Special preparation is required for these beds. Create and maintain a soil that is friable, continuously high in organic matter, naturally high in soil nutrients, and has a pH of 6.5. The soil should have enough clay to hold water for three days. Add 2 in. (52 mm) of composted organic matter approved by the landscape architect by 15 February and again by 15 June. Work the compost into the soil in February, and use as a soil topping in June. Pull weeds every third mowing. By 15 June and again by 15 September, fertilize beds with 8-8-8 granular fertilizer, taking care to avoid getting the granules on plant foliage, or use an approved complete liquid fertilizer. Applications shall follow manufacturers' instructions on the packaging, and rates used shall be noted in the weekly landscape management report submitted to the landscape architect.

GROUND COVER BEDS

Mulch liriope (*Liriope muscari*) with a shredded leaf mulch to a settled depth of 4 in. (102 mm) around clumps by 15 February. Supplement mulch by 31 October to create a total depth of 4 in. (102 mm). Place mulch between clumps or sprinkle over top and water in to wash down between plants. Do not cover plant leaves with the mulch.

Mow the liriope to a height of 1 1/2 in. (38 mm) between the 1st and 15th of February. Collect the clippings and compost them on-site. Fertilize ground cover with 8-8-8 fertilizer by 15 February at a rate according to manufacturer's directions. By 15 May and 15 July, remove intrusive grasses and broadleaf plants. Do this either physically or with herbicides such as Post or Image. If using chemicals for removal, test on a 1 m^2 area of ground cover in order to ensure that plants will not be damaged. Wait three weeks after testing for results before conducting a spray weed removal program. Apply herbicides when there is no wind to prevent drifting of spray.

EXISTING MATURE DECIDUOUS SHADE TREES ALONG THE PERIMETER OF SITE

Regularly examine trees for diseased and weak branches and limbs, and notify landscape architect when a problem is noted. Make a list of proposed mature tree trimming problems and costs for correction by 15 May and provide to landscape architect for evaluation.

NEWLY PLANTED DECIDUOUS SHADE TREES
AT PERIMETER OF SITE

By 15 February fertilize trees with one cup of 13-13-13 slow-release granular fertilizer evenly scattered 3 ft (0.9m) around each tree base. By 15 November, fertilize each tree again with one cup of 16-0-30 granular fertilizer scattered evenly within a 4 ft (1.2 m) radius around the tree base. This fertilizer provides winter hardiness and protection from summer heat stress. Prune shade trees by 1 February to maintain a single trunk. Remove all suckers at the base of trees each site mowing. Shred all tree trimmings and compost on-site.

RAKING

Remove all leaves, pine straw, twigs, and fallen branches by 30 October and again by 15 December. Shred and apply to on-site compost pile.

FIRE ANT CONTROL

Place ant control material such as Orthene, boiling water, lemon juice, or other approved substance, on ant mounds by 15 April, 1 June, and 15 August. Repeat procedure every two weeks if the ants in the mound are not killed.

IRRIGATION

All new trees, shrubs, and ground cover during the growing season will be irrigated with drip and microspray irrigation. Evaluate all irrigation every two weeks to ensure that plants are getting the proper amount of water and are not being overwatered. Operate the low water volume systems beginning 1 July and ending 1 October. Operate the drip system for three hours, twice a week, and three days apart. Operate the spray system for the ground cover once a week for 30 minutes. Reduce operation time if runoff or significant rain events occur. Conduct all irrigation during the early morning hours. Note irrigation schedule used in weekly landscape management reports.

MANAGEMENT NEEDS OF SPECIFIC PLANTS

Sweet Bay Magnolia (*Magnolia virginiana*)

Fertilize with a cup of 8-8-8 granular fertilizer by 15 February. By 15 November fertilize with a cup of 16-0-30. Scatter fertilizer evenly within a 4 ft (1.2 m) radius around tree. Do not prune branches of this tree. Remove suckers from the base as they appear.

Magnolia "Little Gem" (*Magnolia grandiflora* "Little Gem")

Allow branches to grow to the ground. Place 4 in. (102 mm) of shredded bark mulch in a 3 ft (0.9 m) radius ring around each tree by 15 February. Fertilize over this ring of mulch with 8-8-8 granular fertilizer by 15 February. By 15 November fertilize with a cup of 16-0-30. Scatter fertilizer evenly within a 4 ft (1.2 m) radius around tree. Do not prune this tree.

Japanese Magnolia (*Magnolia soulangiana*)

Prune branches up from these multitrunk clump trees as the shrubs beneath them grow taller. The ultimate form should be a clean, multitrunk 6 to 8 ft (1.8 to 2.4 m) above the ground. It may take seven to ten years for the tree to reach this form. Fertilize with a cup of 8-8-8 fertilizer by 15 February. By November 15 fertilize with a cup of 16-0-30 per tree. Scatter fertilizer evenly within a 4 ft (1.2 m) radius around tree.

Manhattan Euonymus (*Euonymous kiautschovica*)

Fertilize with 1/2 cup of 8-8-8 spread 2 ft (61 cm) evenly around the base of each shrub in February. Once this shrub reaches a size of 6 ft (1.8 m) in diameter, begin to prune it back one branch at a time with handheld "parrot type" pruning shears. Carry out the pruning task in a naturalistic manner by alternating tip pruning with pruning 12 in. (31 cm) into the shrub. This will produce a naturalistic look as opposed to a "sheared" look.

Japanese Boxwood (*Buxus microphylla*)

This fast growing shrub needs little attention except for pruning. Once the shrub reaches 3 ft (91 cm) in diameter, prune in a naturalistic manner with parrot type pruning shears by 15 April and 30 June. Do not shear this plant with hedge clippers.

Azaleas (*Azalea* spp.)

Fertilize azaleas with two cups of cottonseed meal (without the salt) placed 2 ft (0.6 m) around the trunk of each shrub by the 15th of May. The landscape architect shall test the soil pH yearly in the spring to ensure the pH is below 6.5, and if above 6.5 pH, iron sulphate will be recommended to help lower the soil pH to a range suitable for azalea growth. Soil pH adjustment will be an addendum to the contract. Do not shear this plant with hedge clippers. Instead, when leggy growth occurs or the plant becomes larger in diameter than 4 ft (1.2 m), prune naturalistically by alternating tip pruning with pruning 6 to 8 in. (53 to 203 mm) into the shrub. This will produce a naturalistic look as opposed to a "sheared" look. All pruning shall be completed within three weeks after the blooming period. Place pine straw by 15 February under and 2 ft (0.6 m) beyond the drip line of the azaleas to a depth of 4 in. (10 cm). Place pine straw again by 1 November to a maximum depth of 4 in. (102 mm).

Elephant Ears (*Alocasia* **spp.**)

Cut foliage back to within 3 in. (76 mm) of the ground after the first killing frost. Compost foliage and stalks. Mulch 12 in. (31 cm) deep and 2 ft (0.6 m) beyond the outer edge of these tropical rhizomes by 15 November with shredded leaves capped with a 4 in. (102 mm) layer of pine straw.

Banana Trees (*Musa paradisiaca sapientum*)

Cut foliage back to the ground after the plant top is killed by frost. Compost clippings. Mulch 12 in. (31 cm) deep and 2 ft (0.6 m) beyond the outer edge of the plant with shredded leaves, capped with a 4 in. (102 mm) layer of pine straw to protect the cold-sensitive root system.

Oakleaf Hydrangia (*Hydrangea quercifolia*)

This plant must have good drainage around its roots to survive. Once the plant reaches 5 ft (1.5 m) in diameter, prune in a naturalistic manner immediately following flowering so next year's flower buds can still be formed during the summer. Prune naturalistically by alternating tip pruning with pruning 12 in. (31 cm) into the shrub. This will produce a naturalistic look as opposed to a "sheared" look. Fertilize with one cup of 8-8-8 or three cups of cottonseed meal by 15 February each year. Scatter fertilizer evenly in a 4 ft (1.2 m) radius around the base of the shrub.

Leatherleaf Mahonia (*Mahonia bealei*)

These free-form shrubs will need little attention until they reach a height of 4 ft (1.2 m). At that time, cut one-third of the longest canes back to the ground by 15 February. Fertilize with one cup of cottonseed meal scattered 2 ft (0.6 m) evenly around the plant. By 15 February mulch beneath and 2 ft (0.6 m) beyond the plant with pine straw to a depth of 4 in. (10 cm). Place pine straw again by 1 November to a cumulative depth of 4 in. (102 mm).

Muscadines (*Vitis rotundifolia*)

Prune muscadines back to two buds between 15 January and 15 February. Shred all pruned material and compost on-site. Train the vines to follow the steel trellis. Keep trunk clean of branches for 4 ft (1.2 m) above ground, then let branches grow, keeping a central branch. Prune after the first frost in the fall or early winter. All new growth is to be pruned back to two buds and thinned. The landscape architect will meet the contractor on the site to instruct on pruning procedures. Fertilize by 15 February with one cup of 8-8-8 per vine. Scatter evenly in a 3 ft (0.9 m) radius around the base.

Index